A. Hastings Ross

The Church-Kingdom

Lectures on Congregationalism

A. Hastings Ross

The Church-Kingdom
Lectures on Congregationalism

ISBN/EAN: 9783337173104

Printed in Europe, USA, Canada, Australia, Japan

Cover: Foto ©Lupo / pixelio.de

More available books at **www.hansebooks.com**

THE CHURCH-KINGDOM:

LECTURES ON CONGREGATIONALISM,

DELIVERED

ON THE SOUTHWORTH FOUNDATION IN THE ANDOVER
THEOLOGICAL SEMINARY, 1882–86.

BY

A. HASTINGS ROSS,

PASTOR OF THE FIRST CONGREGATIONAL CHURCH, PORT HURON, MICHIGAN;
LECTURER IN THE OBERLIN THEOLOGICAL SEMINARY, AND AUTHOR
OF THE "OHIO MANUAL," "THE CHURCH OF GOD: A CATE-
CHISM," AND "THE POCKET MANUAL."

BOSTON AND CHICAGO:
CONGREGATIONAL SUNDAY-SCHOOL AND PUBLISHING SOCIETY.

Electrotyped and Printed by
Stanley and Usher, 171 Devonshire Street, Boston.

It should be understood that, in issuing theological books, the Congregational Sunday-School and Publishing Society is not to be held as approving every principle and opinion advanced in them.

PREFACE.

DURING the present century there has been a wonderful movement among Christian nations towards equality in all things. The laborer, the citizen, the layman, are coming to the front, and the future is theirs. Freedom is in the air. Wild theories of brotherhood and socialism are freely promulgated. To this whole movement questions of government, in order to liberty and security, are fundamental. The churches, busy as never before with the evangelization of the world, feel this ground-swell of re-adjustment, and are freeing themselves from bondage to the State, that they may teach the root-principles of all government. And the movement is back towards the liberty and unity of the primitive churches, with their equality and care for the people. It is coming to be felt that this world was not made for the few but for the many; that the welfare of the people is above the pleasure of the rich or the ambition of the ruler. This movement can not be stayed; it may be guided. And believing that Christ Jesus our Lord put into his churches not only equality but also brotherhood, — love of our neighbor, — we find in their government a model for the future State. To cast a handful of salt into the bitter fountain of human passion already flowing, we publish these Lectures.

The title may seem strange, but it expresses better than any other the contents of the Lectures. Christ dwelt largely on "the kingdom," which became his Church and which is still coming. Hence organized and manifested Christianity is this very kingdom of heaven coming. The Church is the human side of the kingdom, and the kingdom is the divine side of the Church. In other words, the Church is the kingdom in manifestation. From this central point, polity has been considered in these Lectures; for which no better name could be found than The Church-Kingdom. Whether we have given all the elements of this divine institution or not, and whether we have treated them in their normal relations or not, we must leave it with others to judge. We can only add that we have desired to cover all the elements and to give their normal development.

If our view of the origin of polities be correct, the divisions in Christendom have more honorable foundations than many have supposed. But the same view of their origin presents also the stubborn obstacles which must be overcome before those divisions can emerge in ecumenical unity.

A special call for a full discussion of Congregationalism is found in the action of the last National Council (1886) respecting ministerial standing and the pastorate (§ 124: 8). The inadequacy of ordaining and installing councils to secure purity has led the churches to turn to ministerial standing in associations of churches or conferences as an adequate safeguard easily applied. But in the transition from one safeguard to another, there is danger lest some abnormal principle or practice be introduced which shall work evil. It is hoped that the following discussion may be helpful in avoiding this danger, and at the same time assist in securing uniformity in principle and practice among the free churches of Christendom. The one doctrine of the Christian Church has but one constitution that is normal, whatever incidental peculiarities national life may give it.

All who understand the significance of the action of the National Council, above referred to, will exonerate the Congregational Sunday-School and Publishing Society from all responsibility for views deemed peculiar to any portion of our churches, that may appear in these Lectures.

We have given to this doctrine of the Church an ecumenical comprehension, hoping that the time is not far distant when a general council of free churches throughout the world, including especially mission churches, shall be held in London, at the call of our English brethren, to confer upon all matters of faith and polity.

These Lectures were given in the Andover Theological Seminary in 1883, 1885, and 1886, on the Southworth Foundation, and are an enlargement of the Lectures given in the Oberlin Theological Seminary since 1872, and outlined in the Pocket Manual.

We ask the blessing of the Great Head of the Church and the King of the kingdom upon this humble attempt to present the principles and development of his Church-kingdom.

A. HASTINGS ROSS.

PORT HURON, MICHIGAN, 1887.

CONTENTS.

LECTURE I.

		PAGE
§ 1.	The scope of these Lectures is the Church of God	1
§ 2.	Limited to outward forms, instead of the inner life	2
§ 3.	Polity largely fashions doctrines	2
§ 4.	Forms in which the Church has appeared	3
§ 5.	Christendom divided over the visibility of the Church	4
§ 6.	Definition of the Church of God	5

I. THE PATRIARCHAL DISPENSATION.

§ 7.	Origin of society in the family	6
§ 8.	Antiquity of this dispensation	6
§ 9.	Beginnings of the Church of God	6
§ 10.	The Church continued to the Exodus	7
§ 11.	The simple form of the Patriarchal dispensation	8
	(1) The Sabbath. (2) Sacrifices. (3) The Priesthood. (4) Initiatory rite: when introduced. (5) Creed.	
§ 12.	This form not unifying	9
§ 13.	Nor did it conserve piety	9
§ 14.	Little separation between saints and sinners	10

II. THE CEREMONIAL DISPENSATION.

§ 15.	Developed out of the preceding dispensation through a family covenant	11
§ 16.	This covenant did not rigidly separate between the good and the bad	12
§ 17.	The law followed the renewal of the covenant	12
§ 18.	The worship being national, tended to unity	12
§ 19.	The priesthood national and exclusive	13
§ 20.	The ritual minute and inflexible	13
§ 21.	The creed of this dispensation	14
§ 22.	The dispensation a Theocracy	14
§ 23.	It honored the family	15
§ 24.	This church form unifying	15
§ 25.	Origin of synagogues in the inadequacy of this dispensation for an ecumenical religion	16
§ 26.	This dispensation superseded	16

§ 27. Yet not wholly set aside.. 17
    (1) Attempted return to the family Church. (2) Attempted return to the national Church.
§ 28. Reforms to become permanent must have two elements — a religious element and an ecclesiastical element............. 18
§ 29. The permanent separated from the transient.................. 19

LECTURE II.
III. THE CHRISTIAN DISPENSATION.
I. *The Kingdom of Heaven.*

§ 30. The kingdom, the foundation of the Christian Church, neglected by writers on Congregationalism................ 21
§ 31. The kingdom already set up in the world..................... 22
    (1) Its establishment predicted. (2) A forerunner of it sent. (3) The gospel — the gospel of the kingdom. (4) The kingdom preached. (5) Set up in that generation. (6) Put in contrast with the Ceremonial dispensation. (7) The command to evangelize the world rests on Christ's assumption of royal power.
§ 32. The kingdom of heaven defined............................. 24
    Its elements are: (1) Loyalty. (2) Unity. (3) Holiness. (4) Invisibility. (5) Infallibility. (6) Perpetuity. (7) Universality. (8) Equality among subjects.
§ 33. These notes distinguish this kingdom from all others......... 27
§ 34. Conditions of admission also help to define it............... 28
§ 35. The kingdom distinguished from the Church universal........ 28
§ 36. The kingdom partly on earth and partly in heaven............ 29

II. *The Kingdom of Heaven in Manifestation.*

§ 37. It must appear in life and continued organism............... 30
    (1) The Ceremonial dispensation organically bound to the Patriarchal. (2) The Christian dispensation organically bound to the Ceremonial.
§ 38. Its development into organic manifestation not understood by the Jews.. 31
§ 39. The true Israel perpetuated through Christ's disciples: the remnant.. 32
§ 40. The transition rejected and retained much of the old dispensation.. 33
§ 41. It retained the synagogue form of worship................... 34
    (1) The synagogue originated in a religious want. (2) It met a universal need. (3) Its worship was local, congregational, weekly, lay. (4) It could be carried and conducted anywhere — ecumenical.

§ 42. The kingdom chiefly manifested in and through local churches. 36
(1) The Holy Spirit uses fellowship as the channel of blessing. (2) Hence the apostles planted churches everywhere. (3) Churches ever appear wherever the kingdom extends.
§ 43. Fellowship unites these churches in associations 38
§ 44. Therein church polity arises in one of four radical forms 39
§ 45. Polity has a nobler origin than bigotry, ambition, or corruption, in theories of the Christian Church.................. 41

LECTURE III.

THE ROMAN CATHOLIC AND THE EPISCOPAL THEORY OF THE CHRISTIAN CHURCH.

§ 46. Early change in thought and language, as the kingdom became visible in churches 42
§ 47. The true relation of churches to the kingdom expressed by one theory, not by many.. 43
§ 48. Theories reduced each to its constitutive principle and its development 45

1. THE PAPAL THEORY OF THE CHRISTIAN CHURCH.

§ 49. Its imposing nature — Macaulay 46
§ 50. Its origin in confounding the visible and the invisible Church . 47
(1) This confusion seen in Ignatius, Irenæus, Cyprian. (2) The confusion born naturally of the Ceremonial dispensation. (3) Its removal would have prevented the Papacy. (4) The distinction between the visible and the invisible Church of the utmost present practical value. (5) To confusion in thought must be added the primacy of St. Peter. (6) Also an environment favoring papal pretensions.
§ 51. The Papal Theory stated 51
§ 52. Its constitutive principle — not infallibility — but............. 52
(1) Infallible primacy. (2) Not determined until 1870. (3) The principle active and passive.
§ 53. This principle developed in an infallible system 53
(1) Covering doctrine, rites, worship, morals. (2) Under the Pope as supreme ruler on earth.
§ 54. Proofs on which the system rests 55
§ 55. Observations on the Theory 56
(1) It is a living power. (2) It can not be assailed by argument. (3) It can not be reformed. (4) Its alternative is victory or death.— Syllabus of Errors and Papal Infallibility. (5) The Roman Catholic churches reformable when the Papacy perishes. (6) If the Papacy should prevail, it could express the unity of the kingdom of heaven.

II. THE EPISCOPAL THEORY OF THE CHRISTIAN CHURCH.

§ 56. This Theory older than the Papal........................... 59
§ 57. Origin of the Theory, in presiding presbyters............... 59
§ 58. The Theory stated 62
§ 59. Its constitutive principle.—Apostolic succession 62
§ 60. Alleged proof of it 63
§ 61. Develops into a minute and exclusive system............... 64
§ 62. Different Episcopal Churches.............................. 65
       (1) The Greek Church. (2) The Anglican Church. (3) The Protestant Episcopal Church. (4) The Moravian Brethren.
§ 63. Observations on the Episcopal Theory 67
       (1) It is a system of government. (2) It is aggressive and exclusive. (3) Only the Greek Church in it claims infallibility. (4) It is an incomplete system, not ecumenical.

LECTURE IV.

THE PRESBYTERIAL AND THE CONGREGATIONAL THEORY OF THE CHRISTIAN CHURCH.

III. THE PRESBYTERIAN THEORY OF THE CHRISTIAN CHURCH.

§ 64. This theory in its elements older than the Episcopal, but later in formal statement.. 70
§ 65. Origin of the Theory...................................... 71
§ 66. The Theory stated 71
§ 67. Its constitutive principle—Authoritative Representation..... 72
§ 68. Developed into the following system: 72
       (1) Particular or local churches. (2) Church Sessions. (3) Presbyteries. (4) Synods. (5) General Assemblies. (6) Presbyterian Alliance, ecumenical. (a) Its Powers. (b) Its foreign principle.
§ 69. The claimed proof of this system.......................... 75
§ 70. This system embraces: 76
       (1) The Presbyterian Churches. (2) The Methodist Churches; the Methodist Episcopal Church mixed and unstable.
§ 71. Observations on the Presbyterian Theory 77
       (1) It is a simple, consistent, incomplete system. (2) It is not dependent on lay ruling elders. (3) It does not claim infallibility. (4) It is reformable, if proved unscriptural.

IV. THE CONGREGATIONAL THEORY OF THE CHRISTIAN CHURCH.

§ 72. This Theory the oldest in principle, but the latest in full development.. 79
§ 73. The Theory stated 79

§ 74. Its constitutive principle — Independence under Christ of the local church 80
§ 75. Its developed system 81
    (1) The local church of believers. (2) These churches in fellowship. (3) Associated in occasional councils. (4) Associated in bodies meeting statedly. (*a*) District Associations of churches. (*b*) State Associations of churches. (*c*) National Associations of churches. (*d*) An Ecumenical Association of churches (not yet formed).
§ 76. This Theory embraces all Independents or Congregationalists, Baptists, most Lutherans, and some others 83
§ 77. Proof of the Theory 83
§ 78. Observations on the Congregational Theory 83
    (1) It develops a simple, consistent, comprehensive system. (2) It is not infallible. (3) It is a living and revolutionary Theory.

V. COMPARISON OF THESE FOUR THEORIES OF THE CHRISTIAN CHURCH.

§ 79. They are the only simple Theories of the Christian Church.... 84
§ 80. These Theories are mutually exclusive. 85
§ 81. Each Theory is capable of becoming ecumenical in comprehension 87
§ 82. Their influence on civil government, giving liberty or tyranny. — Papacy, Episcopacy, the Puritans, both Presbyterian and Congregationalist 88
§ 83. Each Theory determines the activities of its adherents 93
§ 84. The utility of this divine evolution of Ecclesiastical systems, a forecast of the outcome 94

LECTURE V.

THE DOCTRINE OF THE CHRISTIAN CHURCH.

MATERIALS. — CONSTITUTIVE PRINCIPLE.

§ 85. Recapitulation of the chief points reached 97

THE DOCTRINE OF THE CHRISTIAN CHURCH.

§ 86. Explanation of terms 98
§ 87. Confusion through various standards of belief 98

I. THE MATERIALS OF THE CHRISTIAN CHURCH.

§ 88. Definition of the term "materials" 100
§ 89. Materials of the Patriarchal Church 100
§ 90. Materials of the *kahal*, or the Ceremonial Church 100
§ 91. Materials of the Jewish synagogue 101
    Excommunication from *kahal* and synagogue.

§ 92. Materials of the kingdom of heaven 102
§ 93. Materials of the Church of Christ. — Church and kingdom: how differ 103
§ 94. Materials of local churches....................................104
    (1) The manifestation and the thing manifested need to correspond. (2) The New Testament confirms this principle. (*a*) Churches addressed as holy. (*b*) Spiritual conditions of membership required. (*c*) Baptism symbolizes a changed life. (*d*) A credal test required. (*e*) Purity through church discipline. (*f*) Wide difference between a church and its congregation. (3) The apostolic churches confirm the same.
§ 95. This argument not invalidated by imperfections. Nor by infant baptism 108
§ 96. This position a development 108

II. THE RELATION OF ONE LOCAL CHURCH TO OTHER LOCAL CHURCHES.

§ 97. All local churches spiritually one and inseparable 109
§ 98. This unity makes each independent of the rest 110
§ 99. The rule of discipline rests on this normal relation 111
    (1) The "church" in Matt. 18: 17 the local church. (*a*) It was not the company of believers before Pentecost. (*b*) It was not the Jewish synagogue. (*c*) The rule not given for Ceremonial Dispensation. (*d*) It was given to local churches. (2) The action of the local church final. (3) Its finality confirmed by "binding" and "loosing."
§ 100. The election of officers rests on the independence of each church 114
    (1) The election of an apostle. (2) The election of the seven almoners, or deacons. (3) The election of delegates. (4) The election of elders, or presbyters.
§ 101. Their general relations indicate their independence 116
§ 102. They thus follow their model, the synagogue 117
§ 103. The Apostolic Fathers confirm this independence 118

III. THE PRIMITIVE CHURCHES NOT SUBORDINATE TO ANY CENTRALIZED ECCLESIASTICAL AUTHORITY.

§ 104. Their spiritual unity seeks visible union under Christ 119
§ 105. Reasons why the *ecclesia* dropped the authority of the *kahal* ..119
    (1) The authority of the *kahal* in the ceremonial law fulfilled and abolished. (2) The authority of the *kahal* in the state abolished in the *ecclesia*. (3) The *ecclesia* thus stripped of authority.
§ 106. Hence the churches not subject to an Infallible Primate 121
§ 107. The churches not subject to an Episcopate 123
§ 108. The churches not subject to a Presbytery or General Assembly 125

§ 109. The independence of the primitive churches conceded 126
§ 110. Authority beyond itself not an element of any *ecclesia*, but instead independence 128
    (1) Congregationalism therefore follows. (2) The only escape is in other standards than the Bible. (3) The Presbyterians have no such escape. (4) The evolution of Congregationalism has the promise of the future.

LECTURE VI.

THE DOCTRINE OF THE CHRISTIAN CHURCH.

THE CHRISTIAN MINISTRY.

§ 111. The ministry precedes the churches, and is not an official relation 131
§ 112. The Christian ministry not a priesthood.......................132
    (1) A priest is one who offers sacrifices. (2) Christ the Christian's Priest and High Priest. (3) He absorbed and abolished the priesthood. (4) A priesthood and mass impeach Christ's atonement.
§ 113. The ministry of the Word a function of the Church-kingdom. 134
    (1) The ministerial function not exclusive. (2) The ministry prepared and called by Christ. (3) Recognition of the divine call in ordination distinguishes the ministry from the laity. (4) The ministry in what sense independent of the churches. (5) The ministry not prelatical. (6) The ministry a special and a permanent function.

I. THE TEMPORARY MINISTRY OF THE WORD.

§ 114. The apostles of our Lord 138
§ 115. The qualifications of the apostles 138
    (1) Personal selection by Christ. (2) Personal instruction by Christ. (3) Inspiration by the Holy Spirit. (4) Special miraculous power. (5) Special authority. (6) Equality in rank and order.
§ 116. The apostolate temporary 140
    (1) Its special nature proves its temporary nature. (2) Its qualifications not continued. (3) No successors of the apostles. (4) Church organization completed during the apostolate.
§ 117. The Prophets 142
    (1) Distinguished from the Old Testament prophets. (2) Had the gift of inspired utterance. (3) Their ministry temporary.

II. THE PERMANENT MINISTRY OF THE WORD.

§ 118. This ministry called by different names 143
    (1) Teachers. — Three lists of ministers. (2) Evangelists,

or missionaries. (3) Elders, or presbyters. (4) Bishops the same as elders and pastors. (5) Pastors, shepherds. (6) Rulers in the churches. (7) Leaders, chiefs. (8) "The angels of the churches."

§ 119. The qualifications of the Permanent Ministry 147
 (1) Personal character. (2) Personal reputation. (3) Domestic relations. (4) Natural and spiritual gifts. (5) Preparation and study. (6) Examples to the people.

§ 120. Provision for the perpetuity of the ministry..................149

§ 121. The ministry recognized in ordination 150
 (1) Ordination of some sort to be expected. (2) Ordination by imposition of hands and prayer. (3) Significance of ordination. (4) Ordination an ecclesiastical recognition of the ministerial function, not of the pastorate. (5) Ordination is by the churches. (6) Ordination confers no special gift or grace.

§ 122. The ministerial standing of the ordained. — Meaning of the term 154

§ 123. All communions hold to ministerial standing. — Congregationalists 155

§ 124. Where ministerial standing should be held 157
 (1) Not in the civil courts. (2) Not in local churches. (3) Not in a council of churches. (4) Not in unassociated churches. (5) Not in ministerial associations. (6) But in associations of churches. (7) Standing therein safe and essential. (8) Ministerial standing recognized by the National Council.

§ 125. This ministerial standing protects and completes our polity..163

LECTURE VII.

THE DOCTRINE OF THE CHRISTIAN CHURCH.

THE CHURCHES AND THEIR OFFICERS.

§ 126. Meaning of the words "church" and "churches" in the New Testament. Acts 9: 31 no exception 166
 (1) It may mean the scattered church of Jerusalem, or (2) It may mean the whole body of believers, "the holy Catholic Church."

§ 127. The city churches severally one congregation................168
 (1) Many converted at Pentecost returned home. (2) May have met in several places for worship. (3) Under the same officers. (4) Consistent with Congregationalism.

§ 128. Definition of a local church 170

§ 129. A church not a voluntary society..........................171

§ 130. Members in a church on an equality................ 171

CHURCH OFFICERS.

§ 131. Church elders or pastors 172
    (1) Their appointment by the church. (2) A plurality in every primitive church. (3) Duties of church elders or bishops. (4) Elders have a twofold membership — as Christians — as ministers. (5) Their accountability also twofold. — Their church accountability. (6) Inauguration into the pastorate. — Installation.
§ 132. Deacons, or the ministry of tables 178
    (1) Origin of the office. (2) Duties of deacons. (3) A lay office. (4) Qualifications for the diaconate. (5) Deacons should be ordained. (6) Their authority one of function. (7) Elected sometimes for a term of years.
§ 133. Ruling elders 181
    (1) Two theories of the ruling eldership — ministerial and lay. (2) Duties of ruling elders under each theory. (3) The primitive ruling elders ministers. — No lay elders in the New Testament. (4) Theory of lay eldership falling.
§ 134. Need of a board of rulers in a church 184
§ 135. How Scripturally met. — A Church Board 185
§ 136. Duties of such Church Board 186
§ 137. The church clerk 186
    (1) Qualifications for the office. (2) The duties of the clerk.
§ 138. The church treasurer 187
    (1) A perpetual need makes the office permanent. (2) Qualifications of a treasurer. (3) Duties of a church treasurer and of a parish treasurer.
§ 139. Special church committee. — Sunday-school superintendent ... 189
§ 140. Church officers rulers in a church 190
    (1) Church can remove them. (2) No officer has the right of veto.
§ 141. Church officers guides of the church 191

LECTURE VIII.

THE DOCTRINE OF THE CHRISTIAN CHURCH.

WORSHIP AND SACRAMENTS.

§ 142. Worship essential to the idea of a church 194
§ 143. The nature of Christian worship 195
    (1) Worship must be in spirit and truth. (2) It must be offered in the name of Christ. (3) It must be in faith and penitence.
§ 144. The ends of church worship 196
    (1) The glory of God its chief end. (2) Christian edification. (3) The conversion of unbelievers.

§ 145. The form of worship should meet both the nature and ends of worship 197
(1) No Christian form revealed. (2) The best form flexible and changeable. (3) Hence liberty to change given the churches.

§ 146. Variety in the worship of the primitive churches............198
(1) Worship of the Jewish synagogue. (2) Elements of worship in apostolic churches. (3) Later form of worship. (4) The three oldest Liturgies. (5) The Great Reformation changed forms of worship. (6) A clearer conception of worship appearing.

§ 147. The value of Liturgies in church services 202
(1) No liturgy imposed by Christ or his apostles. (2) Liturgies have been generally used. (3) Liturgies not essentially connected with polity.

THE CHURCH SACRAMENTS.

§ 148. The Christian worship centers in the sacraments.............205
(1) Their number — seven or two. (2) Only Baptism and the Lord's Supper are sacraments. (a) Confirmation. (b) Penance. (c) Orders. (d) Marriage. (e) Extreme Unction. (f) Feet-washing. (3) Confirmed by the nature of a sacrament. — Quaker view. — Church view.

§ 149. Baptism 207
(1) It superseded circumcision in the covenant of God. (2) Baptism required of all believers after Pentecost. (3) John's baptism not Christian baptism.

§ 150. The essential elements of baptism 209
(1) Water, the purer the better. (2) The intent to baptize. (3) Into the name of the Trinity. (4) But once administered.

§ 151. The mode of baptism various 210
§ 152. The subjects of baptism 211
(1) They are unbaptized converts. (2) Also infant children of believers. (3) But not the children of unbelievers.

§ 153. The relation of baptized children to the church. Theories....213
(1) Made full members by baptism. (2) Baptism and confirmation make full members. (3) Baptism and an orderly life make full members. (4) Baptism with public confession makes full members. (5) Baptism only a consecration, having no effect on membership. (6) The Baptist position contrary to the covenant of grace.

§ 154. The Lord's Supper. — Names 216
(1) A memorial, not a sacrifice. (2) It superseded the passover. (3) To be often repeated. (4) The elements used, bread and wine. (5) The mode of celebrating the supper

CONTENTS. xvii

diverse. (6) Should be celebrated by members in both kinds.
§ 155. The communicants 218
 (1) Determined by different conditions in different churches. (2) All agree in requiring these prerequisites: (*a*) Belief in Christ. (*b*) Baptism. (*c*) Church membership. (*d*) Confirmed by the communicants of the passover. (3) These terms confirmed by Scripture, history, and nature. (*a*) Judas Iscariot did not participate in the supper. (*b*) Primitive churches excluded all but full members from the room. (*c*) The nature of the case excludes non-members from the Eucharist. (*d*) These terms regulate our fellowship at the table. (4) These terms may not be increased in number.
§ 156. The invitation to the Eucharist should conform to these terms.224
 (1) The common invitation regards them. (2) The pastor can not control the invitation.
§ 157. Who may administer the sacraments 225
 (1) Ordinarily ordained ministers. (2) Laymen may sometimes administer; since (3) Validity and efficacy not dependent on the administrator; but laymen should administer. (*a*) Only in pressing exigencies. (*b*) Only by vote of the church. (4) Ordination not an essential element, but required ordinarily for administering the sacraments.

LECTURE IX.

THE DOCTRINE OF THE CHRISTIAN CHURCH.

DISCIPLINE.

§ 158. A church must have some form of discipline 229
§ 159. This discipline covers the general management, as: 230
 (1) The order of church services. (2) The times of church meetings. (3) The rules of procedure. (4) The regularity of procedure.

DEALING WITH OFFENDERS.

§ 160. Preliminary considerations 231
 (1) Discipline determined by the theory of the Church. (2) Defects in discipline of little weight. (3) Drift in discipline decisive. (4) Study of discipline needed. (*a*) Because discipline is common. (*b*) Because mistakes in discipline rend churches. (5) Congregationalism has essentially one discipline.
§ 161. The permanent authority of discipline, where located 233
 (1) This authority not original but derived. (2) Placed by Christ in local churches. (3) This authority limited.

§ 162. The subjects of church discipline 235
      (1) Lay officers. (2) Ministers require a twofold process — one as church members, another as ministers. (3) Baptized children not subjects.
§ 163. The offences demanding discipline 235
      (1) Denial of cardinal doctrines. (2) Scandalous offences. (3) Private wrongs, violations of covenant.
§ 164. The duty of discipline...238
      (1) Authority joined with discretion. (2) The function of the church involves discretion. (3) Discretion varies discipline. — Intemperance.
§ 165. The ends of church discipline....................................240
      (1) The reclamation of the offender. (2) The purity of the church.
§ 166. The rule, or steps, of discipline...............................241
      (1) The first step. (2) The second step. (3) The third step. (4) The final step. (5) These steps complete and final.

SOME QUESTIONS RESPECTING CHURCH DISCIPLINE.

§ 167. Should all cases be treated alike? 244
§ 168. When should the first step be taken?...........................244
§ 169. Should a second private interview be sought? 245
§ 170. Does asking for a letter forestall discipline?.................245
§ 171. Does granting a letter preclude discipline? 246
§ 172. How should a case be brought before the church? 246
§ 173. How should the church conduct the case?........................247
§ 174. May not discipline be had by jury trial? 249
§ 175. What rules control evidence in discipline? — Hearsay evidence? 250
§ 176. May legal counsel plead in church trials? 252
§ 177. What censures may be inflicted? — Lifting the censure........254
§ 178. Should the censure be announced publicly? 255
§ 179. Are witnesses and others protected by the law? 255
§ 180. When do irregularities in procedure invalidate action? 256
§ 181. Who may vote in church matters? 257
§ 182. What is the validity of votes when a majority do not vote?....259
§ 183. Can members be dropped from the church roll? 259
§ 184. What part may a pastor take in discipline? 261
§ 185. Can a local church complete the discipline of a ministerial member? 261
§ 186. What redress is there if a church do wrong? 262

LECTURE X.

THE DOCTRINE OF THE CHRISTIAN CHURCH.

FELLOWSHIP.

§ 187. Independent churches bound in the closest fellowship 264

§ 188. Church fellowship is the communion of churches 264
§ 189. Church fellowship a necessity..................................265
§ 190. Church fellowship not peculiar to any polity 265
§ 191. The vehicle of centralization 266
§ 192. Church fellowship fully exhibited under liberty 266

OCCASIONAL COUNCILS.

§ 193. Origin of the system of councils 267
    (1) It has a warrant in the New Testament. (2) Early general councils. (3) The system of councils in New England born of the union of Church and State. (*a*) Otherwise it would have appeared elsewhere. (*b*) If normal, the system would have spread. (*c*) Its political fostering in New England. (4) Councils limited by nature and call.

§ 194. Description of the system of councils........................272
    (1) Definition of a council. (2) By whom called. (3) Assembled by letters missive. (4) Those calling determine the membership. (5) Rights of members in councils. (6) A quorum of a council. (7) Objects of councils. (8) Scope of councils narrow. — Communion more comprehensive than advice. (9) The size of councils. (10) Kinds of councils. (*a*) Councils called by one party — *uni parte*. (*b*) Councils called by parties in agreement — *duo parte*. (*c*) Councils called by parties in disagreement — mutual. (*d*) Councils called by one party in a controversy — *ex parte*. (11) Some councils easily confounded with others. (*a*) As councils in lay discipline — *uni parte* with *ex parte*. (*b*) As councils of friends — *duo parte* with mutual. (*c*) "The third may," when *ex parte*. (12) Mode of procedure in councils. (13) The "result" of councils. (14) Councils dissolved on adjournment without day.

QUESTIONS ON COUNCILS.

§ 195. What is the force of usage in Congregationalism?............279
§ 196. Is the result of a council divisible? 280
§ 197. Is there the right of challenge in selecting councils?........280
§ 198. Is there not danger of packing councils? — Associations better, with appeal to mutual councils 280
§ 199. Can an association be a party to a council? 282
    (1) Parties most interested may call councils. (2) Past usage can not prevent change. (3) Similar councils have been called. (4) The need of such councils urgent. (5) They adjust our polity to its expanding conditions.
§ 200. What part have councils in ministerial discipline? 284
    (1) Ministers amenable to the churches as ministers. (2) Churches in any locality have "the inalienable right" to

give or withhold fellowship. (3) The method of using the right separable from the right itself. — Councils render the right practically inoperative. (4) The inalienable right demands change to ministerial standing in associations of churches. (5) Mutual councils then needed for redress of wrongs or for completing process of discipline.

§ 201. May a council depose a minister? 287

(1) The ministerial function and call. (2) Ordination the recognition of these. (3) Not the conferring of character, grace, or the Holy Spirit. (4) Withdrawal of ordination by council deposition.

§ 202. Why may not councils yield to associations of churches in ordination and in deposition? 288

(1) Nothing to prevent the change but usage. (2) An association of churches better than a council. (a) It includes the churches in any locality, which a council may not do. (b) It can correct mistakes, which a council can not. (c) Neither method interferes with church independence. (d) If an association ordain, it should depose. (e) Economy favors associations in many states. (3) These reasons favor associations of churches.

§ 203. May not installation give place to recognition? 290
§ 204. Are councils adequate safeguards? 290

(1) They reach only one third of our pastors and one fourth of our ministers. (2) This decadence has occurred in the face of urgent appeals for installation. (3) Councils are thus failing safeguards and inadequate.

MINISTERIAL ASSOCIATIONS.

§ 205. Ministerial associations express church fellowship in an indirect way 292

(1) Definition of ministerial associations. (2) Their origin. (3) Their object. (4) Ministerial standing sometimes held in such associations. (5) Ministerial associations temporary in nature.

CHURCH ASSOCIATIONS.

§ 206. Definition of associations of churches. — Names 295
§ 207. Importance of church associations 295
§ 208. Origin of church associations 296

(1) The General Court as a lay association. (2) Earliest associations in America. (3) Earliest associations in England.

§ 209. Membership and functions of church associations 298
"The inalienable right of churches in any locality."
§ 210. Associations possess no authority over churches 300

§ 211. Process of expulsion from an association of churches 301
  (1) An association ordaining should depose. (2) An association bound to labor with and depose the unworthy. (3) Difference between pastoral representation and ministerial membership or standing in associations. (4) Expulsion cuts off from connection; deposes.
§ 212. Relief from injustice in a mutual council 304
§ 213. Credentials of ministers and churches. — Dual contents of Presbyterian credentials 304
§ 214. Our churches evolving this normal system of church associations 305
  NOTE. — Origin of The National Council of the Congregational Churches of the United States. 306

LECTURE XI.
THE DOCTRINE OF THE CHRISTIAN CHURCH.
ACTIVITIES AND RELATIONS.

§ 215. The churches commissioned to evangelize the world 312
§ 216. Work committed to each local church 312
  (1) Training the children and candidates for admission. — Sunday-schools. (2) Parish evangelization.
§ 217. Churches should coöperate in common labors 314
  (1) In ministerial training. (2) In home evangelization. (3) In foreign missions.
§ 218. Methods of coöperation among independent churches 314
  (1) Coöperation of the primitive churches. (2) Coöperation through voluntary societies. (3) Coöperation through permanent boards of trust. (4) Coöperation through individual and delegated trust. (5) Coöperation through association of churches.
§ 219. The normal method of church coöperation 317
§ 220. Obstacles to be overcome in reaching the normal method 319
  (1) Reverence for the ways of our fathers. (2) Regard for charters and trust funds. (3) Fear of unwarranted centralization.
§ 221. Obstacles: how removed in attaining the normal method 320
§ 222. Advantages of churches managing their common labors 321
§ 223. Churches, not individuals, the true factors 322

LEGAL RELATIONS OF CHURCHES.

§ 224. Churches must touch in some points the civil power 323
§ 225. Churches independent of the State, and dependent upon it 324
§ 226. Their true relation lost in the union of Church and State 325
§ 227. The Reformation but a partial return 326

§ 228. Full return in America to the primitive relation 327
§ 229. The parish system an inheritance from the State 328
§ 230. The parish contained the legal existence of a church 331
§ 231. This inheritance should be rejected for the normal relation, in which 332
 (1) The State may legislate respecting church property. (2) The State may exempt or tax church property. (3) The State may require the teaching of morals and religion in its schools. (4) The State may suppress disorder in a church and enforce Sunday rest. (5) The State may prevent church fines and imprisonment. (6) The State may regulate the alienation of church property and trust funds.

COMITY AMONG CHURCHES.

§ 232. Different theories of the Church give different communions and require comity 337
 (1) Comity assumes the right of private judgment. (2) Comity divides churches into evangelical and unevangelical. (3) Comity requires limited fellowship with the evangelical churches. It is to be remembered: (*a*) That the Lord established independent churches. (*b*) That union efforts end in denominational results. (*c*) That other polities deny church independence and liberty. (4) Comity can not fellowship unevangelical churches.

RELATION OF CHURCHES TO THE WORLD.

§ 233. The churches are commissioned to evangelize the world, not to conform to it 341

LECTURE XII.

THE DOCTRINE OF THE CHRISTIAN CHURCH.

CREED. — OBJECTIONS.

§ 234. Church Creeds of the utmost importance 344
§ 235. The General Confessions of Congregational Churches 345
§ 236. The Doctrinal Bases of State Associations 346
§ 237. Creeds of local churches 347
§ 238. Assent of members and pastors to church creeds 347
§ 239. Safeguard in church councils 348
§ 240. History vindicates these guards of Orthodoxy 348
§ 241. The people the best custodians of faith 350
§ 242. The people the best guardians of liberty 352
§ 243. Congregational discipline and purity in the faith 353
§ 244. These safeguards complete 354

CONTENTS. xxiii

SOME OBJECTIONS TO CONGREGATIONALISM CONSIDERED.

§ 245. The force of objections......................................355
(1) Some objections have no force whatever. (2) Some objections lie against faulty administration. (3) Some objections have real but not conclusive force. (4) Objections test polities and show the best.

§ 246. Objection from public discipline............................357

§ 247. Objection respecting unity among churches 357

§ 248. Objection respecting efficiency. Efficiency : 359
(1) Hindered by union efforts. (2) Hindered by union of Church and State. (3) Hindered by the parish system. (4) Hindered by the "Plan of Union." (5) Hindered by defects in discipline. (6) Efficiency from use of wisdom. (7) Efficiency from use of resources. (8) Complete efficiency from the union of wisdom and resources.

§ 249. Objection from centralization in unity 363
(1) The Master prayed for unity. (2) Fellowship devoid of authority. (3) Votes devoid of authority. (4) Our churches freed from personal leadership. (5) Our churches relieved of ministerial control. (6) They have rejected consociationism. (7) They avoid all dangerous centralization in their associations. (8) These associations rightly balance liberty and unity.

§ 250. Congregationalism, it is objected, would have been an anomaly in the first centuries 368
(1) The gospel not an evolution of nature. (2) The gospel was, then, an anomaly in the first century. (3) The synagogues were democratic. (4) Democratic independent churches conceded as a fact in the first century.

§ 251. The edifice too large for the foundation, it is said. — The constitutive principle can bear ecumenical unity................370

§ 252. Government not given prominence enough in Congregationalism. — The Scriptural warrant exhausted 370

§ 253. Church government discretionary, it is said 370
(1) Polity belongs to the essence of the church. (2) Confirmed by convictions of men. (3) The constitutive principle of Congregationalism given in the New Testament. (4) The New Testament commands obedience in polity, as in doctrine. (5) The future belongs to the primitive polity. Conclusion.

Index 377

·THE CHURCH-KINGDOM:

LECTURES ON CONGREGATIONALISM.

LECTURE I.

THE PATRIARCHAL DISPENSATION AND THE CEREMONIAL DISPENSATION.

"God having provided some better thing concerning us, that apart from us they should not be made perfect." — Epistle to the Hebrews.

§ 1. WE are called upon in these Lectures to examine as we may be able the external forms of an institution which had its origin in heaven, which expresses the highest wisdom and love of our Father in heaven, which, including the richest part of human history, will find its full consummation in heaven, and which is called in its final earthly form " the kingdom of heaven." This wonderful institution, in its widest comprehension, is named the Church of God.

No one who takes this wide view of our subject can feel cramped in its study. For what engages God's wisdom and love, all through the ages, from Eden to the end of the world, " to the intent that now unto the principalities and the powers in the heavenly places might be made known *through the Church* the manifold wisdom of God, according to the eternal purpose which he purposed in Christ Jesus our Lord "(Eph. 3: 10, 11), — what thus engages God's wisdom and love and purpose ought certainly to engage also the reverent study of every believer: but especially the most devout inquiry of all who are aspiring to be ministers in this holy Church of God.

§ 2. It is true that we are confined to the outward forms of this divine institution, to the exclusion, in large degree, of the inner life that animates and fashions those forms; but there is such a reciprocal relation between form and life, and organism and the vital energy which develops it, that no one who regards the life can disregard the form. Indeed, in nature we study life only in and through its organic manifestation; and in grace we study the life of God in the hearts of men, as an energy leavening society and restoring righteousness and worship, chiefly in and through the Church, the organic manifestation of that life. In the development of the life hid with Christ in God there may have been changes of outward form to suit an altered environment; but in every case the life must be examined in and through the organism by which it chiefly manifested itself at the time. Alter the organism, and, if the life demanded it, a richer development follows, as when Judaism passed upwards into Christianity; but if the life did not demand it, decay follows, as when Christianity partially passed backwards into Judaism again. Thus a change in the outward constitution of religion is the most momentous that can come to any people. For "the real history of man is the history of religion — the wonderful ways by which the different families of the human race advanced towards a true knowledge and a deeper love of God. This is the foundation that underlies all profane history : it is the light, the soul, and life of history, and without it all history would indeed be profane." [1] This close relation between form and life in religion, and between religion and the history of man, gives to church polity a place next to theology.

§ 3. Indeed, the outward form of the Church goes beyond the inner life and fashions theological systems with its moulding touch. "It is a significant fact that in the primitive churches the earliest departure from the gospel was not in the false statement of doctrine, but in the perversion of

---

[1] Max Müller's Chips from a German Workshop, 1, 20.

church government and ordinances. Sacerdotalism and sacramentarianism led the way to the later corruption of Christianity in its doctrinal form."[2] Hence doctrinal reforms should have as their aim the purification of the fountain whence the chief doctrinal errors have flowed. And such in fact has been their aim. "All the endeavors truly reformatory down to the Reformation had the idea of the true Church in some form for their basis." And the great Reformation was "the setting forth of a new conception of the Church, which . . . derived church authority not from a particular order, but from the whole communion."[3] "The doctrine of the Church, its due constitution, discipline, and worship, is a doctrine of no mean order in the Christian system of truth. It is intimately connected with the doctrine of sacred Scripture and with the doctrine of the Holy Spirit. The doctrines of regeneration, of the sacraments, of sanctification, and even of Christ as the sole Mediator and Teacher of men, are intimately connected with it."[4]

The nature of the Church as a divine institution, the vital influence that outward forms have on the inner life in its unfolding, and the irresistible power with which the doctrine of the Church has historically moulded, and, in the nature of things, must ever mould, other cardinal doctrines, combine to enforce a study which the superficial brush aside as trivial.

§ 4. We ask, therefore, all who are filled with the spirit of Christ to study the organic forms which the life-giving and redeeming grace of Christ has taken in its unfolding. It appeared first in the family form, which was capable of universal extension, but which lacked due expression of "the communion of saints," and which, therefore, was not suited to a world-wide religion. Then it grew into a national form, which, from ethnic and geographical reasons, was provincial and exclusive, fostering within narrow limits

[2] The Church, by Prof. H. Harvey, D.D., 16, 17.
[3] Herzog's Ency., condensed trans. vol. 1, 681.
[4] Principles of Church Polity, by Prof. George T. Ladd, D.D., 180.

the fellowship of the saints, but totally inadequate for an ecumenical religion. From this it flowered into a third and final form, which, through the union of particular congregations, exhibits fully "the communion of saints," and which is thus fitted to be an ecumenical and everlasting form. We shall pass hastily through the first and second forms, as through porches of the true temple, that we may dwell in the glory of the third. As we believe the porches were built, after divine patterns, so we believe that the temple itself was not left to the art of men, but is of God, fashioned after an imperishable model.

§ 5. Christendom is divided into two great sections over the definition of the Church of God, especially in its Christian form. "One great body, following Calvin and embracing a majority of Protestant communities, maintain that the Church is invisible; while the Lutherans, the Roman Catholics, the Oriental Christians, and the great bulk of the more famous Anglican divines (in accordance with the Anglican formularies) maintain it to be visible."[5] This line, of course, is broadly drawn. Few, if any, on the one side deny that the invisible Church becomes visible in suitable organizations, and that too by the operation of its own inherent forces; and few on the other side, except the Roman Catholics, deny that the visible Church has an invisible boundary not precisely conterminous with the visible. And some Roman Catholics admit that a few outside their communion will be saved through invincible ignorance. The issue is one of adjusting boundary lines. Are the lines of the spiritual realm and the lines of the visible organization identical? If they are, then the marks or notes of the invisible Church are the marks or notes of the visible Church; for both are the same thing. Are the lines that bound the invisible Church different from those that bound the visible Church? Then the notes or marks of the one are not the notes or marks of the other, but they separate

[5] Ency. Brit. 9th ed. v, 759.

in varying degrees, even unto entire divergence. We shall find, we believe, that in no one of the three great forms of the Church of God were these lines identical, but instead more or less divergent, proving that the visible Church is not identical with the invisible. But this will be more fully treated hereafter.

§ 6. But what is the Church of God as manifested in its threefold form? We answer in the words of Prof. Samuel Harris, D.D., of Yale Theological Seminary: " The Church is the organic outgrowth of the life-giving and redeeming grace of Christ penetrating human history in the Holy Spirit."[6] On this definition, note : (1) That it applies to all three dispensations of the Church of God, though particularly designed to define the Christian Church. (2) That it makes the life of Christ penetrating humanity and redeeming it the germ and root of the Church. (3) That this life penetrates history through the Holy Spirit. That life enters the individual heart in regeneration and is nurtured in sanctification. The Church is not therefore independent of Christ and the Spirit in its inception, progress, and consummation. (4) Yet the Church is not this life, but the organic outgrowth of the life-giving and redeeming grace of Christ. The Church of God is more than the number of the redeemed ; it is more than the fruits of the Spirit in the hearts of the redeemed ; it is more than the atoning work of Christ its Head ; it is also an organic outgrowth, "the communion of saints." (5) This organic outgrowth or manifestation may be, or it may not be, exactly conterminous with the redeeming grace of Christ penetrating human society in the Holy Spirit. The Church is an organic manifestation of an invisible life, which may gather into itself some foreign elements, and which may continue to exist as an organism for a time after its life-giving energy has been withdrawn.

Now this Church of God, born of the grace of God,

[6] 29 Bib. Sacra, 114.

begun in Eden, destined to fill the world with glory, and to be consummated in heaven (1 Cor. 15 : 24-28), has had three forms of organic manifestation, above alluded to, called the patriarchal dispensation, the ceremonial or Mosaic dispensation, and the Christian dispensation — the family, the national, and the ecumenical forms.

We will now trace this organic outgrowth of the grace of God in Christ penetrating human society.

I. — THE PATRIARCHAL DISPENSATION, OR THE FAMILY FORM OF THE CHURCH OF GOD.

§ 7. We assume the patriarchal theory of the origin of society, which has been stated by Sir Henry Maine to be, "'the origin of society in separate families, held together by the authority and protection of the eldest valid male ascendant. . . . The strongest and wisest male rules. . . . All under his protection are on an equality.' This is also Darwin's view. . . . At present it must be concluded that the most probable theory of the structure of early society is that, in a more or less developed form, the family was the original unit; sexual and parental affection point to it, and early law and custom confirm it."[7]

§ 8. But, whatever the origin of human society, this earliest form of the Church of God can not be carried back beyond man's apostasy. The Church begins where so many sermons begin, at Adam's fall. Had Adam stood in his integrity, the worship he and his posterity would have offered unto God would have expressed the beauty of their own native holiness. The confession of sin and the redemptive element would have found no place in it. It would have been like that of the angels. The Church of God, as we know it, could not in that case have existed. This is evident.

§ 9. The beginnings of the Church of God were in this wise. The life-giving and redeeming grace, of which the

[7] Prof. George Harris, D.D., 5 Andover Rev. 662, 664.

Church is the organic outgrowth, was announced to our apostate parents in the garden of Eden in a most comprehensive and germinant promise that the seed of the woman should bruise the serpent's head (Gen. 3: 15). When this proto-evangel opened the door of hope, there was no Church, and no material for a Church, except as sinners could be brought to repentance. The love and wisdom of God in a plan of redemption had been dimly hinted at, but the prime condition essential to the beginning of the Church, penitence, had not yet been wrought in the heart of man.

The first recorded appearance of the Church of God in germ was in the sacrifices offered by Cain and Abel (Gen. 4: 3, 4). And it is significant that the scriptural list of saints begins with the name of the first martyr (Heb. 11: 4). When the second son of Adam became righteous, we do not know; but worship, both eucharistic and expiatory, either by command of God or by the demand of fallen human nature, had been instituted long before the special sacrifice which God respected and which angered Cain. It seems certain that the faith of Abel began the Church of God.

§ 10. But the life of saints continued to the exodus of Israel. There may have been breaks in the succession, even after Seth renewed it; but the great promise of a Saviour was handed down through Enoch, Noah, and others, until it was confirmed in a covenant with Abraham and with his seed. The meager record gives only the great events; and saints seem always to have been few. Indeed, twice the Church became almost extinct — at the flood and at the call of Abraham. The mingling of the sons of Seth with the daughters of Cain ended in the deluge. Through Noah God sought to people the earth again with a godly seed. But this seed became corrupt, until a single family was called, and, to keep it pure, was made to wander up and down the promised land. Many others, like Melchizedek, may have retained belief in Jehovah, but the sacred narrative leads apparently to another conclusion. Men knowing

God glorified him not as God, but fell into idolatry, save the few who continued the genealogy of faith, the Church of God, until the giving of the law.

§ 11. The form of the Church in this period was very simple, hardly entitled to the term organic. It is expressed by the word patriarchal. The household was the only visible organism. Its elements of worship and belief were: (1) The Sabbath. The day of rest and of worship was instituted, we believe, before the apostasy. It was ordained of God in man's physical constitution and announced (Gen. 2: 2); and it was observed after the fall in some fashion, as indicated in the moral law (Ex. 20: 8). (2) Sacrifices. These were eucharistic and expiatory (Gen. 4: 3–5). Wherever men called upon the name of the Lord, it is probable that they did so in connection with such sacrifices. Noah (Gen. 8: 20), Abraham (Gen. 12: 7, 8; 13: 18; 15: 9; 22: 1–13), Isaac (Gen. 26: 25), and Jacob (Gen. 28: 18; 33: 20; 35: 14) sacrificed unto the Lord. Their sacrifices had in remembrance God's blessings, and also man's sin and the promised Saviour; and were therefore eucharistic and expiatory. They were continued down to the giving of the law (Job 1: 5; 42: 8; Ex. 10: 25); that is, from the beginning to the end of the period. (3) A priesthood. The patriarch was the priest of his household. This is declared of some of the patriarchs; it is presumptively so of the rest. There were no other priests. Hence the term patriarchal has been given the period. (4) There was no initiatory rite at first. Natural birth or purchase or conquest introduced into the household and into all the privileges of the Church estate. But God's covenant with Abraham was sealed by the sign of circumcision. It covered children and slaves (Gen. 17: 10–14). This outward rite was the sign and seal of a spiritual renewal (Deut. 10: 16; 30: 6), of the covenant of promise (Gal. 3: 7, 29), and of the life hid with Christ in God (Col. 3: 3). It therefore binds the three dispensations into one covenant (Col. 2: 11, 12). (5) The creed embraced a few and simple beliefs — God, prayer, salvation, special promises — on which faith lay hold (Heb. 11: 1-29). "To follow up any of the religions thus represented, in the true line of their subsequent history, must certainly land us in a creed recognizing only one God . . . a worship of simple patriarchal sacrifice and prayer, and belief in the favor of a personal and merciful God thereby."[8] This creed was unwritten, traditional, enlarging as God revealed himself to the patriarchs.

§ 12. This form of the Church, though so simple, was not unifying. Natural selection may have drawn the pious into some forms of fellowship; but the only recorded attempt at consolidation or solidarity by building the tower of Babel was frustrated (Gen. 11 : 1-9). The Jacobs and the Esaus could not agree or live in peace; but neither gathered a following after his kind from beyond his own household. The form was narrow, clannish, isolating. It could not make the people of God one congregation. There was no fellowship wider than that of the family circle, unless at rare intervals (Gen. 14 : 18-20).

§ 13. Nor did this form of the Church conserve piety. Twice in its progress the Church ran almost out; but God interposed to save it, first, by the ark of Noah (Gen. 6 : 1-

[8] Comp. Hist. Religions, by Prof. J. C. Moffat, D.D., part 1, 246. The Veda are to the Aryan or Indo-European family of nations including the English, what Genesis is to the Semitic family of nations, including the Hebrew. Max Müller, in his Chips from a German Workshop, vol. i, sect. 1, says: "The religion of the Veda knows of no idols;" "God has established the eternal laws of right and wrong;" "He punishes sin and rewards virtue;" "the same God is willing to forgive; just, yet merciful;" "the idea of faith is found in the Veda, including trust in the gods, and belief in their existence; a belief in personal immortality, without a trace of metempsychosis or the transmigration of souls." "The Veda is the earliest deposit of the Aryan faith." "The religion of the Veda is Polytheism, not Monotheism;" but "not what is commonly understood as Polytheism. Yet it would be equally wrong to call it Monotheism." 27-44.

The development in the Bible is upwards into greater clearness and fulness; that of the Veda downwards, until in Buddhism religion is lost in a system "without a God," "without what goes by the name of 'soul,'" "without an objective heaven," "without a vicarious saviour," "without rites, prayers, penances, priests, or intercessory saints." It is only by accommodation that such a system can be called a religion. "The word 'religion' is most inappropriate to apply to Buddhism, which is not a religion, but a moral philosophy." Olcott's Buddhist Catechism, ques. 128, 1, note.

8), and second, by the call of Abraham (Gen. 12: 1-3). By keeping Abraham, Isaac, and Jacob moving to and fro as pilgrims and strangers, and by special revelations, God preserved a holy seed until it should become a nation. The development was in all other cases away from God. This is declared by Paul (Rom. 1: 21-23), indicated by the record in Genesis, and supported by a comparison of ancient religions. It is said "that the fundamental elements of religion are the same in all the ancient records we possess; and the further into antiquity the history is pursued, the more does that in which they differ diminish. Consequently, the reasonable presumption is that if we could follow them all up through their history, we should find that the primitive religion in each of the cases was identical with that in all the rest."[9] Fitted to the condition of the race in its primitive needs, this form of the church did not conserve piety, nor fellowship nor unity. It was preparatory, not permanent.

§ 14. There was in the patriarchal dispensation no marked separation between saints and sinners. Cain and Abel seem to have worshiped together, until God signified his approval of the one and disapproval of the other. In that act of discrimination a distinction was made between an external worship and a service springing from true faith in God; but that distinction aroused the anger of Cain, and murder soon silenced the first saint and martyr. Cain was driven out, and Seth revived the line of saints. But when "the sons of God saw the daughters of men that they were fair," the line of Seth mingled again with the line of Cain (Gen. 6: 2), until the flood established anew a godly seed (Gen. 7: 1). The call of Abraham was a more marked separation, followed by the expulsion of Ishmael and the choice of Jacob instead of Esau.

Then, as now, children of the same parents were not the same; but good and bad shared in the rites and worship of the household. The outgrowth of the divine life in the

[9] Moffat's Comp. Hist. Relig. 1, 246.

hearts of men took no discriminating form; it was bounded only by the sacredness of the family. The birthright had in it the priesthood of the family and the promise of the father. But the faithful and the unfaithful, the righteous and the wicked, were in the same household until they instituted households and clans of their own, when each followed his own bent, the many into idolatry, the few into monotheistic beliefs, like the patriarchs of Israel, Melchizedek, and even Balaam (Gen. 14: 18; Heb. 7: 1; Num. 22: 9, 18).

While this family form of the Church could easily have become ecumenical, it lacked the essential element of universal fellowship. It could not express the communion of saints, and did not, therefore, foster piety. Even the covenant which runs through the three dispensations is a family covenant. The life, begotten by the Holy Ghost, began in the family relation (Gen. 3: 15), was nurtured long in the household, and is still largely dependent on the family; but in due time it outgrew this narrow limitation, and entered upon a second stage of development.

II. — THE CEREMONIAL DISPENSATION, OR THE NATIONAL FORM OF THE CHURCH OF GOD.

§ 15. Near the close of the preceding dispensation, God prepared the way for the evolution of a new and better out of the old and inadequate form of the Church. This he did by confining the promised seed to the family of Abraham. He entered into a covenant with one man, to train him and his posterity, in one line, as a peculiar people, the chosen of God, until the Messiah should appear to bless "all the families of the earth" (Gen. 12: 3). This covenant he ratified in a solemn vision (Gen. 15: 5-18); and confirmed unto Isaac (Gen. 17: 19; 26: 3) and Jacob (Gen. 28: 13). When the sons of Jacob became twelve tribes, and were consolidated into one people by the bondage of Egypt, God led them into the wilderness to train them, and there he renewed this covenant with them as a united people. He purposed to weld them into one political and religious life. He said unto all Israel: "Ye shall be unto me a kingdom of priests, and an holy nation. And all the people answered together, and said: All that the Lord hath spoken we will do" (Ex. 19: 6, 8). Thus the whole people as a nation became consecrated unto God in church relations (Acts 7: 38); it was henceforth the *kahal*, or "the congregation," or Church of Israel, and was so treated in all sacred history. The family Church thus became a national Church.

§ 16. This covenant involved true religion, or the life of God in the heart, but did not distinguish by rigid tests between the holy and the wicked. It required circumcision of the heart (Lev. 26: 41, 42), but the outward sign and seal were applied only to males. To observe every ordinance and keep every commandment was to be holy; and yet the inner observance is not confounded with the outward performance (Rom. 2: 28, 29). This distinction runs in varying degrees of clearness through the whole sacred record. "The sacrifices of God are a broken spirit," and similar utterances, show that the pious understood the law as exacting more than external compliance (John 3: 3-10).

§ 17. The law followed immediately upon the renewal of the covenant. As the nation was also the Church, moral, religious, ceremonial, civil, military, and sanitary laws were intermingled in one code. Rulers and courts had jurisdiction in all matters. The code was specific and inflexible, covering the dress of the priests, the form of the tabernacle, the kinds of sacrifices, the time and number of feasts, every thing, indeed, that pertained to its gorgeous ritual.

§ 18. The place of worship tended to national unity. That place was at first the tabernacle, afterwards the temple. During the disorganized period of the judges (Judges 17: 6), there was no fixed capital nor stable government, but the tabernacle was a movable sanctuary. The law, however, was explicit, making one place the center of all worship (Deut. 12: 5-7), and so securing "the communion of saints." The unifying power of this law was such that Jeroboam, the son of Nebat, who rebelled, set up a counterfeit system to counteract it (1 Kings 12 : 26–29). He ordered his subjects to worship at Dan and Bethel. The civil power, he thought, needed the backing of the ecclesiastical, and so he caused Israel to sin.

§ 19. The priestly function of the father was now confined to Aaron and his posterity. Of this priesthood it may be said : (1) That it existed in three orders : the high priest, the priests, and the Levites. The Levites, taken instead of the firstborn of Israel, could not even see the holy things while uncovered ; but they carried and cared for the sacred utensils when covered by the priests. The priests offered sacrifices as mediators between God and the people. The high priest made annual atonement for the whole nation. (2) This priesthood was national, chosen from among the children of Israel to offer for all the people. (3) It was also exclusive. Only the male descendants of Aaron could be priests. " The stranger that cometh nigh shall be put to death " (Num. 18 : 7). (4) The priests were not, as such, rulers in Israel. Priestly, not civil, functions belonged to them. The rulers were at first chosen by the people. (5) To this priesthood the irregular order of the prophets did not belong. The prophets were inspired teachers, whether lay or priestly. They came from all classes and conditions in society, and were the moral and religious teachers of Israel.

§ 20. The ritual was minute and inflexible. Nothing in it was optional. It was a yoke which could with difficulty be borne (Acts 15 : 10). Passing minor matters, it required: (1) A bloody initiatory rite, which every male born into the nation or admitted to citizenship had to undergo. There was one law for the home-born and for the stranger (Ex. 12: 48, 49). No male could possess national rights without enduring this ecclesiastical rite. (2) The annual festivals brought all males three times a year to the ecclesiastical capital, if they obeyed the command respecting them (Ex.

23 : 17 ; Deut. 16 : 16). (3) Their memorial feast was the passover, which was a type of Christ (1 Cor. 5 : 7). This, when last observed by Christ, passed over into the Lord's Supper. It was observed in small companies. Thus the passover and circumcision became the germs of the Christian sacraments.

§ 21. The creed of this dispensation gathered about a belief in one personal and holy God, in the promised Messiah, in the law revealed on Sinai, and in the revelations made by the prophets. It became fuller as the prophets disclosed the glories of the coming reign of the promised Seed. Samuel founded the school of the prophets — regular societies for the purposes of instruction, the original of colleges, seminaries, universities. "Long before Plato had gathered his disciples around him in the olive-grove, or Zeno in The Portico, these institutions had sprung up under Samuel in Judæa." [10]

§ 22. God was the Ruler of this nation and Head of the Church. He instituted all laws, ceremonies, rites. He inspired the prophets. He decided causes when appealed to him (Deut. 1 : 17). God was the recognized Ruler of the people, the judges being his deputies, and the kings his viceroys. A "Thus saith the Lord," if properly authenticated was the end of controversy. The prophets were God's interpreters. To withhold tithes was to rob God (Mal. 3 : 8), and idolatry was adultery (Jer. 3 ; 13 : 27). This dispensation was a pure theocracy. There was no falling away from belief in a personal God, as in other religions; instead, God was made the national Ruler and constant Revealer. The prophets, whose writings we possess, would not let Israel forget God. Though they could not counteract the evils of Jeroboam's separate ecclesiastical establishment for the ten tribes, called the kingdom of Israel, they saved the kingdom of Judah from a similar fate, and attested to both kingdoms the existence, power, justice, and grace of an ever-living, personal God.

[10] Hist. Jewish Ch., Dean Stanley, i, 422.

§ 23. It is worthy of mention that this second, or national, form of the Church did not set aside the family, but continued it in all its integrity. It did not build a national establishment upon the foundation of the individual, but upon the foundation of the household. The home continued, though its priesthood was absorbed in the Aaronic priesthood. The family of Jacob had become the nation. That the family continued in full force under this dispensation is evident from the laws respecting marriage, the relation of children to parents, the Levirate marriage, the punishment of adultery, and the law of inheritance. The law recognized and fostered the existence and continuance of families. The family was the unit of organization. The people were numbered after their families, and circumcision was a household rite, as well as a national (Gen. 17 : 12 ; Josh. 5 : 2, 5, 9). Circumcision was the chief sign of the covenant, which, taking its origin in the family, became, as we have seen (§ 20) national.

This most important institution, the family, like the day of rest, was perpetuated also in the final and ecumenical form of the Church of God, the Christian dispensation. Development in ecclesiastical matters thus retains the primitive type, and what is added to suit new conditions is not destructive of the original form. Christianity fosters the home.

§ 24. Yet in this church form there was the greatest possible unity and concentration. There was one place of worship; one priesthood, culminating in one high priest; one initiatory rite; one ritual; one system of feasts; one congregation, or church; one Head and Ruler, the one living and true God. It was a close, exclusive, centralized, unifying system, in complete contrast with the preceding dispensation. The Church of God was a holy nation, which all believers in God must join. This concentration, together with its particularity, made the system burdensome in the extreme. Centering in the capital, to which all males must go three times a year, and filled with minute requirements, this "tutor" became intolerable (Gal. 3: 24; Acts 15: 10). It was in striking contrast both with the liberty of the gospel (Gal. 4: 3–7; 5: 1, 13) and with the cruel tyranny of other religions.

§ 25. This national Church became inadequate. The festal journeys were too severe for the young and aged, too long for the distant, and too infrequent for the needs of growing spirituality. The temple worship could not be carried into Babylon or into the dispersion. How much less could it meet the wants of all nations, if converted to Judaism? It conserved unity and fellowship, and thereby preserved the rich promises of God, but its limitations precluded its ever becoming the religious establishment of the world. It became conscious of this fatal inadequacy: for when it had largely served the ends for which it was ordained, the life which it had preserved and nourished found its provisions inadequate, and added thereto a form of worship in synagogues which became the germ of the Christian congregational worship. While Mosaism was old and vanishing away; while the temple was closed and the Church was in exile, and the required worship could not be rendered, social neighborhood worship sprung up, without prophet or priest, which soon spread wherever the Jews were scattered, and which met the wants of the pious, in reading the sacred books, in prayers, and in praise. We have seen how circumcision was the link which, extending four hundred and thirty years into the patriarchal dispensation, bound it to the ceremonial dispensation; and we shall see how the congregational worship of the synagogue became the organic link that, extending nearly six hundred years into the ceremonial dispensation, bound it to the Christian dispensation. The life of God begotten in the hearts of men prepared for enlargement in external forms centuries before the actual development occurred.

§ 26. Nor was the extra-legal synagogue worship the only prophecy of the coming fulfillment and supersedure of the ceremonial law. Moses, who had founded this dispensation, had especially predicted its temporary nature (Deut. 18: 18, 19). The Law-giver, like unto Moses, should establish a new covenant, which should include the Gentiles (Is. 42: 6). Daniel became very explicit: "The God of heaven shall set up a kingdom, which shall never be destroyed" (Dan. 2: 44). The Jews understood these predictions; for they looked for a coming One, even at the time of his appearing, to establish a kingdom.

It is hardly necessary to add that the ceremonial dispensation has been superseded by the Christian. Christ came to fulfill and destroy it (Matt. 5: 17, 18). When he said: "It is finished," the veil of the temple was rent in twain, from the top to the bottom (Matt. 27: 51), opening the most holy place in the sacred temple to the gaze and tread of all men. This ended the second form of the Church of God, a fact repeatedly declared in the Acts and Epistles. The partition between Jew and Gentile was broken down (Acts 11: 12-17; Eph. 2: 14, 15); circumcision was abolished (Acts 15: 1, 24-29). Christ "abolished the law of commandments contained in ordinances" (Eph. 2: 15), and brought in "a better hope" (Heb. 7: 18, 19), under another priest (Heb. 4: 14) and law (Heb. 7: 12).

§ 27. In concluding this imperfect glance at the preparatory dispensations, it is of importance to note what parts of them, if any, are properly taken up into the Christian dispensation. We have already referred to the family as running through all three dispensations (§ 23); so also the Sabbath and the covenant of grace (§§ 16, 23). Other common elements will appear in our discussion. Here let us mark two tendencies: (1) The attempt has sometimes been made to return to the family form of the Church. All church organizations and all associations of ministers and churches, of whatever name, are denounced. Christianity is to be, in the view of such, wholly unorganized. Individual and family nurture is all that is needed. But the results of such nurture, whether in the primitive or in modern times, do not satisfy. Indeed, they indicate that the disintegration of organic Christianity would be fatal to piety and missions. Hence this tendency is sporadic and transient. (2) The more extended and less fatal tendency is the transplanting of the ceremonial dispensation into the Christian. The priesthood, the ritual, the union of Church and State, the infallibility of teaching, have been transferred into the major part of Christendom, from which reformations have only secured a partial deliverance.

§ 28. If any one still fancies that polity is of trifling importance, he needs to recall the price at which the liberties of Protestantism have been bought; for it was on the field of church polity and through a sea of blood that they were won, and it is only on the same field that they can be maintained. The Protestant and the Puritan reforms had been lost altogether, had they not rested ultimately on a theory of the Church, that is, church government. Calvin wrote his Institutes, we are told, in order to convert Francis I., king of France. "It was a decisive moment in the history of the kingdom of God. Had the king, to whom all were looking, been converted, the nation would have been converted, and the conversion of France would have given a new character to this portion of history." [11] To have done this, however, the king's conversion must have led him to break with Rome; and his spiritual renewal must have also become an ecclesiastical conversion. For had he been regenerated by the Spirit, the conversion which Calvin desired would have occurred only in part. The reformers looked for more, for the adoption also of the great Protestant doctrine of the right of private judgment in matters spiritual, out of which has come all our liberties. Only such a conversion would have changed the history of France and of Europe. For systems of theology may come and go under the same polity, like floods in a river; even reforms may arise under any mode of ecclesiastical government; but unless they reform

[11] Henry's Life of Calvin, 53.

the polity by changing its nature, or break loose from it, or are cast out by it, the on-rushing stream soon obliterates all traces of the reformation. In proof of this, put the histories of Germany, Holland, England, and Scotland in contrast with the histories of Italy, Spain, France, and Bohemia. Great awakenings in the former countries changed their histories, but only because they broke away from the polity brought over from Judaism; but similar awakenings in the latter countries failed utterly, because not carried, from various causes, into separation from the Papacy. It has been the ecclesiastical reformations that have saved the doctrinal and spiritual from beating like tides against the solid rock. As before said: "All the endeavors, truly reformatory, down to the Reformation had the idea of the true Church in some form for their basis." "The Reformation was the setting forth of a new conception of the Church." Reforms from papal errors and oppressions have failed whenever a new conception of the Church has for any reason been unable to assert itself as an accomplished fact, and such reforms must ever fail.

§ 29. The difficult task falls, therefore, to the lot of church polity of separating what is permanent from what is transient in the preparatory dispensations, and of embodying the permanent while rejecting the transient in the final Christian polity. In other words, we are called upon to trace the normal development of the outgrowth of the life of God in human history from its primitive germs to its perfect realization. We have seen its growth from the family form into the national, which itself looked forward to an ecumenical and everlasting form. It is the part of students of church polity to unfold the true doctrine of the Church of God in its principles and details, while keeping it free from all attempted regressions into the outgrown and superseded, and from all abnormal developments. Communions, like fragments, have been broken off from the perverted Christian forms, and they have approached more or less closely the normal and final polity. We seek the true; for we are taught by history that a false theory of church government carried Christendom to Rome, as it has carried many back to Rome since the Reformation. Reforms in false theories, until they reach and establish a better doctrine of the Church, are floods in a river, tides in the ocean, which come and go, and leave things essentially as they were before.

LECTURE II.

THE KINGDOM OF HEAVEN AND ITS MANIFESTATION.

"*Preaching the kingdom of God, and teaching the things concerning the Lord Jesus Christ.*" — Luke, of Saint Paul.

III. — THE CHRISTIAN DISPENSATION, OR THE ECUMENICAL FORM OF THE CHURCH OF GOD.

§ 30. IN tracing the outgrowth of the life of Christ in the hearts of men, we passed hastily through the preparatory forms, until they developed into the Christian dispensation, which is only the kingdom of heaven in manifestation. It is evident from the Gospels that Jesus Christ looked upon the kingdom of God, or the kingdom of heaven, as the foundation of his Church, or perhaps we should rather say that he viewed his Church as the manifestation of his kingdom. Hence he dwelt almost exclusively, in his teachings, on the kingdom. The kingdom of heaven is his common phrase. So much the greater, therefore, is our wonder that writers on Congregationalism have so largely ignored all discussion of the nature and relations of the kingdom of heaven;[1] for the study of the kingdom is the natural approach to the study of organic Christianity. Christ viewed his mission as the setting up of a kingdom, whose characteristics he took great pains to disclose. Church polity should therefore be studied from the stand-point of the kingdom, from

[1] Hanbury, at great pains, has gathered into three large volumes of Historical Memorials the history and writings of English Congregationalists from their modern beginning to the Restoration, in 1660, but the word kingdom does not occur in his elaborate index. The same is true of Felt's Ecclesiastical History of New England, in two volumes, covering the period from 1620 to 1678. These volumes of Hanbury and Felt cover the fruitful formative periods of Congregationalism in England and America. Dr. Leonard Bacon, Dr. Henry M. Dexter, The Congregational Dictionary, and others, do not treat of the kingdom of heaven, while setting forth its manifestation. John Cotton's Keyes of the Kingdom devotes only a few lines to the nature of the kingdom of heaven. This general silence is ominous, since the term is found so frequently in the New Testament and since writers of other polities discuss it at length.

which Christ and his apostles viewed it. Historical Congregationalism ought not to be separated from the kingdom of heaven as its normal development. Hence we shall seek to unfold the external form of the Christian Church, not from the imperfect vision of those who revived its primitive manifestation under the restrictions of an unfavorable environment, but from the clear vision of its Founder and his apostles, who gave the interior formative principles. We hope thus to reach a wider and completer view of the unity and comprehension of the Church than could be obtained by any merely historical treatment. We approach this inner, central, and comprehensive view with reverence.

I. — THE KINGDOM OF HEAVEN.

§ 31. It would seem superfluous to prove that Christ established a reign in the world which he called the kingdom of heaven, or the kingdom of God, or the kingdom, were it not that some have questioned its present establishment. We must, therefore, show that the kingdom has been already set up, of which the Church is the manifestation.

(1) The establishment of a kingdom had been predicted. God revealed that he had anointed a King whose rule shall include the nations and the uttermost parts of the earth (Ps. 2: 6, 8), whose kingdom shall never be transferred or destroyed, but which shall become universal and endure forever (Dan. 2: 44; 7: 14, 27). The birth-place of this King was declared (Micah 5: 2), so that the Sanhedrin promptly answered Herod's question where the Christ should be born (Matt. 2: 5), and the star led the magi to the feet of the Prince of Peace, when born in Bethlehem. The character of this kingdom, in some of its features, and the time and place of the birth of its King were foretold.

(2) Lest the Jews should not be prepared to welcome their King and his kingdom, a forerunner came to announce both. He cried: "Repent ye; for the kingdom of heaven is at hand (Matt. 3: 2; Mark 1: 1–8). Even the King himself

took up the same cry (Matt. 4: 17), and he commanded his apostles to proclaim: "The kingdom of heaven is at hand" (Matt. 10: 7). The seventy were charged to cry in every city and place where Jesus was about to come: "The kingdom of God is come nigh unto you" (Luke 10: 9), and no opposition was to prevent their crying it (Luke 10: 11). Such urgency proves that in the mind of Christ the kingdom was not a remote reign, not even now begun, as some teach, but instead a near and almost present reign, which enabled him even then to say: "Then is the kingdom of God come upon you" (Matt. 12: 28).

(3) Indeed, the gospel is declared to be the gospel of the kingdom. Jesus preached the gospel of the kingdom (Matt. 4: 23; 9: 35; Luke 8: 1); and he said to the Pharisees: "The law and the prophets were until John: from that time the gospel of the kingdom of God is preached" (Luke 16: 16). Philip preached in Samaria "good tidings concerning the kingdom of God and the name of Jesus Christ" (Acts 8: 12). And Paul in Corinth reasoned and persuaded as to "the things concerning the kingdom of God" (Acts 19: 8).

(4) Hence it was a natural expression they used when they spoke of preaching the kingdom of God. Christ sent the Twelve "to preach the kingdom of God" (Luke 9: 2), and another to "publish abroad the kingdom of God" (Luke 9: 60). Paul "went about preaching the kingdom" (Acts 20: 25), "testifying the kingdom of God," and "preaching the kingdom of God" (Acts 28: 23, 31).

(5) The kingdom was to be set up immediately. Christ's words are emphatic: "I tell you of a truth, There be some of them that stand here, which shall in no wise taste of death, till they see the kingdom of God" (Luke 9: 27). In other passages he asserted not a distant, but a present or immediate, kingdom (Matt. 11: 12; Luke 22: 29).

(6) The kingdom as already set up is contrasted with the ceremonial or Mosaic dispensation. This is done by

Paul as respects meats (Rom. 14: 17), and also as respects glory. "For if the ministration of condemnation is glory, much rather doth the ministration of righteousness exceed in glory" (2 Cor. 3: 9). So glorious a thing it is to be a Christian that the least in this kingdom are greater than the greatest in the ceremonial dispensation (Matt. 11: 11).

(7) Christ based his command to evangelize the nations on his assumption of regal power. His words are: "All authority hath been given unto me in heaven and on earth. Go ye therefore, and make disciples of all the nations" (Matt. 28: 18, 19).

Thus it seems clear that Christ now reigns in the kingdom of heaven, a kingdom so glorious that Mount Sinai ceases to be glorious (2 Cor. 3: 10, 11), and that his kingdom is put into sharp contrast with the preceding dispensations. The preparatory are merged in the permanent, so far as this world is concerned; though, in the final consummation, even this kingdom shall be delivered up unto God the Father, that God may be all in all (1 Cor. 15: 24–28). Meyer remarks that the expressions, the kingdom of heaven, the kingdom of God, the kingdom, "never signify any thing else than the kingdom of the Messiah, even in those passages where they appear to denote the (invisible) Church, the moral kingdom of the Christian religion, or such like."[2]

§ 32. The kingdom of heaven is the reign of Christ in the world as respects redeemed humanity, with its divinely revealed destiny, manifesting itself in the Christian dispensation. There are certain characteristics or notes which define the kingdom more accurately, and are more or less essential to its existence.

(1) A kingdom involves the loyalty of its subjects to the king. It is so here. Christ is King, and loyalty to him is essential. He has the sole power to enact laws. In him rests the sole power of executing those laws. If any claim

[2] Com. on Matt. 3: 2.

to act for him, they must present their commission. For the King is supreme and over all, God blessed forever. He is Head over all things to the Church, which is his body (Eph. 1: 22, 23). Hence none but he can be called Master (Matt. 23: 10). Personal allegiance, or loyalty, is due from each and every one, and exists, so far as his reign extends, in human hearts. "My sheep hear my voice, and I know them, and they follow me" (John 10: 27), are his tender words. There can be neither neutrality (Matt. 12: 30) nor divided service (Matt. 6: 24). To guide them into all the truth, he sent his Spirit to take his place with his disciples (John 14: 26; 16: 13), so that what the apostles taught was "the commandment of the Lord" (1 Cor. 14: 37). This loyalty involves love, faith, obedience, all secured and nourished by the abounding grace of the King.

(2) Unity is also an essential element of the kingdom. The kingdom is one, and not many. It can not be divided. A part can not be severed from the rest and remain still a part of the kingdom. To be separated from it is to apostatize. It is one and inseparable, now and forever (Matt. 12: 25).

(3) Another essential characteristic is holiness. It is a holy kingdom. Its King is sinless; and his life, penetrating humanity through the Holy Ghost, begets a kindred holy life, while the past sins are forgiven (Rom. 3: 25, 26). Christ abides in the believing subject "the hope of glory" (John 14: 23; Col. 1: 27), and the saint becomes thus a partaker of the divine nature (2 Pet. 1: 4). The kingdom is righteousness and peace and joy in the Holy Ghost (Rom. 14: 17), which the wicked can not enter into or inherit (John 3: 3, 5; 1 Cor. 6: 9; Gal. 5: 21; Eph. 5: 4, 5).

(4) This kingdom is invisible; that is, while it manifests itself in life and institutions, and must do so, that manifestation is neither identical nor conterminous with the kingdom. Hence while in the world the kingdom is not of the world (John 18: 33, 36); its subjects can not be known exactly

except by the King (2 Tim. 2 : 19) ; many claiming to belong to it do not (Matt. 7 : 21–23) : for its tests are not outward rites, but a new creature (Gal. 6 : 15). Such a kingdom has no metes and bounds that are every-where discernible by men. Judas and Ananias and Magus deceived the apostles. Hence invisibility characterizes the kingdom. We see the manifestation, but we can not discern precisely where the Spirit operates (John 3 : 8). We stand here at the parting of the ways, and the wrong road, as we shall in due time see, leads to Rome (§ 32 : 5).

(5) Infallibility may also be predicated of the kingdom: for a kingdom includes king, laws, and subjects. The King is infallible; his laws are infallible ; and so we may speak of the kingdom as infallible, though its subjects err in judgment and in heart. The inspiration given by the King to prophet and apostle was also infallible. Make the kingdom and its manifestation identical, as the Romanists do, and we have, by one short step, Papal infallibility. Through fear we will not deny the fact that infallibility belongs as an essential element to the kingdom of heaven. For its King is infallible ; the Spirit animating the kingdom is infallible; its law is infallible (John 1 : 1; Col. 2 : 3; John 16 : 13; 1 Cor. 14 : 37). But, notwithstanding this, infallibility can not be predicated of the manifestation of the kingdom, since that manifestation passes through a fallible medium, human nature. Yet the nearer an ecumenical agreement among saints is reached, the more is individual infirmity eliminated and ecclesiastical infallibility attained. This arises from the working of God in believers' hearts, for his good pleasure (Phil. 2 : 13). The Romish error runs nearer the truth than Protestants have imagined. If the bold assumption that the kingdom of heaven and the Roman Catholic Church are one and identical be granted, Papal infallibility follows. We hold the infallibility of the kingdom, but deny the infallibility of the churches: for the kingdom and the visible manifestation are not identical.

(6) The kingdom is without end, everlasting, perpetual (Dan. 7: 14; Luke 1: 33). It is called "the eternal kingdom of our Lord and Saviour Jesus Christ" (2 Peter 1: 11). Its subjects are bought with "an eternal redemption," and rewarded with "eternal life," "eternal comfort," "eternal salvation," "the eternal inheritance," and an "eternal weight of glory." Perpetuity is therefore a characteristic of it. This perpetuity precludes change. The Christian is not to give place to another dispensation. It will continue to the end of the world, when the mediatorial King will "deliver up the kingdom to God, even the Father . . . that God may be all in all" (1 Cor. 15: 24-28); yet the kingdom exists in glory forever.

(7) Before that great and notable day the kingdom will gather into itself all the nations. It will become universal in extent and comprehension (Matt. 13: 31-33; 28: 19; Rev. 11: 15; Dan. 7: 13, 14). Universality is a distinguishing mark of the kingdom.

(8) Among the innumerable subjects of this kingdom, there is equality. It is not a kingdom of classes and hierarchies. It has no aristocracy. It is a brotherhood and therefore a democracy, the republic of God. The greatest in the kingdom are those who serve and obey best (Matt. 5: 19; 23: 11). Ambition for place is repressed, and all must become as little children (Matt. 18: 1-3). There is but one Master; all others are brethren (Matt. 23: 8-10). To enter the kingdom all must be born anew, and all must have love, faith, repentance. The same privileges are opened to all, and the same trials are to be endured by all. All have essentially the same duties and the same rewards. Even the King humbled himself to the condition of a servant, that he might be the firstborn among many brethren (Phil. 2: 5-11; Rom. 8: 29). All in it are one (Gal. 3: 28).

§ 33. The kingdom of heaven is thus marked by loyalty, unity, holiness, invisibility, infallibility, perpetuity, universality, and equality. The notes, or characteristics, are sometimes carried up to fifteen and sometimes reduced to four. But whether less or more, they distinguish the kingdom of heaven from all other kingdoms. It is peculiar. It is unlike the preceding dispensations. It is the consummate outgrowth of the life of God in human history and is worthy the admiring study of angels (1 Peter 1: 12) and the acceptance of all men (Rev. 15: 3, 4). It has been defined as "The gathering together of men, under God's eternal law of righteous love, by the vital power of his redeeming love in Jesus Christ, brought to bear upon them through the Holy Spirit." [3]

Dr. Candlish makes the kingdom cover, as we have done, both reign, or exercise of kingly power, and realm, or subjects of such power. The kingdom is "a society bound together by certain laws and ruled by a power which guides the action of the parts and of the whole to an end that is adequate and good." [4] We can but think that the best definition is that which enumerates the characteristics of the kingdom.

§ 34. The kingdom is still more clearly defined by observing the conditions of admission into it. Those conditions must correspond, of course, with the nature of the kingdom. As the kingdom is spiritual and holy, a man is not admitted by natural birth, but by the renewal of the heart (John 1: 13; 3: 3, 5); nor can outward rites admit to it, but only a new creation (Gal. 6: 15), which issues in "repentance toward God, and faith toward our Lord Jesus Christ" (Acts 20: 21). And these conditions are essentially the same as were required under the preparatory dispensations, as is shown in the eleventh chapter of Hebrews. They, through grace, make a man holy, spiritually minded, a true child of Abraham (2 Chron. 7: 14; Is. 55: 7; Rom. 2: 28, 29; 8: 5-8; Gal. 3: 29).

§ 35. The kingdom is still to be distinguished from what

---

[3] The Kingdom of God, by Prof. J. S. Candlish, D.D., 197.
[4] Ibid. 399.

is called the Church universal, which includes all the saved. There is one flock and one Shepherd (John 10 : 16), one body and one Head (Eph. 5: 29, 30), one Mediator (1 Tim. 2 : 5), and one Name by which men can be saved (Acts 4: 12). To be out of this Church is to be destitute of love, faith, penitence, salvation. Here again we see the perversion which Rome makes in applying to the Roman Catholic Church what is true only of the Church universal, namely: "Out of the Church there is no salvation." In making its own visible communion the only true Church of God, the Roman Church must make baptism essential, or "necessary unto salvation." "It is impossible to be saved without it."[5] The Church of God, or the Church universal, includes all the saved in all the dispensations of grace and is wider than the kingdom of heaven.

§ 36. (1) The kingdom of heaven is partly on earth and partly in heaven, and is constantly coming. Its incarnate King ascended into heaven at his inauguration, saying, "All authority hath been given unto me in heaven and on earth. Go ye therefore, and make disciples of all the nations," etc. (Matt. 28: 18, 19). He reigns King of kings and Lord of lords, synchronizing, or timing, his providential rule with the work of his Spirit, so as to bring the best results out of the labors of his disciples, while preparing the nations for evangelization. He shall thus govern until every knee shall bow, and every tongue confess that Jesus Christ is Lord, to the glory of God the Father (Phil. 2: 10, 11), and until he shall deliver up his kingdom unto the Father (1 Cor. 15: 24). He thus reigns in heaven. Besides this, all who die in him go to be with him where he is (Luke 23: 43 ; Acts 7: 59; Rev. 7: 9). They are in the kingdom still, but enjoying its glory. Others are in the kingdom on earth, training in the school of Christ, under the eye of the Master, for the same blessed abode. Thus a part are over the river, a part are crossing now, a part are following on — all cheered by the smile of their ascended and glorified King.

[5] Canons of Trent, on Baptism, v; Cat. of Perseverance, 210.

(2) It is manifest that the kingdom must be constantly coming, or else all the saints would soon be in heaven. The Spirit is continually renewing the hearts of men and sanctifying them, and so the leaven is working, the mustard-seed is growing, and the kingdom is extending. The line of progress is not steady; it wavers here and there; it advances and recedes now and then: but on the whole, it is advancing, with the promise of final conquest. Christ "must reign, till he hath put all his enemies under his feet" (1 Cor. 15: 25). The prayer, "Thy kingdom come," is being answered.

Thus Christ has already set up a kingdom upon earth, peculiar in its notes or characteristics. Such a kingdom must manifest itself, and, coming into a world of sin, it must cause strife and stir (Matt. 10: 34-36). It is revolutionary, overturning whatever opposes, and reconstructing on the principles of righteousness and peace and joy in the Holy Ghost. This will go on until the final consummation.

II. — THE KINGDOM OF HEAVEN IN MANIFESTATION.

§ 37. It is the nature of life to manifest itself in some organism; and the life of Christ, penetrating human history, — constituting a spiritual, holy, progressive kingdom, — must manifest itself in human conduct and institutions. It can not be hidden. The leaven, by the law of its being, must work. The seed must grow or die. Light must shine, and fire burn. So in a world "dead through trespasses and sins" (Eph. 2: 1), the life of God, to reach its ends, must renew the heart of the individual, establish the communion of saints, and found institutions for fellowship and nurture. The redemption of a lost world must be a manifested work. But as the kingdom of heaven is a development from the preceding dispensations, its manifestation must show close connection with them. There is more than a mere succession; there is also a continuation. There is a unity of life running through the patriarchal, the ceremonial, and the Christian dispensations, as unity of life runs through the larva, the chrysalis, and the butterfly. We can trace this continuity.

(1) The ceremonial dispensation was bound to the patriarchal, not only by love, and faith, and repentance, and the redemptive scheme, but also by a special covenant made with Abraham and sealed by circumcision. The Seed of the woman, the Messiah, constitutes the central unity, the divine bond of continuity, as the covenant and seal constitute the organic lines of development.

(2) The Christian dispensation was bound to the ceremonial as a flower to its stem, not only by love, faith, repentance, the covenant, and the Messiah and King, but also by rites and forms of worship. "The Church polity of our first century does not present itself as a fresh creation, but rather as a continuation of a *régime* already there, simply modified to fit the needs of the new spiritual life and purposes."[6] Here too there was more than a succession: there was a continuation, a development.

§ 38. But the method of this development, and hence of manifestation, was not comprehended by the Jews. How the Son of David should ascend the throne of his father and rule the world was by no means clear, not even to his chosen apostles (Acts 1: 6), while his disciples held a most perverted conception respecting it (John 6: 15). Yet the spiritual nature of the kingdom had been revealed, and it was in ways suited thereto that Jesus sought to establish and manifest his glorious kingdom. A process of separation along a spiritual line was begun by John the Baptist in the baptism of repentance. He separated the Jews, imperfectly indeed, on the line of faith and repentance (Matt. 3: 5, 6), as they were separated from others on the line of carnal descent from Abraham (John 8: 39). He laid the axe unto the root of the trees (Matt. 3: 10), thus beginning a process of separation which the winnowing-fan of Christ should

[6] Prof. E. B. Andrews, in 40 Bib. Sac. 51.

continue (Matt. 3: 12). Christ took up the process of his forerunner and carried on the winnowing, thoroughly cleansing his threshing-floor, until a complete separation was effected on or along the spiritual boundary of his kingdom. The multitudes that followed him were divided; those who looked for the establishment of a world-wide temporal kingdom more and more deserted him; while those who dimly discerned a spiritual realm, after long and patient training (John 16: 31), clung hesitatingly to him. His fan was in his hand. The process of separation hastened. He journeyed, and preached, and warned, and wrought miracles, and prayed, until the great majority rejected and crucified their Messiah. "He came unto his own, and they that were his own received him not. But as many as received him, to them gave he the right to become children of God" (John 1: 11, 12). That is, all Israel, the nation of priests, the *kahal*, or congregation, or Church of God, as externally organized, were cut off from all the privileges and promises of the covenant as children of Abraham, and from the law of Moses as the *kahal*, or congregation of Israel, by the one act of crucifixion, except the little band of Christ's recognized disciples. They remained the true *kahal* of Israel. All other Jews therein became apostates. The process of winnowing had cleansed the threshing-floor.

§ 39. Thus through Christ's first disciples the Church of God was continued. They then constituted it on earth. They were the wheat separated from a nation of chaff, the true seed of Abraham, the "little flock," to whom the Father gave the kingdom (Luke 12: 32). They became the Christian Church, recognized and ordained as such on the day of Pentecost (Acts 2: 1-4). They had fulfilled all righteousness in keeping the ritual law, and so needed not to be baptized and were never baptized with Christian baptism. They were the Church in transition. All that joined them, after their divine recognition as such on Pentecost, were baptized into Christ (Acts 2: 38, 41; 8: 38; 11: 16;

etc.). A striking case was the baptism of John's disciples at Ephesus, A.D. 56 (Acts 19: 3-5). As the winnowing, or separation, had left all who had not become disciples of Jesus outside the Church, no one could be admitted to fellowship except through the rite of Christian baptism, as Christ had enjoined (Matt. 28: 19). There was no cleavage, no mere succession, but instead continuity, development, evolution, the passing of the family Church into the national, and the national into the ecumenical form. The three dispensations are not three precious stones placed in divine succession, but the same life of God in human history, growing out of the limitations of narrower forms into the universal and unlimited: one Church in three forms.

§ 40. As was natural and inevitable, the manifestation of the kingdom rejected much which belonged to the ceremonial dispensation and retained what could be used. The national could not be stretched into the ecumenical, and every attempt to do it has fettered the feet of the Christian Church. Paul regarded the Jews as "kept in ward under the law," as under a "tutor," and not as sons in true liberty. The Aaronic priesthood, the ceremonial law, the altar, the sacrifices, the feasts, the temple, the place and mode of worship, the dress of those officiating, were all fulfilled in Christ. They have been outgrown and abolished, as is elaborately declared in Hebrews (see especially 9: 12, 25, 26; 10: 12, 18; 7: 18, 19): "The bond written in ordinances," . . . Christ took it "out of the way, nailing it to the cross" (Col. 2: 14). Men thereafter could worship God acceptably anywhere and in any way, if in spirit and in truth (John 4: 21-23). Hence adhesion thereafter to the ceremonial law is rightly called bondage (Gal. 5: 1) and a falling away from the scheme of grace, if relied on for salvation (Gal. 5: 2-4).

But the kingdom retains in its manifestation the Sabbath; the family; the Sacred Scriptures, adding to them the law of the New Covenant, which all communions hold to be inspired; the cardinal virtues, which here find their fullest development; the vicarious atonement through sacrifice, for Christ offered once for all his own life a ransom for the world; and the priesthood in Christ, a new order, "after the power of an endless life" (Heb. 7: 16). In short, the manifested kingdom retains all the essentials of the preceding dispensations and so many of the incidentals as could be adapted to a free, spiritual, ecumenical Church, and rejected all the rest.

§ 41. One of these incidentals retained in substance is the synagogue form of worship. We have already alluded (§ 25) to this outgrowth of the religious life of the Jews, but it needs fuller treatment. For "as the Christian Church rests historically on the Jewish Church, so Christian worship and the congregational organization rest on that of the synagogue and cannot be well understood without it."[7] As the kingdom of heaven manifests itself chiefly in and through local congregations, and worship therein, we call attention to the origin of this kind of worship.

(1) The synagogue form of worship had its origin in a want which the national worship could not itself satisfy (§ 25). The Babylonian captivity revealed the inadequacy of the temple service, from which relief was found in synagogues. These the dispersion made universal and popular. Without a temple, sacrifices, feasts, and the ordained worship, there sprung up, how we do not know, an unauthorized kind of worship in local congregations, which was both a necessity and a prophecy, a sign of the decadence of the national establishment and the hope of better things, if not of a new dispensation.

(2) Born in the sorrows of captivity, when Israel's harps hung upon the willows in Babylon, the synagogue would have been rejected after the return as the remembrancer of exile, had it not met a universal want — a want so common that, in Christ's time, " not a town, not a village, if

[7] Hist. Christ. Ch. 1, 456, by Dr. Philip Schaff.

it numbered only ten men . . . but had one or more synagogues." The number in the city of Jerusalem was about four hundred. It is held that a synagogue invaded the holy temple — "an incongruous mixture of man-derived worship with the God-ordained typical rites of the sanctuary." Yet Christ sanctioned synagogue worship by regular attendance upon it (Luke 4: 16; John 18: 20). The synagogue was more than the temple in the nurture of religious life and faith.

(3) For the synagogue worship was local, congregational, weekly; laymen, women, and children could and did meet every Sabbath to hear the law and the prophets and to offer praise and prayer. A building suited to the needs of the place was built. The worship consisted in reading the law and prophets, the nineteen prayers, the chanting, the preaching or expounding of the Scriptures, and the amen responded by the people. "Any Jew of age might get up to read the lesson, offer prayer, and address the congregation."[8] Each synagogue elected its own officers, the ruler and his two associates, the three almoners, or deacons, and the council. "Each synagogue formed an independent republic, but kept up a regular correspondence with other synagogues. It was also a civil and religious court, and had power to excommunicate and to scourge offenders."[9] All the affairs of a synagogue, worship and government, were under the exclusive control of laymen. No priest had any part in them. Each synagogue was independent of the rest, whether taken singly or collectively.

(4) It is clear that synagogue worship could be carried anywhere and offered by any Jew of age. It was perfectly suited to ecumenical extension. It had already extended wherever the Jews had been dispersed, before Christ came. It could be carried throughout the world. The apostles and disciples at first were all laymen, but as such they could

[8] Hist. Christ. Church, Dr. Schaff, 1, 459.
[9] Ibid. 458.

preach Christ in any synagogue. They availed themselves of this privilege. When, therefore, the kingdom was set up, this familiar and capable mode of worship had been prepared for it. It was known to all Jews and devout Gentiles. The kingdom seized upon this mode of worship for its extension (Acts 9: 20; 13: 5; 14: 1; 17: 1, 2, 10, 17; 18: 4, 19, 26; 19: 8); for Christian worship in local churches had both its starting-point and model in the Jewish synagogue. More recent investigations tend strongly to show that among the Gentiles a similar preparation for the Christian *ecclesia* had been made in the heathen clubs that abounded.

§ 42. And it is in and through these local churches that the kingdom of heaven chiefly manifests itself in the world. It is true that it must show itself also in the lives of the renewed. The divine life begotten in regeneration bears the fruit of the Spirit in holy living (Matt. 5: 16; Gal. 5: 22, 23). " By this shall all men know," says the King, " that ye are my disciples, if ye have love one to another" (John 13: 35). A love that treats all men as brothers will distinguish those that possess it, until the whole course of human history has been changed. Without it, we are nothing (1 Cor. 13: 1–3). But we mistake greatly if we regard individual holy lives as the chief manifestation of the kingdom of heaven; for such lives do not appear where local churches do not exist. The Christian life is not an isolation, but a fellowship. It constitutes believers one flock, one body. The communion of saints is essential to its nurture, if not to its begetting. Hence it appears almost exclusively in communities. It is hardly too much to say that if the fellowship found in, and fostered by, local churches were to cease, individual holy living would largely cease from among men.

(1) The Holy Spirit makes fellowship the channel of blessing. When, on the day of Pentecost, the disciples were baptized of the Spirit for their work, they were not taken singly while at private prayer, but when "they were all together in one place." "The tongues parting asunder" "sat

upon each one of them" (Acts 2: 1, 3). It has been so ever since; the collected Church, and not the individual member, being the channel of the Spirit's blessing. Revivalists seldom labor where the Church or churches can not be aroused to concerted prayer and labor, thus confirming this fundamental law of the kingdom, that "through the church the manifold wisdom of God," "in Christ Jesus our Lord," is "made known" (Eph. 3: 10, 11). The same is confirmed by the failure of those who discard organization (§ 27: 1). The local church in any place, not the ministry, not any outside organization, is the organ of the Spirit, a fact needing emphatic assertion at the present time.

(2) Hence we can see why the apostles founded churches every-where. They preached in synagogues and formed their followers into churches. The separation from the synagogues was, however, slowly effected. But as necessity arose, churches were planted alongside the synagogues, as organic centers of life and labors. For "the apostles do not rest satisfied with the conversion of individuals as such, nor with leaving with each believer a book or a rule of life for his own personal guidance. Every-where they seek to organize a society: the 'brethren,' the 'disciples,' the 'saints,' are formed into a church, that is, an *ecclesia*, or congregation; and that society receives a distinct and definite constitution."[10]

(3) For the same reason the kingdom has ever appeared in local churches wherever it has obtained a foothold. It matters not what theory of the Church has been held, neighborhood churches have been formed by this law of fellowship. Christ honors the smallest church with his presence (Matt. 18: 20). This local organization is the universal manifestation of the kingdom. Its subjects thus behave in all lands and ages, therein revealing a law of the kingdom, which surmounts all obstacles. As the law of gravitation has its way, so this law of fellowship has its way in the realm

[10] Introd. to Acts, by Prof. Plumptre.

of Christ. Persecution, even death, has not been able to prevent church assemblies. If harried out of one country, believers brave the wilderness in obedience to it. Similarity of wants, experiences, hopes, trials, labors, tends to foster fellowship in local churches; but the origin and continuance of churches lies deeper, in a law of the one indivisible kingdom of heaven.

§ 43. But the lives of believers and the local congregations are not the whole manifestation of the kingdom of heaven among men. The boundaries of fellowship for each Christian are wider than the roll of the church to which he belongs. Its membership is not the limit of communion and labors. The kingdom includes all true churches, and hence coming into the kingdom brings one into union with all such churches, while each church from its constitution and nature is in fellowship with all the rest. It is not a separate integer, but a related factor; and hence each church seeks to express in some suitable way its relation to all other organically manifested parts of the one kingdom. The law that binds individual saints into local churches binds those churches into normal associations for fellowship and coöperative labors. This law is the gravitation which makes the kingdom one and its manifestations one. Hence the communion of saints, though obstructed, can not be wholly prevented since it is the visible expression of the fundamental law of the invisible kingdom of heaven. That this communion might become ecumenical, with neither family, nor national, nor race limitations, the kingdom at the start seized upon the synagogue or club form of organization and worship, which gathers the believers of one place together into a church and joins all churches together in fellowship. Thus there are many churches, but one comprehensive manifestation. We must broaden our conception of local churches into an ecumenical comprehension if we would attain an adequate idea of the kingdom of heaven in manifestation.

Through changes in the lives of individuals making them

holy, through local churches as the channel of the Spirit's working, and through associations of churches, human society will be wholly leavened, and the world will be led to believe in an atoning Saviour (John 17 : 21).

But in this manifestation of the kingdom we must not for a moment forget that the local church is the great factor. It is the nurturing home into which believers are spiritually born. It is the integer of wider fellowship. It is in and through local churches that the kingdom becomes the light of the world and the salt of the earth. They are the worshiping and working forces. In them life is nurtured and from them evangelization flows. Through them chiefly the kingdom manifests its power of redeeming the world. Whatever holy living there may be in individual Christians, and whatever the method of exhibiting the union of the local congregations, the world sees practically and chiefly the worship and labors of local churches. By and in these churches the kingdom comes into conflict with the powers of darkness. Little is done through other instrumentalities. Hence we repeat that the kingdom of heaven chiefly manifests itself in the world in and through local churches.

§ 44. This manifestation of the kingdom brings us to the origin of church polities. Here, in the necessity of unity between church and church, lies the parting of the ways. Here, in the communion of saints beyond the bounds of local congregations, emerge the various theories of the Church which are embodied in the great ecclesiastical communions. Here, one road leads to Rome, another to Constantinople, another to Geneva, and another to Plymouth; and all Christians must walk in one of these ways. If each local church were wholly independent in matters of authority and of fellowship, that is, an absolutely independent integer, no polity need emerge. If any polity should arise, it would be abnormal, unnatural, man-made. But since all churches are united in one kingdom of heaven, they stand to one another, not as absolutely independent integers, but as factors in a common whole, towns in a united realm. If we add together, not only all the individual Christians, but also all the local churches, we do not obtain the kingdom of heaven in manifestation. The kingdom itself is a unit, and not a collection of units; an integer, and not a collection of integers. And the normal manifestation of that kingdom must disclose its oneness. "In conceiving the Church as in one sense single, in another plural, the thought of the New Testament writers does not begin with plurality and pass thence to unity by abstraction and generalization, but moves from unity of essence to plurality of concrete manifestation. Unity is first and highest." [11]

It is the fact that at bottom all Christian churches are one, which compels their combination under some theory or doctrine of the Church. Whatever independence one local church or communion of churches may have, that independence must be subordinate to the essential, underlying oneness of all. This oneness compels the unity of external manifestation which all polities seek to express. There is an earnest, pervading, prevailing, irrepressible desire of believers, begotten of the Spirit, to manifest in organic, visible form the unity of the kingdom of heaven, which will sometime find adequate, normal, and ecumenical expression. The attempts to realize it have given rise to the following theories or doctrines of the Christian Church, namely: —

(1) Fellowship and unity on the principle of infallible primacy, which emerges in the Papacy.

(2) Fellowship and unity on the principle of apostolic succession, which emerges in Episcopacy.

(3) Fellowship and unity on the principle of authoritative representation, which emerges in Presbyterianism.

(4) Fellowship and unity on the principle of church independency, which emerges in Congregationalism.

We see that fellowship is the common factor and unity the common end of these four theories; but the end is sought

[11] Prof. E. B. Andrews, 40 Bib. Sac. 55, 56.

to be reached on the common factor by a different principle in each. These theories are actual, and respectively dominate large communions. Singly or combined they constitute all the polities that divide Christendom. Each will be considered hereafter with less or more fullness.

§ 45. While we shall endeavor to show which one of the four is Scriptural and normal, we wish at the outset to protest against ascribing to any polity that has dominated large bodies of churches a superficial origin. Our discussion will prove that church polities penetrate to lines so narrow, and principles so subtile, that learned and good men have been led to adopt and defend each one of the theories above given. These theories did not take their origin in ambition, priestcraft, or corruption; no, not one of them. Their primary causes lie deeper, in things more honorable alike to human nature and the grace of God. Ambition, priestcraft, corruption, may have been the rich soil nurturing wrong conceptions of the nature of the Christian Church; but the seed and root of the gigantic outgrowths which have divided Christendom were something better than human depravity. Nor is it altogether bigotry that builds so many churches of different orders in small towns, but loyalty, often at great costs, to ecclesiastical belief. The waste in money and labor is deplorable, but the devotion that gives both money and labor is admirable. Let us not accuse those falsely who long to have their community one flock in faith and worship, but whose adhesion to principle — as they view it — divides that community into separate churches. We may deplore, as we should, the conflict of theories, but we can not but regard loyalty to convictions a priceless element of character. We shall not, therefore, try any one's patience by cataloguing corruptions. Instead, we will endeavor to set forth the normal relation of church to church in the indivisible kingdom of heaven.

LECTURE III.

THE ROMAN CATHOLIC AND THE EPISCOPAL THEORY OF THE CHRISTIAN CHURCH.

" That they may all be one . . . that the world may believe that thou didst send me." — Jesus Christ.

" But be not ye called Rabbi : for one is your teacher. and all ye are brethren. And call no man your father on the earth [pope means father] : *for one is your Father, which is in heaven. Neither be ye called masters : for one is your master, even the Christ."* — Jesus Christ.

IN fulfillment of the prayer : " Thy kingdom come," and in obedience to the command : " Make disciples of all the nations," the apostles and primitive Christians entered upon their mission. And such was their activity and success that they soon compassed the known world. For Paul wrote, in A.D. 62, that the gospel had been preached "in all the world," "in all creation under heaven " (Col. 1: 6, 23). Wherever they preached, with rare exceptions, churches were gathered of Jewish and Gentile believers. In consequence of the unity of the kingdom, of which they were visible manifestations, these churches stood in the closest possible relation to one another. Life was clothing itself with organic form. And from the fundamental law of fellowship, the communion of saints was emerging in some form of polity.

§ 46. There soon appeared, therefore, a change in thought and language corresponding with the change of the invisible kingdom into visible churches. The Christ had spoken of his kingdom as near at hand, the apostles saw it in manifestation. It was natural that in thought and language the idea of the kingdom should recede into the background while the idea of its manifestation in churches should fill the foreground. And such was indeed the fact. Christ used the phrase kingdom of heaven, or its equivalent, as recorded by Matthew, thirty-six times; but he used the word church in only two passages (Matt. 16: 18; 18: 17). On the contrary, his apostles used the phrase "kingdom of heaven," or its equivalent, in the Acts and Epistles, thirty-one times, and the word "church" one hundred and twelve times. The kingdom was becoming visible in organic form, and men spoke of the kingdom less and less, but of the churches more and more. This change has been recognized by modern theologians. "An explanation of it has been sought in two different and indeed opposite ways, some regarding it as an indication of advance in the conception of Christian truth, and others again seeing in it a proof that the apostles did not fully apprehend or retain the great ideas of the Master."[1] It seems more rational to regard the change in thought and expression as due to the natural and inevitable development of the invisible kingdom into concrete organic manifestations of that kingdom, the churches, in its coming among men.

§ 47. These organic manifestations called churches hold some relation to the kingdom out of which they grow, not in virtue of their planting by the apostles, nor of their common faith and worship, but in virtue of their being churches of Christ. This relation dominates their faith and worship and makes them one while many. The human mind is so constituted that it will express the relation existing between the kingdom and its organic manifestation, and consequently between church and church, in some tangible form or working system; and that form or system constitutes a theory or doctrine of the Christian Church, whether true or false. Four such theories have divided Christendom and demand attention. For it is manifest that there can be but one normal or true development of the kingdom into organic manifestation. Whatever theories of the universe science in its infirmity may from time to time present, no one is so foolish as to imagine that God has constructed the universe on a plurality of conflicting plans. He has built it on one

[1] The Kingdom of God, by Prof. Candlish, D.D., 180.

sublime plan, and all the theories of science are tentative efforts to comprehend and state that plan. We hold the same to be true of God's sublimer scheme of grace in its organic manifestation. Rising from the inferior and preparatory to its perfected and permanent dispensation, each stage had one divine model and not many models. In this the Christian is not inferior to the patriarchal and the ceremonial dispensations. It has one normal manifestation. If it were possible to deduce from the Federal Constitution several distinct and incompatible forms of civil government, what could be said of the wisdom of its framers or of the stability of this Republic? To suppose that Christ or his apostles put into the New Testament, or framed into the primitive churches, several conflicting doctrines of the Christian Church, is to impeach their wisdom and inspiration. If they did it, they had not common wisdom. However fruitless human efforts have hitherto been in finding and stating the divine doctrine of the Christian Church, we must believe in such a doctrine, or surrender our belief in the inspiration of the founders of that Church. The true doctrine must be in the New Testament, if these writings were given by inspiration, as the true doctrine of the material universe must be in nature; but in either case it may be hidden for wise purposes. Nowhere is unity expressed by plurality, whatever incidental varieties may appear. This is so self-evident that the advocates of every theory of the Christian Church instinctively feel it. They can not be made to believe that Christ ordained a fourfold polity as the normal development of his one kingdom. And they take a still more superficial view who affirm that Christ ordained no principles of church government for a kingdom which is to subdue all nations. The kingdom is one fellowship, and fellowship involves polity, and that polity must be one like the kingdom. This is not saying that other polities must be in all respects wrong, that there can be nothing good in them, but that they are in some one or more essential respects wrong. Nor is it saying that a detailed system has been revealed, but only that the essential elements of the normal polity have been given. The want of some detailed book of discipline in the New Testament is no proof whatever that the principles of a consistent, complete, and normal polity are not found therein. Because God has not written his plan of the universe in distinct characters, science is not justified in denying any plan, but is instead stimulated to ascertain the hidden plan. The numerous theories which have been held and then rejected are the scaffolding needed in the building of the true edifice. It is so in church polity. The polity has not been revealed in detail; but it exists in the mind of Christ; it has been revealed in principle; and the theories which have sprung up and become embodied in great ecclesiastical systems are efforts to express in organic form those principles. That erroneous theories should have arisen in ecclesiology, as in science, is not surprising. That unity of view and expression will some time be reached in both ecclesiology and science is certain. That men have clung tenaciously to their theories, believing them to be true, is no more surprising in polity than in science. A man can not do otherwise without impeaching his own faith. The more logical and conscientious a man is, when possessed of a theory of any sort, the less can he countenance opposing theories. Nor is this bigotry; it is logic.

§ 48. We turn then to the four great theories of the Christian Church which divide Christendom, to ascertain, if possible, what is true in them, and which one comes nearest to the divine model. They are properly named the Papal, the Episcopal, the Presbyterial, and the Congregational theory. We shall reduce each one to its simple constitutive principle, and then give the development of that principle into a complete and ecumenical system. And we mean by constitutive principle of any polity, that principle which gives it individuality, distinguishes it from all other polities, pervades all its institutions, and gives the answer to every query regarding the peculiar constitution outward and inward of that polity. This is substantially the definition given by Cardinal Wiseman. It will simplify matters very much to find in each theory of the Church the one principle that controls and so constitutes it what it is, and gives life to it; for that one principle seeks to give to the visible churches the unity of the invisible kingdom of heaven out of which they spring. Each principle develops into a system elaborate and minute and peculiar. Some of the systems have been perversions from others, settling at last each around its constitutive principle, while others arose from a clear perception of their constitutive principles. In the former case, foreign elements may have been borne along for centuries, until gradually eliminated. But in each polity the drift has been more and more to crystallize about its constitutive principle, until that principle dominates all parts. We shall seek accuracy in brevity of presentation.

I. — THE PAPAL THEORY OF THE CHRISTIAN CHURCH.

§ 49. This theory has developed a church establishment imposing in its nature and extent. Macaulay, writing in 1840, before the theory had flowered in the dogma of the immaculate conception (1854), and fruited in the dogma of papal infallibility (1870), said : " There is not, and there never was, on this earth, a work of human policy so well deserving of examination as the Roman Catholic Church. . . . She saw the commencement of all the governments, and of all the ecclesiastical establishments, that now exist in the world; and we feel no assurance that she is not destined to see the end of them all. . . . And she may still exist in undiminished vigor when some traveler from New Zealand shall, in the midst of a vast solitude, take his stand on a broken arch of London Bridge to sketch the ruins of St. Paul's."[2] This is not quite as truthful as it is beautiful, though no one can

[2] Review of Ranke's Hist. of the Popes.

question the accuracy of the impression intended to be produced. The brilliant essayist forgot the patriarchal despotism of China, that such as the government was in the time of Confucius and his predecessors, so it is, essentially, at the present day.[3] He overlooked also the Eastern, or Orthodox Greek Church, out of the bosom of which the Roman Catholic Church was born, "both the source and the background of the Western."[4] The Papal Church did not therefore see the commencement of all the governments, and of all the ecclesiastical establishments, that now exist in the world, and we shall show why it will not see their end. Imposing and grand as it is, its completeness in papal infallibility bears in it the doom of death.

§ 50. The origin of the Papal system is not in the constitution of the primitive churches. "This volume further demonstrates," says Bishop A. Cleveland Coxe, "what I have so often touched upon — the historic fact that primitive Christianity was Greek in form and character, Greek from first to last, Greek in all its forms of dogma, worship, and polity." And he refers to Dean Stanley as inviting "us to reform the entire scheme of our ecclesiastical history by presenting the Eastern apostolic churches as the main stem of Christendom, of which the Church of Rome itself was for three hundred years a mere colony, unfelt in theology except by contributions to the Greek literature of Christians, and wholly unconscious of those pretensions with which . . . the fabulous decretals afterwards invested a succession of primitive bishops in Rome, wholly innocent of any thing of the kind."[5]

(1) There arose among the primitive churches a confusion of thought over the nature of the Christian Church. The outward manifestation in local churches with their ministry began to be identified with the invisible kingdom, a confusion which we have seen (§ 5) still exists, dividing Chris-

---

[3] 5 Ency. Brit. 668. [4] 11 Ency. Brit. 154.
Introd. Notice to Am. Ed. Ante-Nicene Fathers, vol. vi, pp. v, vi.

tendom into two great sections. This confusion is both the source and the support of the Papal Theory of the Church. Ignatius (A.D. 80–107) wrote: "If any man follow him who makes a schism in the Church, he shall not inherit the kingdom of God."[6] Irenæus (A.D. 120–202) confused the kingdom and the visible Church in the famous passage: "'For in the Church,' it is said, 'God hath set apostles, prophets, teachers,' and all the other means through which the Spirit works; of which all those are not partakers who do not join themselves to the Church, but defraud themselves of life through their perverse opinions and infamous behavior. For where the Church is, there is the Spirit of God; and where the Spirit of God is, there is the Church."[7] Here the Church is the visible body with its officers, and it is made identical with the invisible Church or kingdom of heaven. He makes true of the former what is true only of the latter. Both these quotations imply that there is no salvation outside the visible Church. But this identity between the visible and the invisible Church more largely dominates the thought of Cyprian (A.D. 200–258), who may be called the father of the Roman Catholic system. He cries out: "How can he be with Christ who is not with the spouse of Christ, and in his Church?"[8] "Whoever he may be, and whatever he may be, he who is not in the Church of Christ is not a Christian."[9] "For it has been delivered to us that there is one God, and one Christ, and one hope, and one faith, and one Church, and one baptism ordained only in the one Church, from which unity whosoever will depart must needs be found with heretics. . . . Moreover, Peter himself, showing and vindicating the unity, has commanded and warned us that we cannot be saved, except by the one only baptism of one Church."[10] Thus the implication of Ignatius and Irenæus became hardened into the dogma of Cyprian: "Out of the Church there is no salvation." And this in due time came to mean in the

[6] Phil. iii. [7] Ad. Hær. book iii, ch. xxiv.
[8] Ep. xlviii, 1. [9] Ep. li, 24. [10] Ep. lxxiii, 11.

Occident: "Out of the Roman Catholic Church there is no salvation."

(2) This confusion of thought was born of the ceremonial dispensation, in which the civil and the spiritual realms were, in the minds of the ordinary Jew, conterminous and identical. It was natural, therefore, for the Jewish Christians to overlook the lines of distinction between the kingdom and its manifestation, which Christ and his apostles had drawn. The apostles did not get rid of similar notions under the teaching of the Master until the illumination of Pentecost. Their successors did not have the same degree of illumination, and hence as we recede from the days of the apostles the lines between the visible and the invisible Church become dimmer until they disappear. So, too, the order of Jewish priests, with dress and ceremonies and sacrifices, would in time be brought over.

(3) If this confusion in thought could have been removed, and the distinction drawn by the apostles and their Master retained, the Papal Theory of the Church would not have been born. "Such a distinction might have led," says Neander, "to an agreement between Augustine and the Donatists. Augustine endeavored to establish the distinction, but he was afraid to follow out the idea to the full extent, and his notions became obscure."[11] Had this greatest of uninspired theologians been bolder as a reformer, he by clearness of thought might have prevented the birth of the Papacy. He faltered; left the distinction in obscurity still; and the natural result followed. "The idea of the Church had become confounded with its external manifestation, and thus the way was prepared for all the abuses of the Romish hierarchy and the development of the Papacy."[12] It was thus left to the reformers of the sixteenth century to draw the lines between the visible and the invisible Church, the organic manifestation and the spiritual kingdom, so deep and distinct that they can not again become obliterated. We say,

[11] Hagenbach's Hist. Doct. i, 354.   [12] Ibid. ii, 71.

again, because they were before clearly drawn in the teachings of the New Testament. But while the confusion lasted the Papal Theory grew almost to its completeness.

(4) We greatly err if we fancy that this distinction between the visible and the invisible Church is of no practical present use. It is of the utmost value in evangelizing the world, as in determining the form of the Church. Hagenbach states it exactly when he says: "In the view of the Romanist, individuals come to Christ through the Church; in the view of Protestants, they come to the Church through Christ."[13] The question confronts each minister and missionary: Shall I labor to bring sinners to Christ through the door of the Church, or shall I bring them to the Church through Christ the door?

By the Roman Theory a horde of savages is brought to Christ by the church sacraments; by the Protestant Theory, sinners are brought to the sacraments by conversion to Christ in faith and penitence. Make the visible and the invisible Church one and identical, and you make therein baptism and regeneration identical — baptismal regeneration is the outcome. Baptism thus becomes necessary unto salvation. But draw the line where the Scriptures do, between the kingdom of heaven and its organic manifestation in churches, and you ascribe salvation, not unto the Church, but unto Christ; not to the sacraments, but to repentance and faith. We see how closely together the widest theories and practices lie in their origin. We see also that nothing touches purity in faith and practice with a more controlling hand than theories of the nature of the Christian Church.

(5) In seeking the origin of the Papal Theory we must add to this confusion of thought and consequent identification of the manifestation of the kingdom with the kingdom itself, this further element, the elevation of the chief spokesman of the apostles to the position of primate among them, and consequently the making of his so-called successors primates in the whole Church. Of this we speak hereafter.

[13] Hagenbach's Hist. Doct. II, 290.

(6) To these two elements must also be added an environment adverse to the primitive polity. The great Roman Empire had dazed men with its glory. Church officers were drawn by the unnoticed drift of their surroundings into hierarchical claims. The conversion of the emperor, and the union of Church and State, carried at a bound the persecuted Church into power. The consequent fearful ingress of heathen multitudes, with their heathen customs, into the Church, corrupted it, and Rome, the capital of the known world, aspired to a greater ecclesiastical empire. These constituted an environment in which the germs of the Papal Theory took root and growth; but of which we can not speak more particularly.

§ 51. The Papal Theory is, that "the Holy Catholic Apostolic Roman Church is the mother and mistress of all churches;"[14] that it is the only true Church of Christ; that "the Church has the power of defining dogmatically that the religion of the Catholic Church is the only true religion;"[15] that "the primacy of jurisdiction over the universal Church of God was immediately and directly promised and given to blessed Peter, the apostle of Christ the Lord;" that the same primacy "must, by the same institution, necessarily remain unceasingly in the church," and "in his successors, the Bishops of the Holy See of Rome. . . . Whence whosoever succeeds to Peter in this See does by the institution of Christ himself obtain the primacy of Peter over the whole Church;" and that "the Roman Pontiff, when he speaks *ex cathedrâ*, that is, when in discharge of the office of pastor and doctor of all Christians, by virtue of his supreme apostolic authority, he defines a doctrine regarding faith or morals, to be held by the universal Church, by the divine assistance promised to him in blessed Peter, is possessed of that infallibility with which the divine Redeemer willed that his Church should be endowed for defining doctrine regarding faith or morals; and that, therefore, such definitions of the Roman

[14] Tridentine Faith.   [15] Papal Syllabus of Errors (1864), 21.

Pontiff are irreformable of themselves, and not from the consent of the Church." "But if any one — which may God avert — presume to contradict this our definition : let him be anathema." [16] More briefly : the Roman Catholic Church is the community of the faithful united to their lawful pastors, in communion with the See of Rome, the infallible Pope, the successor of St. Peter, and vicar of Christ on earth.

§ 52. The constitutive principle of this theory is the infallible primacy of the Pope. Before the theory had developed into papal infallibility, Cardinal Wiseman thus defined the constitutive principle : " The doctrine and belief that God has promised, and consequently bestows upon it [the Church], a constant and perpetual protection, to the extent of guaranteeing it from destruction, from error, and fatal corruption. This principle once admitted, every thing else follows." [17] This principle did not, however, distinguish, even then, between the Roman Catholic Church and the Orthodox Greek Church ; for the latter holds that " the bishops united in a General Council represent the Church, and infallibly decide, under the guidance of the Holy Ghost, all matters of faith and ecclesiastical life." [18] Infallibility, or rather the claim of it, does not, therefore, alone distinguish the Roman Church from all others. If, therefore, infallibility be admitted, every thing else does not follow.

(1) Primacy would seem to distinguish the Roman Church, but it has not dominated the whole development of that Church. If we join the two terms — infallibility and primacy — we cover perhaps the whole normal development until the final consummation of the theory. This gives infallible primacy as the constitutive principle of the Papal Theory of the Church. It is nothing against the accuracy of our position that this principle did not emerge into full recognition until A.D. 1870 ; for we do not know fully a plant or a tree until it has blossomed and borne ripened fruit. The Papal Theory did not mature until the Vatican Council.

[16] Vatican Decrees, on Church, chap. i, ii, iv.
[17] Quoted in Romanism as It Is, 107.   [18] 11 Ency. Brit. 159.

(2) Before that council settled it, the infallibility claimed by the Romish Church was an unlocalized quantity. It was held by one party that it was focused in general councils of the Church. Another party found it in the decrees of such councils when ratified and confirmed by the Pope. A more recent and third party, led by the Jesuits, placed it in the popes, speaking *ex cathedrâ*. The Vatican Council was called to remove this confusion, which it did. For by the decree of this general council, confirmed by the Pope, the perpetual seat of infallibility was infallibly located in the See of Rome. Hence the popes, from Peter to the present incumbent, have been infallible in their official though contradictory utterances. No one in the three parties could reject this Vatican dogma of infallibility, however much he opposed the passage of it; for the infallible organ of the Church, in the belief of each party, infallibly decreed the said dogma. Whatever the struggles by which the constitutive principle has reached final recognition, the main currents of the system from the earliest claims of infallibility and primacy have been towards this principle.

(3) While this principle is active and authoritative in the popes, it is passive and submissive in all other prelates and in the laity. For it is the function of the popes to define, teach, and rule; but of the prelates and laity to learn, believe, and obey. Thus, what Christ is to the kingdom, his vicar, the Pope, is to the Church, "setting himself forth as God" (2 Thess. 2: 4).

§ 53. This constitutive principle develops into an inflexible and intolerant system. It requires the submission of every Christian every-where to the Pope, as unto Christ; indeed, no one can be a true Christian who does not submit to the Pope. All private judgment in religion is denied, since the infallible Pope must define what is to be believed and what not; and the infallible can not err. If any of its dogmas appear strange and unscriptural, the system finds in tradition or in decrees of councils and popes their infallible justification. Schism becomes, too, the greatest sin, since it is apostasy from the kingdom of heaven. There is hence a necessity for conformity or unity in religious faith and ecclesiastical ritual. It becomes the duty of the popes to repress by anathema, excommunication, and sword all attempts to broach new opinions, since the popes have decreed the use of such weapons against error, heresy, and schism. The reigning Pope has supreme power over churches and ministers, to rule them in faith and morals; to enact canons, rites, dogmas; and to do whatever else may be thought conducive to the welfare of the Church in ritual, doctrine, morals, politics, and science. He has even indicted the science of the nineteenth century, and declared the separation of Church and State a heresy, and liberty in religious belief "the insanity."[19] The system is intolerant in the extreme.

(1) In doctrine it has infallibly declared that baptism is necessary unto salvation; that the mass or eucharist is a real but bloodless sacrifice of Christ, as truly a propitiatory offering, as was his death on the cross; that there is a purgatory for the purifying after death of imperfect saints; that indulgences are beneficial; and that the great catalogue of errors, with which reason and Scripture and history have successfully indicted this system, are to be believed.

(2) The government of the Roman Catholic Church is monarchical, the Pope being its supreme and infallible ruler. The people have no vote or voice in its management, in any particular. Below the Pope as his executive council are the cardinals appointed by himself. Every decision of this council is subject to revision by the Pope. The full number of cardinals is seventy-two. There are two sorts of bishops, bishops in ordinary and vicars apostolic. Their jurisdiction on every point is clear and definite. They control the inferior orders of clergy. In most Catholic countries the bishops have a certain degree of civil jurisdiction. Below the bishops in government are chiefly the parochial priests. Besides.

---

[19] Encycl. 13 Aug. 1832; 8 Dec. 1864, Appleton's Annual Cycl. 1864, 702.

these there is a considerable body of ecclesiastics, who do not enter directly into the governing part of the Church, although they help to discharge some of its most important functions. The most solemn tribunal is a general council, that is, an assembly of all the bishops of the Church, who may attend either in person or by deputy, under the presidency of the Pope or his legates, whose appointment necessarily emanates from the Pope. All church property is held in trust and controlled by the bishops.

§ 54. The proof of this stupendous system to those who accept it is easy: The infallible Church has ordained it. But to those who deny its infallibility, the proof is indeed slender. Here is the Scriptural argument as given in the order of citation in the decree of papal infallibility: "That they may all be one; even as thou, Father, art in me and I in thee, that they also may be in us" (John 17: 21). "Thou shalt be called Cephas" (John 1: 42). "Blessed art thou, Simon Bar-Jonah: for flesh and blood hath not revealed it unto thee, but my Father which is in heaven. And I also say unto thee, that thou art Peter, and upon this rock I will build my Church; and the gates of Hades shall not prevail against it. I will give unto thee the keys of the kingdom of heaven: and whatsoever thou shalt bind on earth shall be bound in heaven: and whatsoever thou shalt loose on earth shall be loosed in heaven" (Matt. 16: 16-19). This would indeed be a strong passage had not Christ given the same power to all the apostles (John 20: 23) and to each local church (Matt. 18: 18). What was so expressly distributed by the Lord of all can not be made applicable only to one. But there is added: "Feed my lambs;" "Feed my sheep" (John 21: 15-17). "But I made supplication for thee, that thy faith fail not: and do thou, when once thou hast turned again, stablish thy brethren" (Luke 22: 32).

This is the whole Scriptural proof cited in the decree of papal infallibility. In other connections several other passages are quoted or referred to, but they apply to the whole apostolate, and not to Peter alone. On this slender Scriptural basis the huge fabric rests. But what is lacking in Scripture the system finds in the coördinate standards of faith and practice, namely, tradition, and decrees of councils and popes (§ 87).

Such is the Papal Theory of the Christian Church in its present completed development. It is grand, imposing, consistent, reducible to one constitutive principle, and claiming with logical daring to be the one only true Church of Christ because identical with the kingdom of heaven. We can hardly wonder that some Protestants are so awed by its grandeur that they turn back to Rome.

§ 55. Yet on this Papal Theory, as it has risen to completeness, it is obvious to note several things: —

(1) The Papal Theory is a living power. It is met everywhere, full of vigor and hope, with unbroken front, and until recently confident of a speedy and universal acceptance or conquest. It had great consistency and strength as a system even while maturing; and now, while a fatal cleavage is going on, separating the governing clergy from the Roman Catholic laity, its power is tremendous. It was the laity of Roman Catholic Italy that stripped the Pope of his temporal power the very year in which the clergy decreed his infallibility. And all other Catholic countries acquiesced in spite of papal anathemas.

(2) The Papal Theory is unassailable by argument. The infallible is above argumentation. No proof can reach it; no logic can harm it. For more than three and one-half centuries the theory has flourished and gained some lost ground, under the convicting proofs which reason, history, and the Bible hurl against it.

(3) The Papal Theory is irreformable. The infallible can not, of course, err. Hence the Papacy can never be reformed. This hope must be abandoned.

(4) The alternative with the Papal Theory is either vic-

tory or death. There can be no compromise, no middle ground. The Syllabus of Errors, issued by Pope Pius IX in 1864, is the formal indictment of modern progress in science and liberty. It denounces, as a principal error, that "every man is free to embrace and profess the religion he shall believe true, guided by the light of reason" (Error 15); that "Protestantism is nothing more than another form of the same true Christian religion, in which it is possible to be equally pleasing to God as in the Catholic Church" (18); that "the Church has not the power of availing herself of force, or any direct or indirect temporal power" (24); that "national churches can be established, after being withdrawn and plainly separated from the authority of the Roman Pontiff" (37); that "the Church ought to be separated from the State, and the State from the Church" (55). Among other errors infallibly stigmatized is this: "The abolition of the temporal power, of which the Apostolic See is possessed, would contribute in the greatest degree to the liberty and prosperity of the Church. . . . N. B. Besides these errors, explicitly noted, many others are impliedly rebuked by the proposed and asserted doctrine, which all Catholics are bound most firmly to hold, touching the temporal sovereignty of the Roman Pontiff" (76). The next day after the Vatican Council, in 1870, had declared the Pope infallible, which made this syllabus and all it contains infallible, France declared war against Germany, in consequence of which the Roman Pontiff was soon stripped of every vestige of temporal sovereignty and power. The King of Italy, on entering the States of the Church, proclaimed: "In the first place, all political and lay authority of the Pope and Holy See in Italy is abolished and will remain so."[20] By the decision of the supreme court of Italy the king has jurisdiction within the walls of the Vatican, the palace of the Pope. The infallible primate, the vicar of Christ, is thus made subject to the laws of Italy.[21] This is

[20] Appleton's Cycl. for 1870, 414.   [21] 2 Andover Review, 171.

the reason the Pope keeps up the fiction of being a prisoner in the Vatican, being deprived as he is of his temporal power. For unless he can recover that temporal power, so necessary to "the liberty and prosperity of the Church," that "all Catholics are bound most firmly to hold it," the Pope will have been proved by the providence of God to be a false teacher the very year the Vatican Council declared him to be an infallible teacher. It was the stress of this contradiction, unless speedily remedied, of which there appeared no hope, that wrung from the very Pope who called the council to decree his infallibility the despairing cry: "All is lost!" To recover his temporal power, and so to escape the demonstration of his fallibility, which this contradiction involves, the Pope, as the Hon. William E. Gladstone shows,[22] has been, and still is, engaged in stirring up a general European war, that out of the strife he may emerge clothed with temporal sovereignty again. Necessity compels him thus to feign imprisonment, and to foment strife, until he wins or the Papacy dies. We may hope with confidence that the cleavage going on between the Papacy, which is clerical government wholly, and the Roman Catholic population will end in the overthrow of the Papal Theory, in a conflict indeed of its own making. With violence shall it be cast into the sea.

(5) When the Papal Theory perishes, and not till then, the Roman Catholic churches may be reformed. Parts may possibly again be broken off, separated entirely, and so reformed. But its adherents can not be reformed until there ceases to be a Papal Theory on the earth. For it is the Papal Theory that divides the Greek and Protestant communions from the Roman Catholic. Were there no Pope, the local churches in the Roman communion could break into provincial or national bodies and be reformed, as preparatory to a more comprehensive union. And, if it be true, as held by some, "that the order of bishops was craftily abolished by

[22] Vaticanism, 85.

the Council of Trent (A.D. 1563), and the theory of certain schoolmen was made into dogma, to this effect, namely, the Pope is universal bishop, and possesses the whole episcopate; all other bishops are but papal vicars, that is, presbyters only," — then the end of the Papacy is the end of the episcopacy in that great communion. Be this as it may, we have no doubt that the rise of this theory into completeness in papal infallibility is the beginning of its end.

(6) If, however, the Papal Theory should prevail — which it will not — it could easily become ecumenical. It once embraced, with the exception of the Greek Church, all Christendom. It has now all the ecclesiastical machinery and institutions needed to express in itself, in visible form, the unity of the invisible kingdom of heaven.

II. — THE EPISCOPAL THEORY OF THE CHRISTIAN CHURCH.

§ 56. The Episcopal Theory is older but less imposing than the Papal. The church of Jerusalem and not the church of Rome was the mother church. The gospel was preached, beginning at Jerusalem. The Eastern or Greek Church is the source and background, as we have shown (§§ 49, 50), of the Western or Roman Church. There can be no doubt of this, nor of the fact that Episcopacy arose before the Papacy in the Christian Church. That the former is less imposing than the latter does not result so much from the nature of the system as from its incomplete development. Episcopacy has for some reason been largely confined to national boundaries. It has never called, in modern times, a central council having authority over, and giving laws and unity to, all the communities and nations embracing the theory. Lacking this central, authoritative, and unifying body, the Episcopal Theory does not impress the imagination as profoundly as does the Papal.

§ 57. The origin of the Episcopal Theory may be quite accurately traced. In many, if not all, of the primitive churches or particular congregations there was a presbytery; that is, each local church had a plurality of elders or presbyters. Luke speaks of such elders or bishops in local churches (Acts 14 : 23 ; 20 : 17, 28 ; 21 : 18), and Paul calls them a presbytery (1 Tim. 4 : 14) ; of which we shall speak more particularly in another Lecture. In this local church presbytery, or board of elders, there would naturally arise by choice, or otherwise, a presiding officer, who would receive in time some distinguishing title, though only the first among equals. The name bishop, though originally and everywhere in the New Testament synonymous with presbyter or elder, — the three words being used interchangeably, — at length became the title for distinguishing the presiding presbyter. Thus, in the genuine Ignatian Epistles, we read of "being subject to the bishop and the presbytery;"[23] of a "justly renowned presbytery," being "fitted as exactly to the bishop as the strings are to the harp;"[24] of "obeying the bishop and the presbytery with an undivided mind, breaking one and the same bread;"[25] of being "subject to the bishop as to the grace of God, and to the presbytery as to the law of Jesus Christ ;"[26] and of similar expressions in ten other passages, showing how common the distinction had become, if indeed these expressions are not in part or wholly interpolations. The bishop and presbytery were in the local or particular church, the only diocese then known. In later writings presbyters are also spoken of as presiding over the local churches,[27] while the bishop and his presbytery are at a still later writing again conjoined.[28] The bishops of the early churches were pastors of local churches.

Under the persecutions which every-where met the preachers of Christ, and the want of church edifices in which to meet, the presbytery of each church, under its chosen leader, called a bishop in honor, not in order, would teach and feed the flock as best they could, in the homes or

[23] Ep. Eph. ii.   [24] Ibid. iv.   [25] Ibid. xx.   [26] Ep. Mag. ii.
[27] Pastor of Hermas, 2, iv.   [28] Apostol. Const. book ii, xxviii; book viii, iv.

wherever they could most safely or conveniently assemble the whole or a part of the church. The presbyters would also labor in adjacent territory, which labor would require some overseeing, and this would naturally fall to the lot of the bishop of the local presbytery, the *primus inter pares*. Vice-Principal Edwin Hatch, in his famous Bampton Lectures, says that "the weight of evidence has rendered practically indisputable" the identity of the primitive bishops and presbyters; that, in the course of the second century, the bishop came to stand above the rest of the presbyters of the local church; that "the episcopate grew by the force of circumstances, in the order of Providence, to satisfy a felt want;" that "the supremacy of the episcopate was the result of the struggle with Gnosticism;" that "dioceses in the later sense of the term did not yet exist" in the fourth century; and that the first diocese was that of which Alexandria was the centre.[29] "By degrees a systematic organization sprang up, by which neighboring churches were grouped together for the purposes of consultation and self-government. The chief city of each district had the civil rank of the 'metropolis,' or mother city. There the local synods naturally met, and the bishop — styled 'metropolitan,' from his position took the lead in the deliberations, as '*primus inter pares*,' and acted as the representative of his brother bishops in their intercourse with other churches. Thus, though all bishops were nominally equal, a superior dignity and authority came by general consent to be vested in the metropolitans, which, when the churches became established, received the stamp of ecclesiastical authority. A little higher dignity was assigned to the bishops of the chief seats of government, such as Rome, Antioch, Alexandria, and subsequently Constantinople; and among these, the bishop of Rome naturally had the precedence."[30] Thus slowly, under a favoring environment, the

[29] Org. Early Christ. Chhs. (1880), 38; 82, 83; 98, 99; 215; 195, 194.
[30] 8 Ency. Brit. 488.

bishop from being a mere presbyter became a presiding presbyter over equals, then a metropolitan among neighboring churches, and finally a bishop with authority, when Christianity became the state religion in the Roman Empire.

§ 58. The Episcopal Theory of the Christian Church when fully developed may be thus stated: "In order to be a valid branch of the Church of Christ, the Church must have (1) the holy Scriptures; (2) the ancient catholic creeds; (3) the ministry in an unbroken line of succession from the apostles; (4) this ministry must be in the exercise of lawful jurisdiction; (5) the Christians of any nation with these conditions constitute a national branch of the Church of Christ, totally independent of the jurisdiction and authority of any foreign church or bishop, subject only under Christ to the authority of the universal Church in general council assembled; and (6) as such they have jurisdiction over all their members and authority in matters of faith to interpret and decide, and in matters of discipline and worship to legislate and ordain such rites and ceremonies as may seem most conducive to edification and godliness, provided they be not contrary to the Holy Scriptures."[31] This theory is sometimes stated more briefly and broadly, but with less accuracy.

§ 59. The constitutive principle of this theory may be found in apostolic succession; that is, that "episcopal ordination in an unbroken line of succession from the apostles is necessary to valid jurisdiction and the due administration of the sacraments anywhere."[32] If this line be broken anywhere, the life ceases in the branches thus severed, and can not again be restored, except by ordination at the hands of some bishop, in lawful jurisdiction, who has himself been ordained in unbroken line of succession from the apostles. Hence the children are taught: "How is the life of the church preserved? By the Holy Ghost, through the Apos-

[31] Appleton's Am. Cycl. vii, 249.   [31] Ibid. 250

tolic Succession of her ministry." "What is necessary to make any particular church a true branch of the Catholic Church? It must hold to the Creed of the Church, to the Apostolic Ministry, and to the Apostolic Succession."[33] The touch of a bishop's fingers in succession is the essential principle, since neither faith nor worship nor works avail any thing without his official touch. On this "fiction," as Archbishop Whateley calls it, the renewing grace of God in Christ Jesus is made to depend.

§ 60. This constitutive principle needs ample and convincing proof, but instead it rests on assumption largely. "Bishop Stillingfleet declares that 'this succession is as muddy as the Tiber itself.' Bishop Hoadley asserts: 'It hath not pleased God, in his providence, to keep up *any proof* of the least probability, or moral possibility, of a regular uninterrupted succession; but there is a general appearance, and, humanly speaking, *a certainty to the contrary*, and that the succession hath often been interrupted.' Archbishop Whately affirms that 'there is not a minister in Christendom who is able to trace up, *with an approach to certainty*, his spiritual pedigree.'"[34] It is admitted that the New Testament does not even set forth the fact of an episcopate, much less the constitutive principle of the Episcopal Theory, which has come into such power in Christendom; and the supposed traces of it have been largely removed by the revision of the New Testament. "The care of all the churches" (2 Cor. 11: 28) is simply "anxiety for all the churches." James is sometimes called "the bishop of Jerusalem," but there is no evidence that he was any thing more than a presiding presbyter, if not one of the apostles. Jerome is quoted to show that episcopacy was called into being to repress heresies and supplement the authority of the rapidly diminishing body of the apostles, and that the superiority of bishops over presbyters was rather due to the custom of the churches than to the ordinance of Christ.[35] The constitutive principle has no

[33] Trinity Church Catechism, Qs. 77, 79.
[34] Orthodox Congregationalism, by Dr. Dorus Clarke, 23.   [35] 8 Ency. Brit. 484, seq.

proof, but stands in direct antagonism to the tests given in the New Testament of what constitutes true believers, ministers, and churches. Christ refused to let his apostles forbid a man casting out devils in his name, because he did not follow them (Mark 9: 38, 39). God made the gift of the Holy Spirit the test, and taught Peter so in a vision (Acts 10: 9–16). The apostles and church at Jerusalem, in two test cases, followed the same rule (Acts 11: 1–18; 15: 1–29). Hence, not apostolic succession, but the gift and graces of the Holy Spirit, distinguish the gospel ministry and the churches of Christ. But this will appear more fully hereafter.

§ 61. This constitutive principle develops into a compact system. (1) There must be different orders of the clergy, some as bishops possessed of functions which others as presbyters do not possess. In fact there has arisen this series — deacons, priests, bishops, archbishops, and patriarchs; but not all these are essential to the system. (2) Lawful jurisdiction must be observed to prevent confusion. The higher orders must have their respective realms; a bishop his diocese; the priest his congregation. The bishop has in his diocese authority over churches and priests and deacons, in matters of admission, discipline, and property. (3) There are national convocations or conventions, composed of two houses, — into the lower of which laymen may be admitted, — which have authority to enact whatever may be needful in matters of faith, discipline, ritual, and worship, that does not contravene the sacred Scriptures. (4) General councils were held in the early centuries, having authority over the whole Church in virtue of the union of Church and State. These have been for many centuries suspended through the divisions in Christendom. They must be restored again in order to complete the theory, and to express the unity of all the national churches. (5) The bishops have the sole power and right to confirm and ordain to holy orders. No one not episcopally ordained is qualified for the ministry, or can be recognized as a minister of the gospel, whatever success may attend his labors. And no congregation of true believers, though worshiping statedly in one place and calling itself a church, can be a true church or be recognized as such, unless ministered unto in orderly connection by one who has been ordained by a bishop in the line of succession from the apostles. And, what is more, no denomination of true Christians, though presided over by bishops, so called, as the Methodist Episcopal Church, can be treated as a branch of the true Church, until the said bishops and the lower clergy shall have been ordained by a bishop in succession from the apostles.[36] Thus is carried out, in logical consistency, the dictum of Cyprian: "It is no avail what a man teaches; it is enough that he teaches out of the Church; where the bishop is, there is the Church."[37] (6) The system descends to minute details with its authority. Thus, on issuing a new hymn-book, in 1871, the Protestant Episcopal Church in the United States of America, "resolved that this Hymnal be authorized for use, and that no other Hymns shall be allowed in the public worship of the Church, except such as are now ordinarily bound up with the Book of Common Prayer." The words both of prayer and of praise must be "authorized," or God can not be worshiped acceptably in public service! Thus the principle develops into a system consistent and exclusive, and capable of universal extension, provided the authority of control can be carried over from national conventions to general councils representing all the nations of Christendom.

§ 62. The Episcopal Theory, however, has not always developed into precisely the same system or form. (1) The Catholic and Apostolic Church of the East, commonly called the Greek Church, is its oldest form. Under this general name or title, several national churches with their peculiarities are included. It has its three orders of ministers,—

[36] A Churchman's Reasons, by Dr. Richardson, 150, seq.
[37] 5 Ency. Brit. 759.

deacons, priests, and bishops, — under four patriarchs of equal rank, but who are themselves of the order of bishops. The Eastern Church runs so nearly in the line of the development of the Western until we reach the question of the primacy, that we might almost define it as a truncated Papal Theory; for it holds to seven sacraments and to infallibility.

(2) The Anglican Church had its birth in a political revolution and a spiritual reformation. It broke off from Rome; but, as might be supposed from the compromises in which it originated, its connection with the civil power as a state establishment, and the corruptions from which it was only a partial reformation, it contains discordant elements, in its liturgy, its polity, and its doctrine. The Prayer Book opens towards Rome and towards Geneva, containing both papal and evangelical elements. "An impartial estimate of the Anglican formularies would probably be found to support that view of coördinate authority of Scripture and the Church which is taken by a large body of her divines, . . . though many of her adherents would undoubtedly incline, more or less completely, to that more Protestant view, which subordinates the Church to Scripture."[38] In polity the Anglican Church is also incongruous, since it places a layman, the king or the queen of England, at its head. Hence a writer truly says: "She is a Janus, and her temple is always open." Still the controlling factor in this incongruous establishment is that of apostolic succession. The grounds of fellowship, however, as set forth in a manifesto issued for visitors of the World's Exhibition in London, in 1862, are wider, namely: "The remission and regeneration through Baptism, the gift of the Holy Ghost in Confirmation, the objective presence of the body and the blood in the Eucharist, as well as its sacrificial character, Apostolic Succession, Absolution, and the authority of the Ancient Creeds."[39] The Anglican Church stands, therefore, more closely identified with the Greek Church in polity, and with the Greek

[38] 5 Ency. Brit. 759. [39] Ecclesia; or, Ch. Problems Considered, 115.

and Roman Churches in doctrine, than with the Protestant Churches.

(3) The Protestant Episcopal Church, having no connection with the State, and freed from an adverse environment, is perhaps the normal development of the constitutive principle. There remains a Low Church element in it, which is foreign to the system, and which in time must be eliminated from it, but which can find no distinctive life and place outside. The Reformed Episcopal Church, having no distinctive constitutive principle, must fail, ceasing to be, or returning to the fold whence it went out.

(4) The Moravian Brethren have an episcopal government in part. "The ministers are bishops, presbyters, and deacons. The bishops alone can ordain, but they are not diocesan. They are appointed by the general synod, or by the elders' conference of the Unity, and have official seats both in the synods of the provinces where they preside, and in the general synod." " The general synod which governs the whole Church meets every ten years." " The worship is liturgical."[40]

These are differing forms of the same theory of the Church of Christ, and constitute the chief manifestations of Episcopacy.

§ 63. There are several things to be noted in connection with the Episcopal Theory of the Christian Church.

(1) It is a systematic form of church government. It has a central formative principle and a logical development, notwithstanding the fact that its historical forms have been modified by extrinsic circumstances. Strip off the abnormal elements, and the polity will be invigorated. " The decided growth of the Episcopal Church (in the United States) dates from the period when it clearly enunciated its distinctive theory."[41] The theory referred to is Apostolic Succession.

[40] 16 Ency. Brit. 812.
[41] Prof. Diman, in Centennial No. North Am. Review, 36.

(2) It is a living, aggressive theory. It shows a most vigorous vitality. Denying to non-Episcopal ministers and churches, of all names, all right and claim to be true Christian ministers and churches, Episcopacy consistently invades their mission fields and parishes. Logically it can not do otherwise. Hence the more consistent the system is, the more intolerant and exclusive it must become. It dominates large and active communities, as we have seen, husbanding and using its vast resources and energies in its own enlargement. It, like the Papacy, contends for the mastery of Christendom, and thus of all nations.

(3) Only one branch, the Eastern Church, claims infallibility for its general councils. As a system, infallibility can not be predicated of it; reform of it is therefore possible. It can surrender any doctrine or principle, even its constitutive principle, whenever its adherents see sufficient cause for so doing, and become another polity.

(4) It is at present an incomplete system. It does not now as formerly express the unity of the kingdom of heaven. The last of the so-called ecumenical councils was held in A.D. 680. Since then this theory has found no way of exhibiting the unity of its adherents. The Pan-Anglican Conferences, and the Episcopal Congresses, held in later years, have been limited in scope, without authority to govern even those taking part in them, and are consequently abnormal. Indeed, it would seem impossible, in this age of liberty, to convoke a general council which should have authority over national churches. Passing beyond national boundaries, this theory of the Church meets a barrier of liberty which since the Reformation it has not had strength to pass. To convoke a general council to deliberate and advise, is to expose the weakness of the theory and introduce a foreign and divisive principle. Hence the system stands incomplete, and must remain incomplete, unless it can restore authoritative general councils. Moreover, being incomplete, it is inadequate to answer the sacerdotal prayer

of Christ the Head, that all his disciples may be one, that the world may believe in Him (John 17: 20-23). Unless it can again find a way to set up general councils with authority, the theory fails to reach the goal of ecumenical unity, and, sooner or later, must yield to the theory which shall best fulfill this prayer of Christ on the principles of liberty.

LECTURE IV.

THE PRESBYTERIAL AND THE CONGREGATIONAL THEORY
OF THE CHRISTIAN CHURCH.

"*Let the elders that rule well be counted worthy of double honor, especially those who labor in the word and in teaching.*" — Saint Paul.

"*Tell it unto the church: and if he refuse to hear the church also, let him be unto thee as the Gentile and the publican.*" — Jesus Christ.

HAVING examined the Papal and the Episcopal Theory of the Christian Church, we come next to the Presbyterial Theory.

III. — THE PRESBYTERIAL THEORY OF THE CHRISTIAN CHURCH.

§ 64. This theory in its elements is older than the Episcopal, but later in its development. As we have seen (§ 57), the primitive churches had a plurality of elders in each, called by Paul a "presbytery." These presbyters, like the elders or rulers in the synagogue, had the oversight and rule in the church in which they were bishops. Hence the writer of the Hebrews could say: "Remember them that had the rule over you" (Heb. 13: 7, 24). And Clement Romanus, writing before the death of the Apostle John, says: "Being obedient to those who had the rule over you, and giving all fitting honor to the presbyters among you." "Ye, therefore, who laid the foundation of this sedition, submit yourselves to the presbyters, and receive correction so as to repent."[1] Whatever came before Presbyterian rule over churches united in organic bodies, it is certain that the rule of presbyters, as a church board, in local churches, came before the

[1] Ep. Cor. 1, lvii.

Episcopate or the Papacy. But such local Presbyterian rule did not develop into what is now known as Presbyterian government. Presbyterianism as a polity does not date earlier than John Calvin. But there had been similar theories proposed before Calvin, though "limited, fragmentary, and abortive." The aim of Calvin was to formulate a theory or form of government, which should prevent the disintegration caused by the Reformation, and at the same time match the power of Rome. He would have separated it also largely from the control of the State. Each church, at the first, had as many presbyters as it chose to elect.

We learn the respect shown the presbyters of the primitive churches by what is said to the churches about obeying them. Thus Polycarp tells the members to be "subject to the presbyters and deacons, as unto God and Christ;"[2] and Ignatius speaks of being "subject to the presbytery, as to the apostle of Jesus Christ."[3] But whatever the honor paid the local church presbytery, there was no association of such presbyteries in the early days with authority over particular churches.

§ 65. Not until the Great Reformation did the theory emerge, and then only through a wrong interpretation of a single passage of Scripture. It was held that two kinds of elders, ministerial and ruling lay elders, are mentioned by Paul in the words: "Let the elders that rule well be counted worthy of double honor, especially those who labor in the word and in teaching" (Tim. 5: 17). It is now conceded by good Presbyterians that only one kind of elders is here referred to.

§ 66. The Presbyterian Theory is government of churches by sessions, presbyteries, synods, and assemblies, or by similar judicatories. It is the union of all churches in one body, under the rule of chosen representatives of the churches; on the principle that the greater shall rule the less, in enlarging judicatories, until all become united in one

² Ep. Phil. v.   ³ Ep. Tral. ii.

supreme court, to which appeals can be taken from the smallest tribunal. It thus seeks visible unity under orderly government, for all churches.

§ 67. The constitutive principle which controls the whole development is authoritative representation. This pervades and guides every thing. By this we mean that the chosen representatives of a particular church have in virtue of their election the power to rule or govern that church; and that the chosen representatives of several or many churches have in virtue of their election the power of government over those churches; and so on until an ecumenical unity is reached.

The principle of authoritative representation is thus the formative principle in the Presbyterian Theory. It matters not, so far as the theory goes, whether the representatives chosen to govern be ministers or laymen, or partly ministers and partly laymen. The principle is separate from the character of the representatives, and from the historical development of the principle into any system.

§ 68. Yet in the development of the principle, it is best to take the purest historical form as the example, which is the Presbyterian Church in the United States. It is free from all modifications caused by the union of Church and State, which can not be said probably of any European example of the theory. The constitutive principle develops in the Presbyterian Church in the United States into the following simple and efficient order : —

(1) The believers in any locality are united in a particular church, the primary seat of power, and called the church of that place.

(2) Each one of the churches so gathered chooses from among its members any needed number of ruling elders, who, together with the pastor or pastors of that church constitute the session, with power to admit, discipline, dismiss, or excommunicate members of said church. It elects also from itself delegates or representatives, called

commissioners, to the higher judicatories of the presbytery and the synod within whose jurisdiction the church falls.

(3) "A presbytery consists of all the ministers, in number not less than five, and one ruling elder from each congregation, within a certain district."

"The presbytery has power to receive and issue appeals from church sessions, and references brought before them in an orderly manner; to examine and license candidates for the holy ministry; to ordain, install, remove, and judge ministers; to examine and approve or censure the records of church sessions; to resolve questions of doctrine or discipline seriously and reasonably propounded; to condemn erroneous opinions which injure the peace or purity of the church; to visit particular churches for the purpose of inquiring into their state, and redressing the evils that may have arisen in them; to unite or divide congregations at the request of the people, or to form or receive new congregations; and in general to order whatever pertains to the spiritual welfare of the churches under their care."[4]

The presbyteries are thus clothed with power to control the churches in them in matters of doctrine and discipline, and also to ordain, remove, and judge ministers. This includes the power to vacate a pulpit, and to dissolve the pastoral relation, at their own discretion.[5]

(4) "A synod is a convention of the bishops and elders within a larger district, including at least three presbyteries." The synods have the power to do for the presbyteries, over which each has jurisdiction, what the presbyteries may do for church sessions, in matters of references, appeals, records, wrongs, evils, order; in forming, uniting, or dividing presbyteries; and in general oversight. They have also the right "to propose to the General Assembly, for their adoption, such measures as may be of common advantage to the whole Church."[6]

[4] Form of Government, x, sec. i, viii.
[5] Moore's Digest (1873), 144–180; Minutes Gen. Assembly, 1874, 83, 85.
[6] Form of Government, xi, sec. i, iv.

(5) "The General Assembly is the highest judicatory of the Presbyterian Church. It shall represent, in one body, all the particular churches of this denomination. It consists of an equal delegation of bishops and elders from each presbytery," in a specified proportion.

It receives and issues appeals and references duly brought before it; reviews records of synods; gives constitutional advice and instruction; constitutes a bond of union; decides all controversies respecting doctrine and discipline; bears testimony against errors and immorality in any church, presbytery, or synod; erects new synods; superintends the concerns of the whole church; corresponds with foreign bodies; suppresses schismatical contentions; and reforms manners in all churches under its care.[7]

(6) There was organized, in 1875, a Presbyterian Alliance. Its first general council met in 1877, and thereafter meets "once in three years." "Any church organized on Presbyterian principles which holds the supreme authority of the Scriptures of the Old and New Testaments in matters of faith and morals, and whose creed is in harmony with the consensus of the Reformed Confessions, shall be eligible for admission into the alliance."

(*a*) "Its powers. The council shall have power to decide upon the application of churches desiring to join the alliance; it shall have power to entertain and consider topics which may be brought before it by any church represented in the council, or by any member of the council, on their being transmitted in the manner hereinafter provided; but it shall not interfere with the existing creed or constitution of any church in the alliance, or with its internal order or external relations."[8]

(*b*) It will be noticed that the constitutive principle of Presbyterianism is expressly abandoned in "The Alliance of the Reformed Churches throughout the world holding the

---
[7] Form of Government, xii, sec. i, ii, iv, v.
[8] Constitution of Presby. Alliance, art. ii, iii, 3.

Presbyterian system." Authoritative representation is dropped on passing national boundaries, and a foreign principle introduced, which substitutes deliberation and the expression of opinion for the decrees of a judicatory with authority. In attaining ecumenical unity Presbyterianism by constitutional provision surrenders, for the time being at least, the very principle which makes it Presbyterian.

§ 69. This theory claims to find the proof of its constitutive principle in the New Testament. In a paper read before the second council of the Presbyterian Alliance, held in 1880, it was said that "there is not a scintilla of evidence for any other form of government in the New Testament."[9] Yet the author was chary of Scriptural proof, adducing only the conceded identity of presbyters and bishops, and, further, the ordination and discipline of presbyters. The whole system has been claimed to be Scriptural, the *jure divino* constitution of the Christian Church. This claim has, however, been so shattered that Prof. E. D. Morris, D.D., of the Lane Theological Seminary, is constrained to say: "In explaining and justifying this polity on Scriptural grounds, nothing more than such general warrant will be affirmed." He then surrenders the *jure divino* claim for Presbyterianism; and justifies Presbyterianism (1) by reference to the synagogue as the model of the Church; (2) by the claim that the apostles ordained elders, who taught, governed, and had general oversight in the churches; (3) by "the conception of government, as a distinct characteristic of the Church;" (4) by "the fellowship of the churches, and the unity of the Church, as well in government as in more general forms of administrative association." "Such in outline are the Scriptural foundations on which the Presbyterian polity claims to rest."[10]

We shall have occasion to examine the texts on which this claim rests, and so we pass them now, only saying here

[9] Report and Proceedings, 152.
[10] Ecclesiology (1885), 139–143.

that the identity of presbyters and bishops is not a doctrine peculiar to Presbyterianism; that the whole synagogue service was conducted by laymen; that each synagogue was independent of the control of other synagogues, though in fellowship with them; and that the "presbytery" of the New Testament was confined to a local, or particular, church, like a modern Presbyterian session, and nothing more.

§ 70. The constitutive principle of Presbyterianism has had several forms of development, more or less differing in general character and in details.

(1) There is a large number of churches called Presbyterian. There are fifty such on the roll of the second council of the Presbyterian Alliance. Ireland enrolled two Presbyterian churches; Scotland, five; the United States, eight; Austria, three; France, two; Germany, two; Italy, two; Switzerland, four; thus revealing the inability of authoritative representation to unify churches within national limits, even when those boundaries are very narrow.

(2) The Methodist-Episcopal Church is not strictly Episcopal, but is essentially Presbyterian. Its bishops are presbyters raised to a defined superintendency, but not constituting a third order in the ministry. Before this Church can be recognized as Episcopal, its bishops and presbyters must be ordained, in the line of apostolic succession, by the bishop, rightly ordained, of some other Church.[11] The government of this Church is chiefly by presbyters, on the principle of authoritative representation. On this the Wesleyan Methodists and the Episcopal-Methodists essentially agree.

But Methodism as a polity is not a simple, but a compound, and hence it is unstable. The following changes may be noted in the Methodist-Episcopal Church: (1) At first bishops alone ordained, now the conferences have the power to participate; (2) the bishops can not now, as formerly, decide appeals, (3) nor control the press, which is now in the hands of the conference; (4) ministers can not

[11] Churchman's Reasons, 150-167.

now, as formerly, set members back on trial; (5) nor expel them without trial; (6) nor appoint all the stewards.[12] To these changes may be added a most fundamental one (7), the introduction, after long delay and secessions, of lay representation. This radical change from clerical rule to the admission of a lay element in the government of the Church was effected in 1872. Before that date "not a layman ever touched his finger to the making of the laws of discipline" by which that great communion had been governed. These changes are steps toward greater liberty and the fuller recognition of the principle which is dominant in their polity. Yet the conflicting elements still remaining will cause trouble and possibly division again.

§ 71. We remark, on the Presbyterian Theory of the Christian Church: —

(1) That it is a simple, consistent, but incomplete system. At present the theory stops at national boundaries. It has become another theory and polity in the Presbyterian Alliance. To reach ecumenical unity on its own peculiar principle, the alliance must be clothed with power to rule the churches that compose it. Whether the Presbyterian Alliance will be able in time to gain and apply the constitutive principle of Presbyterianism to itself or not, the future must determine; but as the matter now stands, the head of gold is in antagonism with the body of silver and brass and iron and clay. It has borrowed from another polity the principle of fellowship without authority, on which to show its ability to attain ecumenical comprehension in fulfilling the prayer of Christ for unity.

(2) This theory is not dependent upon there being in each church a board of ruling lay elders, as the General Assembly of the Presbyterian Church in America has declared.[13] If the lay elders should be ordained presbyters, or if a board of laymen should take the place of ruling elders,

[12] Eccl. Polity, by Rev. A. N. Fillmore, 193, 194.
[13] Moore's Digest (1873), 115.

the representation would be clothed with equal authority to govern. Presbyterianism does not, therefore, fall with the surrender of Calvin's wrong interpretation of 1 Tim. 5 : 17.

(3) This theory of the Church does not claim infallibility. It has surrendered, or, more accurately, is surrendering, its *jure divino* claim. It is surrendering its theory of ruling elders. It has waived aside its constitutive principle in the formation of the Presbyterian Alliance. It may surrender also other positions, as greater light comes to it. Its highest judicatory in America in 1832 inhibited women from speaking in promiscuous assemblies;[14] but the same General Assembly in 1874 declined to express an opinion on the question, but committed "the whole subject to the discretion of the pastors and elders of the churches."[15] The General Assembly thus vacated, in this instance, its right and power "of deciding in all controversies respecting doctrine and discipline,"[16] and remanded such a question to church sessions, which by the Form of Government have no such power.[17] This transference recognizes the principles of another polity and has great peril in it to the Presbyterian Theory.

(4) The theory, not being infallible, is reformable. We have noted some changes. Others may arise. Once, cases of discipline were appealed from the church session to the presbytery, thence to the synod, and finally to the General Assembly, thus involving the whole Church perhaps in a petty quarrel. The annual sessions of the assembly were burdened with such appeals. In order to carry on the other business more satisfactorily, these appeals are now carried to a judicial commission, whose decisions are final except in matters of law and all matters of constitution and doctrine. This is an important change inasmuch as the voice of the whole Church is not uttered by the commission, as it is by the General Assembly. This change was made in 1884. It raises the question why a shorter reference may not be had

[14] Moore's Digest, 304.
[15] Minutes, 66.
[16] Form of Government, xii, v.
[17] Ibid. ix, vi.

and one equally trustworthy. All these modifications are toward greater liberty.

IV. — THE CONGREGATIONAL THEORY OF THE CHRISTIAN CHURCH.

§ 72. The last of the four theories of the Christian Church is the oldest in principles and the latest in development. It is conceded by historians that the primitive churches, like the synagogues or clubs from which they came, were absolutely independent one of another (§ 109) and that they had at first no organic system of fellowship. When such fellowship arose, it was without the exercise of authority. Not even a vote of the body could bind dissentients until the Church was united with the empire under Constantine, about A.D. 313. The principles of this polity go back to Christ, but its development in harmony with those principles dates since the Reformation. Hatch, in his Bampton Lectures, 1880, traces all the elements found in the primitive churches to sources external; to institutions civil, eleemosynary, or religious.[18] This shows the preparation providentially made for Christianity as an organism. We shall discuss this polity in detail in subsequent Lectures.

§ 73. The Congregational Theory of the Christian Church is that the kingdom of heaven, being itself one, has but one normal manifestation, or natural development, which appears first in individual churches, equal in origin, rights, functions, and duties, which are consequently independent one of another in matters of control; then in associations of churches without authority by which the fraternity and unity of all Christians are expressed and the churches coöperate in Christian labors, all being subject to Christ alone and to his revealed will. It shuns independency on the one hand, with which it is sometimes confounded, and on the other hand the exercise of authority by associated churches. It also avoids all ministerial or prelatical rule.

[18] Org. Early Christ. Churches, 208, passim.

§ 74. The constitutive principle of the Congregational Theory of the Christian Church is not the participation of all the members of a local church in the government of that church. "The exercise of all government by the church collectively, and not by the office-bearers alone," is held by some to be its determining characteristic.[19] But a church governed by adult members, or by adult male members, or by a board of control elected for the purpose and reporting to the church, is Congregational if independent of outside control and united by fellowship to other churches.

(1) Its constitutive principle is the independence under Christ of each fully constituted Church of Christ, or the autonomy under Christ of every local congregation of believers duly organized. This church independence is the principle which makes Congregationalism what it is. It governs all its institutions and determines all questions that arise touching order. And we mean by independence here the right and duty under Christ of each fully constituted local church to manage its own affairs, elect and ordain all its officers, administer its discipline, and determine its mode of fellowship, without external accountability and control, but in harmony with the fellowship of unity in the kingdom of heaven. Each church is thus complete in itself, possessed of the whole functions of the Christian Church, so that if all other churches should cease to be, it could become the mother church of another Christendom. The independency of the local church controls the entire development of the system, and distinguishes Congregationalism from all other systems.

(2) It is sometimes claimed that fellowship is a distinctive principle of Congregationalism; but this we believe to be a palpable mistake. The fundamental idea of the Church of Christ is "the communion of saints;" and every theory of that Church uses fellowship as its common element, but each after its own peculiar formative principle. As against strict

[19] Church of Christ, Prof. Bannerman's, ii, 314, 315.

CONGREGATIONAL THEORY. 81

independency — were such a thing possible — fellowship is a peculiar principle, occupying one of the foci of an ellipse, but against all actual polities, fellowship is not peculiar to the Congregational polity, since they have church fellowship in presbyteries, conferences, conventions, or councils. Fellowship is common therefore to all polities, and should never be spoken of as a peculiar principle of any one of them.

§ 75. In the development arising from the constitutive principle of the Congregational Theory, there is: —

(1) The local congregation of believers, gathering the true Christians of a place into church relations for worship and work, each such church having power of self-government under Christ, to manage all its internal affairs. It is complete, autonomous, independent of external control.

(2) These independent churches, sustaining the same relation to the indivisible kingdom of heaven, stand in the closest relation to one another in fellowship, a fraternity or brotherhood, with obligations and duties that bind them into associations of communion, assistance, coöperation. No church can live unto itself alone. The oneness of the kingdom constrains all useful modes of fellowship.

(3) This fellowship may find expression in occasional councils of churches, to inquire and advise in matters of common concernment, or of church discipline and peace, or respecting any questions where light and advice may be needed.

(4) But as fellowship is a constant force wider than advice, and should therefore have stated and systematic expression, the churches should meet statedly for consultation and coöperation, in bodies that should have and exercise no authority of coercion, but only the right of self-protection. This systematic fellowship of churches has found regular expression in the following bodies: —

(*a*) District associations, or conferences. These are composed of ministers and delegates of the churches situated within a small territory. They usually meet twice a year, and possess no ecclesiastical authority over the churches and ministers composing them, except what is essential to self-protection, a right and power which every organization possesses.

(*b*) State associations, or conferences. In these the churches of a State or Territory are united under a constitution, defining membership, and excluding the exercise of ecclesiastical control or authority over the ministers and churches belonging to them. Yet here too the body has the inalienable and self-evident right and duty of enforcing the terms of its constitution, and the covenant of association, whether written or unwritten.

(*c*) National associations, called the National Council in the United States, but Unions in England and her Colonies. These include the churches of the nation or province, in some proportionate representation specified in their constitutions. The independence of the local churches is secured by such provisions as these: " This National Council shall never exercise legislative or judicial authority, nor consent to act as a council of reference." "The Union recognizes the right of every church to administer its affairs, free from external control, and shall not, in any case, assume legislative authority, or become a court of appeal."

(*d*) This theory, to be complete, must hold general councils of all national associations, in other words, an ecumenical association. The reasons for this are the same as under the other three theories, the communion of saints and the prayer of Christ for universal unity (John 17: 20-23). These we have already discussed in another place.[20] When organized, as it some time will be, the Congregational Theory of the Christian Church will have reached ecumenical comprehension. This development will be normal from beginning to end, with no introduction of foreign elements, with no damage to the liberty of local churches. Its consti-

[20] 16 Cong. Quarterly (1874), 291, seq.

tutive principle dominates fellowship in every stage of its widening development.

§ 76. The constitutive principle of this theory controls the following communions: The Independent, or Congregational, churches of Great Britain and her Provinces; the Congregational churches of the United States; the Baptist churches of all names and lands; the Christian and some other minor bodies.

The Lutheran communions generally hold it, but modified by modes of ministerial discipline which are somewhat Presbyterian. " The [Lutheran] churches undoubtedly retain the authority to call, to elect, and ordain ministers." " Ecclesiastical power really vests in the church itself, or in the members constituting the church. Each individual congregation, embracing pastor and people, has full authority under Christ to act for itself." [21] The European Lutherans, being connected with the State, are less Congregational than the American Lutherans.

§ 77. As the other Lectures will be given to the proof, development, and relations of the Congregational Theory of the Christian Church, it is enough to say here that the proof is rational, Scriptural, and ecclesiastical. Its impregnable citadel is in the New Testament and the conceded constitution of the apostolic churches (§ 109). Its relations to religious and civil liberty prove its fitness to be the coming polity (§ 82).

§ 78. This Congregational Theory demands a few special observations: —

(1) It develops into a simple, consistent, comprehensive system, able to express the unity of believers the world around. It must have been by neglecting its modes of fellowship, and fixing the eye on the impossible claims of strict independency, that Professor Bannerman, of New College, Edinburgh, could call it a "no church system," in this passage: "It is not in the church system — or, rather, no

[21] 25 Bib. Sacra, 489, 490.

church system — of Congregational Independency, that we see an approach to the model exhibited for our imitation in the Apostolic Church."[22] It will appear, we think, in due time that Congregational Independency is a simple, consistent, comprehensive scheme, suited to all the functions and emergencies of the churches of Christ, and possessing as good a claim to inherit the earth as can be produced for any other theory.

(2) Still it puts forth no claim of infallibility in its development. Whatever has been incorporated in it that is abnormal, or whatever is normal that has been neglected, in its bitter struggle for existence, can be removed or replaced, as light shall reveal more clearly the vast comprehension of its principles.

(3) This is a living and revolutionary theory. It bears in its bosom popular governments, democracies in the nations, because first in the churches. It makes all men brothers, under one Father, in essential equality. It makes the people of the Lord free — a kingdom and priests unto God. It withholds from elders the power of "lording it over the charge allotted to them" (1 Peter 5: 3). Because of its leveling power, this theory has incurred the hatred of aristocracies and hierarchies as no other polity has ever done or can ever do. Yet it still lives, to contend for the mastery: for the life of God is in it.

V. — COMPARISON OF THESE FOUR THEORIES OF THE CHRISTIAN CHURCH.

We have drawn out with some degree of particularity the four theories of church government which are competing for the mastery of Christendom, and so of the world. We may say of them: —

§ 79. They are the only simple theories of the Christian Church. They can each be reduced to one constitutive principle, with a normal manifestation covering the main features

[22] Church of Christ, II, 330.

of their historical development. The abnormal features mentioned are due to extraneous conditions, and constitute no impeachment of the claim that each theory is a simple and not a compound theory. The formative principle which gives life and shape to each system, and answers all questions touching it, has been definitely stated; and with them all we compass the whole possible circuit of church polity. Hence they are the only simple theories of the Church. When we place the government of the visible Church in the hands of an infallible primate, or in the hands of a few bishops, the successors of the apostles, or in the hands of authoritative representatives of the churches, or in the hands of independent churches, we cover the whole ground of possible simple systems. Thus the Papacy, Episcopacy, Presbyterianism, and Congregationalism, are the only stable systems, because simple. They may be compounded to some degree in unstable systems, tending ever to become simple and so engendering strifes and secessions; but such systems must severally become, sometime, one of the above four simple systems, when its dominant principle shall have thrown off the foreign elements. We have noted the changes in Episcopal Methodism, but " Methodism," says one of its advocates, "will be found to be a regular and systematic combination of the three principles of church government, namely: Episcopal, Presbyterian, and Congregational."[23] Whatever Methodism has borrowed from Episcopacy and Congregationalism, it has not borrowed the constitutive principle of either polity; and cleavage and change will go on in it, until it becomes a simple, dominated by one formative principle.

§ 80. These theories are mutually exclusive. One does not lead to another, or grow out of another, though the conditions for the development of one may have also conduced to the development of another, as the environment of the Roman Empire helped Episcopacy in the East and Papacy in

[23] Eccl. Polity, by Rev. A. N. Fillmore, 122.

the West. The rule of the presbyteries in local churches opened the door, through the presiding presbyter, historically but not logically, for Episcopal succession and rule; and Episcopacy opened the door in the same way for the Primacy: but logically the constitutive principles of all these theories are separate and exclusive. As one did not emerge from another, so one can not be harmonized with another. They are mutually exclusive. If any two of them be bound together by green withes, as is sometimes done in so-called union churches, they will wrestle and contend and divide until one or the other is expelled or the church is killed. As in large communions so in the individual churches, a mixed government struggles to become homogeneous. Hence the celebrated dictum of Dr. Nathanael Emmons: "Consociationism leads to Presbyterianism; Presbyterianism leads to Episcopacy; Episcopacy leads to Roman Catholicism; and Roman Catholicism is an ultimate fact,"[24] is only partly true. Consociationism is indeed a compound, with a dual interpretation of it,[25] but whose essential element was declared in 1799, by the Hartford North Association of Congregational ministers to be Presbyterian.[26] Each other polity mentioned is an ultimate fact, Presbyterianism as really as Roman Catholicism. The most that can be said of this dictum is that its first and last clauses are correct.

While the Papacy holds the "figment" of apostolic succession, its formative principle of an infallible primate would hold its theory of the Church in unabated vigor, were the whole episcopate besides abolished, as Bishop Coxe claims that it has already been abolished by the Council of Trent. While the Episcopacy allows, in some degree, authoritative representation by presbyters and even laymen, yet neither its unity nor its life inhere therein, and it would exist in unabated vigor were that representation abolished, which is only a concession to popular demands. It is not strictly a

[24] Memoirs, by Rev. Edwards A. Park, D.D., 163. [25] Contrib. Eccl. Hist. Ct., 40, seq.
[26] Hist. Presb. Ch., by Dr. E. H. Gillett, 1, 438.

part of the Episcopal system. The three other theories give no countenance to the Congregational Theory of the Christian Church, nor can they: for the independence of the local church is subversive of all aristocratic or hierarchical pretensions and systems. There is nothing in common as to principles between this popular theory and the others.

It follows that no one of these theories can be reformed into another of them, without there being first a destruction of its formative principle. By no development or modification can one be otherwise transformed into another. If it lose its place among existing polities at any time, it must be by the annihilation of its constitutive principle, and thus by regeneration. They stand opposed, each against all the rest, not in incidentals, not in degrees of development, but in their constitutive principles. He dreams who thinks of uniting them in some perpetual Christian union. If the Papacy were destroyed, its episcopate would make it Episcopal, unless its episcopate was absorbed in the Papacy, as has been claimed; in which case the abolition of the Papacy would make the Roman Catholic Church Presbyterian. If the Episcopacy be destroyed, Presbyterianism is left with its authoritative representation. If Presbyterianism be given up, the individual churches are then left in their independence to be united on the principle of free fellowship. Or this process may be reversed. But only in one way or in the other can ecumenical unity be reached.

§ 81. Yet each theory is capable of exhibiting the unity of Christ's invisible kingdom. This has been shown. But, as we have seen, the Episcopal and the Presbyterial Theory, in seeking to become ecumenical in their comprehension, will be, or has been, obliged, owing to the modern environment of liberty, to introduce a foreign principle into their highest assemblies, which is subversive of their constitutive principles. In their ecumenical tribunals the national churches must at present meet to consult and express an opinion, not to govern. One act of authority would probably shatter them. If liberty has come to stay with Church and State, removing all oppression, then these two systems will never be able to overleap the barrier of liberty, so as to express consistently the unity of the Christian Church. And their failure to do so must doom them.

The Papal Theory consistently expresses the ecumenical unity of its adherents, wherein lies its great strength. But it does it by completely suppressing liberty, which it calls "the insanity." Its infallible words are: "From this totally false notion of social government, they fear not to uphold that erroneous opinion most pernicious to the Catholic Church, and to the salvation of souls, which was called by our predecessor Gregory XVI (lately quoted) 'the insanity' (Ency. 13, August, 1832), (deliramentum), namely, that 'liberty of conscience and of worship is the right of every man; and that this right ought, in every well-governed state, to be proclaimed and asserted by the law,'" etc.[27] This is the quintessence of tyranny.

The Congregational Theory, in the fullest exercise of liberty, can easily express in associations of fellowship and consultation, without authority, the ecumenical unity of all particular, local churches throughout the world. The Holy Spirit sent by the great Head of the Church to take his place is steadily drawing the communion of saints into wider circles of fellowship, and will not cease to do so until the prayer of Christ for unity is visibly answered. It is of the utmost importance, therefore, to the common people which of these great church polities shall prevail to the exclusion of all the rest. For —

§ 82. The relation of church polity to civil government is most intimate. The profoundest foresight was shown in the maxim of King James: "No bishop, no king." The grandeur of the Puritan movement, which included both the

---

[27] Ency. Letter, Pius IX, 1864, Dec. 8. Appleton's Ann. Cycl. 1864, 702.

Presbyterians [28] and the Congregationalists, is seen, not in robes and miters and triple crowns, not in hierarchies and exaltation of the clergy. The highest grandeur of any government lies in the good it does the people. Measured by this standard we must accord the greatest glory to the Puritans. The Papacy denies to the people all that is comprehended under the term liberty or freedom, stigmatizing it as insanity. With it liberty is a popular craze. The relation of Episcopacy to liberty in the state is exactly expressed by the maxim above given : "No bishop, no king." But the relation of the Puritans to civil liberty may be learned from the historians, as also their relations to religious purity and liberty. "That the English people became Protestants is due to the Puritans." [29] "As the priest of the Established Church was, from interest, from principle, and from passion, zealous for the royal prerogatives, the Puritan was from interest, from principle, and from passion, hostile to them." [30] Hume says : "It was only during the next generation that the noble principles of liberty took root, and spreading themselves under the shelter of Puritanical absurdities, became fashionable among the people." [31] Liberty, indeed, as well as righteousness, was one of the "Puritanical absurdities." Froude says : "Whatever exists at this moment in England and Scotland of conscientious fear of doing evil is the remnant of the convictions which were branded by the Calvinists into the people's hearts." [32] The English Puritans were Calvinists. The Puritans gave righteousness and liberty to England, and through her to the world. The greatest glory of the nineteenth century, in political affairs, the abolition of slavery, and the enlargement of popular liberty, is the fruit of the Puritan movement. "One hundred and eighty

---

[28] As the Puritan movement was a reformation of the Reformation in England, the Presbyterians here referred to are those of England, and not those on the continent or in Scotland.
[29] Bancroft's Hist. U. S., Rd. Ed. (1876), 1, 224.
[30] Macaulay's Hist. Eng., i, 47, Ed. Phillips, Sampson & Co. (1856).
[31] Hist. Eng., v, 499.
[32] Calvinism : an address delivered at St. Andrews, 44.

million Europeans" have been raised during the present century, "from a degraded and ever dissatisfied vassalage to the rank of free and self-governing men." [33] This is the rising monument to the Puritans.

But the greater share of this glory belongs to the Congregational Puritans who went beyond the Presbyterian Puritans as respects liberty, in their theory of government. Archbishop Laud, in his sermon February 6, 1625-6, at Westminster, before Charles I, said: "And there is not a man that is for parity — all fellows [that is, equals] in the Church — but he is not for monarchy in the State." [34] Prof. James S. Candlish, of the Free Church College, Glasgow, points out the difference between the Presbyterian and the Congregational Puritans. "The Presbyterians were anxious to reform the Church of England more thoroughly, but they desired still to retain its national character. They would have a Church in alliance with the State, and embracing as far as possible all the people, not only preaching the gospel and dispensing the sacraments, but exercising discipline, and in all these functions aided and supported by the civil power." The Congregationalists on the contrary "sought an entire and unlimited toleration." "Cromwell contended that godly men should not be excluded from the public service because they would not take the Covenant." This position landed the Congregationalists in "a political theocracy, the Church being merged in the State, and the kingdom of God conceived as a Christian State." [35] Thus the Congregational Theory emerged as a Christian State both in England and in New England; but it soon was forced to correct its error in England by the Restoration, and in New England by a slower process. Yet while thus embarrassed by inherited notions from state establishments, the influence of this theory of the Church upon liberty in the State has been immense. It laid the foundations of this Republic and may

[33] Mackenzie's Hist. 19th Century, 459. [34] Hanbury's Hist. Memorials, 1, 476.
[35] Cunningham Lectures, 1884, 294-296.

even claim the form of its development. "The Church was the nucleus about which the neighborhood constituting a town was gathered." No institution "has had more influence on the condition and character of the people" than the republics called towns, which for several generations were churches or parishes acting in civil and political relations.[36] The germ of our state and national institutions was this town-church, and this church was democratic and Congregational. Thus it was that this "government of the people, by the people, and for the people," became the guiding star of all nations in civil and religious liberty. " To Robert Browne belongs the honor of first setting forth, in writing, the scheme of free church government." " Such was the commencement of that great movement on behalf of the independence of the churches which has electrified the globe and wrought out the most stupendous political and moral revolution of modern times."[37] There was an earlier but abortive attempt in Germany. The synod of Homburg, in 1526, gave the first formal development of Congregationalism since the Reformation,[38] but it was too revolutionary to suit the times. No statesman can omit to study the forms of church government of the country he governs, for they have the closest relations to, and the most controlling bearing upon, the liberties of that country.

It has been said that "the Presbyterian Church is the most republican church, the most American church, so far as political institutions can be assimilated to religious institutions;" but close inquiry does not justify such claim. The word republican means "pertaining to a republic; consonant with the principles of a republic;" and a republic is "a state in which the sovereign power is exercised by representatives elected by the people." The particular churches under the Presbyterian polity elect their respective sessions only in part. Such sessions are composed of pastors and ruling

[36] Palfrey's Hist. New Eng., ii, 11, seq.
[37] Orthodox Congregationalism, Dr. Dorus Clarke, 39.   [38] 6 Cong. Quart., 276-280.

elders. Each Presbyterian church elects and ordains its own ruling elders; but its pastor, the presiding officer of the session, must receive his call through the presbytery, subject to its discretion; for election by the church is considered as only a petition for installation, and his acceptance as only a request for installation. Hence the session is not wholly elected by the people. The session of each church within a specified district chooses one ruling elder, and these ruling elders with the ministers of those churches, and possibly other ministers, constitute a presbytery. The synod is made up in the same way, but from a wider district. But the general assembly consists of an equal delegation of ministers and ruling elders chosen by the presbyteries, in some specified ratio. Thus the ruling elders are the only representatives fully and directly elected by the people. Until quite recently the ruling elders were chosen for life; and they are still generally so chosen. Hence after the first election of the church session, there may be no other election by the people for a full generation, and then only to fill vacancies. This infrequent choice of ruling elders, and the choice of petition for a pastor, are all that the people have to do in "the most American church." For the presbyteries and synods are made up of ruling elders elected by the sessions, together with the ministers. The presbyteries choose from themselves the commissioners of the general assembly. Thus every election after the choice of the session is made by church officers from their own number. If our political institutions were of this sort, then the election of town and city officers generally for life by the people would exhaust the people's right and duty. For the city and town officers would elect from their own number both county and state officers; and these again from their own number would choose all national officers, as the legislative, the executive, and the judicial. From the beginning to the end, the people would have but one choice, the election of town and city officers. Every thing beyond this initial point would be done by officers holding generally life tenures, who would elect from themselves, directly or indirectly, county, state, and national officials. This is not so much republican as aristocratic in its principles and operation.

This brief statement of Presbyterianism, as given in its Form of Government, does not justify the claim that the Presbyterian Church is "the most American church." It is almost wholly a government of officers elected for life, by officers chosen from among themselves and by themselves. It is not a government of the people, by the people, and for the people.

A nearer approach is found in Congregationalism, as lately developed into district, state, and national associations of churches. It is true that the element of authority is lacking in this system, an element not Christian, but introduced by the union of church and state under Constantine. But this return to the plan of the apostles does not deprive Congregationalism of its resemblance to republicanism. Congregational churches elect and install their own officers, choose delegates to ecclesiastical councils, to district and state bodies, and to whatever conventions they may wish to attend. Thus elections are frequent, and by the membership, not by the officers. The election of delegates to the National Council is indirect, as the election of United States senators is indirect. And the candidates are not confined to officials but may include any member. Here is a closer parallel between civil and ecclesiastical institutions, as is fitting between the child and the parent; for our civil institutions had their origin in Congregationalism.

§ 83. It would seem hardly necessary to add that each one of these theories determines the activities of its adherents. Theological differences within the evangelical lines have some bearing upon benevolences and labors. A Calvinist and an Arminian can, however, worship and work together, if brought into the same church, and soon forget their differences in a common brotherhood. There is nothing in church action to raise their doctrinal differences into controlling position. But it is not so in matters of polity. A true Papist can not fraternize with a Congregationalist, though both believe in the consensus of faith of all Christendom; for every church act involves a theory of the Church, and in their theories they are at antipodes. It is so also with an Episcopalian and a Presbyterian. Indeed, the attempt has been made to make two theories standing nearest together coöperate in missions at home and abroad; but the theories were stronger than utilities, and so have drawn them into separate channels of activity. It is not wholly bigotry that keeps churches asunder (§ 45), but often adherence to principle. Conscience lies at the bottom. Doctrine is not so much involved in acts of worship and church action, but polity is involved, and hence must assert itself. And each theory of the Church demands that church acts be in harmony with itself, and that all activities center in itself.

§ 84. The ecclesiastical development indicated by the theories presented has been useful. God's method is: "First the blade, then the ear, then the full corn in the ear" (Mark 4: 28). The theories have been tutors, leading unto the truth. They are experiments needed for the discovery and confirmation of the plan of Christ. The followers of Christ were placed as children under the liberty and unity of love, not under a minute and inflexible law, as were the children of Israel. Grand determinative principles were given to guide them, not minute ordinances like those which Moses gave, and which became a yoke of bondage. In applying these principles mistakes arose which required centuries for their full development, as we have seen, and which may require centuries for their elimination. This is the training of God's providence in his school of grace. We may say of the theories of church government, what has been said of the Christian clergy: " They came to be what they were by the inevitable force of circumstances, that is to say, by the gradual evolution of that great scheme of God's government of the world which, though present eternally to his sight, is but slowly unfolded before ours."[39] As in nature and in science and in theology, so in ecclesiology, there has been development through manifold tentative efforts. "The type remains, but it embodies itself in changing shapes: and herein the history of the Christian churches has been in harmony with all else that we know of God's government of the world." "The history of the organization of Christianity has been in reality the history of successive readjustments of form to altered circumstances. Its power of readjustment has been at once a mark of its divinity and a secret of its strength."[40] In these tentative adjustments, arising from misconceptions of revealed principles, but suited graciously to the environment, the Church has at no time lost its power to bless and save. Its mission though perverted has not been abandoned. We may ascribe much good to theories of the Church, while holding them to be abnormal and wrong. "We are quite willing to concede," with Prof. George P. Fisher, D.D., of Yale Theological Seminary, "that the Papacy itself, the centralized system of rule, which has been the fountain of incalculable evils, was providentially made productive of important advantages during the period when ignorance and brute force prevailed, and when anarchy and violence constituted the main peril to which civilization was exposed."[41] Any theory, whether true or false, whether respecting the Church or the State, when once embraced by large bodies of men, must work itself into its legitimate results; if it prove itself worthy, it will be continued; but if it prove itself unworthy, it will be rejected. Thus the Church, like the world, is in a state of free training under the providence, the Word, and the grace of God.

And what shall be the outcome? We answer in the

[39] Org. Early Christ. Churches, Hatch, 163.   [41] Discussions in Hist. and Theol. 162.
[40] Ibid. 212, 213.

words of one competent to speak, an adherent of the Anglican Church: "It would seem as though, in that vast secular revolution which is accomplishing itself, all organizations, whether ecclesiastical or civil, must be, as the early churches were, more or less democratical: and the most significant fact of modern Christian history is that, within the last hundred years, many millions of our own race and our own Church, without departing from the ancient faith, have slipped from beneath the inelastic framework of the ancient organization, and formed a group of new societies on the basis of a closer Christian brotherhood and an almost absolute democracy."[42] We are working back to the original model: "In the first ages of its history, while on the one hand it was a great and living faith, so on the other hand it was a vast and organized brotherhood. And being a brotherhood, it was a democracy."[43] The bright promise of the future lies in the words: "And all ye are brethren" (Matt. 23: 8).

[42] Hatch's Org. Early Christ. Churches, 215. [43] Ibid. 213.

LECTURE V.

THE DOCTRINE OF THE CHRISTIAN CHURCH.—MATERIALS.
— CONSTITUTIVE PRINCIPLE.

" *But ye are an elect race, a royal priesthood, a holy nation, a people for God's own possession.*" — Saint Peter.

" *With freedom did Christ set us free: stand fast therefore, and be not entangled again in a yoke of bondage.*" — Saint Paul.

§ 85. HAVING covered the field of possible polities in our brief survey of the Christian Church, we need here to note the chief landmarks. God has established his Church to reveal his wisdom and grace unto the world. That Church has had three forms or models, the Patriarchal, the Ceremonial, and the Christian; or, the family church, the national church, and the ecumenical church. Of the latter, four grand conceptions have been developed into four simple, exclusive, ecumenical systems. Each one of these four conceptions or theories we have reduced to its constitutive principle, with its development, in some instances mixed with foreign elements. Each of these systems is contending for the mastery of Christendom. We have shown also that as God has not framed the universe on discordant plans, but on one comprehensive plan, revealing his wisdom, as science even now discloses, so Christ has not built his Church on discordant principles, but on one comprehensive plan, revealing the unity of the kingdom of heaven. Any other supposition impeaches his wisdom and the inspiration of his apostles. Hence the question is forced with irresistible logic upon every believer and every communion of believers: What is the true theory or conception of the Christian Church?

We are prepared to give an answer to this question with charity toward all and with malice toward none, since we have shown how closely the great polities run together in their dominant principles and how each polity is worthy of the profoundest study. We trust that our answer will not be deemed presumptuous; for, if wrong, we shall not part company with the multitude who have spoken as confidently as we, only to be in the end mistaken. We shall exhibit fully what we hold to be the doctrine of the Christian Church under appropriate heads with proofs.

THE DOCTRINE OF THE CHRISTIAN CHURCH.

§ 86. Let us explain terms that we may be understood. We mean by "Christian Church" the manward side of the kingdom of heaven, which Christ set up in the world on the day of Pentecost, in its whole manifestation. The term "Church of God" is more comprehensive, since it includes the three dispensations, which neither the term kingdom (§ 35) nor the term Christian Church includes. We mean by "doctrine" the principles, facts, and development which go to make up the manifested kingdom among men. These principles and facts stand in logical connection by which the development is shaped. We call it "the doctrine" because it seems to us to be the principles and facts given in the New Testament and confirmed by the institutions of the apostolic churches working out into a normal system. The system is the only one, as we view it, which those principles and facts warrant. Hence it must be the doctrine for all who accept the Bible as the only and sufficient rule of religious faith and practice, if our interpretation be correct.

§ 87. But here arises a great difficulty in respect to what shall be regarded as the standard of faith and practice. It is difficult to argue when the parties can not agree upon any common criterion or test by which to determine the value of proof. And this is our trouble here. Christian communions do not agree as to standards and their differences are radical. "All communities of Christendom, with the exception of the Socinians, agree that the divine revelation of truth is contained simply and purely in the Holy Scriptures. But they differ from each other in this: The Protestant confessions alone regard the written volume of revelation as complete in itself; while all others either (1) place in juxtaposition with Scripture certain coördinate sources of Christian knowledge and instruction, the Greeks a so-called tradition, and the Romanists tradition and its living, teaching authority, that is, the Pope, or (2) holding the proper source of the knowledge of the divine things to be a direct illumination of every individual by the Holy Ghost, subordinate the Scriptures to this personal enlightment as merely its testimony (or *regula secundaria*) and witness. These are represented by the Quakers."[1] From this, and from the consensus and dissensus of the creeds,[2] we may classify the standards of belief as follows:—

(1) The Socinians and Rationalists elevate Reason above Scripture, Tradition, Inner Light, and the Church.

(2) The Quakers elevate the Inner Light above Reason, the Scriptures, Tradition, and the Church.

(3) The Anglican Church (generally) elevates the Scriptures above Reason, the Inner Light, and Tradition, but raises the Church to an equality with the Scriptures.

(4) The Greek Church elevates the Scriptures above the Inner Light and Reason, but makes them coördinate with Tradition and the General Councils of the Church.

(5) The Roman Catholic Church elevates the Scriptures above Reason and the Inner Light, but raises to an equality with them Tradition and the Pope.

(6) The Presbyterians, Congregationalists, Baptists, Methodists, Lutherans, and others elevate the Scriptures above Reason, Inner Light, Tradition, Pope, and the Church. With them, as with all true Protestants, the Scriptures are the only and sufficient standard of faith, morals, and polity: for the Scriptures alone are inspired and infallible.

[1] Winer's Confessions of Christendom, I, 1, 37.
[2] Schaff's Creeds of Christendom, 1, 919, seq.

With such confusion respecting the standards by which all arguments are to be tested, the truth of God both in theology and in polity has had hard work to find acceptance. What is conclusive with one has no weight with another. Even where the Scriptures are held to be coördinate with tradition or the living oracle in the Church, they are practically subordinate, as being interpreted by the other standard or standards. Although thus embarrassed by the number of standards of belief, the truth of God must ultimately prevail, until this article of the present consensus: "The Divine Inspiration and Authority of the Canonical Scriptures in matters of faith and morals," and, we add, polity, excludes all other standards.

I. — THE MATERIALS OF THE CHRISTIAN CHURCH.

§ 88. We mean by materials those of whom the Christian Church is properly composed — they who form it. And here, in order to completeness and the understanding of the case, we will consider the materials of the family church, the Hebrew congregation, the Jewish synagogue, the kingdom of heaven or Christian Church, and the local churches or particular congregations of believers.

§ 89. In the patriarchal, or family, form of the Church, the children and servants were members as well as the parents or heads of the family. There was no separation between the pious and the wicked, except in rare instances, as the expulsion of Cain, the casting out of Ishmael, the flight of Jacob, and similar cases (§ 14). The whole household constituted the material of this visible form — parents, children, and servants. Even the seal of the Abrahamic covenant was applied to all males alike (§ 11: 4).

§ 90. "The congregation, or assembly, of Israel" is the translation of *kahal*, which is often used in the Old Testament. "It describes the Hebrew people in its collective capacity under its peculiar aspect as a holy community, held together by religious rather than political bonds. Sometimes it is used in a broad sense as inclusive of foreign settlers (Ex. 12: 19); but more properly, as exclusively appropriate to the Hebrew element of the population (Num. 15: 15). ... Every circumcised Hebrew ... was a member of the congregation, and took part in its proceedings, probably from the time that he bore arms. ... Strangers settled in the land, if circumcised, were with certain exceptions (Deut 23: 1-8) admitted to the privileges, and are spoken of as members of the congregation in its more extended application."[3]

Thus the circumcised became members of the congregation, assembly, or holy community. The sign and seal of the covenant of promise, when applied to Hebrew or heathen and to their children (Gen. 17: 10-14), made them members of the national Church. Circumcision was made a distinguishing test of admission. This external rite was the symbol, however, of an internal relation, which all who were communicants did not possess. Hence the command to circumcise the heart (Deut. 10: 16; 30: 6), and the words of Paul: "For he is not a Jew, which is one outwardly; neither is that circumcision, which is outward in the flesh: but he is a Jew, which is one inwardly; and circumcision is that of the heart" (Rom. 2: 28, 29). The materials of the spiritual realm were not then identical with those of the national Church; the boundaries of the two were not identical and conterminous.

§ 91. The synagogue grew up without express warrant from the law or from a prophet to meet a want (§ 41: 1). The assembly, or congregation, of Israel was divided up in synagogues into many congregations, as many as were needed for neighborhood worship. To become a member of a synagogue, as of the congregation of Israel, a stranger was required to adopt the Jewish faith and ritual and to be circumcised; that is, become a Jew. Such were the materials of the synagogue. But many heathen. after the dispersion

[3] Congregation, Smith's Dict. Bible, Am. Ed.

of Israel, were brought by it into contact with the monotheistic faith and worship, and became "half-proselytes, called, 'proselytes of the gate,' who embraced the monotheism and Messianic hopes of the Jews without submitting to circumcision and conforming to the Jewish ritual. They are called in the New Testament religious, devout, God-fearing persons. They were the first converts [to Christianity], and formed generally the nucleus of Paul's congregations."[4] Such persons were in the process of becoming full proselytes, when Christ was preached to them. And "a full proselyte, called 'proselyte of righteousness,' was one that was circumcised and in full communion with the synagogue."[4]

The materials of the congregation of Israel in its comprehensive sense, as also when divided into many synagogue congregations, were still further defined by the exercise of excommunication. Certain persons were to be cut off from the congregation of Israel (Ex. 12: 19; Num. 19: 20). Christ referred to excommunication from the synagogue (Luke 6: 22; John 9: 22, 23, 34, 35). The third and last step in this process was entire exclusion, so that a man thus excluded would be as a heathen. This discipline of the synagogue did not rest on the law of Moses, since the synagogue was not a Mosaic institution (§ 41: 1), but is the natural right of every organization that it may protect itself from evil men.

§ 92. The kingdom of heaven is composed only of holy persons. No one can doubt this. Christ taught even "the teacher of Israel," Nicodemus, that "except a man be born anew, he cannot see the kingdom of God," and that he must "be born of water and the spirit," or "he cannot enter into the kingdom of God" (John 3: 3, 5). Heart righteousness, and not ceremonial righteousness merely, must be had, or one can "in no wise enter into the kingdom of heaven" (Matt. 5: 20). The unrighteous shall not inherit the

[4] Schaff's Bible Dict., Art. Proselyte.

kingdom of heaven (1 Cor. 6: 9; Gal. 5: 19-21; Eph. 5: 5). The materials of the kingdom of heaven are therefore regenerate, holy persons, sinners renewed in the spirit of their minds (Eph. 4: 23), new creatures in Christ Jesus (2 Cor. 5: 17; Gal. 6: 15).

§ 93. The Church of Christ is the manifested kingdom on earth. Hence Christ is King of the kingdom and "Head of the Church." The Church is subject to Christ as a wife to her husband. "Christ also loved the church, and gave himself up for it; that he might sanctify it, having cleansed it by the washing of water with the word, that he might present the church to himself a glorious church, not having spot or wrinkle or any such thing; but that it should be holy and without blemish" (Eph. 5: 23-27). The Church is Christ's body (Col. 1: 18, 24). This Church can be none other than the invisible, spiritual body or realm which is identical in membership or materials with the kingdom of heaven, above described; and yet not quite identical in conception or idea with the kingdom. The terms "the kingdom" and "the Church" express two somewhat different views of the same realm. The Christward view is called the kingdom; the manward view is called the Church. That is, the redeemed viewed in their relation to Christ their king is the kingdom; but the redeemed viewed in their relation to men is the Church. The kingdom is the Christward side of the Church and the Church is the manward side of the kingdom. Hence "the gospel of the kingdom" appropriately represents Christianity, and so it is used (Matt. 4: 23; 9: 35; 24: 14); but "the gospel of the Church" would not properly represent it, and so it is never used.

This being the case, the materials of both are the same. Those who constitute the kingdom constitute also the Church of Christ. And the conditions of citizenship in the kingdom become the conditions of membership in the Church. What admits to the one admits to the other; and what excludes from the one excludes from the other: for the one is the other, viewed only in a different relation.

This church-kingdom, by the laws of its continuance and growth, manifests itself in the world, and chiefly in and through local churches (§ 42). Hence we must consider their proper membership.

§ 94. The local, particular church should be composed of believers, or holy persons. They should be composed of the same materials as the church-kingdom. This is of the utmost importance, and hence we must prove it.

(1) It is reasonable that the thing which manifests should be of the same material as the thing manifested. The kingdom, as we have seen (§ 42), or the Church, is chiefly manifested among men in and through local churches, which stud Christendom as the stars bestud the sky. But if the churches be composed of others than the members of the kingdom, how can they manifest forth the Church of Christ or the kingdom of heaven? Synagogues of Satan (Rev. 2: 9; 3: 9) can not represent the Church of Christ. And to the degree in which the churches are mixed bodies, partly of the world and partly of the kingdom, they must fail to witness for the spiritual and holy Church. How can a tree bearing bad fruit be a manifestation of a tree bearing good fruit? How can death exhibit life? or darkness light? or error truth? One body can not be a fit manifestation of another body, whether in whole or in part, unless it be of the nature, character, spirit, materials of the body represented. This is too plain for question. Hence it is a thing reasonable and to be expected that local churches should be composed of the same materials or members as the church-kingdom, with the same essential conditions of admission.

(2) This reasonable presumption is confirmed by the teachings of the New Testament, which we need to examine carefully.

(*a*) The local churches are addressed as holy bodies. Paul calls them, "beloved of God, called to be saints" (Rom. 1: 7); "sanctified in Christ Jesus" (1 Cor. 1: 2); "the faithful in Christ Jesus" (Eph. 1: 1); "saints and faithful brethren in Christ" (Col. 1: 2); "God's elect, holy and beloved" (Col. 3: 12). Peter calls them "living stones," to be "built up a spiritual house, to be a holy priesthood, to offer up spiritual sacrifices, acceptable to God through Jesus Christ" (1 Pet. 2: 5); "an elect race, a royal priesthood, a holy nation, a people for God's own possession" (1 Pet. 2: 9). These and similar expressions can properly apply only to churches whose members are citizens of Christ's kingdom.

(b) The conditions of membership indicate that the local churches are viewed as spiritual bodies. We have seen that admission into the church-kingdom requires a new birth, repentance, faith, righteousness. These are made conditions of admission into the visible churches. On the day of Pentecost, when the Christian Church was recognized and inaugurated, repentance was required, and acceptance of the Gospel (Acts 2: 38, 42), by such as "were being saved" (Acts 2: 47). Belief in Christ the only name (Acts 4: 12) made all "of one heart and soul" (Acts 4: 32). But this belief involved a change of heart, as is seen by contrasting Simon Magus (Acts 8: 13, 20-23) with Saul of Tarsus (Acts 9: 1, 5, 15) and the jailer of Philippi (Acts 16: 30, 31). The preaching of the apostles testified, "both to Jews and to Greeks repentance toward God, and faith toward our Lord Jesus Christ" (Acts 20: 21). Without faith it is impossible to be well-pleasing unto God (Heb. 11: 6). These tests, which were ever applied, sought to exclude from the churches all who were not already in the church-kingdom.

(c) The initiatory rite required for admission into the visible churches is symbolic of a changed life. After the day of Pentecost, whoever joined the churches was baptized as the sign of spiritual cleansing. It had been enjoined by Christ himself on his disciples (Matt. 28: 19). Hence, when the new dispensation was inaugurated, and thereafter, all believers were baptized (Acts 2: 41; 8: 12, 38; 9: 18; 10: 48, etc.). Baptism did not renew the heart, or make one a Christian; it was the external symbol of the internal cleansing through the blood of Christ, on repentance and faith. "For in one Spirit were we all baptized into one body" (1 Cor. 12: 13); being "buried therefore with him through baptism into death: that like as Christ was raised from the dead; . . . so we also might walk in newness of life" (Rom. 6: 4; Col. 2: 12). "For as many of you as were baptized into Christ did put on Christ" (Gal. 3: 27). Hence baptism is called by Paul "the washing of regeneration," and is joined with "renewing of the Holy Ghost" (Tit. 3: 5), as the completed work of admission. Ananias said to Saul: "Arise, and be baptized, and wash away thy sins, calling on his [Christ's] name" (Acts 22: 16). But baptism into the name of the Trinity availed nothing without faith (Acts 8: 13, 21; 1 John 2: 19). To avail any thing, baptism must be the sign of a new creation (Gal. 6: 15).

(d) These conditions imply a creed, some rule of faith; and there are hints of such creed other than those given in the preceding conditions of membership. The central article of this creed was, and is, that Jesus is the Christ, the Lamb of God, that taketh away the sin of the world. Hence "the churches were strengthened in the faith" (Acts 16: 5). Paul was heard "concerning the faith in Christ Jesus" (Acts 24: 24). The baptismal formula was, and is, a creed in itself, the norm of the Apostles' Creed and of all others. But there were added to it "the pattern of sound words" (2 Tim. 1: 13), which were received as axioms of the faith from the apostle.

(e) To all these, as the conclusive proof of the identity in materials of the local churches with the church-kingdom, was added the power of church discipline. Judas Iscariot had gone "to his own place" (Acts 1: 25) before the Christian Church was inaugurated. But the sharpness of this discipline was shown when Ananias and Sapphira lied to God the Holy Ghost (Acts 5: 1–11). This was a miraculous interposition; but the ordinary procedure is given by the Head of the Church (Matt. 18: 15–18). Fellowship was not to

MATERIAL OF LOCAL CHURCHES. 107

be held with fornicators, covetous persons, idolaters, revilers, drunkards, extortioners, and the like, no, not to eat (1 Cor. 5: 11). The Church was commanded to put away an incestuous man (1 Cor. 5: 13). Departures from the word are to be treated in the same way (2 Thess. 3: 14, 15), and greetings are to be withheld from errorists (2 John 10, 11). All such go out from the churches because they are not of the church-kingdom (1 John 2: 19).

(*f*) There was a wide difference, then, between a church and its congregation. The local church was a body of believers, of redeemed saints; but the congregation was a mixed body of believers and unbelievers (1 Cor. 14: 23). Men were not made church members, except on conditions which involved a renewed life, and which separated them from the rest of mankind. A church was unlike any other organization that appeared among men: for it was a spiritual body, composed of saints, into which no unrenewed persons could properly be admitted. Hence each church was composed, on Scriptural grounds, of the same sort of persons or materials as the church-kingdom.

(3) This position is confirmed by the attitude of the apostolic churches. "The Teaching of the Twelve Apostles," recently discovered, carries us back near to the year of our Lord 100, and gives as the law of the churches this rule: "And let no one eat nor drink of your Eucharist, but those who have been baptized into the name of the Lord."[5] Clement Romanus (A.D. 30–100), in writing to the church in Corinth, addressed it as "called and sanctified by the will of God, through our Lord Jesus Christ." And the church of Smyrna, which first used the term "holy and catholic," speaks "of all the congregations of the holy and catholic church in every place."[6] Justin Martyr (A.D. 110–165) says: "As many as are persuaded and believe that what we teach and say is true, and undertake to live accordingly, are instructed to pray and to entreat God with fasting, for the remission of their sins that are past. . . . Then they are

[5] Chap. ix. [6] Ep. on Martyrdom of Polycarp.

brought by us where there is water, and they are regenerated in the same manner in which we were ourselves regenerated,"[7] that is, baptized. The early churches also cast out heretics and immoral men.[8]

Hence Hatch says: "In the earliest period, the basis of Christian fellowship was a changed life — 'repentance toward God and faith toward our Lord Jesus Christ.' . . . In the second period, the idea of a definite belief as a basis of union dominated over that of a holy life. . . . In the third period, insistence on Catholic faith had led to the insistence on Catholic order."[9] The churches started on the theory of a holy membership, tested by a changed life.

§ 95. The inability fully to attain that absolute purity in local churches which exists in the church-kingdom does not invalidate this argument drawn from reason, from the New Testament, and from the primitive churches, that only regenerate persons, those born anew, are proper members of local churches because only such are members of the church-kingdom. Only those who have the life of Christ in the heart are the materials of Christian churches. All others are foreigners. Those only who are of faith belong to the household of faith (1 John 2: 19). None others can rationally, Scripturally, and historically be admitted, though the standard be often unattainable.

Nor does infant circumcision and infant baptism invalidate this argument in either of the three dispensations. The one was commanded in the patriarchal and ceremonial dispensations as the seal of the covenant; the other is implied in the Christian dispensation by the continuance of the covenant (Gal. 3: 17, 29), by baptism being substituted for circumcision (Col. 2: 11, 12), by the words of Christ respecting children: "Of such is the kingdom of heaven" (Matt. 19: 14), and by the words of Paul (1 Cor. 7: 14). This, however, will be more fully discussed hereafter. (§§ 149–153.)

§ 96. This discussion regarding the materials of the

[7] Apol. i, ch. lxi.   [8] Canons of Church of Alexandria.
[9] Org. Early Christ. Chhs. 182–184.

Church reveals a gradual development which we do well to note. There was in the family form the slightest possible separation between the saint and the sinner. Under the national form there was a clear separation between the children of Israel and all other peoples, which hardened into a contempt for all Gentiles. But within the national fellowship, the contrast between the faithful Israelite and the unfaithful became more clearly marked than under the preceding dispensation. Certain men were to be cut off from the congregation as incorrigible. The prophets too denounced sins and wicked Israelites in unmeasured terms, in the name of the Lord. And about the time the prophets ceased, the synagogue arose and spread every-where with its social worship conducted by laymen. This worship cultivated the piety of the true Israelite, but hardened the worship of the undevout Jew into the hollow formalism of the Pharisees, which Christ with his woes could not break. There was a still further separation, which went on, until the winnowing-fan of Christ completely separated the wheat from the chaff. Then arose the kingdom of heaven with its organic manifestations, the local churches, whose members are renewed sinners, the same as the members of the church-kingdom. Thus the life of God in the hearts of men has unfolded in more distinctive and characteristic forms, until it appears at last in visible bodies expressive of its holy nature. These bodies are called churches, formed, when normally formed, of the same materials as the church-kingdom.

Here arises the greatest question in church polity, because it dominates all others: —

II. — THE RELATION OF ONE LOCAL CHURCH TO OTHER LOCAL CHURCHES.

§ 97. It is manifest that if local churches are composed of the same materials as the church-kingdom, they must be spiritually one, as the church-kingdom is one. They are all branches of the same Vine, households of the same realm, members of the same body. They possess, how much soever they may fail to exhibit it, unity in the following respects: (1) unity of headship, "one Lord"; (2) unity of belief, "one faith"; (3) unity of sacraments, "one baptism"; (4) unity of confidence, "one hope of their calling"; (5) "unity of the Spirit in the bond of peace"; (6) unity of comprehension, "one body"; (7) unity of government, "one God"; (8) unity of creed, "unity of the faith, and of the knowledge of the Son of God"; (9) unity of brotherhood, "one God and Father of all, who is over all, and through all, and in all" (Eph. 4: 4–6, 13).

This spiritual unity can not be broken, whatever the relation of one church to another. It is indivisible, because the church-kingdom is indivisible (§ 32: 2). Those that leave it, if any ever do, apostatize, and become forever separated from Christ the Head and from his body. Hence every local church is spiritually one with every other similar church. There never has been, is not now, and never can be, a division between them spiritually. Springing from the church-kingdom, they all are one.

§ 98. But in consequence of this spiritual unity they are in their relation one to another independent. Each one sustains exactly the same relation as the rest to the underlying church-kingdom, out of which they equally spring, and of which they are equally the manifestations in organic form. No matter who planted them, or how they came into being, or what their creed or ritual or government; if churches of Christ at all, and not synagogues of Satan, they are equal and independent. For they become churches neither by historical connection, nor by form of government, nor by mode of worship, nor by doctrinal statement; but by possessing the life hid with Christ in God, by being integral parts of the church-kingdom, by having as members converted and, therefore, holy men. God alone gives the increase. His Spirit renews. Hence a church, being composed of renewed men, is born not merely by the will of man but by the grace of God. There is a human element, which is superficial; the divine element is fundamental, and makes the renewed congregation a church.

Hence each church standing in the same relation to Jesus and his church-kingdom as the rest must stand in essential equality with all the rest, subject to no one of them. No one has the right or authority to lord it over another. A large church, or a mother church, or a metropolitan church, possesses no peculiar or superior rights and powers. The natural relation of church to church, in such a church-kingdom, is that of independence as respects control, and brotherhood as respects fellowship and labor. One is equal to another, and independent of another, but subject to Christ the Head.

§ 99. The Christian rule of discipline rests upon this independence of each church. This rule was given by the Master, taken, it may be, from the synagogue, but made by his command the law of Christian churches. We shall use only so much of the rule at present as bears on the relation of church to church. Christ said respecting the one under discipline: "And if he refuse to hear the church also, let him be unto thee as the Gentile and the publican" (Matt. 18: 17).

(1) The church here meant is the local church, or congregation of believers, to which the offender belongs.

(*a*) It is true no local church then existed; and it is equally true that the process of gathering an *ecclesia*, or congregation of believers in Jesus, out of the *kahal*, or congregation of Israel, had not yet been completed, and was not completed until the day of Pentecost, when the followers of Jesus were divinely recognized as the true Church or congregation, to join which thereafter all had to be baptized (§ 39). While the winnowing-fan was in the hand of the Thresher, and the wheat had not been separated from the chaff, it is not probable that Christ regarded those then professing to be his disciples as the *ecclesia* to which he committed the matter of discipline. All Christ's teachings looked forward to the establishment of his kingdom, unless this rule is an exception. That it is not is evident from what he said of his church in Matt. 16: 18.

(*b*) It has also been said that "church" here means the Jewish synagogue. But Christ was a lawgiver like unto Moses, legislating for a new dispensation as Moses did, and the case must be desperate indeed that would confine his law of discipline to a dispensation which he came to fulfill and supersede in about a year.

(*c*) If Jesus added this rule of discipline to the Mosaic law, then that law has not been abolished as Paul taught (Eph. 2: 15; Col. 2: 14).

(*d*) His rule of discipline was given for his churches, and for them alone. Each local church deals with its own delinquents. The words, "tell it unto the church," can not refer to the Church universal; for it never meets. They do not refer to a national or provincial church organization, for each synagogue completed its own discipline; and, besides, if Christ enlarged the synagogue rule which he adopts, the steps by which appeals might be taken ought to have been given. The word can not refer to ecclesiastical rulers, but it refers to the particular local church. If such a church choose a church board for discipline, subject to itself, the church acts through that board. The power lies in the church that appoints, not in the elders or stewards or council. Christ did not make elders or other officers the church, but instead the congregation of believers.

The apostles so understood the word church. Paul required the church to excommunicate a man (1 Cor. 5: 4, 5, 13), which it did by majority vote (2 Cor. 2: 6). This was in A.D. 57 or 58. John, A.D. 96 or 100, did not cast out, but depended upon the church to act when he should be present (3 John 9, 10). The church at Corinth deposed faithful elders,[10] which involved the power of discipline; and the

---
[10] Clement Romanus, Ep. Cor. xliv.

church right is not questioned, but the church is urged to "live on terms of peace with the presbyters set over it."[11] "In earlier days each separate case came for judgment before the whole church."[12] It seems impossible to escape the conclusion that Christ in his law of discipline had reference to the local church, however small that church might be.

(2) The discipline of the local church is final. There is no intervening tribunal or court between the first and last step, and no appeal from the vote of expulsion. There is no passage in the New Testament which impairs this conclusion by intimating some farther process. The Master made the action of the local church in the discipline of its members final.

(3) This finality is confirmed by what Christ says of "binding" and "loosing." His words are: "Verily I say unto you, What things soever ye shall bind on earth shall be bound in heaven: and what things soever ye shall loose on earth shall be loosed in heaven" (Matt. 18: 18). He applied the same words to Peter (Matt. 16: 19), and stronger words to the apostles (John 20: 23). The words "to bind" and "to loose" were common among the rabbis; and "to bind" meant to forbid or prohibit, and "to loose" to permit or allow. Some would confine the authority conferred in them to the apostles, while others would carry it over to the churches also. So also there is question whether legislative or judicial authority is meant, or both together. But whichever interpretation be the correct one the finality of the action of the local church in discipline is equally assured. If Christ ratifies therein the acts of local churches in discipline, then no appeal can be taken from such action to ecclesiastical tribunals. When the king promises to ratify the decisions of a specified tribunal, all other appeals are excluded. If our Lord addressed these words to the apostles alone, then their connection shows that the authority con-

[11] Clement Romanus, Ep. Cor. liv.
[12] Hatch's Org. Early Christ. Chhs. 100.

ferred, whether legislative or judicial, or both, could not be used by them to set aside this law of discipline which he had just given. This rule would stand in full force to guide them, as it did in fact guide them. Peter acknowledged the power of a local church to call him to account for his conduct in the case of the Roman Cornelius (Acts 11: 1-18); and Paul laid the duty of excommunication upon the local church (1 Cor. 5: 4, 5, 13). Whatever view we take, therefore, of binding and loosing, the independence and completeness of the local church in matters of discipline must stand; for we can not believe that after giving a rule of discipline Christ immediately gave his apostles authority to annul it, or to add to it. Whether spoken to the local church, as the connection implies, or to the apostles alone, the promise of ratification makes the discipline of the local church final.

Thus the Christian rule of discipline is founded upon the independence of each local church, as respects other local churches, whose action is final and supreme.

§ 100. The election of church officers is also founded upon the same principle, namely, the independence under Christ of each local church. Of this we shall speak particularly.

(1) When the place of Judas Iscariot was to be filled, the eleven faithful apostles did not presume, in the exercise of their power of the keys, to choose his successor. They referred the election to the company of believers in Jerusalem, the one hundred and twenty, the Christian *ecclesia*, winnowed out of the *kahal*, or congregation, of Israel. They "put forward two"; then "cast lots," which one should be an apostle. "And the lot fell upon Matthias; and he was numbered with the eleven apostles" (Acts 1: 23-26). "It is uncertain whether this putting forward two was the act of the apostles, presenting the two men to the choice of the whole body of disciples, or of the community choosing them for ultimate decision by lot. The Greek word implies that Matthias was 'voted in,' the suffrages of the church unanimously con-

firming the indications of the divine will which had been given by the lot" (Plumptre). "All those assembled 'put forward two'" (Meyer). In the most important election ever held in the Christian Church, then one local body, the whole assembly participated. The use of the lot carried the final choice between the two up to God. The apostles only superintended the election, giving the needed qualifications, and praying before the casting of the lots (Acts 1: 21, 22, 24, 25). This was an election to the apostolate recognized as valid after the baptism of the Holy Ghost in the mention of "the twelve" (Acts 6: 2); and it was not set aside or superseded by the subsequent call of Paul as the apostle to the Gentiles (Acts 9: 15).

(2) The election of seven assistants of the apostles on the occasion of the first dissension in the Church was expressly by "the multitude of the disciples" (Acts 6: 1–6). The multitude chose the men to serve (or deacon) tables, judging of their qualifications, "whom they set before the apostles: and when they had prayed they laid their hands on them." This office gave rise to the order of deacons in Christian churches (Phil. 1: 1). Their ordination by the apostles did not involve the power of confirmation or ratification on the part of the apostles.

(3) When the church-kingdom had extended and appeared in many local churches, the churches held intercommunion by delegates, as the *kahal*, or congregation, of the old dispensation had been dispersed into all nations and appeared in local synagogues with communication between them. A messenger was "chosen of the churches to travel with Paul" with contributions for the poor saints in Judæa (2 Cor. 8: 19). It was by church action, on command by the Spirit, that Paul and Barnabas were sent on their first missionary tour (Acts 13: 1–3). These first missionaries were in fact a deputation from the church in Antioch. It was the same church that "appointed that Paul and Barnabas, and certain other of them, should go up to Jerusalem unto the apostles

and elders" (Acts 15: 2), to consult them about the question of circumcision. These messengers were chosen by the churches, not by the apostles, as bodies independent one of another in matters of control.

(4) There is no account of the election or appointment of elders in the churches. They were the same in the primitive churches as bishops, presbyters, pastors (§ 118: 4). They are first mentioned as receiving contributions from the hand of Barnabas and Saul (Acts 11: 30); then it is said: "And when they had appointed for them elders in every city" (Acts 14: 23). Thus these officers first appear in the churches, "instituted after the manner of the synagogue"; "but certainly the presbyters (Acts 11: 30), as elsewhere (Acts 14: 23), so also in Jerusalem (Acts 15: 22; 21: 18), were chosen by the church, and apostolically installed" (Meyer). "The word for 'appointed' certainly seems to imply popular election (election by show of hands), which is, indeed, the natural meaning of the word" (Plumptre). "They were appointed by *taking the vote of the people*, the apostles merely presiding over the choice" (Schaff, Bannerman, Alford, Lange, Stanley). Later, the custom by which "church officers were freely chosen by the several communities from their adult members," was changed.[13] Others, however, hold that elders were at first appointed by the apostles (Hackett).

We see, then, that local churches, in the exercise of their right arising from their relation to the church-kingdom, elected their own officers and messengers. The action of each was complete in itself without reference to any other church. Or if any superintendency or confirmation were required in ordination, it was found only in the functions of the apostles, which, as we shall show, ceased at their death.

§ 101. If we turn from internal discipline and the election of church officers to the relation of one church to another, we find marks of their individual independence. The primitive

[13] Hatch's Org. Early Christ. Chhs. 202.

INDEPENDENCE OF LOCAL CHURCHES. 117

churches had constant intercourse one with another. Commendatory letters were given (Acts 18: 27; 2 Cor. 3: 1, 2); messengers were sent from one to another (Acts 15: 2); the distress of churches in one country was relieved by the gifts of foreign churches (Acts 11: 29, 30; 1 Cor. 16: 1–3; Rom. 15: 26); and epistles sent to one church were requested to be forwarded to another (Col. 4: 16). "The seven churches, addressed in the seven epistles (Rev. 2; 3), are presented as distinct from each other. No sign of common government is visible; no other bonds of union amongst the churches can be recognized than the interchange of common spiritual sympathies and subjection to a common divine law." [14]

There is no intimation in the New Testament that one church was subordinate to another; but on the contrary each church managed its own discipline, elected its own officers, and conducted all its intercourse with other churches as an independent body, not subject to the supervision or control of any other church.

§ 102. And this is what we should expect both from the relation of the churches to the church-kingdom and from their model, the Jewish synagogue. Nearly every town and city where the apostles preached had one or more synagogues. The separation of Christians from these synagogues was gradual. In these synagogues were "rulers" of the synagogue. "They formed the local Sanhedrin, or tribunal. But their election depended on the choice of the congregation." [15] "The supreme official, like the two other members of the local court" in each synagogue was elected. "His election entirely depended upon the suffrages of the members of the synagogue." The three almoners "had to be elected by the unanimous voice of the people." [16] Synagogues had power to inflict corporal punishment, and to excommunicate, as we have seen. They were also independent one of an-

---
[14] Ecclesia; Church Problems, etc. 12.
[15] Life and Times of Jesus, by Dr. A. Edersheim, i, 438.
[16] Bib. Theol. and Eccl. Cycl., Art. Synagogue.

other in the management of their affairs. "Each synagogue formed an independent republic, but kept up a regular correspondence with other synagogues."[17] "At Alexandria, where the state gave the Jewish colony exceptional privileges, the separate synagogues seem to have been all subject to the ethnarch; but at Rome and elsewhere there are no signs of their having been linked together by any stronger tie than the fellowship of a common creed and a common isolation from the Gentiles."[18] In so far then as the churches were modeled after the synagogue, they were independent one of another.

§ 103. If we turn to the meager record of the churches given by the Apostolic Fathers, we find nothing to contradict the independence of the local churches one of another, but every thing to confirm it. "The church of God which sojourns at Rome," near the close of the first century addressed a letter to "the church of God sojourning at Corinth," as one equal addresses another equal. In it the church in Corinth is reproved for deposing "some men of excellent behaviour from the ministry."[19] There is no intimation of redress by appeal to any man, church, or synod; nor is there any assumption of authority on the part of the church at Rome to correct the wrong. So also when the church at Philippi deposed the presbyter Valens from the ministry, Polycarp, in his letter to the church, approves the act, but grieves for the need of such discipline.[20] Clement Romanus refers also to majority action of a church, and to presbyters appointed by the apostles "with the consent of the whole Church."[21]

Thus the independence of the local churches one of another, which is logically deducible as the only normal relation of church to church, is confirmed by the uniform teachings of the New Testament, the development of the churches from the Jewish synagogues, and the intimations

[17] Hist. Christ. Ch., Schaff, 1, 458.
[18] Hatch's Org. Early Christ. Chhs. 59.
[19] Clement Romanus, Ep. Cor. 1, 44.
[20] Ep. Phil. xi.
[21] Ep. 1, 44, 54.

of the Apostolic Fathers. Each church, as thus independent, completes the discipline of its members, elects its own officers and messengers, and manages its external relations. Among themselves all were equal and independent, as the towns in a commonwealth. But this independence may be conceded, and yet it may at the same time be held that each and all, while managing their own affairs as regards one another, are still subject to some centralized authority. We have therefore a further question to consider before we leave the independence of the local churches.

III.—WERE THE PRIMITIVE CHURCHES SUBORDINATE TO ANY CENTRALIZED ECCLESIASTICAL AUTHORITY?

This is by no means the same question as that which we have been considering. One church may be independent of another, or of all others taken singly, and yet be subject to them taken collectively, or to an order in the ministry, or to a primate, in which case either Presbyterianism, or Episcopacy, or the Papacy follows.

§ 104. Each church is in spiritual union with all the rest in virtue of its being a part of the church-kingdom; and as such is subject to the will of the Lord Jesus Christ, however that will may be made known (§ 32: 1). Each church in consequence of this spiritual oneness is required to exhibit in all suitable ways its unity with all others. No duty is greater than this; and for it Christ especially prayed (John 17: 20–23). Hence Christendom has endured manifold tyrannies rather than break the visible unity of believers.

§ 105. While the *kahal*, or congregation, of Israel before and even in the dispersion was divided up into synagogues independent one of another, there was still a central authority in the ceremonial law with its priesthood, rites, ritual, and ordinances, to which all Jews and full proselytes owed a recognized allegiance. And when the *kahal* became the *ecclesia* (Matt. 16 : 18; Eph. 5: 23–27), and the synagogues became churches, was there not also a transference of the national authority over into an ecumenical power, commissioned to rule all Christian congregations? If not, some reason must be rendered for dropping it. Can we discover any reason which shall find its vindication in the facts of revelation and of history? That reason is found, we think, in the nature of the ceremonial law which Christ fulfilled and abolished, and in the nature of the kingdom of Christ.

(1) The ceremonial law was largely typical of Christ; its priesthood, its sacrifices, its whole economy. Hence it could not but pass away when fulfilled. Its one ordained place of worship, the temple, was superseded in the Christian dispensation (John 4 : 20–24), and the temple predicted to be destroyed (Matt. 24 : 2). The whole Mosaic ritual contained in ordinances was abolished (Eph. 2 : 15 ; Col. 2 : 14, 20), for there was a change in the priesthood (Heb. 7 : 11, 12). A new high priest (Heb. 2 : 17, 18 ; 3 : 1 ; 4 : 14) offered one sacrifice for eternal salvation (Heb. 7 : 27 ; 9 : 12, 25, 26) and became thereby the mediator of a better covenant (Heb. 8 : 6 ; 9 : 11, 12). That whole ceremonial order of things was superseded and abolished in Christ, as the writer to the Hebrews abundantly demonstrates; and with it went its centralized authority as an organized national theocracy.

(2) So Christ separated his kingdom from the State. Church and State were one and the same under Moses; but under Christ they are separate. Christ was emphatic on this point, when Pontius Pilate examined him (John 18: 36). He refused to meddle in civil and political matters (Luke 12: 14; John 6: 15), and distinguished between the two realms (Matt. 22: 21) as did his apostles (Acts 4: 19, 20 ; 5: 29; Rom. 13: 1–7; 1 Peter 2: 13, 14).

(3) The church-kingdom, thus stripped both of temporal authority and of the ceremonial law with its priesthood and

sacrifices and ordinances and ritual, appears a better and higher development than the *kahal*, or congregation, of Israel fettered with both. One is liberty; the other is bondage (Gal. 5: 1). The destruction of these two elements of authority left the *kahal*, or congregation, of Israel with only the moral and religious institutions of the synagogue — water baptism, and what of the sacred Scriptures was not fulfilled in Christ; and as such it became the Christian *ecclesia*, or congregation of believers in Jesus Christ, — a church-kingdom spiritual, not of this world, whose sole central authority is in its Head and King, and whose local churches are independent one of another, and of all centralized power, except that which is found in Christ Jesus. This is, therefore, the normal relation of individual churches to any part of the whole, or to the whole body.

§ 106. Hence the churches of Christ have not been made subject to an infallible primate. There is no trace of such an order of things in the New Testament. We hunt in vain for Scriptural or historical proof that Peter possessed and exercised a primacy of authority. Whatever primacy he had was of another sort. This is so clearly the case, that Paul, not one of the original apostles, but an apostle to the Gentiles, publicly resisted and rebuked Peter, because he was to be blamed (Gal. 2: 11–14). Paul recorded the event, A.D. 56–58.

Many passages quoted or referred to by the Papists in the Tridentine (1545–1563) and Vatican (1870) decrees are so general that they have equal force under all theories of the Christian Church. These we have already given (§ 54). But there are two passages which need special notice. When Andrew brought his brother Simon to the Messiah, Jesus, looking upon him for the first time, said: "Thou art Simon the son of John: thou shalt be called Cephas (which is by interpretation, Peter)" (John 1: 42). Thus, at the outset, Christ, by the change of name, pointed out in the most emphatic way the place Simon Peter should hold in the coming dispensation. This was made more emphatic in the last year of his ministry, when in response to a reply of Peter, Jesus said: "Thou art Peter, and upon this rock I will build my church; and the gates of Hades shall not prevail against it. I will give unto thee the keys of the kingdom of heaven: and whatsoever thou shalt bind on earth shall be bound in heaven: and whatsoever thou shalt loose on earth shall be loosed in heaven" (Matt. 16: 18, 19). This is the text of the Papacy. Whatever may be meant by the keys, to bind and loose, in this passage, was afterwards conferred in the same words upon each local church, however small (Matt. 18: 18); and after his resurrection, in still stronger language, was conferred upon the whole body of the apostles. What was thus distributed could not be claimed by one alone. Peter never claimed this power as peculiar to himself. It is therefore no proof of his primacy in power.

What is meant then by the words: "upon this rock I will build my church"? We answer: (1) One interpretation gives to the words an historical primacy. Peter was the first to preach the gospel to the Jews (Acts 2: 14), and to the Gentiles (Acts 10: 44–48), thus becoming the foundation of the Church. This is the view of Tertullian, who wrote A.D. 192–220.[22] (2) Cyprian, A.D. 246-258, uses the passage to prove "that the Church is founded upon the bishops."[23] (3) Others make the rock Christ himself, since "other foundation can no man lay than that which is laid, which is Jesus Christ" (1 Cor. 3: 11). This was written to a church building on men, on Cephas, as one of them, and has special weight therefore. This view is held by very eminent names in the Church. (4) The confession of Peter has been regarded by some as the rock; that is, faithfulness of confession. (5) But a certain precedence must be ascribed to Peter, which may be called in a modified sense a primacy. Peter held a peculiar personal position among the apostles and in the building of the church. He was the spokesman

[22] On Modesty, xxi. [23] Ep. xxvi, 1.

of the apostles. God chose him first to preach the gospel, after the inauguration of the church-kingdom, to Jews and Gentiles. He laid "the foundations of the church deep and strong on the Rock of rocks"; but even here he was not as active (1 Cor. 15: 10), nor as consistent (Gal. 2: 11–14), nor wrote as many epistles as Paul. "Nor was Peter himself ever bishop of Rome, nor had he any more to do with the founding the church at Rome than the apostle Paul" (Meyer). His primacy was not that of authority; for he was brought before the church at Jerusalem and the other apostles for preaching to Cornelius (Acts 11: 2–18); while in the council at Jerusalem, A.D. 50, he did not hold as high a position in the settlement of the question had in controversy as James (Acts 15: 19); and Paul publicly rebuked him for his conduct (Gal. 2: 11) and then published the account. He does not begin his epistles with the words: "Peter, an apostle of Jesus Christ, bishop of bishops;" but simply: "Peter, an apostle of Jesus Christ," and "Simon Peter, a servant and apostle." He even calls himself, when speaking to the elders of the churches, "a fellow-elder" (1 Peter 5: 1).

Whatever primacy may be ascribed to Peter, in this sole text of the Papacy, it is impossible to find in it the warrant for the infallible primacy. It did not give special authority to Peter. It did not make him bishop of bishops. It did not provide for successors. It did not keep him from error. Whatever power it conferred upon him was afterwards given to local churches and to the other apostles. There is not the least hint of proof that the primitive churches were either united in Peter or subordinate to Peter as primate.

§ 107. The churches of Christ have not been made subject to an episcopate. Their relations to the whole fraternity did not culminate in a hierarchy of bishops; for each local church had more than one bishop. There was no union or convocation of such bishops, with authority, until the fourth century; that is, not until after the Church was united with the State.

It is true that the churches were, in some respects, under the apostles as the inspired teachers of Christ, to give them both doctrine and order. Their words were the commands of Christ (1 Cor. 14: 37). But the apostolate is not the episcopate. We shall see (§ 116) that not one of the characteristics or signs which distinguished an apostle was transmitted to successors. After the election of Matthias no vacancy in the apostolate was filled, and the office with its functions ceased when John at last fell asleep on the bosom of his Beloved.

But the term apostle was not used exclusively of the Twelve, and of Matthias and Paul. The word means "one sent forth," and is applied to Barnabas (Acts 14: 4, 14). Hence we are not surprised to read of "apostles" in "The Teaching of the Twelve Apostles;" but there "apostles and prophets are described as mere evangelists, or itinerant preachers, who were not expected to remain in one place more than a single day."[24] The "Teaching" was written about A.D. 100.

The so-called Council at Jerusalem, A.D. 50, did not represent the churches generally by presbyters, bishops, or delegates except in and through the apostles. And whatever of authority its decree possessed was derived from the apostles and the claimed inspiration of the Holy Ghost (Acts 15: 28). This council was held for an emergency. The earliest synods were held in Asia Minor, but not until the middle of the second century.[25] The earliest general council was held A.D. 325. Previous to this Nicene Council there could have been no general Episcopal rule of the churches, taken collectively. Even Dean Stanley says: "Before the conversion of the Empire, bishops and presbyters alike were chosen by the whole mass of the people in the parish or diocese (the words at that time were almost interchangeable)."[26] Episcopacy is, then, a late growth. The primitive churches were not

---

[24] Chap. xi, note on Hitchcock and Brown's ed.
[25] Hefele's Hist. Councils, i. 2.   [26] Christian Institutions, 175.

therefore subject to a convocation of diocesan bishops in synod or general council. Had there been such a bond of union, we should find traces of it in the seven epistles to the seven neighboring churches in the province of Asia, or in some other place.

§ 108. The primitive churches were not united in, and subject to, a presbytery or general assembly or ecumenical alliance. Each church had its own presbyters, or bishops, called a presbytery (1 Tim. 4: 14) (§ 131: 2). But these presbyteries were not joined together, with the power of rule, into either provincial presbyteries or synods. Not until the middle of the second century did synods appear, and not until A.D. 325 was there a general assembly. Before these periods there was found no way of concentrating the power of the keys, so that a larger part could govern a smaller, and the whole govern, through authoritative representation, the several parts. Indeed, presbyteries or synods did not come into being by the exercise of authority; but, instead, through the exercise of fellowship, and their power came from the union of Church and State. " Some prominent and influential bishop invited a few neighboring communities to confer with his own." " Not even the resolutions of the conference were binding on a dissentient minority of its members." " But no sooner had Christianity been recognized by the State than such conferences tended to multiply, to become not occasional but ordinary, and to pass resolutions which were regarded as binding upon the churches within the district from which representatives had come, and the acceptance of which was regarded as a condition of intercommunion with the churches of other provinces. There were strong reasons of imperial policy for fostering this tendency."[27] The authority of centralized government, even in its mildest form, was not known to the primitive churches until after Christianity had been made the state religion. The germs of such authority are not Christian, but secular or Mosaic, or both.

[27] Hatch's Org. Early Christ. Chhs. 166-168.

The fellowship of the churches is not the mother of hierarchies or aristocracies.

§ 109. Hence the independence of the primitive churches must be admitted. They were not only free from subjection one to another, but free also from all control by external presbyteries, councils, bishops, or primates. One church was not subject to another church; nor was any church subject to any authority or control, except that of its Lord and Head, Jesus Christ. This absolute independence under Christ is now generally conceded by church historians. We reproduce the evidence of a few authorities, none of whom were Congregationalists, given elsewhere: [28]

"Every town congregation of ancient Christianity was a church. The constitution of that church was a Congregational constitution. In St. Paul's Epistles, in the writings of Clement Romanus, of Ignatius, and of Polycarp, the congregation is the highest organ of the Spirit as well as the power of the church." [29] "Still, each church was an absolutely independent community." [30] "Every church was essentially independent of every other." [31] "The apostles founded Christian churches, all based on the same principles, all sharing common privileges . . . but all quite independent of each other." "Nor does Paul even ever hint at any subjection of one church to another, singly, or to any number of others collectively." [32] "Neither in the New Testament, nor in any ancient document whatever, do we find any thing recorded from which it might be inferred that any of the minor churches were at all dependent on, or looked for direction to, those of greater magnitude or consequence; on the contrary, several things occur therein which put it out of all doubt that every one of them enjoyed the same rights, and was considered as being on a footing of the most perfect equality with the rest." [33] "The primitive churches were independent

---

[28] Pocket Manual, § 34.   [29] Bunsen's Hyppolytus and his Age, iii, 220.
[30] Milman's Latin Christ. i, 21.   [31] Waddington's Eccl. Hist. 43.
[32] Whately's Kingdom of Heaven, Essay II, §§ 20, 136, 137.
[33] Mosheim's Hist. Christ. i, 196.

bodies, competent to appoint their own officers, and to administer their own government, without reference or subordination to any central authority or foreign power. No fact connected with the history of the primitive churches is more fully established or more generally conceded."[34] "The constitution of the primitive churches was thoroughly democratic."[35] "The theory upon which the public worship of the primitive churches proceeded was that each community was complete in itself." "Every such community seems to have had a complete organization, and there is no trace of the dependence of any one community upon any other." "At the beginning of the fourth century . . . the primitive type still survived; the government of the churches was in the main a democracy; at the end of the century the primitive type had almost disappeared; the clergy were a separate and governing class." "In the first ages of its history, while on the one hand it was a great and living faith, so on the other hand it was a vast and organized brotherhood. And, being a brotherhood, it was a democracy." "Its unaccomplished mission is to reconstruct society on the basis of brotherhood."[36] We can but add: And, being a brotherhood, it will be a democracy. Surely what is so universally conceded may be asserted without dogmatizing, and may be accepted as the controlling factor in a Scriptural church polity.

The most recent and thorough inquiries into the organization of the apostolic churches exhibit the "influences from club, municipality, and synagogue," in giving form to the Christian *ecclesia;* but they serve to make even more emphatic the constitutive principle under discussion. Prof. Hugh M. Scott, of the Chicago Theological Seminary, in giving the results of such inquiries, says: "Every-where the congregation is independent, autonomous, and self-deciding." "Whether we accept the details of this discussion or not, two things shine forth with greater clearness than ever before:

[34] Coleman's Prim. Christ. 95.   [35] Ency. Brit. 699.
[36] Hatch's Org. Early Christ. Chhs. 141, 213, 216.

an apostolic system, in which every local church was free, self-governed, autonomous, and resting upon a holy brotherhood of believers; and a ministry that was called only of God, charismatic, prophetic, and in very few respects resembling its ordinary modern clerical successor." [37]

§ 110. It is clear, then, that in passing from the *kahal* of the ceremonial dispensation to the *ecclesia* of the Christian dispensation, both the political or civil power and the centralized, ecclesiastical authority were left behind, as something belonging to the inferior and transient. They do not attach to the Church in its last and perfect form on earth. Both the temporal power and the government of churches by any external human rule are foreign to the gospel. Hence "the plan of the apostles seems to have been to establish a great number of distinct, independent communities" (Whately). "No fact connected with the history of the primitive churches is more fully established or more generally conceded" (Coleman).

(1) If this principle of the independence of the local churches be conceded as an historical fact, then Congregationalism follows. This must be so (§§ 47, 48), since Congregationalism is only the development of this principle into the methods of church fellowship. Let the visible manifestation of the church-kingdom in local churches be once controlled by this principle, and all government by authority, all centralized systems of ecclesiastical power, vanish at once; but the union of all Christendom in associations of churches without authority remains to fulfill the prayer of Christ and to bless the world with liberty and unity. This one principle conceded, every thing else follows.

(2) The only escape is in ecclesiastical rationalism, or in an inner light, or in tradition, or in decrees of an infallible church; that is, one or more of the other than Scriptural standards (§ 87) must be the ground of confidence. The competency of the New Testament and of the apostles must

[37] 44 Bib. Sacra, 213, 488.

be denied. This is done by the Roman Catholic Church, the Greek Church, the controlling part of the Anglican Church, the Quakers, the Socinians, and the Rationalists (§ 87). While others declare that "Christ has not definitely specified the form of church polity;" as though a polity not drawn out in detail could not have been determined by revealing its constitutive principle. We have shown that a single principle dominates each of the four great polities that divide Christendom, and that, therefore, no "definitely specified form of church polity" is needed in order to develop a complete system. The oak is in the acorn; and a polity is in its constitutive principle. When, therefore, Christ in his church-kingdom stripped off the political and hierarchal elements of the preceding dispensation, and left the local churches in their normal relation to the church-kingdom, of which they are the chief manifestations, which relation is that of absolute independence one of another and of any collection of churches, he determined definitely what the true development must be in all essential elements. This is in harmony with his revelation of doctrine and ritual for his better dispensation. No one would call a man wise who should reject all doctrine or should embrace any doctrine because Christ has not definitely specified the form of theology to be held by his churches. In the old dispensation details were given until it became a yoke of bondage. The new and better is for heirs, and so gives principles and facts, both in doctrine and in polity, which determine what for substance our theology and our polity must be. We could not therefore have reasonably expected more than we find.

(3) The Presbyterians are especially firm in their belief in the supremacy of the Scriptures, and until recently they have claimed a *jure divino* proof of their polity. We have seen (§§ 68: 6; 71: 4) that they are surrendering their claim, and introducing foreign elements. If Scripture fail them, as it certainly does, and if the independence of the local churches be conceded as the original form of the apostolic churches, even down to the fourth century, and all this is

conceded, then their principle of authoritative representation will have to be surrendered for that of independence. This could easily be effected by carrying the principle of the Presbyterian alliance (§ 68: 6) down to the general assemblies, the synods, and the presbyteries. They could resolve their judicatories into assemblies of fellowship, counsel, and expression of opinion. Their votes then would become what the votes of the conferences of churches were in the early days, down to the union of Church and State in the fourth century, without authority to bind the minority of dissentients. They could retain their beautiful system of fellowship, and unify it from the top to the bottom on the principle of fraternity without authority.

(4) On the principle, too, of development, which we have more than once referred to, the Congregational Theory will possess the field. It comes latest as the consummate flower of all. True, it is not strictly developed out of any theory or theories; for it was "the plan of the apostles to establish a great number of distinct, independent churches;" but the principle then announced and embodied was buried up for more than a millennium by adverse theories. Those theories did not lie in the Congregational Theory as steps in its development, but they came in through an adverse environment to bury the true form. That original form, like a buried seed, when the environment had changed, burst forth into life amidst persecution and death, with the promise of the future in it. The other theories are undergoing testing by the Word and by the providence of God. They fail to express the brotherhood of the saints in its fullness of liberty. Hence they must cease. This expresses brotherhood, and hence makes all in the local church equal, makes all local churches equal, and issues in popular government and liberty. It is able to exhibit the unity of the church-kingdom on principles of fellowship and coöperation, and so to fulfill the prayer of the Master that all may be one, that the world may believe on him. Thus the glorious end is reached on "the plan of the apostles."

LECTURE VI.

THE DOCTRINE OF THE CHRISTIAN CHURCH. — THE
CHRISTIAN MINISTRY.

*"And he gave some to be apostles; and some, prophets; and some,
evangelists; and some, pastors and teachers; for the perfecting of the
saints, unto the work of ministering, unto the building up of the body
of Christ."* — Saint Paul.

§ 111. THE ministry of the Word logically and historically comes before the gathering of churches, whose materials and relation one to another have been considered. As the true religion is not a natural product, but a revelation from God, there must be heralds of it divinely fitted, chosen, and commissioned; and they, in the order of nature, must precede the acceptance of that religion. To make the ministry the creature of the churches, or an office relation in the churches, is therefore to reverse the order; it places the agent as the product of his own work, the effect before the cause. This is the fatal defect of the Pastoral Theory of the ministry. That theory makes the ordinary ministry to depend on there being a church already existing to call and ordain a man as pastor, and also on his remaining a pastor. If he remit his office as pastor he becomes a layman again. Thus the ordinary ministry is made one of office, not of function and service. Where there are no churches, in heathen lands or anywhere else, there can be no ministry; hence on this theory missionaries are laymen until churches are gathered to make them ministers. This partial theory reverses the order of things, both logically and historically; and hence the churches generally have held the ministry to be a function of the church-kingdom for the enlargement of itself, endowed, called, commissioned, and sent by the Head and King. He takes the initiative in calling men to preach his everlasting gospel, not merely at the outset, in a special ministry, but also all the time, in the ordinary ministry of the Word. In every case the function of the ministry is before the pastoral office. Hence the churches, when gathered, are simply to call and ordain whom the Lord has commissioned as his ministers.

Before we consider, therefore, the internal constitution of the independent local churches, we will consider the ministry of the Word.

§ 112. The Christian ministry is not a priesthood. There was a parental priesthood in the patriarchal dispensation, and the Aaronic priesthood in the ceremonial dispensation, and both priesthoods offered bloody sacrifices. So the Christian dispensation has its priesthood, but it is not the ministry of the Word.

(1) A priest is strictly one who offers sacrifices, both expiatory and eucharistic. This is the use of the word in the Scriptures. Presbyter is sometimes shortened into priest, but this is a perversion. A priest must have somewhat to offer on an altar in worship; in doing which he stands as mediator between God and the worshiper. In the sanctuary and the temple, laymen were forbidden to enter even the place where the sacrifices were offered. He who served as priest in the line of Aaron had to be physically perfect, and was consecrated or ordained to the office, being himself separated from the laity.

(2) Jesus Christ was a priest, and a high priest, of a new order. He is called a "high priest," a "great high priest," called of God to be a priest forever, "after the order of Melchizedek," "another priest," which involves a change of the law (Heb. 3: 1; 5: 1; 7: 11, 12). He offered sacrifice, "one sacrifice for sins for ever," having been "manifested to put away sin by the sacrifice of himself" (Heb. 10: 11, 12; 9: 26). Then he entered the Holy of holies in the heavens (Heb. 6: 20); he "through his own blood, entered in once for all into the holy place, having obtained eternal redemp-

tion" (Heb. 9: 12), and "sat down on the right hand of the throne of the Majesty in the heavens, a minister of the sanctuary, and of the true tabernacle," "the mediator of a better covenant" (Heb. 8: 1, 2, 6). He is the Christian's high priest.

(3) Christ gathered the whole priesthood into himself, and so removed it from his church-kingdom on earth. This is argued at length in the Epistle to the Hebrews. "He, because he abideth for ever, hath his priesthood unchangeable" (Heb. 7: 24); "who needeth not daily, like those high priests, to offer up sacrifices . . . for this he did once for all, when he offered up himself" (7: 27); "but now once at the end of the ages hath he been manifested to put away sin by the sacrifice of himself" (9: 26). "We have been sanctified through the offering of the body of Jesus Christ once for all" (10: 10). "Now where remission of these is, there is no more offering for sin" (10: 18).

There are, then, no more sacrifices to be offered for sins forever; and, if no more sacrifices, there is no further need of an earthly priesthood and altar. Christ has gathered into his own priesthood the whole priestly office, and then by the one sacrifice of himself, "once for all" and "for ever," has purchased eternal redemption for all that believe in him, and has thus abolished altar, sacrifices, and priesthood.

(4) The church-kingdom on earth has therefore no priesthood or sacrifices or altar. It is an impeachment of Christ's one atoning sacrifice on the cross, to substitute a priesthood with its altar and sacrifices for the Christian ministry. Yet the Council of Trent (1545-1563) decreed that in the mass the "same Christ is contained and immolated in an unbloody manner who once offered himself in a bloody manner on the altar of the cross;" and that "this sacrifice is truly propitiatory."[1] "If any one saith that the sacrifice of the mass is only a sacrifice of praise and of thanksgiving; or, that it is a bare commemoration of the sacrifice consummated on the

[1] On the Mass, chap. ii.

cross, but not a propitiatory sacrifice . . . let him be anathema."[2] If there be a sacrifice, there must be also a priesthood to offer. Hence the same council decreed that there is in the Christian Church "a new, visible, and external priesthood," for "consecrating, offering, and administering" this sacrifice, with an anathema for all who deny it.[3] With this new and external priesthood to offer the sacrifice of the mass, the table becomes a veritable altar.

The Orthodox Greek Church also holds that the Eucharist is an expiatory sacrifice, and the ministry a priesthood.[4] The Old Catholics reject the idea of a sacrifice in the Eucharist,[5] and hence of a true priesthood. The Anglican and Episcopal churches reject the idea of a sacrifice in the Lord's Supper,[6] though the ritualists in those churches retain it. The Lutherans, in the mother confession of Protestantism, retain the name of mass, but deplete it of its sacrificial character.[7] Other Protestants reject both the name of mass and the idea of sacrifice in the communion, hence also the priesthood and the altar.

No fair interpretation of the New Testament supports the theory of a Christian priesthood, which was introduced from the preceding dispensation. Indeed, the only passage that looks in a priestly direction by the use of the word "altar" (Heb. 13: 10) refers, as the context shows, to Christ Jesus, who "suffered without the gate," as the sacrifices were "burned without the camp."

§ 113. The ministry of the Word is a function of the church-kingdom. "With the exception of the Quakers and Anabaptists, all Christian communities have been agreed in this. But a divergence of sentiment has obtained as to the relation of the ministerial order to the general body of Christians. The Protestants ascribe to that order a distinction from other believers, grounded only on the function of their

---

[2] Canons on the Mass, iii.　　[3] On Sacrament of Order, 1; Canons on Order, 1.
[4] 11 Ency. Brit. 158.　　[5] Creed, Art. xiv.
[6] Creed, art. xxxi.　　[7] Augsburg Conf., part ii, art. xxiv, 3.

THE MINISTRY A FUNCTION. 135

office; but the Romish Church vindicates for its priesthood an indelible character, imparted in ordination, which forever separates them from the laity. It sharply opposes the clergy as the governing, to the laity as the governed, class."[8]

(1) This ministerial function is not exclusive. It does not shut out the general body of believers from active participation in church worship. No line of separation is drawn between the ministry and the laity, as between the priesthood and the people. As in the synagogues every adult male Jew could take part in the services,[9] so in the primitive churches laymen could take part in the worship (1 Cor. 14: 31). The function of teaching or preaching, by the Acts, the Epistles, and the Apostolical Constitutions, was open to laymen.[10] In this respect all are priests, to offer spiritual sacrifices (1 Peter 2: 5). The ministry is a function of the church-kingdom common to all its members, yet specifically manifested in the superior fitness of some.

(2) This ministerial function is prepared and called into service by the Lord Christ. He calls men into his churches by his Spirit; and he calls men into the ministry by gifts, graces, opportunities, and the influences of the Holy Spirit. "No man taketh the honour unto himself, but when he is called of God" (Heb. 5: 4); "who also made us sufficient as ministers of a new covenant" (2 Cor. 3: 6); "separated unto the gospel of God" (Rom. 1: 1); and "approved of God to be entrusted with the gospel" (1 Thess. 2: 4). Hence it can be said: "And he gave some to be apostles; and some, prophets; and some, evangelists; and some, pastors and teachers" (Eph. 4: 11). This divine calling and appointment is every-where recognized; as when Paul addressed the Ephesian elders: "Take heed . . . to all the flock, in the which the Holy Ghost hath made you bishops" (Acts 20: 28). "Take heed to the ministry which thou hast received

---
[8] Winer's Confessions of Christendom, chap. xx, 244.
[9] Schaff's Hist. Christ. Ch. 1 459.
[10] Hatch's Org. Early Christ. Chhs. 114, 115, 123.

of the Lord, that thou fulfil it" (Col. 4: 17). The ministry is thus called of God.

(3) The distinction between the ministry and the laity in the churches is due to the suitable recognition of this divine call. Those who possess the function of teaching or preaching will manifest it to the satisfaction of the churches, or they will be moved by an inward impulse to seek the work and to prepare for it, and such, if they possess the other needed qualifications, are set apart to their work with prayer and the laying on of hands by the churches. But they are not elevated above the laity by any priestly character, nor separated from them by any indelible quality; but they are set apart, in the interest of good order, to a special function for which God has endowed and called them. The churches seek in ordination to recognize the divine call, and by suitable examination to guard against imposition.

(4) The ministry of the Word precedes the churches, and is, therefore, in some sense independent of the churches. The function belongs to the church-kingdom, not to the local churches as such. When Christ had winnowed out the nucleus of his *ecclesia* from the *kahal* of Israel, he chose twelve whom he named apostles (Luke 6: 13), whom he trained for the founding of churches. He afterwards sent out seventy to preach and prepare the way for himself (Luke 10: 1). These, after the setting up of the church-kingdom, went about preaching the Word (Acts 8: 4), preparing the material for churches of Christ. And so it has ever been, the ministry of the Word has preceded the gathering of churches, but has not preceded the church-kingdom, of which it is a function. The minister must go before the local church, the missionary before the congregation of believers. The churches are planted through the instrumentality of this ministerial function.

It follows, then, that the ministry is independent of the churches in some respects. The churches may not stop one called of God to preach the gospel. Their refusal to ordain, though ordinarily sufficient to silence a man, may for cause be disregarded, and should be disregarded, if he has in fact been called by the Master to preach the Word. The whole question of ordination (§ 121) and of ministerial standing (§§ 122-124) respects good order, not the function of the ministry. One's right to preach does not depend on the call of a local church, or on ordination, or on regular standing, but on the commission of Christ, the Head and King. How much less then is the ministry an official relation in a local church, as was once held by the New England churches.[11] This narrow view has been supplanted by the better and normal view of the ministry.[12] The churches do not create the ministry; they only recognize it. He whom the Master calls is the true minister; but he whom the churches call may be still a layman. The power of the keys is for recognizing the true ministry, and regulating their standing for the good of the churches; but the power to create and silence is not theirs, although generally good order requires acquiescence in their action.

(5) The ministry of the Word is not prelatical. A prelate is a clergyman of a superior order, having authority over the lower clergy. It is true that the apostles were empowered to plant and order the churches, to appoint, it may be, and instruct the ministry; but they by reason of death soon ceased. Their function was special and temporary. In the permanent ministry there is no superior and inferior, higher and lower, in rank or order, but equality in function. Christ rebuked the spirit of hierarchy that appeared among his apostles, and said: "Whosoever would be first among you shall be servant of all" (Mark 10: 44). "And be not ye called Rabbi: for one is your teacher, and all ye are brethren. And call no man your father on the earth," etc. (Matt 23: 8-12).

(6) The ministry of the Word appears both as a special

[11] Cambridge Platform, chap. ix, 7.
[12] Boston Platform, part iv, 1, 1.

function and as a permanent function, as occasion demands. In the planting and ordering of the churches at the first, in inaugurating a new dispensation, extraordinary qualifications would be required, with special names, as apostles and prophets; but for the permanent work of the ministry ordinary qualifications would suffice. Hence the ministry is divided, by reason of this difference in qualification and function, into the temporary and the permanent.

I. — THE TEMPORARY MINISTRY OF THE WORD.

§ 114. At the head of the temporary ministry of the Word stand the chosen apostles of our Lord. Their number is fourteen: the original twelve, Matthias, and Paul. Their name signifies "one sent forth, a messenger"; and consequently it is applied to others, as, "one that is sent" (John 13: 16), messengers (Luke 11: 49; Phil. 2: 25), false apostles (Rev. 2: 2), Barnabas (Acts 14: 14), and Christ (Heb. 3: 1). The word is used twice of Simon Peter; fifteen times of Paul, and fifty-five times of the apostolate. Out of the seventy-eight times used, it is a distinctive title seventy-two times of the chosen messengers whom we call apostles.

§ 115. There were certain special qualifications which characterized the apostles and separated them from all others in the Christian ministry, which need to be clearly detailed: —

(1) They were personally selected by Christ himself. The original Twelve were so selected. "He called his disciples: and he chose from them twelve, whom also he named apostles" (Luke 6: 13). In the selection of Matthias, he designated by the lot whom he would put into the vacancy (Acts 1: 23-25). He personally appeared to Saul of Tarsus when he chose him to be the apostle to the Gentiles (Acts 9: 1-9). Thus each apostle was personally selected in the most marked manner, with the exception of Matthias, of whom we hear nothing thereafter, save one indirect reference (Acts 6: 2).

(2) The apostles were personally taught by Christ for their ministry. The Twelve were so taught. Matthias was selected from those who had been so taught from the baptism of John (Acts 1: 21, 22). Paul even was not an exception. He had seen the Lord (1 Cor. 9: 1). He defended his claim to be an apostle on this very ground: "For neither did I receive it [the gospel] from man, nor was I taught it, but it came to me through revelation of Jesus Christ" (Gal. 1: 12). "By revelation was made known unto me the mystery, as I wrote afore in few words, whereby, when ye read, ye can perceive my understanding in the mystery of Christ" (Eph. 3: 3, 4). Thus all the apostles were personally taught the gospel by Jesus Christ, a qualification insisted on by Peter as essential, and by the opponents of Paul.

(3) They were inspired by the Spirit for their mission. They did not plant churches as missionaries now do. They were the founders of the first churches, and gave them in germ their doctrine and order, creed and polity, and that, too, for all churches in all time. They needed a guidance by inspiration which none others need. They had been promised such inspiration (John 14: 26; 16: 13). They were forbidden to begin their work until they had been "clothed with power from on high" (Luke 24: 49), and thus fitted for the proper exercise of the power of the keys, to bind and loose (Matt. 16: 19) and to forgive and retain sins (John 20: 23); that is, to found and order the churches. Hence they waited until the outpouring of the Spirit on Pentecost, before they made converts, or sought to make them. They thereafter claimed inspiration in what they said and did in respect to doctrine and order. Hence in the decree of the council at Jerusalem (A.D. 50) they claimed guidance and inspiration (Acts 15: 28). This inspiration seems to have been conceded to all the apostles except Paul, who had to defend his apostleship. He was not singular, when he said: "Which things also we speak, not in words which man's wisdom teacheth, but which the Spirit teacheth"

(1 Cor. 2: 13); for he thus put his teaching on an equality with that of the other apostles. He asserted that what he wrote was "the commandment of the Lord" (1 Cor. 14: 37). Inspiration was essential to the apostolate.

(4) The apostles had some special miraculous power. Others also had miraculous gifts; but Paul appealed to the working of special miracles in proof of his apostolate, saying, "Truly the signs of an apostle were wrought among you in all patience, by signs and wonders and mighty works" (2 Cor. 12: 12). He here appeals to tests which were recognized as characteristic of the apostles.

(5) The apostles were clothed with special authority, as was necessary for the founders of churches, who should give them creed and duty and polity. This is involved in their inspiration for their work. Yet they exercised the authority of discipline through the local churches (1 Cor. 5: 3–6, 13; 2 Cor. 2: 6).

(6) The apostles were equal in rank or order. There was great inequality in natural endowments and in labors, but in rank or functions there was none. They were brethren. When an ambition for place appeared, the Master checked it, saying, "Not so shall it be among you" (Matt. 20: 26). The primacy of Peter was not in rank or order (§ 106). Paul met Peter and James on terms of equality (Gal. 1: 18, 19). They "who were of repute imparted nothing" to him (Gal. 2: 6). There is nothing to indicate that there was any inequality in power, rank, or authority among the apostles. They were equal.

§ 116. The apostolic office was temporary. It ceased when John fell asleep. We prove this from several considerations.

(1) Its special nature proves its temporary nature. The churches could not be founded in doctrine, duty, and polity more than once. There has been no addition to the permanent law of the churches, the New Testament, since John's death. As the foundations could not be laid more than

once, the apostolate ceased when its function was fulfilled, dying when the apostles died.

(2) The qualifications of the apostolate did not continue. Christ might have continued to choose and instruct and qualify apostles, as he did Paul, until the end of time: and they could have vindicated their claim to be apostles, as Paul did his, by inspiration and miracles. But none since the days of John, when challenged, can produce the signs of an apostle. The term "apostle" was longer retained, "but there are many indications that traveling evangelists were thus termed for some time after the apostolic age."[13] These "itinerant preachers" could claim no authority as apostles, as they were not expected to remain in one place more than one day. If they remained "three days" they are declared to be "false." This description proves that the signs of the original apostles were wholly wanting in them.

(3) The apostles had consequently no successors. No vacancies were filled after the election of Matthias; that is, after the inauguration of the church-kingdom at Pentecost. James was beheaded A.D. 44. It has been said that "after the death of James the elder and James the younger, Paul and Barnabas were chosen in their stead, that the collegiate number might be preserved."[14] But Paul was called (Acts 9: 15) eight years or more before the death of James the elder (12: 2); while neither the death of James the younger nor the death of Barnabas is known. For aught we know, the former may have outlived the latter. But there is no evidence that Barnabas was ever an apostle in the strict meaning of the word. No vacancies after Pentecost were filled. If the office had been deemed permanent and not temporary, it is certain the vacancies would have been filled, and that the successor of James would probably have been recorded. Dean Alford says that "in the New Testament no trace of the fiction" of "successive delegation from

---

[13] Teaching of the Twelve Apostles, xi, note, Professor Hall.
[14] Alzog's Universal Hist. i, 167.

the apostles" can be found.[15] "The fiction of a direct apostolical succession, verified by historic records, with no gap at any point, is now abandoned by most Anglican authorities, though long maintained as the only ground on which the prelatic polity can stand. More moderate advocates hold that such a demonstrated transmission is not essential; that the episcopal office justifies itself rather on general grounds as an ancient and Biblical institution; that it has been widely and happily recognized during the progress of Christianity; and that, although the polity based upon it may not be the only one authorized in Scripture, it is still the polity best adapted to secure the interests and advancement of the Church."[16] Thus the constitutive principle of Episcopacy is yielding its Scriptural and divine claim, and coming down into the arena of expediency. Canon Spence says that "when the 'Teaching' was written, perhaps half a century or little more had scarcely passed since the Master had gone in and out of earthly homes, and the writing *seems* to be telling of an order once great and powerful in the community, but of an order already passing away." "The apostle belongs rather to a past state of things." "The apostle of the first generation, as we have seen, had no successors."[17]

(4) The apostles completed the organization of the primitive churches. They laid foundations which needed not to be relaid. "The autonomy of the early Christian communities was complete during the life-time of the apostles, and was quite independent of the apostolic office and authority."[18] Thus the truth slowly wins its way.

§ 117. Next to the apostles stand the prophets in the two lists of the Christian ministry (1 Cor. 12: 28; Eph. 4: 11).

(1) These prophets are to be distinguished from the prophets of the Old Testament. The few apostles could not be every-where; and so Christ called into his ministry prophets to aid the apostles. There can be no doubt as to such a

---

[15] Com. on John, xx, 23.   [16] Ecclesiology, Professor Morris, D.D., 129.
[17] Excursus on The Teaching, etc. 131, 139, 152.   [18] 5 Ency. Brit. 700.

ministry, since it is mentioned in the lists, since directions are given them how to teach (1 Cor. 14: 29–32), and since the churches were founded upon them as upon the apostles and Christ: "being built upon the foundation of the apostles and prophets, Christ Jesus himself being the chief corner stone" (Eph. 2: 20). The prophets here named were not the Old Testament prophets, but New Testament prophets, who assisted in the planting and instruction of the churches.

(2) These prophets had the gift of inspired utterance. This we have elsewhere shown.[19] Inspiration is inseparable from their function. This inspired teaching was common under the law, and it was resumed in the early days of the church-kingdom. It was needed in expounding the Scriptures, in teaching and in preaching, no less than in foretelling future events. Women sometimes had this gift (Acts 21: 9). Paul speaks of "the mystery of Christ" which "hath now been revealed unto his holy apostles and prophets in the Spirit" (Eph. 3: 5).

(3) The ministry of the prophets was temporary. The prophets were not church officers, nor always, if generally, elders. Theirs was a function, not an office, which ceased when miraculous gifts were withdrawn. Such gifts belonged to the childhood of Christianity, to be laid aside at maturity, as Paul argues (1 Cor. 13: 8–11). They are referred to in the "Teaching of the Twelve Apostles" in connection with the apostles, and are "described as mere evangelists, or itinerant preachers," except those who abode with some church; and such were worthy of support. It is a gross perversion of Biblical usage to call elders prophets, and preaching prophesying.

II. — THE PERMANENT MINISTRY OF THE WORD.

§ 118. When we turn from the apostles and the prophets to the permanent ministry, we find that different names are employed in the New Testament to designate it. Those

[19] 27 Bib. Sacra, 343–347.

called to this ministry are named evangelists, presbyters or elders, bishops, teachers, pastors, leaders or chiefs, and possibly angels — all different names for the same ministry in the same or different relations. This will appear as we proceed.

(1) Teachers are mentioned last in the lists of the permanent ministry. We may reduce the three lists to the following table: —

Acts 13 : 1,   A.D. 45,   Prophets, Teachers.
1 Cor. 12 : 28, A.D. 58,   Apostles, Prophets, Teachers.
Eph. 4 : 11,   A.D. 61,   Apostles, Prophets, Evangelists, Pastors, and Teachers.

To the list in 1 Cor. 12 : 28, there is appended an enumeration of the miraculous gifts, which added much to the success of the ministry of the Word, such as "miracles, then gifts of healings, helps, governments, kind of tongues."

The word translated "teachers" is applied to Jewish rabbis and lawyers, to John the Baptist, to Paul, and to Jesus. It is conjoined with pastors in the latest and fullest list as identical with them. In the first and second lists the word designates the uninspired ministry in a church, which the third and fullest list calls "evangelists, pastors, and teachers." They are designated elders or presbyters and bishops in other places. Pastors, bishops, evangelists, and many elders were all teachers, but it does not follow that all teachers were pastors, bishops, evangelists, or elders. Teachers we may regard as belonging to the class of elders, of which some were teaching, and others were ruling, elders (1 Tim. 5 : 17).

(2) Evangelists were probably itinerant elders or missionaries. Philip is called "the evangelist" (Acts 21 : 8), and Timothy is exhorted to "do the work of an evangelist," and so to fulfill his ministry (2 Tim. 4 : 5); showing that the work of this class of laborers was well known. The word means "a messenger of good tidings" — a missionary. Any

elder could do the work of an evangelist at times, and return to the pastorate again. The evangelists did not form a distinct class or order in the ministry. They discharged a function of the ministry which changes with the need of itinerant and missionary labor.

(3) The word translated elders or presbyters signifies an older person, a senior, the aged, and was used as a title of dignity. It is found sixty-six times in the New Testament: of rulers in the Sanhedrin and in the synagogue, of the ministry in the churches, and of the dignities around the throne of God. The name is one of dignity, and is used of ministers in Christian churches (Acts 11: 30; 14: 23; 20: 17), who are often joined with the apostles as the recognized ministry.

(4) The word translated bishop occurs but five times, once of Christ as the Bishop of souls (1 Peter 2: 25), and four times of ministers (Acts 20: 28; Phil. 1: 1; 1 Tim. 3: 2; Tit. 1: 7). It means "an overseer, watcher, guardian, superintendent." In civil matters bishops were "magistrates sent out to tributary cities to organize and govern them." This title "pointed to the office on the side of its duties."[20]

The words "elders" and "bishops" are applied in the New Testament to the same persons. Thus the elders of the church at Ephesus (Acts 20: 17) are called bishops in that church (Acts 20: 28). Five years later, in A.D. 65, Paul calls elders bishops (1 Tim. 3: 2; 5: 1; Tit. 1: 5, 7). Elders were bishops, and bishops were elders, in the apostolic churches. "Even Jerome, Augustine, Urban II (pope, a. 1091), and Petrus Lombardus admit that originally the two had been identical. It was reserved for the Council of Trent (A.D. 1545–1563) to convert this truth into a heresy."[21] 'Their identity the weight of evidence has rendered practically indisputable."[22] "This subject then may be regarded as finally settled among scholars."[23]

(5) The tenderest word by which the permanent ministry

[20] Bishop Ellicott on 1 Tim. 3: 1–7.
[21] Kurtz's Hist. Christ. Ch. 69, 70.
[22] Hatch's Org. Early Christ. Chhs. 38.
[23] Schaff's Hist. Christ. Ch. i, 494, note.

is designated is pastor, shepherd. Jesus is called Shepherd (John 10: 14; Heb. 13: 20), and Peter was commanded to feed the lambs and tend and feed the sheep of the Good Shepherd's flock (John 21: 15–17). Bishops or elders are to act the Oriental shepherd, leading the flock, carrying the lambs in their bosom, giving their lives for the sheep, not lording it over them (1 Peter 5: 3). Pastors are the same as elders and bishops.

(6) Rulers in the churches are referred to in such passages as: "He that ruleth, with diligence" (Rom. 12: 8); "the elders that rule well" (1 Tim. 5: 17); "and are over you in the Lord, and admonish you" (1 Thess. 5: 12). These rulers were the elders or bishops (1 Tim. 3: 4).

(7) Another word for rule is sometimes employed, which means leaders, chiefs; as, "Obey them that have the rule over you" (Heb. 13: 7, 17, 24). The passages designate elders or bishops.

These, we think, are all the titles applied to the permanent ministry of the Word; and of this list, excluding evangelists and teachers, it has been said by the Encyclopædia Britannica: "All these names are used evidently to express the same kind of officers, for they are continually used interchangeably the one for the other." [24]

(8) The angels of the seven churches mentioned in the second and third chapters of Revelation held an unknown position. Robinson regards them as "prophets or pastors"; Stuart, as "the leading teacher or religious instructor"; Vitringa, as "the superintendent and leader of the worship"; Ewald, as "a kind of clerk, secretary, and sexton"; Alford and Cowles, as "angels"; Barnes, as "pastors"; Dollinger, as "the episcopate"; Trench, as "diocesan bishops." The meaning is doubtful. That they were not in any proper sense "diocesan bishops" seems clear from the facts that each of the seven churches had its angel; that the churches were near together, so near that the whole seven would not

[24] Vol. v, 699.

constitute a single diocese, unless "a church and a diocese" were "for a considerable time co-extensive and identical";[25] that the New Testament and early church history know nothing of diocesan bishops, as bishops and elders and pastors were identically the same at that time; and that each church as well as angel is addressed as an independent body, free from subordination to a bishop or other authority except Christ. The change from the singular to the plural number in these letters shows that the church is addressed through its angel, just as each one of the six hundred and ninety bishoprics in North Africa,[26] a little later, might have been addressed through its pastor. Besides, each letter closes with the injunction: "He that hath an ear, let him hear what the Spirit saith unto the churches," not "unto the diocesan bishops."

§ 119. As the apostles had special qualifications for their calling, so it might naturally be expected that the permanent ministry would be distinguished from the membership generally, and from other officers in particular, by certain permanent requisites for their official work. Though every adult male could take part in the public services, as every adult male Jew could officiate in the synagogue, still not every such church member was fit for a bishop or elder or pastor, or even deacon. Hence, to guide in the selection of this ministry certain qualifications are made requisite for the office of a bishop or elder or pastor. As the list of requirements is sometimes forgotten, we will give it under appropriate heads.

(1) Personal character stands first. A minister must be sober, of good behavior, temperate, sober-minded, orderly, not soon angry, no brawler, no striker, gentle, not self-willed, not contentious, no lover of money, but a lover of good men, meek, just, holy. He must flee youthful lusts, and follow righteousness, faith, love, and peace; not lording it over the

[25] Archbishop Whately's King. Christ. Essay, ii, § 20.
[26] The Church, by Prof. H. Harvey, D.D., 103.

charge allotted to him, but making himself an example unto the flock (1 Tim. 3: 2; 2 Tim. 2, 22; Titus 1: 5, 6; 1 Peter 5: 3).

(2) Then comes personal reputation. The ministry of the Word must be without reproach, must have a good testimony from them which are without, and must be blameless (1 Tim. 3: 2, 7; Titus 1: 6).

(3) Nor are the domestic relations overlooked. The minister should be married, the husband of one wife, one that ruleth well his own house, having his children in subjection with all gravity; (but if a man knoweth not how to rule his own house, how shall he take care of the house of God?); given to hospitality (1 Tim. 3: 2-5). Celibacy is not then a qualification for the ministry, not even for an apostle, or the first of the so-called popes (1 Cor. 9: 5).

(4) Natural and spiritual gifts are needed. Ministers must be apt to teach, able to teach others, in meekness correcting them that oppose themselves; capable of discerning foolish and ignorant questionings, and of speaking the things which befit the sound doctrine, able also both to exhort in the sound doctrine; and to convict the gainsayers; to reprove, rebuke, exhort with all long-suffering and teaching; tending the flock of God (1 Tim. 3: 2; 2 Tim. 2: 2, 23, 25; 4: 2; Titus 1: 9; 2: 1; 1 Peter 4: 11; 5: 2).

(5) In this day of lay and boy preachers, we need to recall the preparation and study required for the ministry of the Word. The minister must not be a novice, lest being puffed up he fall into the condemnation of the devil. He must study that he may hold the faithful Word which is according to the teaching, that he may be able both to exhort in the sound doctrine and to convict the gainsayers. Hence he is required not to neglect the gift that is in him, but instead to give heed to reading, to exhortation, to teaching. He must be diligent in these things; to give himself wholly to them. He must take heed both to himself and to his teaching (1 Tim. 3: 6; 4: 14, 15, 16; Titus 1: 9).

(6) He is to be an example to his people; in all things showing himself an example of good works; in his doctrine showing uncorruptness, gravity, sound speech, that can not be condemned. His conduct and words are to be such that no man can despise him, being an example to them that believe, in word, in manner of life, in love, in faith, in purity (Titus 2: 7, 8; 1 Tim. 4: 12).

With these qualifications for the ministry in mind, it may be said of an elder or pastor or bishop, that "no man taketh the honour unto himself, but when he is called of God, even as was Aaron" (Heb. 5: 4). Though this ministry is a function of the church-kingdom, for the building up of the body of Christ (Eph. 4: 12), not all in that kingdom are qualified for it; and not all who may desire to enter it may have been called unto it. The giving in detail of the qualifications implies some right and power of enforcing them upon aspirants for the ministry; and out of this right and power comes ordination.

III. — ORDINATION.

§ 120. The permanent ministry needed some provision for its perpetuity, as its function is permanent. Christ called and qualified the temporary ministry. He in a formal manner selected the Twelve, whom he named apostles (Luke 6: 13). He designated the seventy, whom he sent out two by two (Luke 10: 1). When the church-kingdom was set up, "he gave some to be . . . evangelists; and some, pastors and teachers; for the perfecting of the saints, unto the work of ministering, unto the building up of the body of Christ: till we all attain unto the unity of the faith, and of the knowledge of the Son of God" (Eph. 4: 11-13). As the apostolate and the prophetic function were soon to cease, there was need of establishing by suitable recognition the permanent ministry. Hence the apostles superintended the election of, if indeed they did not appoint, elders in every church (Acts 14: 23). Paul exhorted Timothy to lay hands hastily on no man (1 Tim. 5: 22), but commanded him to commit the gospel "to faithful men" who should be "able to teach others also" (2 Tim. 2: 2). He left Titus in Crete, "to appoint elders in every city" (Titus 1: 5). And Clement Romanus, who was contemporary with the apostles, says: "They [the apostles] appointed those [to be presbyters] already mentioned, and afterwards gave instructions that when these should fall asleep, other approved men should succeed them in their ministry."[27] Thus the ministry has been continued to the present time; but how were "other approved men" to be designated for the ministry when qualified by the Christ? How was the needed testing of the qualifications to be made?

§ 121. The recognition of the ministry is made in ordination, which is a formal inquiry and setting apart to the work. The inquiry respects the qualifications, and consequent fitness or unfitness, of the candidate, as called of God for the ministry; and the setting apart is an ecclesiastical act or ceremony formally recognizing him as called of God to be a minister.

(1) We should expect to find some setting apart of men to so important and responsible a ministry. It would not only be natural, but expected, since the priests under the ceremonial dispensation were consecrated to their holy office by solemn and elaborate ceremonies. They were anointed and consecrated during seven days, and the ordination separated the priests from the people. None others than the unblemished (Lev. 21: 16-24) and the consecrated could serve at the altar (Ex. 28: 41; 29). In addition, "there was regular ordination to the office of rabbi, elder, and judge" among the Jews, with "the imposition of hands."[28]

(2) The ordination of the New Testament was by the laying on of hands and prayer. The words translated to ordain, in the Authorized Version, are reduced from the prelatical sense into simply, "to become," or "to appoint," by

[27] Ep. Cor. I, ch. xliv.   [28] Edersheim's Life and Times of Jesus, II, 382.

the revision. The seven almoners were set apart by the laying on of hands and prayer (Acts 6: 6). Paul and Barnabas were consecrated in a similar manner as foreign missionaries (Acts 13: 3). Timothy was thus ordained by the presbytery of a local church, assisted by Paul (1 Tim. 4: 14; 2 Tim. 1: 6).

But imposition of hands was had in cases of converts (Acts 8: 17; 9: 12, 17); and in cases of ordination, "the rite was not universal: it is impossible that, if it was not universal, it can have been regarded as essential." [29] In later times, "the form of ordination or consecration varied. In the Alexandrian and Abyssinian churches it was, and still is, by breathing; in the Eastern Church generally by lifting up the hands in the ancient Oriental attitude of benediction; in the Armenian Church, as also at times in the Alexandrian Church, by the dead hand of the predecessor; in the early Celtic Church, by the transmission of relics or pastoral staff; in the Latin Church by the form of touching the head, which has been adopted from it by all Protestant Churches. No one form was universal; no written formula of ordination exists." [30]

(3) The significance of ordination depends upon the theory of the ministry held. If the Christian ministry were a priesthood, as it is not (§ 112), then ordination would be essential to the work of the ministry, and especially to the administration of the sacraments. But since the function of preaching was opened to laymen, ordination put no gulf between the ministry and the laity, but was only an ecclesiastical recognition of the divine call to the ministry. Christ calls men to be his ambassadors, but they stand to his churches in relations of vital moment, which require that his call be recognized, not ratified, but ascertained and recognized. "The conception of ordination, so far as we can gather either from the words which are used to designate it,

[29] Hatch's Org. Early Christ. Chhs. 131.
[30] Dean Stanley's Christ. Institutions, 175.

or from the elements which entered into it, was that simply of appointment and admission to office." "It can hardly be maintained upon this evidence that the ceremony of imposition of hands establishes a presumption, which is clearly not established by the other elements of ordination, that ordination was conceived in early, as it undoubtedly was conceived in later, times as conferring special and exclusive spiritual powers."[31]

(4) Ordination is the ecclesiastical recognition of the ministerial function of the church-kingdom as that function appears in individuals called by Jesus Christ to preach the Word. It is not therefore primarily and fundamentally an inauguration into the pastoral office, as the New England fathers made it,[32] but into the ministry of the Word.[33] The function is wider than the pastoral office; it includes as well all evangelistic and missionary labors; and so ordination is to the ministry, which is as wide in its scope as the wants of the church and the work of Christ.

(5) Ordination is to be performed by the churches. The apostles, as we have seen (§ 115), had the power of the keys; they might therefore set men apart in ordination to the ministry. But the permanent power of the keys was committed to local churches (§§ 99, 109). They had power to prove the spirits, whether they were of God (1 John 4: 1); to try them who called themselves apostles, and they exercised their power in this respect (Rev. 2: 2); and to set apart by the laying on of hands and prayer (Acts 13: 3; 1 Tim. 4: 14). A Baptist writer goes so far as to say: "The ministry alone confer ordination: in these examples (Acts 6: 6; 13: 1–3; 1 Tim. 4: 14), apostles, presbyters, and evangelists appear as officiating, but in no instance unordained persons."[34] But, in this case, if ordination be necessary to an orderly ministry, then the ministry have the sole right and power of opening and shutting the door to a recognized ministry; and

---

[31] Hatch's Org. Early Christ. Chhs. 130, 132.
[33] Boston Plat. part iv, chap. i, § 1.
[32] Cambridge Plat. chap. ix, § 2.
[34] Harvey's The Church, 84.

there results a clerical rule in the churches. We sympathize with our ecclesiastical fathers when they repudiated this clerical ordination. "In general, the ordination of ministers was by the imposition of the hands of their brethren in the ministry; but some churches, perhaps to preserve a more perfect independency, called for the aid of no ministers of any other churches, but ordained their ministers by the imposition of the hands of some of their own brethren."[35] This was sometimes regarded as irregular.[36] But it rests on sound principles. There is no priestly or clerical rule in Christian churches. The body that could "prove the spirits," and try false apostles, and elect its officers, and had the keys of discipline, could recognize those whom the Master sent it as under-shepherds by prayer and the laying on of hands. This is confirmed by the action of the Corinthian church in removing men from the ministry.[37]

The local churches are the only organs of the Spirit provided for this work of ordination. The church-kingdom chiefly manifests itself in and through them. They are the normal repositories of ecclesiastical power, and the only bodies on which such power was conferred for all time. They are chiefly affected by the ministry, and have consequently the highest reasons for keeping out of the ministry all whom the Lord has not qualified and called. Their conceded independence (§ 109) involves the right and power of ordination.

(6) There is no peculiar right or authority conferred by ordination. Ordination does not set the ministry over the churches; it does not end logically or in fact in ministerial rule. No man ordained to the ministry can invade a church to govern it; nor can he unite with others so ordained to form a presbytery to rule it. This ordination is the recognition of those whom Christ has called to the ministry; but a man so ordained must be called to the pastorate (§ 131 : 1)

---

[35] Hutchinson's Hist. Mass. i, 374.   [36] Felt's Eccl. Hist. ii, 267.
[37] Clement Romanus, Ep. Cor. chap. xliv.

by the vote of a church before he can have any authority therein, except as a layman in the church of which he is a member. His position as pastor is distinct from the recognition of his divine call as a minister. He may be a minister and not a church officer. And his ordination to the ministry gives him no authority whatever over or in local churches.

IV. — MINISTERIAL STANDING.

§ 122. The ordination of ministers places them in a peculiar relation to the churches. Those ordained may or may not be officers in a local church, but whether officers therein or not, they by reason of their recognized ministerial call stand as ministers of the Word, and are treated as such in all communions. We call their peculiar relation to the churches ministerial standing. And we mean by it a minister's responsible relation to, and connection with, some association of churches which may vouch for him and call him to account for heresy or immorality. If true ministers at all, they are called to exercise their function in subordination to the church-kingdom, which chiefly appears in the world in and through churches. Their belief and conduct vitally affect these churches. The needed qualifications by which to test them have been given not merely for their guidance, but for the guidance of the churches in ordaining them and dealing with them. They, if church officers, are more than church officers. They owe in fellowship accountability to the churches that recognize them as ministers of the Word. If the Ephesian church could commend by letter Apollos to the disciples in Achaia (Acts 18: 27); and if the council of Jerusalem could notify the churches that the Judaizers who disturbed their peace were not officially sent forth (Acts 15: 24), we may well assume that the relation of recognized ministers to the churches forms a broad and sure basis for their accountability to the churches. As the churches can not create ministers, but only recognize those called by the Great Head of the Church to be ministers, so they may not uncreate ministers, but only withdraw from the unworthy the recognition which they had given in ordination. They may cast the unworthy out of their fellowship, or more formally take away the endorsement already given them in ordination; that is, depose them; and all this in the exercise of their authority to do the things that make for purity and peace. Fellowship requires association, and churches associated may, in the exercise of a common and universal right, keep themselves free from unworthy ministers.

If this right of self-protection exists in neighboring churches in virtue of their common union in the church-kingdom, it may be exercised in any way suitable to the independence of said churches one of another. The way that is simplest, completest, and safest is best. If that way be by occasional councils or by stated associations, the principle is the same. Which is the better way, we will consider hereafter (§§ 204, 209). We here affirm that if the churches can call the ministry to account by councils, they can by associations of churches. Both ways recognize an accountable relation of the ministry to the churches, and hence ministerial standing.

§ 123. This ministerial standing is so natural that all communions require it. Each of the great polities, and all combinations of them, where the ministerial function is recognized at all, have ways of making the ministry responsible, either to itself or to the churches. The General Association (ministerial) of Connecticut, in 1813, by vote affirmed that ministers, whether pastors or not, are amenable to the ministerial association to which they belong.[38] And the Supreme Court of Vermont, in an elaborate decision given in 1879, have held the same.[39] Out of New England and in all foreign countries, we have elsewhere shown [40] that

[38] 9 Cong. Quart. 194; Contrib. Eccl. Hist. Ct. 328.
[39] Shurtleff v. Stevens, 51 Vt. 501; 31 Am. Repts. 704.   [40] 43 Bib. Sacra, 417, 420.

ministerial standing is held among Congregationalists in associations of churches. The General Association of the Congregational churches and ministers of Michigan, in May, 1880, by unanimous vote adopted the following as expressive of the past history of those churches nearly from the beginning, namely: "By 'ministerial standing' this association understands such membership in some local conference or association as makes the said body responsible for ministers connected with it; that is, the conference or association receives its ministerial members on credentials by vote, may arraign, try, and expel them for cause, or dismiss them to corresponding bodies on their own request."[41]

In the leading colonies of New England the State and Church were at first one, and the Legislature was a general association of the churches, possessing civil and ecclesiastical jurisdiction. The General Court of Massachusetts, in 1653, ordered that no one should be "allowed to preach without the approbation of the elders of the four churches next to the place where he may be employed, or by the court of the county in which it is located;" and "that no man be ordained . . . an elder, unless timely notice thereof is given to three or four neighboring churches, so that they may ascertain whether they can approve of him."[42] Similar things were done in Connecticut, even down to the middle of the last century.[43] Their Legislatures were stated assemblages of the churches for ecclesiastical as well as civil matters, and exercised most rigorous authority over churches and ministers.[44] Thus this accountability of the ministry to the churches or to itself has every-where been asserted and exercised. A call to preach the everlasting gospel does not lift one out of responsible connection with the churches. It is only when the churches forbid him to fulfill his divine calling that he can rightly assert his higher commission. He is

[41] Minutes Gen. Ass. Mich. 1880, 20.
[42] Felt's Eccl. Hist. ii, 95, 108.
[43] Ibid. 267, 268; The New Englander for 1883, 472.
[44] Cases cited in The New Englander, 1883, 468–473.

required to have a good testimony from them that are without, and certainly much more is he required to have the confidence and testimony of those that are within, which is expressed in the term ministerial standing.

§ 124. There being such a thing as ministerial standing in all communions, where is it properly lodged? This question will be answered according to the polity held, and we answer it according to the principles of Congregationalism.

(1) It is not the part of the civil power to recognize the call of men to the ministry, and so either to ordain them or to authorize them to preach and call them to account, as did the courts of the New England colonies. Christ separated the Christian Church and the local churches from the State (§ 225), and so took from the magistrates all questions ecclesiastical.

(2) Ministerial standing can not be held in local churches. If the ministerial function were confined to the pastoral relation, and a man ceased to be a minister the moment he ceased to be pastor, — which some have held to be "the necessary verdict of the principles of Congregationalism,"[45] — then ministerial standing would be held in local churches, since a vote to remove a pastor from office would be his deposition from the ministry; and besides, he, while pastor of one church, would be a layman every-where beyond that church. But this theory of the ministry was not embraced by the English or other Congregationalists, and soon ceased to be held in New England.[46] In answer to the seventh point raised by the ministers of Old England, the ministers of New England, about 1638, held that a church might depose from his office an unfit or unworthy pastor; but if one should be set aside without sufficient cause, he would still remain a minister of Christ.[47] This answer rests on the fact of a ministerial function wider than the pastorate, to which Christ calls men. But no sooner was such a position taken than the

---

[45] Congregationalism, Dr. H. M. Dexter, 150.
[46] Mather's Magnolia, ii, 230. [47] Felt's Eccl. Hist. i, 368.

ministerial standing of the ordained passed beyond the control of the local church to give or take away. Other churches recognized the pastor as a minister of the Word, and his responsibility to his own church was not a sufficient guard of purity. Thus a minister is more than a pastor and church member. He is regarded as a minister by the churches generally, and treated in all repects as a minister. If he prove unworthy, all other churches are compromised. If his church call him to account, all other churches in the neighborhood are not only interested but also involved in the result. If his church neglect to call him to account, other churches can not clear themselves of responsibility on the plea that it concerns that church alone, as under the Pastoral Theory; but they must themselves proceed to take action in the case. The National Council, in 1880, after a discussion of ministerial standing, with only one dissentient vote, declared "that the body of churches in any locality have the inalienable right of extending ministerial fellowship to, or withholding fellowship from, any person within their bounds, no matter what his relations may be in church membership or ecclesiastical affiliations."[48] His ministerial standing can not therefore be in the local church.

(3) Nor can it be held in a council of churches. The churches may by a council or otherwise ascertain the call and qualifications of a man for the ministry, and so ordain him. But the council on adjournment ceases to exist. It can not be re-assembled. If all its members be summoned again in council, it is a new body. Such an occasional council can not, in the nature of things, hold the ministerial standing of those it ordains. A dead body can not call to account the living.

(4) The unassociated churches in any locality are not the best depository of ministerial standing. If a minister within their bounds is amenable to them as a body, it is to the whole body, not to a part of the whole, and any council that might

[48] Minutes, 17.

be called to deal with him should include the whole body, not a part of the whole, or any beyond its bounds. If his standing lies around among them as unorganized, which one shall begin the process of dealing with him? What is everybody's business is nobody's. And if he be a pastor of a church, and that church neglect to call him to account, what church will undertake to discipline a sister church's pastor? It is true, we have a way of dealing with such a church for not doing its duty;[49] which is really a way for punishing a church for being deceived by an impostor instead of punishing the impostor that deceives it. But this way has never worked well, and is such a roundabout way of reaching an unworthy minister that it probably will never be tried again. If, then, the standing of a minister be held in an unorganized body of churches, it is not the best place to hold it, because (a) his standing is then an undefined quantity; (b) no body is burdened with the special duty of calling him to account for heresy or immorality; (c) the parties to the process may limit the council to a part of the whole body of churches in the locality; (d) the minister, if condemned, may call another council of other churches from the same locality or from beyond that locality; (e) in any case the council is selected, if not picked; (f) the conflict and confusion thus resulting have discredited councils, and must ever make reliance on them both uncertain and unwise, especially since railroads have rendered all churches accessible.

(5) Ministerial standing ought not to be held in ministerial associations, since that takes it away from the churches and puts it into the hands of the ministry. The churches might still by council ordain and depose, but that would involve a double accountability that might easily end in a conflict of authority. The association might retain as member and so give standing to a minister whom the churches by council have deposed. At any rate ministers ought not to be accountable only to ministers. The opposition to such

[49] Cambridge Plat. chap. xv, 2 (3); Boston Plat. part iii, ch. 1, 2 (8).

standing in ministerial associations is well founded and will ultimately prevail.

(6) The only adequate and proper depository of ministerial standing is associations of churches. They meet statedly, have well defined boundaries, keep permanent records, and are themselves accountable. If a council commit a mistake or do wrong, it can not redress it after adjournment, and all responsibility is precluded by the dissolution of the council into its individual elements; but if an association of churches do wrong or make a mistake, it exists to feel its responsibility, to correct it and record the correction. These associations embrace the churches of their respective localities, and act in the exercise of their "inalienable right" in giving or withholding fellowship. They are not picked or packed bodies. They have also, through proper committees, time to inquire fully, and under favorable conditions, into a minister's character and record, which a council of churches has not. They can watch over and admonish him; but, in the end, they can arraign, try, and expel him for cause; they can join with him in case of grievance in calling a mutual council to review the whole case, and to accredit or depose him; they can redress an injury, restore the expelled on penitence or justification: they can do all these in the exercise of their "inalienable right," without infringing upon the liberties of any church, in the conceded right of self-protection. They are therefore adequate, and the only bodies that are adequate, for the holding of ministerial standing. To go beyond these would be to introduce the elements of some foreign polity.

(7) Such standing in associations of churches with appeal in case of grievance to a mutual council chosen from beyond the bounds of the association acting in the case, is safe and essential. There is not an element of Presbyterianism in it.[50] Councils guard only one third of our ministry in active service, and less than one fourth of the whole Congregational

[50] Pocket Manual, § 64; The New Englander, 1883, 487.

ministry in the United States, and very few indeed elsewhere. And yet the Supreme Court of Vermont but expressed the common sense of Christendom as to ministerial accountable standing, when it said: "If it be suspected that a wolf in sheep's clothing has invaded their ranks, it is not only for the *interest* of all the members of the association to know the fact, but it is their *imperative duty* to make inquiry and *ascertain* the fact." For the association has "the rightful jurisdiction to investigate charges of unministerial conduct affecting its members, and on conviction to administer proper punishment."[51] The case was that of a minister suspended from membership and published in the papers as unworthy, without citation, or trial, or even hearing. Redress he hoped to find in the civil courts, but failed, the court sustaining the association. But no polity can stand the wrong of inflicting the loss of ministerial standing upon a member of an association without trial or hearing, and give him no method of redress. There should, therefore, be in cases of grievance by an association the right of calling a mutual or *ex parte* council, under proper conditions, for review and redress.

(8) This ministerial standing with right of appeal was recognized as Congregational by the National Council in 1886, in the passage of the following resolutions,[52] namely:—

1. *Resolved*, That standing in the Congregational ministry is acquired by the fulfillment of these three conditions, namely: (1) Membership in a Congregational church; (2) Ordination to the Christian ministry; and (3) Reception as an ordained minister into the fellowship of the Congregational churches, in accordance with the usage of the state or territorial organization of churches in which the applicant may reside; and such standing is to be continued in accordance with these usages, it being understood that a *pro re nata* council is the ultimate resort in all cases of question.

2. *Resolved*, That all Congregational ministers in good

[51] Shurtleff *v.* Stevens, 51 Vt. 501; 31 Am. Repts. 704.   [52] Minutes, 43, 44.

standing in their respective states, who have been installed by council, or who have been regularly called to the pastorate by the specific vote of some church, have formally accepted such position, and have been recognized as such by some definite act of the church, should be enrolled as pastors; and we advise that all our denominational statistics, and direct that, so far as possible, our Year Book, conform to this principle.

The above resolutions were reported by a committee. The following resolutions on the same subject were also adopted.

3. *Resolved*, That this National Council commends to the churches, in accordance with our ancient usage, the importance of properly called ecclesiastical councils, ordinarily selected from the vicinage, and especially the great importance of the installation of ministers to the pastorate by councils, when it is practicable, as conducive to the purity of the ministry and the prosperity of the churches.

4. *Resolved*, That the state organizations and local organizations of churches be recommended to consider such modifications of their constitution as will enable them to become responsible for the ministerial standing of ministers within their bounds, in harmony with the principle that the churches of any locality decide upon their own fellowship.

5. *Resolved*, That the Year Book designate pastors who have been installed or recognized by councils called to examine the pastor-elect and assist in inducting him into office by the letters $p. c.$, and pastors otherwise inducted by the letter $p.$, it being understood that these changes shall be first made in the Year Book for 1888.

The first and second resolutions were adopted unanimously; the others almost unanimously. They recognize and allow the usages of the several states to govern in those states. Thus there is liberty in unity.

The fourth resolution recommends the re-adjustment of state and local associations of churches or conferences so as to recognize the holding of ministerial standing in them.

In doing this, care should be had to avoid the trial of a minister before a promiscuous assembly of the churches. Ministerial discipline arouses passions and often creates parties. It should therefore be guarded in all proper ways, that whatever result may be reached, no just charges of unfitness in the tribunal can be made. Some such regulation or rule should be adopted by every conference or association of churches wherein ministerial standing is held as the following, namely : —

When the standing of any church or ministerial member is called in question, and a trial is to be had, a special meeting of the body shall be called for the purpose, which special meeting shall consist of all the ministerial members of the body in good standing, and a single male delegate of lawful age from each church connected with the body.

Such a rule, together with an appeal from the action of the conference or association of churches to a mutual council, will constitute an adequate safeguard.

§ 125. This ministerial standing in associations of churches, with appeal to mutual councils in cases of grievance, protects and completes our polity. The churches in a locality, in the exercise of their "inalienable right" of giving and withholding fellowship, find that the best and safest way is to join together in an association for communion and labor, as expressive of their union in the church-kingdom. Brotherly love binds them into one as the church-kingdom is one. These associations unite in a state or provincial association, and these again in a national union or council, and all in an ecumenical union. In this completed fellowship the local or district associations have the inalienable right to extend or withhold fellowship to individual churches and ministers, but they therein are bound to regard the common faith and discipline of the whole, otherwise they may themselves be cut off from fellowship by other associations in the exercise of their right of self-protection. There is no exercise of authority except that of self-protection, while the unity and the ministerial function of the church-kingdom are both properly recognized and guarded. There is protection without the state control which our early New England fathers claimed and exercised.[53] A few selected churches can not override the inalienable right of the churches in any locality, and by a council picked from anywhere force fellowship upon the great majority of churches. Our polity is also protected in another way. Many ministers, and the number is increasing, after ordination pass from church to church, and from state to state, without any installing council to ascertain their doctrinal belief or ecclesiastical position. They are in good and regular standing in the Congregational ministry, if nothing but an ordaining council be required to give them such standing. Against such unaccountable ministers the churches have been warned by every method, but to little effect, so short are their memories. The only way to reach them is through standing in associations of churches which can call them to account. If a minister refuse to hold such standing, he therein proves his disregard for ministerial accountability, and the churches may and should disclaim any responsibility for him. His ordination does not lift him above accountability to the churches. If he repudiate this form of accountability, let him call a council of installation every time he changes churches. But if he repudiate both methods, the churches stultify themselves in publishing his name in the minutes and Year Books, without at the same time noting their irresponsibility for him. Churches by calling such ministers do not put them into ministerial fellowship and standing, as we shall see (§§ 131, 200), but may themselves be dealt with for breach of covenant relations, if they persist in employing such irresponsible ministers (§ 211).

The complete adoption of this principle of ministerial standing and its consequent mode of ministerial discipline (§§ 211, 214) will give our polity the completeness, unity,

[53] Cambridge Plat. chap. xvii; The New Englander, 1883, 470–473.

and protection, without the coercive element, which characterized it at the outset in this country, but which it has lacked through much of its career. But the bearing of such ministerial standing on the mode of ministerial discipline will be considered in Lecture Tenth, where many questions respecting it will have full consideration.

LECTURE VII.

THE DOCTRINE OF THE CHRISTIAN CHURCH. — THE CHURCHES AND THEIR OFFICERS.

"*All the churches of Christ salute you.*" — Saint Paul.

"*Neither as lording it over the charge allotted to you, but making yourselves ensamples to the flock.*" — Saint Peter.

WE have shown the independence of the local churches, and set forth the ministry of the Word as the function by and through which the church-kingdom enlarges itself into a constantly increasing number of local churches. We turn now to the internal structure, functions, and external relations of the churches.

§ 126. And here we need to recall the meaning of the word *ecclesia*, or church, in its singular and plural number. It is used in the New Testament about one hundred and fifteen times. It is sometimes employed to give the manward side of the kingdom of heaven (§ 35), as the kingdom gives the Christward side of the same body of believers. It is thus used in the Creed: "the holy Catholic Church." But the word is generally employed to designate a local congregation of believers. It never means in the New Testament a larger or smaller collection of local churches. The word is twice used of the Hebrew commonwealth (Act 7: 38; Heb. 2: 12); three times of a civil assembly (Acts 19: 32, 39, 41), but never of a provincial or national collection of particular congregations. The words: "So the church throughout all Judæa and Galilee and Samaria had peace" (Acts 9: 31), form only an apparent exception. They may be explained in either of two ways: —

(1) The word church here refers to the scattered members of the church in Jerusalem. That church had been already

"scattered abroad throughout the regions of Judæa and Samaria," "all" the church, "except the apostles" (Acts 8: 1). These fugitive members "went about preaching the Word." They were successful, and the apostles sent two of their number to Samaria, who, seeing the work, conferred the gift of the Spirit on those who had been baptized, and returned to Jerusalem (Acts 8: 4, 15, 16, 25). Some of the brethren then scattered abroad went "as far as Phœnicia, and Cyprus, and Antioch, speaking the word to none save only to Jews" (Acts 11: 19). Saul pursued the disciples "unto foreign cities," "to make them blaspheme" (Acts 26: 11), even to Damascus (Acts 9: 3); but in all these cases he found the disciples in the synagogues of the Jews, "punishing them oftentimes in all the synagogues" (Acts 26: 11). There is no intimation that at this early and troublous time the disciples had withdrawn from the synagogues and formed churches. It was not until Saul had been converted, had spent three years in Arabia (Gal. 1: 17, 18), and had fled from Jerusalem to escape the wrath of his former coadjutors in persecution, that the Church is said to have had peace. We know that the Jewish believers were slow in breaking away from their old worship (Acts 21: 20-24). The first recorded instances do not occur until much later (Acts 18: 7; 19: 9). We know, too, that the Jewish *kahal* was comprehensive of Jews every-where, and that the term *ecclesia* was in such current use in its theocratic sense that it was natural for Luke to use it in a similar comprehensive sense of the *ecclesia* in Jerusalem when scattered abroad. "Indeed, it is hardly conceivable that churches, in any proper sense of the term, should have been formed thus early 'throughout all Judæa, and Galilee, and Samaria'" (Jamieson, Faussett, and Brown). This view is put beyond question, it would seem, by the fact that Paul afterwards speaks of "the churches of Judæa" (Gal. 1: 22; 1 Thess. 2: 14). If there was a provincial church in the three provinces, composed of local churches, in A.D. 39, the union did not prevent his calling the several congregations in Judæa churches, A.D. 52. It is both a natural and consistent view, and one in harmony with the otherwise universal uses of the word in the New Testament, to make church in this passage to mean the local church at Jerusalem scattered by the persecution into these and even more distant countries. Especially is this so when we consider that the converts were accustomed to synagogue worship at home and the temple worship at Jerusalem, their political and religious capital. As the separation between the synagogues and the Christian congregations was not complete until after the destruction of Jerusalem in A.D. 70,[1] we can not believe that the separation had been effected in Judæa, Galilee, and Samaria as early as A.D. 39. But if churches then existed there, then we reply: —

(2) The word church in this passage means the church-kingdom, the whole body of believers in Christ, "the holy Catholic Church." "The unity or oneness of the Church of Christ is here presented for the first time." "Used for the whole body of believers, or the Church universal."[2]

Whichever interpretation be true, the advocates of a provincial or national Church must reject both before they can claim in favor of their theory this passage as the solitary exception to general usage. It is far more probable that one or the other explanation be correct than that Luke, careful as he was in the use of terms, should have used the word church in an extraordinary sense here. We can not, therefore, regard this passage as an exception.

§ 127. It is alleged that the city churches were too large to constitute single congregations. Three thousand were added on the day of Pentecost to the one hundred and twenty in Jerusalem (Acts 2: 41), and after a period, "probably not very brief," "the number of the men came to be about five thousand" (Acts 4: 4). How could such a great number of males, to say nothing of women and children, constitute one congregation in a city where they had up to

[1] Schaff's Hist. Christ. Ch. 1, 460.   [2] Lange's Com. in loc.

this time certainly, and probably much later, no meeting-house or hall?

(1) Many of those at first converted were foreign Jews who had come up to Jerusalem from fifteen countries in three continents, stretching from Rome in Europe, to Cyrene in Africa, and to Mesopotamia in Asia (Acts 2: 8-12), and who shortly afterwards returned to their homes, though baptized, numbered, and enrolled in Jerusalem. The form of expression, "came to be" (Acts 4: 4), would seem to include all from the day of Pentecost that had been baptized. Many of these, no doubt, after a brief period of instruction in the new faith, returned to their own countries to preach the glad tidings to their countrymen. But allowing for these, the number of members left in the Jerusalem church was great.

(2) The city churches may generally have met in several places for worship and instruction. Believers in Jerusalem met in the temple and worshiped there (Acts 2: 46; 3: 1), also in synagogues there and elsewhere (Acts 13: 5, 14; 26: 11). "There is no record of any effort to set apart a place of worship for the members of the new society. They met in private houses (Acts 2: 46; 20: 8; Rom. 16: 5, 15, 23; 1 Cor. 16: 19; Phil. 2) or in a hired class-room (Acts 19: 9), as opportunities presented themselves."[3] Persecuted as they often were, without halls, public edifices, or meeting-houses of their own, the members of the city churches probably met wherever they could for worship and instruction, the same church being divided for this purpose into convenient sections. Such a course would seem to have been the natural and inevitable way of doing in this formative period of the churches.

(3) But each city church was under the same officers. The twelve apostles abode for years in Jerusalem, to instruct all believers; and besides, there were elders in every church, a plurality of elders in each (Acts 14: 23; 20: 17, 28;

[3] Plumptre's Introd. to Acts.

1 Tim. 4: 14). These elders constituted a corps of laborers sufficient to conduct services in many places at the same time. But these elders and their assistants the deacons were, however, officers in the church electing them, in the whole church, where the ultimate authority to elect and discipline resided (§§ 99, 100).[4] The same thing is seen to-day in some city churches which hold stoutly to independency.

(4) There is nothing in such a condition of things in the early city churches inconsistent with Congregationalism. Presbyterianism does not follow from it. If we concede, as we are willing to do, that the primitive city churches were so large that each probably met in several places under its presbytery of elders, we do not concede that each section of the one city church was itself a particular church with its separate officers. The division of a large church into neighborhood congregations, or different congregations meeting in the same place but at different times, for convenience of worship and instruction, is one thing; but the union of two or more completely organized congregations in an association, with authority to govern, is quite another. The former is Congregationalism, but the latter is Presbyterianism. We find no germ of a provincial or a national church here in city churches; and, if not here, then nowhere in the New Testament or in the ante-Nicene period.

§ 128. We may define a local or particular church to be the congregation of recognized believers in a place, assembling statedly under a mutual agreement to observe Christ's ordinances in one society. There are five things here which need to be specially noticed in this definition: (1) Those constituting a Christian church must be believers, true followers of Jesus Christ (§ 94); (2) they must live near enough together to meet statedly for worship, business, and labor; (3) there must be some recognition of one another as Christians, with the proper tests in life, belief, and disci-

---

[4] Neander's Planting, 151; Davidson's Eccl. Pol. lect. ii; Ecclesia, or Church Problems, 61.

pline; (4) there must be some agreement to observe the ordinances of Christ together. This agreement is a covenant, whether written or understood, and constitutes the body a church; and (5) they must become one society; that is, one body, under the same officers, with one record, and doing as an organized unit whatever it does, in worship, business, and evangelization. Any such organization is a church of Jesus Christ, named after the place where it exists.

§ 129. A church is not strictly a voluntary society; for the word "voluntary" makes the will or option of the members a fundamental thing in its formation. This is false and pernicious in the extreme, implying as it does that a believer may rightly stay out of the local church, if he choose to do so. The believer is already in the church-kingdom in virtue of being a believer, of which church-kingdom every true church is a normal and fundamental manifestation. He can not stay out of the local church, therefore, without violating the essential law of the church-kingdom, as well as the express command of Christ. He virtually denies the Lord that bought him. He refuses to manifest with others what he is as a redeemed sinner. And no wonder, when such is the case, that it soon became a maxim of the Roman Catholic Church: "Out of the church there is no salvation." This maxim, hardened into a universal rule, is less pernicious, when we take a true conception of local churches as manifestations of the church-kingdom, than the position that churches are voluntary societies. The very close connection of baptism with faith (Matt. 28: 19; Mark 16: 16; Acts 2: 38, 41; 1 Peter 3: 21) removes all option from the believer, except as to which of two or more true churches he shall join. He is bound as a believer to be in some local church.

§ 130. The members in a local church stand on an essential equality one with another. There is no aristocracy within the household, but common rights and privileges and responsibilities. Those chosen to office are not essentially, but only officially, above the rest. Their position is one of function, not of order or rank. This is assumed every-where in the Acts and Epistles. We might argue the same from the origin of the churches in the Jewish synagogues. But it is conceded. "Hence it appears that the church was at first composed entirely of members standing in an equality with one another, and that the apostles alone held a higher rank and exercised a directing influence over the whole."[5] "The whole body of Christians was upon a level. 'All ye are brethren.' The distinctions which Saint Paul makes between Christians are based not upon office, but upon varieties of spiritual power. . . . They do not mark off class from class, but one Christian from another. . . . The gift of ruling is not different in kind from the gift of healing."[6] Elders were not essentially above laymen, hence they are forbidden to lord it over the charge allotted to them, but are required to make themselves examples to their respective flocks (1 Pet. 5 : 3).

CHURCH OFFICERS.

§ 131. The ministry of the Word is in some respects independent of local churches (§§ 111, 113 : 4), but largely it is an office in such churches. This is true particularly of the permanent ministry; that is, of elders, bishops, pastors, and teachers. Whenever these enter upon the duty of tending and feeding a particular flock, they constitute the highest officers in that church.

(1) It is not certain how the elders of the first churches were appointed (§ 100 : 4). The apostles may have "appointed the firstfruits" of their labors "to be bishops and deacons of those who should afterwards believe."[7] Cyprian said that a bishop is "chosen" "by the suffrage of an entire people;"[8] that "they themselves have the power either of choosing worthy priests or of rejecting unworthy ones"; and he stoutly maintains that it is "of divine authority that

[5] Neander's Planting, 32.   [6] Hatch's Org. Early Christ. Chhs. 119.
[7] Clement Romanus, Ep. Cor. xlii.   [8] Epis. liv, 6.

a priest should be chosen in the presence of the people under the eyes of all," and that "God commands it."[9] "A bishop should be elected by all the people."[10] "The Teaching of the Twelve Apostles" says: "Appoint, therefore, for yourselves bishops and deacons."[11] The latest book of the Apostolic Constitutions requires, under the authority of Peter, that a bishop be chosen by the whole people.[12] As the custom of choosing bishops and elders could not have originated in the second or third centuries, it must have been apostolic. We may conclude then that independent churches and all local churches have the right and power of electing their own pastors and bishops.

(2) There was undoubtedly a plurality of elders or pastors in the primitive churches (§ 127 : 3). They constituted a presbytery within the local church. The early custom is approved by our churches,[13] though in practice they lay all the burdens of the primitive eldership upon the head and heart of one frail man. The Sunday-school teacher, however, has in later years come to relieve him in part. Our large city churches greatly need a presbytery of elders in each, to do the varied and exacting duties of the pastorate.

(3) The duties of the bishops or elders in a church may be summed up in these words: To preach the Word; to administer the sacraments; to have the spiritual oversight of the flock; generally, to preside at all church meetings; and to exercise the rule of wisdom, counsel, and love. We do not regard the expressions: "he that ruleth" (Rom. 12 : 8); "them that . . . are over you" (1 Thess. 5 : 12); "the elders that rule well" (1 Tim. 5 : 17); and "that have the rule over you" (Heb. 13 : 7, 17, 24), as implying the complete authority of government, or the power of the keys. Peter gives a charge needing ever to be recalled: "Tend the flock of God which is among you, exercising the oversight, not of constraint, but willingly, according unto God; nor yet for

---

[9] Epis. lxvii, 3, 4.   [10] Canons Ch. Alexandria, Can. ii.
[11] Chap. xv.   [12] Book viii, iv.   [13] Boston Plat. part ii, ch. iv, 5.

filthy lucre, but of a ready mind; neither as lording it over the charge allotted to you, but making yourselves ensamples to the flock " (1 Peter 5 : 2, 3). That such exhortation was needed is clear from history. "The office of the presbyter-bishops was to teach and to rule the particular congregation committed to their charge. They were the regular 'pastors and teachers.' To them belonged the direction of public worship, the administration of discipline, the care of souls, and the management of church property."[14] An Oriental shepherd (pastor) is a fit pattern for the presbyter-bishop to imitate.

(4) The membership of elders is twofold, since they are both Christians and ministers. As Christians, membership should be in some local church; but as ministers, it should be in an association of churches. The latter, with ministerial standing, has been sufficiently discussed (§§ 123–125). As to church membership, it should properly be held in the church where the man is pastor, but it is not essential that it be held there.[15] Rev. John Mitchell said, in 1838: "It is insisted on by some that a minister shall be a member of the church of which he is pastor, and subject, like any other member, to its watch and discipline. But neither the reasons nor the passages from Scripture which are adduced in support of the position are satisfactory; and by a great majority of the denomination it is not, I believe, admitted." Later, quoting from Upham's Ratio Disciplinæ a passage giving the opposite custom,[16] he says: "Mr. Upham must have been misled by the practice, probably, of his own vicinity, or by some of the early writers whom he consulted. As it regards the great body of the denomination, it is believed that the *contrary* is settled both in principle and practice."[17] It is asserted that in England also church membership almost never follows changes in pastorates. This question of membership rests on the principle that there is a ministerial func-

---

[14] Schaff's Hist. Christ. Ch. I, 495.   [15] 43 Bib. Sacra, 405, 406.
[16] § 135.   [17] Guide to Principles and Practice Cong. Chhs. of New England, 237.

tion in the church-kingdom not wholly dependent on the local churches (§ 113 : 4). If we reject this function, and reduce the ministry to the pastorate,[18] then church membership should go always with the pastorate.

Whether a member of the church he serves or not, the pastor has the right to preside over church meetings; for the call to the office of pastor includes this right among others. Of course, if the meeting pertain to himself, his call, salary, dismissal, or discipline, propriety requires that he vacate the chair and, in other matters than discipline, the room. This right was recognized by Upham as early as 1844, for he says: "The practice of the churches permits him to act as the moderator of the church *ex officio;* and that, too, whether he has become a member or not, . . . because, holding the pastoral office, he has the implied consent and approval of the brethren in the discharge of that duty."[19] If a member of the church, he can vote, like any other member, and break a tie-vote as moderator; but if he be not a member of the church he serves, his election as its pastor does not give him the right to vote, or the right to break a tie-vote as moderator. This right can, however, be conferred on him as pastor by the standing rules of the church. It is seldom wise to determine church action by a tie-vote. A measure which can not command a majority of lay votes should ordinarily be allowed to fail.

(5) As the membership of ministers is dual, so their accountability is dual. As Christians they are subject to the care and discipline, like other members, of the churches of which they are members; but as ministers they are subject to the association or confederation of churches where they belong. Of this we have spoken elsewhere (§§ 123–125). Of their church accountability we need to speak. Paul said to the Ephesian elders: " Take heed unto yourselves, and to all the flock, in the which the Holy Ghost

---

[18] Cam. Plat. ch. lx, 6, 7; Dexter's Congregationalism, 150, with notes.
[19] Ratio Discip. § 85, 2.

hath made you bishops" (Acts 20: 28). They were in the church, not over it, subject to its watch-care in some particulars no doubt, like other members (Matt. 18: 15–18). The right of election involves the right of removal and discipline. Even the apostles were not above all responsibility to the brethren. Peter was called to account for visiting Cornelius (Acts 11: 2, 18). The church at Antioch sent out missionaries and received their report on returning (Acts 13: 2; 14: 27). The same church took the initiative in healing dissensions (Acts 15: 2). The church at Ephesus called those claiming to be apostles to account (Rev. 2: 2). The church in Thyatira is blamed for suffering a false prophetess to seduce its members (Rev. 2: 20).

These passages would seem to go beyond church membership, and refer to ministerial membership or functions, and so make bishops subject in all respects to the churches they serve. This is confirmed by "The Teaching of the Twelve Apostles" on bishops and deacons. The churches were to appoint for themselves these officers; were told not to despise them, but "reprove one another, not in anger, but in peace, as ye have it in the gospel." [20] The church in Corinth went so far as to depose elders, "men of excellent behaviour," from their office.[21] At a time when the confederation of independent churches could not be had, each church, while recognizing the ministry of other churches, had no way of conferring with other churches about them, and had therefore to act for itself. This right belongs to the essence of church independency. But while holding this right firmly, another principle comes in to modify it, namely: the fellowship of the churches. It is a matter of concern to all, touching the welfare of all, what the ministry shall be. Hence in the recognition of the ministerial function and call in ordination, those churches in the vicinity most affected thereby should be consulted in said ordination. The same is true of the discipline and deposition of ministers. While each church can ordain and

[20] Chap. xv. [21] Clement Romanus, Ep. Cor. xliv.

depose its own bishops, in virtue of its autonomy, yet if ordination be an ecclesiastical recognition of a divine call into the ministry, the function and call can not be limited to one local church. Hence the ecclesiastical recognition should be wider than that of one church, and the ministerial standing and accountability should also be wider. Thus by reason of the fraternity of the churches and the ministerial function of the church-kingdom, ministers, whether pastors or not, should be dealt with in a way that recognizes both the independence of local churches and their ministerial function. They are more than church members: they are also church officers. They are more than church officers: they are also ministers of Christ; and they should be so treated. Hence there arises accountable ministerial standing in associations of independent churches (§§ 123-125).

(6) The inauguration of ministers into the pastorate. This may have been by the laying on of hands and prayer at their ordination, but we have no proof of it. The Revised Version changes "ordain" to appoint (Acts 14: 23; Titus 1: 5). Whatever ceremony was had on the inauguration of pastors, it was performed by the church itself or by the apostles on behalf of the church, for only to these was the power of the keys given. No ceremony was necessary, no council of churches was necessary, to constitute an elected minister a pastor. He is pastor in virtue of his acceptance of the office. "The essence and substance of the outward calling of an ordinary officer in the church doth not consist in his ordination, but in his voluntary and free election by the church, and in his accepting of that election. . . Ordination doth not constitute an officer nor give him the essentials of his office."[22] "Officers chosen by the church are also to be ordained by it with prayer, and, customarily, with laying on of hands."[23]

Installation, then, is not essential to the pastorate. Elec-

---

[22] Cam. Plat. chap. ix, 2.
[23] Boston Plat. part ii, chap. v, 4; Minutes National Council, 1883, 72, 73.

tion and acceptance are its essence and substance. There is no fundamental difference therefore between a pastor installed and a pastor uninstalled, or, as it has hitherto been published in our minutes and Year Books, but not in any other Congregational Year Books in the world, between "pastors" and "acting pastors." This has been fully discussed in another place.[24] The object of this "invidious distinction" is ministerial accountability. But even here it fails to reach two thirds of those in our active ministry, and three fourths of our whole ministry. It consequently fails as a safeguard of purity. A complete and safe mode of ministerial accountability in associations of churches must speedily replace it (§§ 122–125).

§ 132. There were also deacons in the churches. They were church officers after elders or bishops, and are four times mentioned in the New Testament (Rom. 16: 1; Phil. 1: 1; 1 Tim. 3: 8, 12). The word translated deacon signifies "a waiter, attendant, servant, minister." It is used thirty times in the New Testament, and is in the Revised Version rendered servant, deacon, minister. "Bishops and deacons" are joined in "The Teaching of the Twelve Apostles"[25] as the permanent officers of a church.

(1) The office of deacon originated in a want. The charitable ministration of the apostles did not suit all members of the church at Jerusalem. Hence they called for the election by the church of seven almoners to have charge of this ministration (Acts 6: 1–6). These seven are nowhere called deacons, but the office and name are to be traced to their election, as their great duty is given as serving tables — "to deacon tables." No elders had yet been appointed, as the apostles gave themselves — twelve in this one church — steadfastly to prayer and the ministry of the Word. Henceforth there was to be a division of labors in the church.

(2) The duties of deacons are learned from the cause of their election. "Widows were neglected in the daily minis-

[24] 43 Bib. Sacra, 401–422. [25] Chap. xv.

tration," and so the apostles said to "the multitude of the disciples": "It is not fit that we should forsake the word of God, and serve tables." Then seven men "of good report, full of the Spirit and of wisdom," were elected and ordained "over this business," that the apostles might "continue steadfastly in prayer, and in the ministry of the word." A clear distinction is here drawn between the business and charitable affairs of a church, and the proper work of the ministry. The elders are concerned with the ministry of the Word and prayer; but it is the duty of deacons to look after the benevolences and other business. The deacons were not also ministers of the Word. Their duties were: to care for the poor and sick; to look after the business affairs of the church; to counsel with and advise the pastor; to assist at the sacraments; and to exercise a subordinate oversight of the church in spiritual matters, but not to preach the gospel.

(3) The office in its nature is therefore lay and not clerical. The diaconate is not an order in the ministry of the Word; it is expressly an office for the ministry of tables. This is proved from their original appointment, their qualifications, and the appointment of women to this office (Rom. 16: 1; 1 Tim. 3: 11), who are excluded from the ministry of the Word (1 Cor. 14: 34–36).

(4) The qualifications for the diaconate may be given, since not every one fit to be a church member is fit also to be a deacon — a fact made clear by the following prerequisites: deacons must be (1) spiritual: "full of the Spirit"; (2) orthodox: "holding the mystery of the faith in a pure conscience"; (3) wise: "grave," "full of wisdom"; (4) moral: "not double-tongued, not slanderers," "temperate," "not given to much wine," "not greedy of filthy lucre"; (5) faithful: "faithful in all things," "ruling their children and their own houses well"; (6) reputable: "men of good report," "blameless"; (7) approved: "and let these also first be proved; then let them serve as deacons"; and (8) married: "let deacons be husbands of one wife" (Acts

6: 3; 1 Tim. 3: 8–12). Many are fit to be church members who have not attained unto this high standard. No qualification refers to ability to teach or preach, or limits the office to males. Women filled the office, since the customs of those days precluded in many cases the ministry of men where deaconesses could be serviceable. There still is need of deaconesses in missionary churches, and even in home churches.

(5) Deacons and deaconesses should be set apart to their office by the laying on of hands and prayer. They were in this manner at first ordained (Acts 6: 6). This ordination ought still to be had, that the office may be more honored. It is a great loss to the churches that the functions of the diaconate have in the public estimation shrunken into the distribution of the elements at the Eucharist. Ordination lifts the office into a higher standing.

(6) The authority of the diaconate is more of function than of rule. It is a church's hand caring for its non-ministerial wants. As those wants continue, the diaconate continues, and will ever continue. The office is one of great honor and has its rich rewards for all who fill it well (1 Tim. 3: 13). The church which elects can also for cause vacate the office. Deacons are under the pastor and the church in a rule of love. Blessed is the church that has wise deacons, full of the Spirit, and of good report. Polycarp (A.D. 100–155) speaks of "being subject to the presbyters and deacons, as unto God and Christ."[26] But Ignatius (A.D. 30–107) says that a deacon is "subject to the bishop as to the grace of God, and to the presbytery as to the law of Jesus Christ."[27]

(7) Some churches, in order to secure the best men for deacons, and to have an easy relief from unsuitable deacons, by standing rule elect deacons for a term of three or five years, one going out annually, with the proviso that no one shall be reëlected to the office until the expiration of one year from the time he ceased to be deacon. This prevents

[26] Ep. Phil. chap. v.   [27] Ep. Mag. chap. ii.

friction, as each vacancy that occurs must be filled by another than the retiring deacon.

§ 133. We need to examine the supposed office of ruling elder in the churches. We have already seen that there was a presbytery of elders in each church. These presbyters are sometimes spoken of as ruling, as ruling well, as having the rule. What were these elders? Importance is given the question in certain quarters by the action of the General Assembly of the Presbyterian Church in the United States in 1833, which declared the ruling, or lay, eldership to be "essential to the existence of a Presbyterian Church."[28]

(1) There are two theories of the ruling eldership. One is that of our Congregational fathers, which makes ruling elders, presbyters, bishops, pastors, or ministers, all being of one and the same grade, class, rank, or order of officers in the churches, with a diversity of functions only. The five most distinguished Independent divines in the Westminster Assembly (1643-1647) held that ruling elders are ministerial, not lay, persons.[29] The Cambridge Platform (1648) takes the same view.[30] This has always been the view of Congregationalists.

The other theory, and the one of the Presbyterian standards, is that ruling elders are laymen and not ministers, and hence that they can not ordain or join in the imposition of hands in ordination, or administer the sealing ordinances.[31]

(2) The duties of ruling elders depend somewhat upon the theory of their office, whether it be a lay or a ministerial office. "Most of the churches of New England, for some time after the settlement of the country, had, besides a pastor and a teacher and two or more deacons, a ruling elder, or ruling elders, whose 'business,' says the author of Ratio Disciplinæ, 'it was to assist the pastor in visiting the distressed, instructing the ignorant, reducing the erroneous,

---

[28] Moore's Digest (1873), 115.
[29] Hanbury's Memorials, ii, 224.
[30] Chap. vi, 4; vii, 1, 2.
[31] Moore's Presby. Digest (1873), 114–118; Hodge's Ch. Polity, 127, 128, 285–294.

comforting the afflicted, rebuking the unruly, discovering the state of the whole flock, exercising the discipline of the gospel upon offenders, and promoting the desirable growth of the church.'"[32] "When a minister preached to any other than his own church, the ruling elder of the church, after the psalm sung, said publicly: 'If this present brother hath any word of exhortation for the people at this time, in the name of God let him say on.' The ruling elder always read the psalm. When the member of one church desired to receive the sacrament at another, he came to the ruling elder, who proposed his name to the church for their consent. At the communion they sat with the minister."[33]

Under the theory of a lay eldership, ruling elders exercise in the Presbyterian Church "government and discipline, in conjunction with pastors or ministers." They may not "participate in the ordination of ministers by the laying on of hands," nor "administer sealing ordinances," but may "explain the Scriptures and exhort in the absence of the pastor." They, with the pastor or pastors, constitute the session of a particular church, which session is "charged with maintaining the spiritual government of the congregation"; to receive, discipline, and dismiss members; "to concert the best measures for promoting the spiritual interests of the congregation, and to appoint delegates to the higher judicatories of the church."[34]

(3) The ruling elders of the New Testament were ministers, and not laymen. There is no evidence whatever that they were laymen elected to rule. The passages adduced for a lay eldership do not support it. The words: "he that ruleth, with diligence" (Rom. 12: 8), apply equally to either theory, if they refer to church officers at all. The immediate context would make them apply to private Christians or to the deacons. No proof can be drawn from the passage. "Governments" (1 Cor. 12: 28) is rendered in the margin

---

[32] Form and Covenant of Old South Ch. Boston, 1841, 4.
[33] Hutchinson's Hist. Mass. 1, 376.   [34] Moore's Presby. Digest, 114, 116, 117, 127.

"wise counsels." It may cover "elders, bishops, pastors, rulers, presidents, or moderators," and is no proof for lay eldership. Nor is such an eldership found in the crucial text: "Let the elders that rule well be counted worthy of double honour, especially those who labour in the word and in teaching" (1 Tim. 5: 17). For, in the first place, the honor referred to is not of place, rank, dignity, power, but of support. This is proved by the context. Tertullian alone of the ante-Nicene Christian writers refers to this "double honour," and reproves the giving of a double portion to "presiding bishops" at meals.[35] And, in the second place, the word translated "especially" always distinguishes between members of the same class, and never between members of different classes. This is conclusive against lay eldership. These three texts are all that can be found for lay elders. "No footsteps are to be found in any Christian church of lay elders, nor were there for many hundred years."[36] The ruling eldership of the New Testament is ministerial.

(4) The theory of the lay eldership is falling. This is manifest. In a paper read before the Second General Council of the Presbyterian Alliance (1880) on "Ruling Elders," it is not once claimed that ruling elders are laymen. The opposite seems to have been silently conceded.[37] Prof. E. D. Morris, D.D., of the Lane Presbyterian Theological Seminary, says: "1 Tim. 5: 17 really exhibits no distinction in office, but simply a recognition of superiority in the primary function of instruction."[38] Dr. Philip Schaff says of the distinction between two kinds of elders: "It is a convenient arrangement of Reformed Churches, but can hardly claim apostolic sanction, since the one passage on which it rests only speaks of two functions in the same office."[39] Dr. R. D. Hitchcock, professor in the Union Presbyterian Theological Seminary, in reviewing a work by Rev. Dr. P. C. Campbell, of Scotland, in which the lay eldership is surren-

[35] On Fasting, xvii.
[36] Lange's Com. on 1 Tim. 5:17.
[37] Proceedings, 165-176.
[38] Ecclesiology, 141.
[39] Hist. Christ. Ch. 1, 496.

dered, says: "The drift of critical opinion is now decidedly in this direction. It is beginning to be conceded, even among Presbyterians of the stanchest sort, that Calvin was mistaken in his interpretation of 1 Tim. 5: 17; that two orders of presbyters are not there brought to view, but only one order; the difference referred to being simply that of service, and not of rank. . . . The *jure divino* theory of the lay eldership is steadily losing ground." "We might easily be rid of it any day by ordaining our lay elders and making them ministers of the Word and dispensers of the sacraments."[40] Such a change in Presbyterianism would make its government "a clerical despotism."[41] It would rule out the people completely, since the power of ordination in that polity resides wholly in the ministry, lay ruling elders not being permitted, as we have seen, to have part in it.

§ 134. There is need of some board of rulers in the local churches. This need is met by either theory of the ruling eldership; but one, and the only true, theory makes that rule clerical or ministerial; the other and failing theory makes it laical, since the elders are the "representatives of the people, chosen by them for the purpose of exercising government and discipline, in conjunction with pastors or ministers."[42] Our early New England fathers had two ways of escaping clerical rule on their true theory of the eldership: the first was in reserving to the church itself the right and power of admissions, dismissals, discipline, and general management of affairs; and the second was in relying on the magistrates, elected chiefly by laymen, for protection from heresy, schism, and disorders.[43] In a Congregational church the power of ruling elders is subordinate to the church itself; while in the Presbyterian polity the session governs the church and chooses all representatives to higher judicatories. To retain its popular element, that polity must justify its lay eldership somehow. Its *jure divino* claim is being surrendered and will

[40] Presby. Theol. Rev. for 1868.
[42] Presby. Form of Government, chap. v.
[41] Hodge's Church Polity, 128, 129.
[43] Cam. Plat. chap. xvii.

have to go. But Professor Hitchcock says: " A better support is sought for it in the New Testament recognition throughout of the *right* and *propriety* of lay participation in church government; in the general right of the church, as set forth by Hooker in his Ecclesiastical Polity, to govern itself by whatsoever form it pleases." [44] This is a sad descent from a *jure divino* claim, a " Thus saith the Lord," to expediency or ecclesiastical rationalism. With the fall of lay ruling eldership falls the claim of a Scriptural warrant for the higher judicatories, and Presbyterian government becomes clerical rule.

§ 135. The need of a governing board within the church may be Scripturally met in this way: There was at first a presbytery of presbyters, or bishops, in every church (§ 131: 2), and there may be again, as occasion demands; there are deacons in each church (§ 132); each church has the right to delegate its powers and functions, in certain particulars, to committees or commissioners (§ 100: 3); let now the pastor or presbytery, the deacons, and a committee chosen by the church for the purpose, constitute a church board, whose action must in matters of general concern be endorsed by vote of the church to become effective, and we have an authorized board within the church. Nearly all our churches have such a church board, named by different names, but composed as above described. The church board is, perhaps, the best name for it. All the elements composing it are authorized in the Word of God, as also the limitation of its powers (§§ 98, 99: 2, 3). Such a board of rule does not discredit the diaconate, as the lay ruling eldership has done, until in some instances it ceases to be filled at all. Hence the appointment of deacons in Presbyterian churches has to be urged and enjoined; for " the disuse of this Scriptural and important office, it can not be doubted, has done great injury to the churches, as well as induced vague and erroneous views in regard to the nature and importance of the office." [45]

[44] Presb. Theol. Rev. 1868.   [45] Bird's Presby. Digest, 64, note.

§ 136. The duties of such a church board may be defined as the examination of candidates for admission to church privileges; the general oversight and control of the spiritual interests of the church; all preliminary inquiries into complaints against church members; the presentation of cases of discipline to the church; the trial of all difficult cases, if so ordered by the church, with recommendations for action thereon; and the devising of ways and means for the purity, peace, and prosperity of the church; but in all these cases the board must report to the church for final action its doings and recommendations.

The function of such a board is most important for the welfare of any church. Its scope may well be enlarged, and that too without danger. Such a church board is not the plural eldership of the primitive churches, nor the ruling eldership of the Reformed Churches, nor a wholly unwarranted body. It does not make a church Presbyterian. It does give a local church rulers such as the Scriptures and the apostolic fathers warrant, who are not over and above the church, but in it, responsible to it, doing its work, reporting to it. So far as the ministry of the Word is concerned, such church board does not equal in efficiency the primitive plurality of elders in every church; but it does put into every church a board of administration and stability which is greatly needed, and will be of untold value when fully and rightly worked.

§ 137. In every well-organized society there must needs be a clerk or record keeper. The fact that there is no mention of such an officer in the primitive churches is no proof that they had none, or that churches should not have a record keeper in after times. It is of the utmost importance, though not essential to the being of a church, that the proceedings of a church be properly entered on some record, and so preserved. It tends to order, regularity, peace, prosperity, legal security, to keep a journal. Each church should elect a clerk.

CHURCH CLERK. 187

(1) The qualifications for the office of clerk are of nature and of grace. Not every good man is capable of being a good scribe or clerk. He must have natural gifts and acquired habits. He must see to it that all things in church meetings are done legally, decently, and in order, and that a true record be made of the proceedings. He needs to be versed in Congregational usages and parliamentary rules. He needs to know what business should come before the church meeting, and how it should be introduced, that he may aid the moderator in the public business. He should be the fittest person in the church, except the pastor. The pastor is moderator, and should in no case be also clerk.

(2) The duties of a church clerk are similar to those of the secretary or scribe of any permanent body. He is to take minutes of all proceedings, which, however, are private memoranda, though recorded in the church book, until adopted by the church; he must see to it, therefore, that the minutes are properly adopted. He conducts correspondence for the church; gives notices of all business meetings, unless otherwise provided for; keeps a roll of church members, with additions, dismissions, excommunications, deaths, baptism of infants and adults; preserves on file, or otherwise, all letters, reports, communications, notices, papers, books, journals, etc., and transmits them to his successor. He is not their owner, but their custodian. He has no right to withhold them from the church, or committee of the church, or any legal representative of the church, or to destroy them. He must not allow any alterations of the minutes after they have been approved by the church. He should prepare the reports for state minutes. He should prepare for each business meeting an order of business for the use of the moderator.

As he is the proper channel of communication between the church and other bodies or persons, it is important that his name be published in the minutes of state associations.

§ 138. A very important office is that of treasurer. Judas the traitor, who had "the bag," who was "a thief," and who "took away what was put therein" (John 12: 6), was not a church treasurer; for the apostles were not a church, and besides, he lived and died under the Mosaic dispensation. The apostles were, after the day of Pentecost, the first church treasurers. Their duties became in time so burdensome that seven almoners were chosen for "this business" (Acts 6: 1-6). Their services included the support of the ministry of the Word as well as assistance for the widows and the poor and sick.

(1) This pecuniary function of the church is perpetual, and needs therefore recognition in an appropriate office. Paul, though declaring that his hands had ministered unto his necessities (Acts 20: 34), claimed the right of support at the hands of the churches (2 Thess. 3: 9; 1 Cor. 9: 4-14), and claimed support for the ministry, saying, "Even so did the Lord ordain that they which proclaim the gospel should live of the gospel" (1 Cor. 9: 14). Such being the permanent law of the Christian dispensation, it follows that some one or more in every church should be assigned to this special duty of receiving and disbursing funds for that and other purposes. They who are called to this duty are called treasurers. As in all fiduciary trusts, they must keep an accurate account of all moneys received and disbursed, obey the vote of the church, be prompt in all payments, and make an itemized report of the treasury statedly to the church.

(2) The church should choose the man best fitted for the position as treasurer. He needs to be honest, capable, exact, prompt, affable, one who can dun without offence, and who feels the wants of the pastor as his own. Men will not freely contribute through a treasurer whose honesty or even accuracy they question. The treasurer must be above suspicion.

(3) Many Congregational churches are fettered by parish societies (§§ 229-231), making an unscriptural division between the spiritual and the secular affairs of a church, compelling two organizations, with separate functions, records,

treasurers. We must therefore distinguish, when such is the case, between the church treasurer and the parish treasurer.

(*a*) The church treasurer, in this case, confines his official duties to the missionary, benevolent, and charitable funds of the church, leaving all the other financial concerns to the parish treasurer.

(*b*) The parish treasurer, on the other hand, confines his official oversight to the funds given or bequeathed for church or parsonage building, repairs, pastor's salary, salary or pay of others, and whatever expenses are incurred by the legal corporation, leaving missionary and benevolent and charitable funds to the church treasurer.

(*c*) Hence one man ought not generally to be treasurer of both organizations. The two bodies, with their funds and objects, are so separate and yet so interwoven that to avoid confusion, or the subordination of one of them to the other, the treasurers should be different men with different books and reports. It is to be hoped that the parish, born of the union of State and Church, will soon give way, and leave the churches in the normal simplicity of the New Testament.

§ 139. A church, like any other independent society, can appoint special committees at any time for any legitimate purpose. Such committees are needed. A committee may be empowered by vote of a church to conduct as a jury a trial of a member in case of great length or delicacy (§ 174). There may be committees on supply of the pulpit, on music, on any matter of interest. The church acts through these committees, and more efficiently than it could as a body. These committees, after they have finished their work, report to the church; and thereupon, unless they are standing committees, cease to exist. "A committee ceases to exist as soon as the assembly receives the report," "and can not act further unless revived by a vote to re-commit"[46] or to continue the committee.

We have now considered all actual and possible church

[46] Robert's Rules of Order, §§ 28, 30.

officers in an independent church. Any new need may be met by some special committee. Even the Sunday-school superintendent of the home church should thus be a church officer (§ 216); and a church can appoint members to have charge of mission schools, and designate the teachers in the home and mission schools.

§ 140. We need to remind all church officers that they are in the church, not over it. The ministry is especially liable to forget this, because of its independence, in some respects (§ 113 : 4), of the churches. Their ministerial function (§ 111), recognized in ordination (§ 121), gives them in itself no right, authority, or privilege in any church, until that church by vote empowers them to act as its officers. In other words, those called of God and ordained to the ministry to be church officers must be called by vote as pastors. A neglect to distinguish between the ministerial function and the pastoral relation has troubled both ministers and churches. A wide distinction must be made, for it exists in fact. Then no minister not also a pastor of a church will presume on the exercise of authority in any church; and when he is also a pastor of a church, he needs to remember that he is in it and not over it. This is true of deacons, clerk, treasurer, committees. Hence certain things follow from this: —

(1) The church that elects them to office can also remove them from it. The power exists in the church for both election and removal; but it should not in either case be exercised without sufficient cause. But all church officers need to remember that it is no infringement upon their rights of office for the church to remove them. Of course all legal contracts must be kept inviolate; but a pastor, because he is a minister, has no claim upon pulpit or salary when once the church by vote properly terminates his relation as pastor to them. This has come reluctantly to be conceded as true of pastors, but it is no less true of deacons and other officers.

(2) No officer has the right of veto upon the action of a

church. Not even an installed pastor may refuse to put a motion when properly made, much less can he refuse to declare the vote or veto church action. He may vacate the chair and resign his pastorate; but should he presume to lord it over the church in any one of these three ways, the church may remove him from the chair by electing another moderator in his stead. The pastor, as moderator, is bound by the ordinary parliamentary rules, except as they are modified by Congregational usages. In like manner, the clerk can not withhold papers, documents, or records belonging to the church, or correspondence as clerk, on the plea that they are private property, but must, instead, as the servant of the church, produce them when required. He is only custodian for the church. Church officers are the servants of the churches that elect them, and they that serve best are the greatest.

§ 141. Church officers are also more than servants: they are the chosen guides of the churches electing them. They are to see to it, each officer in his place, that the church they serve shall be trained and guided thoroughly in every function for the duties and labors required of it as a church of Christ. The pastor, as being the leader, or chief, or shepherd, by patience, loving suggestion, example, instruction, should secure the prompt and complete performance of every organic function, that his church may be thoroughly equipped, and active in every good work; so trained that every service and duty will go on regularly if the pastor be absent. Hence, though a pastor may in a noble sense be all things to all men, if by any means he may save some (1 Cor. 9: 20-23), yet he can not wisely be all the officers in a church. Nothing is more destructive of organic life and power than such dependence on the pastor, unless it be an unquestioning devotion to him. The first duty of the pastor is the development of the organic life of a church, so that it shall not be a congregation merely, but a trained band of workers, able to stand alone and carry on its functions and labors for a season as a church, whether it has a pastor or not. Hence, if there be no fit and trained men in the several offices, the pastor must find and train them, fitting one for one office, and another for another, until, like a regiment or an ocean steamer, the organization is perfect, with every man in the right place and each with his specific duty. Christ had more than a rabble following him: he had a band of apostles in training, to continue and enlarge his work. A minister and a crowd of admirers do not make a strong church; the crowd scatters when the minister goes: but a strong church is one organized with a full corps of officers, all trained to do their appointed work. A pastor should strive to keep his church, like a ship carrying a priceless cargo, well officered, well trained, well trimmed, able to care for itself and do its work, hold its meetings, transact its business, carry on its benevolent and missionary labors, whether the pastor be present or absent.

There is great evil also in laying all, or a large number of, the offices in a church, other than the pastorate, upon one man who has leisure or ambition or self-denial for every thing. Offices should be as widely distributed as possible, that many may be in training. If one man runs the church, others lose interest in it; opposition to the one-man power surely arises, and the church is paralyzed. If that one pillar should fall, the church, if not utterly demoralized by its long idleness, will rally and prosper, and wonder what ailed it all the years of its feebleness. The offices must be distributed as widely as possible, and men trained in them, if a church would become what it ought to be. Hence the pastor should quietly see to it that the greatest efficiency be secured in the church under the greatest number of the best guides it can command. This is a part of his official business.

Yet the officers must shun in practice, as in theory, the definition of a church given by Rev. Samuel Stone, "the famous colleague of the more famous Hooker," pastor of the First

Church, Hartford, Conn., from 1633 to 1663, when he said: "A church is a speaking aristocracy in the face of a silent democracy;"[47] that is, "The elders only were to speak in the transaction of church affairs; the brethren were to give their consent in silence."[47] If any pastor has this conception of a church, at the present time, he will attempt to be more than a guide. He will lord it over his people, and will soon find, like Noah's dove, no rest for the soles of his feet. The church, not the pastor nor the officers, is the depository of ecclesiastical power, and it can speak in business meetings and in all other meetings.

[47] Dr. L. Bacon's Hist. Discourse, Contrib. to Eccl. Hist. Ct. 16.

LECTURE VIII.

THE DOCTRINE OF THE CHRISTIAN CHURCH.—WORSHIP AND SACRAMENTS.

"*God is a Spirit: and they that worship him must worship in spirit and truth.*" — Jesus Christ.

"*Baptizing them into the name of the Father and of the Son and of the Holy Ghost.*" — Jesus Christ.

"*As often as ye eat this bread, and drink the cup, ye proclaim the Lord's death till he come.*" — Saint Paul.

THE local churches are manifestations of the church-kingdom for worship, sacraments, fellowship, and labors. No one of them exists for itself alone, and entertainment does not enter into its constitution and relations.

THE WORSHIP OF CHRISTIAN CHURCHES.

§ 142. Christian worship is largely social. It is the communion of saints in prayer and praise. The individual believer may worship God in private; it is indeed his duty (Matt. 6: 6); he may meet with a few others in occasional worship; but this is not enough: he must worship in church relations. Out of this inherent tendency to communion, born of the Spirit, come the local churches in every place, all arising from, and exemplifying, the unity of the church-kingdom. Hence worship inheres in the idea of a Christian church. It constitutes an essential element of a church. We can not dissociate worship from a church without destroying our conception of a church. The life that makes men saints and unites saints in a church estate is a life of prayer and praise, of fellowship in the worship of Christ Jesus our Lord. It is this life that causes believers in times of persecution to dare death itself that they may meet together. Take worship away, and a church would become a synagogue of Satan. The unity of the church-kingdom appears in this necessity for social worship; and as this worship is a matter of ecclesiastical regulation, its discussion belongs to church polity.

§ 143. As all regulations respecting worship in churches should conserve the nature and end of true worship, we must, at the outset, determine what its nature and end are.

(1) Christian worship must be in spirit and truth, for God is a Spirit, and "such doth the Father seek to be his worshippers" (John 4: 23, 24). It need be no longer at Jerusalem, but it may be offered every-where. If only two or three agree together for worship in spirit and truth, Christ promises to be in the midst of them (Matt. 18: 20). There must be the genuine worship of the soul, not the formal offering of accustomed service.

(2) This worship must be offered in the name of Christ, or it is not Christian worship. Christ said: "Hitherto ye have asked nothing in my name: ask, and ye shall receive, that your joy may be fulfilled." "If ye shall ask anything of the Father, he will give it you in my name." "In that day ye shall ask in my name" (John 16: 23, 24, 26). This marks a radical change in the prayers of Christ's disciples: before, they had not used the name of the Son of God; thereafter, they were to use it. Their worship was to cease being Jewish and become, for the first time, Christian. Monotheistic worship should give place to Trinitarian, "that all may honour the Son, even as they honour the Father" (John 5: 23). This puts a limit to Christian fellowship (§ 232: 4).

(3) Christian worship must be in faith and penitence. Without faith, it is impossible to please God (Heb. 11: 6). "Now he commandeth men that they should all everywhere repent" (Acts 17: 30). The preparation needed for true worship is, to testify, "both to Jews and to Greeks, repentance toward God, and faith toward our Lord Jesus Christ" (Acts 20: 21).

The nature of Christian worship requires the offering of praise and prayer, in faith and repentance, in the genuine adoration of our spiritual natures, unto God the Father, in the name of Jesus Christ the Son of God. Neither the simple household form, nor the gorgeous ritualistic form of the preceding dispensations, strongly fostered true worship. The Christian form needs to foster it, or it misses its end.

§ 144. The end of church worship is threefold.

(1) First of all, the end of worship is the glory of God. We are to do all things for his glory (1 Cor. 10: 31); and if in the necessary acts of life, how much more in the very highest act of which the soul is capable, the worship of Almighty God! The whole plan of redemption has God's glory as its chief and final consummation. In it he has made known the riches of his glory (Rom. 9: 23), that he may cause the thanksgiving to abound unto the glory of God (2 Cor. 4: 15). But this is not all.

(2) Church worship is for Christian edification. All the spiritual gifts bestowed upon the primitive churches were given, says Paul, "that the church may receive edifying" (1 Cor. 14: 5). Hence he wrote: "Seek, that ye may abound unto the edifying of the church" (1 Cor. 14: 12, 18, 19). If edification was the end of supernatural gifts, it is also of natural gifts. Every thing in the worship must promote spiritual building up. This excludes from church services spectacular exhibitions, dead languages, vain rantings, whatever fails to edify the saints.

(3) Church services are for the conversion of unbelievers. The gift of tongues was a sign for this purpose (1 Cor. 14: 22) — a sign, a monitor, but nothing more. "But if all prophesy, and there come in one unbelieving or unlearned, he is reproved by all, he is judged by all; the secrets of his heart are made manifest; and so he will fall down on his face and worship God, declaring that God is among you indeed" (1 Cor. 14: 24, 25). If that was true of inspired teaching in language that all could understand, it will be

true, in its degree, of uninspired teaching, the Spirit applying the Word for the conviction and conversion of sinners. Hence it is the law of all church worship: "Let all things be done unto edifying."

§ 145. The form of church worship should be that which best satisfies the nature and end of worship. That form may change in details to suit the environment, but must be essentially the same to meet the wants of saints and the conversion of sinners. Hence: —

(1) No fixed form of Christian worship has been revealed. There was large liberty under the patriarchs, though there bloody sacrifices and a right spirit were essential (Gen. 4: 4, 5). But under Moses liberty was excluded in a fixed and minute ritual (§ 20). Under Christ again there is liberty, with no ritual, no imposed and fixed form of worship, as becomes an ecumenical religion. A few things are enjoined in the New Testament, but the order and details are not given. Even the Lord's Prayer is not given twice alike (Matt. 6: 9–13; Luke 11: 2–4), and to reduce it to a liturgical form, a doxology had to be added. No one can find a ritual or liturgy, or even a full order of services in the New Testament. "The Teaching of the Twelve Apostles" gives three short eucharistic prayers, but adds: "But permit the prophets to give thanks in such terms as they please." [1] Nor is there any claim that the prayers given must be used, though the implication is that they are to be used Yet we learn from Justin Martyr that prayer was offered by the leader "according to his ability;"[2] that is, extemporaneously. "There is no trace of a uniform and exclusive liturgy; it would be inconsistent with the liberty and vitality of the apostolic churches."[3]

(2) The best form of Christian worship is that which best meets the nature and end of worship, which have been given. But the conditions are not the same in all ages, communities, and peoples; and, indeed, these conditions

[1] Chap. x.   [2] First Apol. chap. lxvii.   [3] Schaff's Hist. Christ. Ch. 1, 463.

change in the same communities. The same essential wants vary in their demands among different classes of men; and a variety of forms would seem best adapted to satisfy these wants. The Sunday and the week-day services are quite diverse; and a wise discretion will vary the services to meet the demands of the occasion. An ecumenical religion should be flexible in its form of worship, so as to comprehend all races, nations, tribes, tastes, conditions, wants, classes, and give to each church the worship which shall best suit its needs.

(3) To secure this flexibility Christ gave complete liberty to his churches in matters of worship. This liberty is one of the inherent rights of independent churches, which no one can take from them. This freedom in worship was one of the things "ordained in all the churches" by the apostles. Each church, whether chiefly coming from Jews or Gentiles, could regulate its own worship, changing it to suit its own needs. Many churches might have many forms, substantially alike, but varying somewhat. And so now, were all churches of one faith and order, there might be found in any city all the varieties of worship which we now see, save the mass. One might use the Prayer-Book, another the Lutheran ritual, another the baldest services, each meeting the wants of its worshipers, but each and all in the sweetest fellowship and most cordial coöperation. Congregationalism not only allows, but also encourages, this broad and catholic liberty.

§ 146. This liberty gave variety to the forms of worship among the primitive churches. Rituals were not unknown, as we shall show, but they were not one and the same for all.

(1) Their model was no doubt that of the Jewish synagogue, which has been thus described: "The people being seated, the minister, or angel of the synagogue, ascended the pulpit and offered up the public prayers, the people rising from their seats and standing in a posture of deep devotion. The prayers were nineteen in number, and were closed by

reading Deut. 6: 4–9; 11: 13–21; Num. 15: 37–41. The next thing was the repetition of their phylacteries, after which came the reading of the law and the prophets. . . . The last part of the service was the expounding of the Scriptures and preaching from them to the people. This was done either by one of the officers or by some distinguished person who happened to be present. . . . The whole service concluded with a short prayer or benediction."[4] There was singing or chanting in the synagogue services. As the synagogue was not itself expressly authorized under the law, and as each one was independent of the rest, the ritual of the synagogue can not be regarded as divinely authorized.

(2) We catch a glimpse of the primitive church worship through the door of disorders, and find that they had in the services inspired prophesying, speaking with tongues, interpretation of tongues, revelations, all which were supernatural gifts; then, reading the Scriptures, prayers, singing or chanting, and preaching. But the order in which these occurred is not given. Any adult male could participate.

The synagogue prayers may have been used at first, called perhaps "the prayers" (Acts 2: 42); but they would not long suffice, since prayer was to be offered in the name of Christ. The Psalms too would no longer meet their wants, since the coming Christ of the Old Testament had become the crucified and ascended Redeemer of the New Dispensation. Hence new prayers, "hymns and spiritual songs," arose and were used (Eph. 5: 19; Col. 3: 16). "Psalms, hymns, and unpremeditated bursts of praise, chanted in the power of the Spirit, such as those of the gift of tongues, were the chief elements of the service. The right of utterance was not denied to any man (women even seem at first to have been admitted to the same right) (Acts 21: 9; 1 Cor. 11: 5) who possessed the necessary gifts (1 Cor. 14: 26–33) and was ready to submit to the control of the presiding elder or apostle. There were in the unwritten traditions of the

[4] Schaff's Bible Dict. Synagogue.

church; in the oral teaching as to our Lord's life and teachings (1 Cor. 11: 23; 15: 1–8); as to the rules of discipline and worship (2 Thess. 2: 15; 3: 6); in 'the faithful sayings' which were received as axioms of the faith (1 Tim. 1: 15; 4: 9; 2 Tim. 2: 11; Titus 3: 8), the germs at once of the creeds, the canons, the liturgies, the systematic theology of the future."[5]

"The frequent use of psalms and short forms of devotion, as the Lord's Prayer, may be inferred with certainty from the Jewish custom, from the Lord's direction respecting his model prayer, from the strong sense of fellowship among the first Christians, and finally from the liturgical spirit of the ancient Church, which could not have so generally prevailed, both in the East and the West, without some apostolic and post-apostolic precedent."[6]

(3) The later worship appears in the so-called Constitutions of the Apostles, "a collection of ecclesiastical laws and usages which grew up gradually during the first four centuries." From them we draw a picture of a church assembly in the latter half of the ante-Nicene period (A.D. 100–325).

In the middle of the church was the bishop's throne, and on either side of him sat the presbytery, and the deacons stood near at hand, in close and small girt garments. The laity sat on either side, the men, women, the young men, the young women, and the married women with children, by themselves. The reader stood upon some high place; and after two lessons, some one sang a hymn of David, the people joining in the conclusion of the verses. Then a portion of the Acts, of Paul's Epistles, and of the Gospels was read by a deacon or presbyter, all standing while the Gospels were read. Then the presbyters, one by one, and last of all the bishop, exhorted the people. Then all rose up, and, after the catechumens and penitents and all non-communicants had gone out, prayed to God eastward. After this came the holy kiss. Then the deacon prayed for the whole world, and

[5] Plumptre's Introd. to Acts.   [6] Schaff's Hist. Christ. Ch. 1, 463.

the several parts of it. This was followed by a prayer for peace upon the whole people, with a blessing, and a prayer by the bishop; after which came the Eucharist, no unbeliever or uninitiated person being allowed to be present. During the service a deacon was to see to it that nobody whispered, slumbered, laughed, or nodded.[7]

(4) The ritualistic tendency of the early days developed into full liturgies, three of which, in the ante-Nicene period, have been preserved: The Divine Liturgy of James (about A.D. 200), which is thirty-five octavo pages long; The Divine Liturgy of Mark (about A.D. 225), twenty-five pages long; and the still later Liturgy of the Blessed Apostles, sixteen pages long.[8] As they do not agree in length, so also in other respects, proving that uniformity did not exist prior to the union of Church and State under Constantine. With the incoming of the Gentile masses after the conversion of the Roman Empire came a "prodigious number of rites and ceremonies." "They had both a most pompous and splendid ritual. Gorgeous robes, miters, tiaras, wax tapers, crosiers, processions, lustrations, images, gold and silver vases, and many such circumstances of pageantry were equally to be seen in the heathen temples and the Christian churches."[9] With the coming in of the papacy came greater uniformity, spectacular worship, fixed liturgies, and the utter perversion of Christian worship from its spiritual nature and true end.

(5) The great Reformation sprang out of a different conception of the Christian Church, and changed worship as well as doctrine, polity, and morals, but in varying degrees. The Lutheran, the Anglican, and the Protestant Episcopal Churches, and some others, retained elaborate and fixed liturgies; but the Reformed Churches and the Puritans carried the reform in worship much farther. The reaction from the corruptions and persecutions of Rome and Canterbury drove

[7] Apostolical Constitutions, book ii, lvii; book viii, xi.
[8] Ante-Nicene Christ. Library, T. and T. Clark's ed.
[9] Mosheim's Eccl. Hist. book ii, part ii, chap. iv, § 1.

the Puritans into the extreme of ritualistic barrenness. The public reading of the sacred Scriptures without comment was stigmatized as "dumb reading," and for a time the reading of the Bible was dispensed with in the pulpit, and that quite recently. The sermon, without liturgy and Scripture, rose in dignity above worship, until, to hear the preacher was in thought and speech and fact the chief business in public worship. This introduced into the worship of God a most obnoxious human element. The preaching, and so the preacher, became the center of attraction or of repulsion; that is, man, not God, received the chief honor in the sanctuary. And so it has come to pass that if the preacher is popular, the church will be crowded; if, like Paul, he is not attractive, — "his bodily presence is weak, and his speech of no account" (2 Cor. 10: 10), — the church is largely empty. Church attendance depends, therefore, upon the preacher. Thus a personal, human element, which in the worship of Almighty God should have little or no place, controls largely church going and church worship. And so again, on the other hand, reaction into barrenness of ritual has perverted public worship from its spiritual nature and end.

(6) A clearer conception of worship begins, however, to appear. The Bible has its place in the services; responsive readings, praise, the Lord's Prayer, chanting, organs, in some cases, short liturgies, any thing that may edify in worship, are coming in to give variety and freshness to worship. The admiration of a preacher is giving place to the worship of God in the churches. For it is found that there is no hierarchy in an organ, nor priesthood in a liturgy, nor bondage in responsive readings; but instead, edification of all classes and conditions of men in the worship of God.

§ 147. This variety of services, arising from the liberty of independent churches, raises a question as to the value of liturgies in church services. This is a different question from that which vexed our non-conforming Puritan fathers. They rebelled against a fixed, complete, and enforced liturgy, covering prayers and hymns (§ 61). In our use of rituals and liturgies, we must not forget the price they paid for our liberties. We should remember: —

(1) That no ritual or liturgy has been imposed by Christ Jesus. This is so clearly the case that Dean Stanley quotes "the positive statement of Saint Basil, that there was no written authority for any of the liturgical forms of the Church in his time" (A.D. 329–379).[10] Had any liturgy been imposed by Christ and his apostles, it would have appeared both in the record and in uniformity prior to the fourth and fifth centuries. Nor has Christ given any one the power to enforce liturgies. The local churches are severally independent under Christ, and may not be brought into subjection to any other authority. True, the cut of a vestment is nothing; but when the state or a hierarchy attempts to enforce any style or form, we, like our ecclesiastical fathers, should remember Paul's course, and give place to them, no not for an hour (Gal. 2: 5). Men suffered, and some died, to purchase the liberty to wear or not to wear, as edification might determine, any form of dress, and to use or not to use any ritual, liturgy, service, that may meet the spiritual nature and end of public worship. We have entered into their labors: but any attempt to enforce either the most barren form of service or the most gorgeous liturgy, or any thing between, would arouse the old Puritanic spirit, and set our churches in battle array against it, as of old.

(2) Yet it must be confessed that the synagogue had its ritual; that the heathen temples had their rituals; that the primitive Christians consequently were used to liturgical worship; that they would naturally bring it over, in some of its parts, at least, unless expressly forbidden, into the churches; that there is no such prohibition recorded; that, on the contrary, there are supposed hints of liturgical worship in the New Testament (Acts 2: 42; 4: 24–30; 1 Tim. 3: 16); and that liturgies came early into use and have

[10] Christ. Institutions, 52.

continued in use ever since in the major part, even of the Reformed Churches. Much may be said for them and much against them; but if they were made free and short, so that a part of the services should be liturgical and part extemporaneous, but all optional, the best results would probably follow. This liberty our Congregational churches enjoy, each one regulating its own mode of worship to suit its own wants, and the practice ranges from the baldest service up to the Book of Common Prayer. One church may be better edified with a liturgy, another without one, another with a mixture of both written and extemporaneous forms. One minister may excel in extempore worship, another in reading services. Let each minister and church study the things that edify and save.

(3) It is entirely a wrong view of the matter to identify liturgies with church polity. The right and power to enforce their use is claimed of course by centralized ecclesiastical systems, but this claim is separable from the liturgies themselves. A Congregational church does not lose its independence by adopting a ritual or even the Prayer Book. In the exercise of that independence it controls its own worship for its own edification. This liberty and right needs to be exercised by our churches until they meet all needs arising from the various classes, tastes, gifts, etc., of a versatile civilization. The mode that suits one church may not suit another; very well, let each meet its own needs: in modes of worship diverse, in spirit and polity one. Not ecclesiastically, if historically, is it uncongregational to use a liturgy. The Lutherans have always had a liturgy.

Worship is rooted deepest in renewed human nature, and its heaven-illumined top rises the highest of human acts. Slowly, but surely, in the exercise of liberty, will the churches purify their worship of foreign and hindering elements, until those forms alone remain which conform exactly to the spiritual nature and end of Christian worship. Thus shall the churches worship God more and more in the beauty of holiness.

THE CHURCH SACRAMENTS.

§ 148. The highest part of worship centers in the sacraments. Yet Christendom is divided as to their number and nature.

(1) "The Roman Church, like the Greek, reckons seven sacraments: that is, baptism, confirmation, eucharist, penance, extreme unction, orders, marriage." "But the Romish Church does not attribute an equal dignity to all the seven." "The Protestant Church, including all parties, admit only two: baptism and the holy supper." "The Mennonites join feet-washing (John 13: 5-14) with the sacraments."[11]

(2) We hold the Protestant view to be correct, because only baptism (Matt. 28: 19; Mark 16: 16; John 3: 5; Acts 2: 38, 41; 10: 48; 22: 16) and the Lord's Supper (Matt. 26: 26-30; Mark 14: 22-25; Luke 22: 14-20; 1 Cor. 11: 24-26) are perpetually enjoined, and are of the nature of sacraments.

(*a*) Confirmation is an unction, or chrism, an anointing from the Holy One (1 John 2: 20, 27) or from God (2 Cor. 1: 21), or the conferring of the gifts of the Holy Ghost (Acts 8: 17). There is nothing to indicate that it was commanded, that it was designed to be continued, or that it in its essence has been continued.

(*b*) Not a passage quoted for penance as a sacrament (Mark 1: 4, 5; Matt. 18: 18; John 20: 22, 23; 2 Cor. 7: 10; Acts 10: 43; Ex. 33: 19) indicates that it is more than repentance and forgiveness and the apostolic power of the keys.

(*c*) And the proofs of the sacrament of orders (1 Cor. 6: 1; Acts 20: 28; Titus 1: 5; 1 Tim. 5: 22) prove no more than this, that the Christian Church has a ministerial function, and not that the recognition of such a ministry in ordination is a sacrament.

(*d*) Marriage is as old as Eden, and the references to it relied on to prove it a Christian sacrament (Eph. 5: 31, 32;

[11] Winer's Confessions of Christ. § 14.

Matt. 19: 11, 12; 1 Cor. 7: 8, 9, 32, 33, 38) have no such meaning. The heathen marry and are given in marriage.

(e) There would seem to be more ground for regarding extreme unction as a perpetual duty, though not as a sacrament (Mark 6: 13; James 5: 14, 16), were it not for the fact that it refers to miraculous cures, not to an anointing of the dying. "The prayer of faith shall save him that is sick, and the Lord shall raise him up" (James 5: 15); this is any thing but extreme unction as practised in the churches. Miracles were predicted soon to cease (1 Cor. 13: 8), and they soon ceased.

(f) Feet-washing as a sacrament or rite has had little countenance, although Christ said of it: "For I have given you an example, that ye also should do as I have done to you" (John 13: 15). The churches generally have made this example to cover all menial acts of service for the Master done in humility, and not to mean a sacrament of feet-washing.

As, therefore, there is no proof that these six things — confirmation, penance, orders, marriage, extreme unction, and feet-washing — were designed to be sacraments in the churches, and as they in nature are unlike sacraments, Protestants rightly reject them and hold only two sacraments, baptism and the eucharist.

(3) This view is confirmed by the nature of a sacrament. It is true that the Quakers regard the sacraments as simply inward spiritual rites, and not as outward, visible signs. They say that "baptism is not the washing of the body with water . . . but the powerful work of the Holy Spirit in the hearts of all who submit thereto, refining them from the pollutions of sin. . . . That the communion of the body and blood of Christ is not the partaking of outward bread and wine, but is inward and spiritual, a real participation of his divine nature in measure, through faith in him and obedience to his Spirit in the heart."[12] Hence it is truly said that "the

[12] Hodgson's Hist. Memoirs, 37, 38, who quotes Barklay's Apology, prop. xii, xiii.

Quakers reject both the idea and the name of sacraments."[13] But all Christendom besides regard the sacraments to be outward, visible signs and seals of an inward state and relation. Baptism is the sign and seal of an inward spiritual cleansing, and hence it is called "the washing of regeneration" (Titus 3: 5). So the eucharist expresses the communion of the saints with Christ, and is the sign and seal of their covenant relations with him. That both were regarded as outward and visible signs and seals is proved by the fact that the apostles, after the day of Pentecost, baptized all believers and celebrated with them the Lord's Supper. Of this there can be no reasonable doubt.

BAPTISM.

§ 149. Baptism is an outward initiatory rite standing at the door of the visible churches. It is the sign of spiritual cleansing, and so of fitness to enter into the visible household of saints.

(1) Baptism supersedes circumcision as the sign and seal of the covenant of promise. God entered into a formal covenant with Abraham, and with his seed after him (Gen. 15: 7-21), whose sign and seal he afterwards made to be circumcision (Gen. 17: 10-14). This "covenant confirmed beforehand by God, the law, which came four hundred and thirty years after, doth not disannul, so as to make the promise of none effect" (Gal. 3: 17). Hence the covenant of promise abides still; and if so, then its sign and seal, so that if we are Christ's, then we are Abraham's seed, and heirs according to promise (Gal. 3: 22-29). Christ ordered all his disciples to be baptized (Matt. 28: 19); his apostles, under the guidance of the Holy Spirit, set aside circumcision as no longer treated by Christ as the sign and seal of the covenant (Acts 15: 1, 28, 29), baptism having taken its place. Paul's words are conclusive here: "In whom [Christ] ye were also circumcised with a circumcision not made with hands, in the

[11] **Winer's Confessions of Christ. § 14.**

putting off of the body of the flesh, in the circumcision of Christ; having been buried with him in baptism, wherein ye were also raised with him through faith in the working of God, who raised him from the dead" (Col. 2: 11, 12). Thus "the circumcision of Christ" is baptism, receiving which, one receives the sign and seal of the covenant of promise. The command of Peter to baptize the uncircumcised Cornelius (Acts 10: 47), instead of circumcising him, for the first time indicated the supersedure of circumcision by baptism. The rite of blood, confined to males, was given that "Abraham might be the father of all them that believe" (Rom. 4: 11); yet believing Gentiles were only required to be baptized, a sign and seal applied to males and females, Jews and Gentiles. Every-where thereafter baptism is put as the substitute for circumcision in admitting believers into covenant relations with God. It became, and has ever continued, the initiatory rite, the sign and seal of the covenant of promise.

(2) Hence baptism is required of believers in Christ Jesus, as circumcision was required from Abraham to Pentecost. The initiatory rite was an everlasting ordinance, as the covenant was everlasting (Gen. 17: 13), and Christ enjoined its new form upon all disciples (Matt. 28: 19; Mark 16: 16), and no one, Jew or Gentile, joined the church after Pentecost but through baptism (Acts 2: 38, 41; 10: 48; 22: 16, etc.). Those who before that day believed were, as we have shown (§§ 39, 105), separated by the winnowing-fan of Christ into the spiritual *kahal* of Israel, which became on Pentecost the Christian *ecclesia*, or church-kingdom. They were the church, and needed not to join it. All others were left outside as rejected Jews or unconverted Gentiles. The circumcision of the rejected availed them nothing (1 Cor. 7: 19; Gal. 5: 6; 6: 15), and so, on believing, they renewed the covenant in baptism.

(3) John's baptism was not Christian baptism. The apostles generally had been baptized unto repentance, but John the Baptist lived and died under the law of Moses, as Christ

himself did. The preaching and the baptism of the forerunner were preparatory. This baptism unto repentance availed nothing under Christ. As a rite it was not enough. This is put beyond question by the twelve disciples whom Paul found at Ephesus. They had been baptized "into John's baptism" only, and when he knew it, he commanded them to be baptized also "into the name of the Lord Jesus" (Acts 19: 1-7).

Thus all believers after Pentecost entered the visible churches through the door of baptism. This substitute for circumcision as the sign and seal of the covenant became the initiatory rite of the Christian churches.

§ 150. But what are the essential elements of true baptism? What constitutes valid baptism? This is a practical question.

(1) Water is the element used, and the purer the better. One must be "born of water and the Spirit" (John 3: 5). Water was always used in baptism (Acts 8: 36, 38; 10: 47), living or running water. "But if thou have not living water, baptize into other water; but if thou canst not in cold, in warm."[14]

(2) There must be the intent to baptize. No mock baptism is valid. This intent ought to include all parties to the rite. Neither of them may be worthy, but they should religiously intend to do what they do. Yet, if the administrator be an impostor, or the recipient a hypocrite, if the rite be performed as a religious ceremony with intent of baptism, the baptism is valid.

(3) Baptism must be into the name of the Father, and of the Son, and of the Holy Ghost; that is, it must be into the Trinity (Matt. 28: 19). This is twice repeated in "The Teaching of the Twelve Apostles," in the four verses of the seventh chapter. Unitarian baptism is not, therefore, valid; but the baptism of the Greek, the Roman Catholic, and all Protestant churches that use the Trinitarian formula is valid, if with intent.

[14] Teaching Twelve Apostles, chap. vii.

(4) Hence baptism should be but once administered. If one has been baptized, with intent, into the name of the Trinity, he should not be baptized again. Thus a Roman Catholic should be received without rebaptism. This is the almost unanimous view, though Presbyterians reject it by a divided vote.[15] Those not baptized into the name of Christ need to be so baptized (Acts 19: 4, 5). In case one has been baptized in infancy and desires confession in baptism, there is no prohibition against such rebaptism, though his infant baptism is valid. It is better that he be rebaptized than that he should be kept out of church relations. Quakers have never been baptized.

§ 151. The mode of baptism is various. The Greek Church uses trine immersion; all Baptist churches, and some others, single immersion; the Roman Catholic Church, and most Protestant communions, sprinkling. The New Testament does not determine the mode or lay stress on it. "The Teaching of the Twelve Apostles," which goes back quite, or near, to the death of the apostle John, says: "Baptize into the name of the Father, and of the Son, and of the Holy Spirit, in living [or running] water. But if thou have not living water, baptize into other water; and if thou canst not in cold, in warm. But if thou have not either, pour out water thrice upon the head into the name of Father, and Son, and Holy Spirit."[16] This confirms the view of church historians that "the usual form of baptism was immersion. . . . But sprinkling also, or copious pouring rather, was practised at an early day with sick and dying persons, and probably with children and others, where total or partial immersion was impracticable."[17] The mode of baptism is declared by God, in the gift of his Spirit in regeneration and sanctification and revivals, to be non-essential. The rule by which the apostles and the churches settled the question of circumcision (Acts 11: 15-18; 15: 7-11, 24-29) settles also

---

[15] Moore's Presby. Digest (1873), 660; Hodge's Church Polity, 196, seq.
[16] Chap. vii.   [17] Schaff's Hist. Christ. Ch. 1, 468, 469.

MODE OF BAPTISM. 211

the question of the mode of baptism. Indeed, that rule remands the dispute as to the mode to the limbo of dead issues. And we may say to those who insist that immersion alone is baptism, what Peter said to the Judaizing Christians in the council at Jerusalem: "Why tempt ye God, that ye should put a yoke upon the neck of the disciples?" since God makes "no difference between us and them, cleansing their hearts by faith" (Acts 15: 9, 10). As all modes are thus recognized by God as valid, churches should not scruple to baptize by immersion or affusion or sprinkling, as the subject may desire.

§ 152. There is still an unended controversy over the subjects of baptism.

(1) All are agreed that unbaptized converts should be baptized before admission to church privileges. All communions, except the Quakers, make baptism the indispensable initiatory rite into membership.

(2) The infant children of believers should be baptized. Here lies the contention, the Baptist churches on one side, all other communions on the other side and in favor of such baptism. If baptism takes the place of circumcision, as we have stated (§ 149: 1), then infant baptism follows logically, as the children are included with their parents in the terms of the covenant of grace. The Baptists reject infant baptism on the ground that it wants positive commandment and tends to corrupt the churches. Other communions believe in and practise it on the ground that no positive command is needed, since baptism takes the place of circumcision, as Sunday takes the place of the Sabbath, without positive commandment. On the same principle, no command was given to baptize children, because the covenant itself applied its seal to children by express command (Gen. 17: 12); and because Paul puts all Christians under the Abrahamic covenant (Gal. 3: 7, 29). In harmony therewith we read of the baptism of households (Acts 16: 15, 33; 1 Cor. 1: 16), and the express teaching: "For the unbelieving husband is sanc-

tified in the wife, and the unbelieving wife is sanctified in the brother: else were your children unclean; but now are they holy" (1 Cor. 7: 14). It does not appear easy to break this chain, when we add to it the words of the Master: "Suffer the little children, and forbid them not, to come unto me: for of such is the kingdom of heaven" (Matt. 19: 14). This is confirmed by the silence of the early Christian writers. Infant baptism seems to have displaced infant circumcision so naturally that when it for the first time is referred to by them, it is neither attacked nor defended, as if it were a new and unusual thing, but instead, is spoken of as a common practice. Tertullian (A.D. 145-220) says that "the delay of baptism is preferable; principally, however, in the case of little children."[18] Later, infant baptism is enjoined: "Do you also baptize your infants, and bring them up in the nurture and admonition of God."[19] Liberty, however, should be allowed on this point, both of belief and of practice.

(3) The children of other than pious parents may not be baptized. This is the position of the Reformed Churches, since they regard baptism as the sign and seal of covenant relations, which makes their children alone holy (1 Cor. 7: 14);[20] and it is the position of our churches.[21] Those not in covenant relations with God can not of course claim or share in the promises, nor properly engage to train their children in "the chastening and admonition of the Lord" (Eph. 6: 4). Their unbelief does not sanctify their seed. The Roman Catholics, believing that baptism is necessary unto salvation, permit the children of those outside their communion to be baptized, and that, too, in peril, by any body. Some Lutherans hold that all children are by birth, through the abounding grace of God in Christ Jesus (Rom. 5: 12-21), brought into covenant relations with God, and consequently are entitled to the sign and seal in baptism, what-

---

[18] On Baptism, xviii.   [19] Apostolical Constitutions, book vi, chap. xv.
[20] Moore's Presby. Digest, 663, 664.   [21] Camb. Confession, chap. xxix, 4.

ever their parents may be. Hence they would baptize all infants. If any do not grow up to be true disciples, it is because they have apostatized. It is not wise to press the position of the Reformed Churches with such rigor as not to baptize dying children of believing parents who are not members, but who stand ready to become members. Yet an indiscriminate baptism of infants is unwarranted and pernicious, and should therefore be avoided.

§ 153. The relation of baptized children to the Church is of great importance, since a false relation easily corrupts the churches and becomes the strong argument of the opponents of infant baptism. Historically, infant baptism has corrupted the churches. But does the normal relation of baptized children to the churches corrupt the churches and fill them with unconverted members? We believe not. But, in answer, let us consider the actual and possible relations of baptized children to the churches.

(1) It might be held that baptism makes children full members in the church and entitles them to all the rights and privileges of the church. This would seem to be the view of the Greek Church, which administers the eucharist to babies; but still it holds to the sacrament of confirmation. The same would seem to follow from the doctrine of baptismal regeneration, since confirmation is reduced by that doctrine from a testing as to the fitness of the candidates and approval of the worthy, to a formal ceremony, the candidates having been already fitted for the visible Church by baptismal regeneration. Still, confirmation is held and practised where baptismal regeneration is taught,[22] perhaps as an ancient and episcopal recognition of said regeneration.

---

[22] The Trinity Church Catechism teaches respecting baptism: —
"*What are we made thereby?*
Members of Christ's body, the Church.
What is the result of this?
We become God's adopted children, and heirs of heaven.
And what else?
We are cleansed from sin, and our bodies are made temples of the Holy Ghost," p. 47.

(2) Baptism with confirmation makes children full members of the Church. Here confirmation is separated from baptism, and is to be applied to youth, on approval. With those who hold to baptismal regeneration, it is a rite for the invigoration of the spiritual life begun in baptism as the effect of baptism, and should be administered to all baptized children as the logical consequence of baptism, bringing them into full membership in the visible Church. This theory of baptism and confirmation would put all the children of Christian parents into the Church, good and bad alike, and has been one of the chief causes of the corruption of the churches in past and present times. By it the whole population soon becomes church members, while bearing few or none of the fruits of faith and the Spirit (Matt. 7: 15-23; Gal. 5: 22-24). The charge that infant baptism corrupts the churches finds here its cause and ample justification.

But there might be a sufficient guard to purity here, if confirmation should be made a proper test of religious faith and experience, as it could easily be made. If at the proper age of discretion, candidates were to be examined as to the fact of a changed heart and life, and admitted or rejected according to the evidence, confirmation added to infant baptism would in such case be as sure a guard to purity as a similar testing without infant baptism could possibly be.

(3) Baptism makes children presumptive members of the church, so that, if free from scandal and possessed of sufficient intelligence, they may become full members. This is the position of the Presbyterian and Reformed Churches. "Children born within the pale of the visible Church, and dedicated to God in baptism, are under the inspection and government of the Church. . . . And when they come to years of discretion, if they be free from scandal, appear sober and steady, and to have sufficient knowledge to discern the Lord's body, they ought to be informed it is their duty and privilege to come to the Lord's Supper."[23] For "all baptized

[23] Presby. Directory for Worship, chap. ix, 1.

persons are members of the church, are under its care and subject to its care and discipline; and when they have arrived at the years of discretion, they are bound to perform all the duties of church members."[24] These baptized children, who are members of the church, are not required to "make a public profession of their faith in the presence of the congregation," for only unbaptized persons are required to do this.[25] This position rests on the church membership of baptized children and on the presumption that they are, unless scandalous, regenerate persons, fit at discretion for full communion and membership. It has proved no better guard than confirmation, except where modified, as among the New School Presbyterians in this country, by another theory. At this point of the relation of baptized children to the Church, the Congregational churches took decided and radical issue with the Presbyterians. They did not hold such children to be in full membership, nor that they were presumptively regenerate persons, nor that they should be admitted to church privileges without public profession; but they held that: —

(4) Baptism with public confession of Christ makes them full church members. The children, in virtue of the covenant, may receive the sign and seal; but because the Church is a spiritual body whose members are holy (§ 94), the baptized children, like the unbaptized adults, "must credibly show and profess their own repentance towards God and faith towards our Lord Jesus Christ, before they come to the Lord's table, or are recognized as members in full communion"; "and otherwise they are not to be admitted thereunto."[26] This has been the Congregational position from the beginning, except as partially suspended for a brief period by what is known as the Half-way Covenant. This position regards baptized children as children of the Church, not as full members, until they give credible proof of con-

---

[24] Presby. Discipline, chap. 1, vi.
[25] Presby. Directory of Worship, chap. ix, iv.
[26] Camb. Plat. xii, 7; Boston Plat. part. ii, chap. vii, 4.

version and publicly confess Christ. No church requires more than this for adult baptism. Hence no guard to purity can be stronger than this. Nor is this a recently assumed position. It is one of the points that divided the Congregationalists and Presbyterians from the beginning. It separates the former also from all other old communions.

(5) The only remaining relation of children to the Church is that of consecration in baptism. This consecration gives no membership in the Church, but leaves the children in this regard as though they had not been baptized. This consecration seems foreign to the covenant of grace. Infant baptism is more than this, or it is not baptism.

(6) The Baptist position that children hold no relation to the Church of God is contrary to the covenant which binds the three dispensations into one. That covenant from the beginning embraced the seed of the pious. It was expressly made to embrace them when renewed with Abraham, and later with the children of Israel at Sinai. Children are not expressly excluded from, but are presumptively included in, the covenant which is continued into and completed in the Christian dispensation. This presumption has convinced the vast majority of Christian churches that God cares still for the children of his people.

This beautiful rite of infant baptism need not subvert the holy nature of the churches. The children thus presented are not made church members, can not become full members until they publicly profess their faith in Christ; yet they are the children of the Church, to be enrolled, watched over, and cared for, trained up for Christ, and so fitted for the public confession. It is needful, therefore, that a church keep a roll of its baptized children, and provide special means for their Christian nurture.

THE LORD'S SUPPER.

§ 154. The second sacrament of the churches is the Lord's Supper, or the eucharist, the communion. It is called "the Lord's Supper" (1 Cor. 11 : 20) because it is eating and drinking together as the Lord ordained. It was early named the eucharist,[27] from the prayers of thanksgiving that precede it. It is also called the communion, or the holy communion, because it is the communion of the body and blood of Christ (1 Cor. 10 : 16), and the fellowship of believers together and with their Head. Each name brings into prominence some essential element of the feast, and is therefore appropriate.

(1) It is the ordinance that commemorates the dying love and sacrifice of Christ for the sins of the world. It is not a sacrifice or a bloodless propitiatory offering up of the body and blood of Christ (§ 112: 4). It should never therefore be spoken of as the mass or a sacrifice. It is a memorial feast; for in it we "proclaim the Lord's death till he come." It is also a sign and seal of the covenant of promise. Hence it is enjoined as a perpetual requirement (1 Cor. 11 : 25, 26).

(2) This sacrament supersedes the passover. It was instituted when Jesus had eaten the Jewish feast with the Twelve and the traitor had withdrawn (Matt. 26 : 20 ; Mark 14: 20; John 13: 30; Matt. 26 : 26–29). Christ was himself the Paschal Lamb sacrificed for sin (John 1: 29; 1 Cor. 5: 7). The passover as a sacrifice was fulfilled and abolished in his death; but as a feast of thankful commemoration, it is still continued in the Lord's Supper.

(3) Unlike baptism, this sign and seal of the covenant is to be often repeated; but how often has not been revealed. "As often as" implies, however, frequency. It was at the first probably observed daily, then weekly. In some churches it is now celebrated weekly; in others, monthly; in others, bi-monthly; but in others less frequently. A bi-monthly observance avoids the evils of a too common observance and the evils of infrequent communions.

(4) The elements to be used in the eucharist are bread and the juice of the grape. Christ used, we believe, unleavened bread and wine. Leavened bread is now generally

[27] Teaching Twelve Apostles, chap. ix; Ignatius, Ep. Phil. iv.

used, and wine or the unfermented juice of the grape. Christ in instituting the supper did not use the word wine. Nothing but the juice of the grape in wine or in some other form should ever be employed, never water or any other liquid.

(5) The mode of celebrating the eucharist is quite diverse, although the way Christ instituted it is well-nigh certain. He was in an upper room, reclining with the eleven at a table in the ordinary mode of eating at that time. Why such stress is laid on the mode of baptism, when that mode is not specified, and so little stress is laid on the mode of the eucharist, when that mode is well-nigh certain, seems indeed strange. Yet Baptists do not recline when they celebrate. They, with others, sit in pews; others partake standing or kneeling; none reclining. The mode has in all cases been changed, but the substance has been retained. The bread and the cup in all communions but that of the Quakers "proclaim the Lord's death till he come."

(6) The sacrament was instituted in two kinds, was commanded in both the bread and the cup (Matt. 26: 27; Mark 14: 23; 1 Cor. 11: 26), and should be administered to all in both kinds. "It was the frequent accidental spilling of drops of wine at the eucharist that first led to the withholding of the cup from the laity."[28] So also the non-officiating Roman priests only partake in one kind.[29] Protestants are right in returning to the way commanded by the Master of the feast.

§ 155. The question about who may commune in this most holy sacrament has more vital bearings than might be supposed. It needs, therefore, careful examination.

(1) Communicants are regulated by different conditions in the various communions. Neither the Roman Catholics nor the Baptists extend the privileges of this sacrament beyond their own membership. They are close communionists.

[28] Fisher's Discussions in Hist. and Theol. 60.
[29] Winer's Conf. Christendom, 278.

This is probably true also of the Greek Church, the Ritualists, and some others. Other churches hold intercommunion at the table of the Lord, inviting members of other denominations to partake with them. But all exclude unbelievers, heretics, excommunicates, and, except the Greek Church, infants.

(2) They agree in requiring the following things as conditions of participation: —

(a) The communicant must, in the eye of charity, be a believer in Christ. He must by faith be a member of the body of Christ, a citizen of the church-kingdom. The communions differ widely as to this faith or belief and its proof, but all communicants must possess it in some degree and form. To an unbeliever it may be a memorial, but it can not be a communion. Faith is essential.

(b) Baptism is also a necessary preliminary of the eucharist. It is made the first outward duty of the believer (Matt. 28: 19; Mark 16: 16; Acts 2: 38, 41; 8: 38; 9: 18; 10: 48; 16: 15, 33; 19: 4, 5). "Baptism was, by divine precept, the necessary condition of entrance into the Christian Church," says the Roman Catholic historian, Alzog.[30] "Christians of every name, from the apostolic age to the present, with hardly a dissentient voice, have declared baptism to be a prerequisite of the eucharist." "In no case is the Lord's Supper put before baptism, in no case does the narrative recognize any interval between faith and baptism to be filled by the Lord's Supper."[31]

(c) Church membership is implied in baptism as a condition indispensable for partaking of the emblems. Believers were added to the churches by baptism. That rite admitted them to visible membership therein. "In no case are believers brought into the church and afterwards baptized." "Uniting with a local church is, therefore, the immediate sequence and, as it were, the natural counterpart of the baptismal vow."[32]

[30] Universal Ch. Hist. 1, § 55, 277. [31] 19 Bib. Sacra, 145, 151. [32] Ibid. 145, 153.

(d) These three conditions are confirmed by reference to the Jewish passover, which the Lord's Supper supplanted and continues. The passover was instituted at the beginning of the exodus, B.C. 1491, or 1648. Only full members of the *kahal*, or congregation, of Israel could partake of the passover. "A sojourner and an hired servant shall not eat thereof. . . . All the congregation of Israel shall keep it. And when a stranger shall sojourn with thee, and will keep the passover to the Lord, let all his males be circumcised, and then let him come near and keep it; and he shall be as one that is born in the land: but no uncircumcised person shall eat thereof. One law shall be to him that is homeborn, and unto the stranger that sojourneth among you" (Ex. 12: 45–49). Faith is here required, for the passover must be kept "to the Lord," circumcision, and full membership in the congregation of Israel, for the circumcised stranger became as one born in the land. No one could thus partake of the passover who wished, until he had complied with the initiatory rite, which also involved belief in the God of the Jews and admitted to the *kahal* of Israel. Females are included in the consecration and circumcision of the males.

(3) These terms, or conditions, are confirmed by the Scriptures and history. Here we may note: —

(a) That Judas Iscariot ate the passover with Christ, but withdrew before the institution of the Lord's Supper (Matt. 26: 20; Mark 14: 17; John 13: 30; Matt. 26: 26-29). This seems to have been the order of events as held by the ablest harmonists and commentators. Thus we are relieved of the repugnant thought that the traitor partook of the sacrament of the supper with the Betrayed. The guiltiest of men did not probably mar with his presence this holiest of rites.

(b) The primitive churches excluded from the room all who were not full church members. "But let no one eat or drink of your eucharist, except those baptized into the name of the Lord: for as regards this, the Lord hath said:

'Give not that which is holy to the dogs.' "[33] Justin Martyr (A.D. 110–165) says: "And this food is called among us *Eucharistia*, of which no one is allowed to partake but the man who believes that the things which we teach are true, and who has been washed with the washing that is for the remission of sins and unto regeneration, and who is so living as Christ has enjoined. For not as common bread and common drink do we receive them."[34] The Divine Liturgy of James excludes catechumens, the unbaptized, and all unable to join in the prayers, from the room where the eucharist is celebrated. An inspection of those present was required.[35] So the Apostolical Constitutions (A.D. 200–400) says: "But we do not receive them to communion until they have received the seal of baptism and are made complete Christians."[36] "Let the door be watched, lest any unbeliever, or one not yet initiated, come in."[37] "Those that first come to the mystery of godliness (the eucharist), let them be brought to the bishop, or to the presbytery, by the deacons, and let them be examined as to the causes wherefore they come to the Word of the Lord; and let those that bring them exactly inquire about their character, and give them their testimony."[38] This examination is then detailed.

(c) This position is confirmed by the nature of the case, both as to privileges and as to discipline. The prime condition of the existence and prosperity of any organized society is that it furnishes its members privileges which it neither offers to others nor permits them to share. All organizations rest on this common-sense principle, and the primitive churches guarded their most sacred privileges even from the gaze of all not in full membership, as a thing demanded, as the condition of their continuance and growth. The requirements of discipline demand the same. If a church excommunicate a member, it not only nullifies its action, but stulti-

[33] Teaching Twelve Apostles, chap. ix.   [34] Apol. i, chap. lxvi.
[35] § 16.   [36] Book ii, chap. xxxix.   [37] Ibid. lvii.
[38] Ibid. book viii, chap. xxxii.

fies itself, if such an excommunicate be permitted to come to the Lord's table the same as before. To permit him to commune would turn discipline into a farce; and yet some have presumed to set Scripture, history, and common sense aside, and opened the door to all who desire to commune. This position logically ends in one of two things: either in the extinction of the churches that adopt it, or in turning them into parish churches, including the whole community of worshipers as members.[39]

(*d*) In 1865 our churches in National Council re-affirmed the position taken in 1648, in the Cambridge Platform, and declared that not only unbaptized adults, but also baptized children, "must credibly show and profess their own repentance towards God and faith towards our Lord Jesus Christ, before they come to the Lord's table."[40] A few churches have foolishly ventured to open the table of our Lord to all who claim to love him. The result will be evil, and only evil. Even in the case of fresh converts, it is better for their Christian nurture that they wait in patience until they can commune in an orderly way, than that the church should set them an example of disorder on the threshold of their entrance into it. They should be taught that the good order of the church is more than their convenience, not that their convenience is to override church rules or necessary usages.

(4) But these terms or conditions of communion — faith, baptism, church membership — may not be increased. They can not be enlarged at pleasure. No church can rightly bar from its communion by unscriptural tests, — such as total

---

[39] The Arlington Street Unitarian Church of Boston, in 1870, opened the eucharist to all who wished to commune, whether members of any church or not. But for thirteen years no one joined the said church; and to prevent its members from becoming too few to administer certain trust funds, it voted, in 1884, that all persons of full age who habitually attended its services should be regarded as members, and should have their names entered on the roll of the church as full members, unless they declined to be so enrolled. — *The Congregationalist*, May 15, 1884. This is the logical end of such looseness. Hence the communions which have opened this sacrament to all report not "churches," but "societies," their churches having largely become parish societies.

[40] Boston Plat. part ii, vii, 4.

abstinence, the singing of the Psalms only in church worship, the immersion of believers in baptism, and the like, — for such legislation has not been granted it. The Lord and King can alone make laws for the guidance of his own. Churches have no right therefore to exclude from their communion the members of other churches which God recognizes as his churches by the gift of the Holy Spirit. If God never recognized as his, by revivals and the fruits of the Holy Spirit, churches that sing hymns, or used intoxicating liquors, or baptized by sprinkling or pouring, then his true churches would be justified in imposing such terms as tests of communion; but since God makes no such distinction, his churches should not. This reasoning is Scriptural, reasonable, and conclusive. It is that which was used in settling the dispute about circumcision in the days of the apostles. When Peter was brought before the church at Jerusalem for his visit to the Roman Cornelius, he vindicated himself by his vision, and by the fact that God gave unto the uncircumcised the like gift as he did unto the circumcised, and asked: "Who was I, that I could withstand God?" (Acts 11: 1-18). The controversy that caused the council at Jerusalem was settled on the same principle exactly, that God, in the gift of his Spirit, "made no distinction between" the one side and the other, cleansing the hearts of all by faith (Acts 15: 9, 28, 29). So we say to all who insist on tests which God does not command or regard: "Why tempt ye God in so doing?" And there is no answer; for God knows the hearts of men and the bearing of acts, and where he makes no distinction his churches can claim no right to make one. When God makes immersion necessary unto the gift of his Spirit, his churches may make it necessary unto communion; but not till then. And so of all other terms of communion.

This argument covers all doctrines, rites, ceremonies, and polities. It covers also all organizations and unorganized believers. At first the test was more easily applied than afterwards, for the gift of the Spirit was then attended with miraculous powers (Acts 2: 4; 8: 17–19), but not in later times. Yet here time reveals the gift of the Spirit in revivals and graces, or the absence of these shows that the Spirit is withheld.

§ 156. The invitation to the eucharist should be conformed to these terms or prerequisites. It should include only such as have confessed their love for Christ in baptism and are in orderly connection with some evangelical church. The invitation should not ignore faith, baptism, and church membership, but treat them all as prerequisites.

(1) This is the common invitation: "All members in good standing in sister and evangelical churches are cordially invited to commune with us," or words to the same effect. It should have regard for three essential things: (*a*) church membership, which implies faith and baptism; (*b*) the evangelical faith; and (*c*) church discipline.

But it is sometimes said that the table is the Lord's, and that therefore whosoever will may freely partake. But the Church is also the Lord's, and on the same principle any body and every body may join it, without conditions, who will. The communion table is no more the Lord's than the local church. The Lord has imposed conditions for admission to each (§§ 94: 2 (*b*); 155: 2), and it is the duty of every church to enforce them. Unless a church can open its doors to every body, it can not its communion table. It has the same right and power of exclusion from one as from the other. If no restriction can be placed on communicants, none can be or will be placed on membership. If the responsibility be thrown upon each individual to commune or not, as he likes, then the Church vacates its divine authority and admits excommunicates, those who deny the Lord that bought them with his precious blood, and infidels, to its holiest act of communion and worship. It is no justification for the Church to say: "The fault is not ours, but that of the unworthy communicant"; for the fault lies partly in the invitation it gives. It is not only the right, but also the duty, of a church to use the authority given it in keeping its highest act of worship free from the enemies of the cross of Christ, as the apostles and primitive churches did; and it must not open the door by its invitation to such enemies.

(2) Nor can the pastor presume to control the invitation to the eucharist. He is not the church; he is not greater than the church. He has no right to alter or set aside the customary invitation of a church to the supper, much less the Scriptural conditions of communion. If a pastor usurp such authority, the church should at once curb his papal pretensions.

A church should control its invitation to the Lord's Supper, and should make it conform to the prerequisites above given, and allow no pastor to alter or neglect said invitation.[41]

§ 157. The question, Who shall administer the sacraments? has very important ecclesiastical bearings. Does their efficacy depend upon the administrator? and, if so, in what sense?

(1) In ordinary circumstances ordained ministers should administer the sacraments. There is, in the churches a ministerial function (§ 113), recognized by the churches in ordination (§ 121), and good order requires that those thus recognized should ordinarily administer both sacraments. "The ministerial authority committed to the pastorate consists, on Romish and Protestant principles, in the preaching of the Word, the administration of the sacraments,"[42] etc. "The mother confession of Protestantism" declares "that no man should publicly in the church teach, or administer the sacraments, except he be rightly called."[43] Our platforms teach that the work of the ministry is, among other things, "to administer the seals of that covenant, unto the dispensation whereof they are alike called;"[44] "to administer the sacraments."[45] All the communions which believe in a ministerial function recognized in ordination

[41] 20 Cong. Quarterly, 275, seq. [42] Winer's Confessions of Christ. § 20.
[43] Augsburg Conf. xiv. [44] Camb. Plat. vi, 5. [45] Boston Plat. part ii, iv, 4.

hold also that "it is a matter of propriety and order that the sacraments should be administered by those only who have been duly called and appointed to that service." [46]

The apostles seem to have left baptism largely to others to administer (Acts 10: 48; 1 Cor. 1: 17), as Christ had left it to his disciples (John 4: 2); for their chief business was preaching and founding churches, not in baptizing converts. They committed the administration of the sacraments to the ordinary and permanent ministry, with whom it has since remained.

(2) Yet laymen may sometimes administer the sacraments. Deacons, Presbyterian ruling elders, and licentiates are laymen; and they, as also other laymen, may sometimes, in emergencies, administer. Tertullian (A.D. 145-220) said: "Besides these [bishops, presbyters, and deacons], even laymen have the right [to baptize]; for what is equally received can be equally given. . . . The word of the Lord ought not to be hidden by any; in like manner, too, baptism, which is equally God's property, can be administered by all." [47] Hatch says: "Baptism by an ordinary member of the church was held to be valid." "The functions which the officers performed were such as, apart from the question of order, might be performed by any member of the community." [48]

(3) The validity and efficacy of the sacraments do not depend on the administrator. This is admitted by all communions. "The Roman and Greek Churches permit, under pressing circumstances, baptism by unordained hands, including those of the midwife, or even of persons not Christian, as Jews, infidels, and heretics. The Reformed Church has declared against this baptism in distress." [49] "Lutherans and Reformed agree in teaching that the efficacy of the sacraments does not depend on any thing in him who administers them." [50] The communions that regard the ministry as a

[46] Hodge's System. Theology, iii, 514.
[47] On Baptism, xvii.
[48] Org. Early Christ. Chhs. 115, 123.
[49] Winer's Conf. Christ. xx.
[50] Hodge's System. Theology, iii, 514.

priesthood, the communion table an altar, and the bread and wine a veritable propitiatory sacrifice, permit only priestly hands to administer the eucharist; and Protestants generally hold that, while the efficacy of a sacrament does not depend on the administrator, good order requires that laymen administer only under the following conditions: —

(*a*) There must be some pressing exigency demanding extraordinary relief. No gulf could be wider than that put by the Roman Catholic Church between its priesthood and its laity; yet, its doctrine that baptism is necessary unto salvation,[51] allows, in case of imminent death, that gulf to be bridged, so that women, Jews, heretics, and infidels may administer valid baptism. The exigency here is the eternal loss of a soul, unless such baptism be administered, though it be that of a babe a few minutes old. There is no such pressing exigency among Protestants, who reject the Romish dogma of infant damnation in all cases where baptism is not administered; but there may arise circumstances which warrant lay administration. The inconvenience of a delay or an exchange, or both, does not, however, create such exigency. A licentiate should exchange rather than administer, even though the eucharist be postponed for a Sunday or two. The Pilgrims at Plymouth are a worthy example. They waited nearly five years without the sacraments before they wrote their pastor in Holland about the propriety of their ruling elder administering the sealing ordinances. John Robinson replied to Brewster: "I judge it not lawful for you — being a ruling elder — . . . as opposed to the elders that teach and labor in word and doctrine — to which the sacraments are annexed — to administer them [the sacraments], nor convenient [expedient], if it were lawful."[52] This patient waiting exhibits a strength of character and adhesion to principle which made that Pilgrim church a pattern and model for all the churches of the Bay Colony, and

---
[51] Council of Trent, on Baptism, canon v.
[52] Quoted from Dr. Bacon's Genesis of New England Churches, 402, 403.

whose "form of worship" the churches of Massachusetts "universally followed." [53]

(*b*) The church must recognize this exigency and empower a layman to administer. When an emergency or exigency arises the church will know it, and, after due patience, if it be not removed, the church can, by vote or general consent, empower a layman to administer baptism or the eucharist, or both; but no licentiate or deacon or other layman should presume to administer on his own option. The emergency must be sufficient, in the judgment of the membership, to justify the departure from the usual order; lest a division of opinion disturb the peace of the church.[54]

(4) It was not essential to the validity of circumcision that it be performed by a priest, and no priest was required to be present at the eating of the passover, and no priest was present at the synagogue worship; and in the churches of Christ no ordained ministry is essential for their worship, or for baptism, or for the eucharist. Yet, as Christ has appointed a ministerial function in his churches, and calls men to exercise that function, and has given his churches the right to recognize those he calls in ordination, good order and propriety require that public worship, baptism, and the Lord's Supper be committed into the hands of this ministry, except in the most pressing exigencies.

[53] Hutchinson's Hist. Mass. 1, 369.
[54] See 17 Cong. Quarterly, 525, seq.

LECTURE IX.

THE DOCTRINE OF THE CHRISTIAN CHURCH.—DISCIPLINE.

"*Brethren, even if a man be overtaken in any trespass, ye which are spiritual, restore such an one in the spirit of meekness; looking to thyself, lest thou also be tempted.*"—Saint Paul.

"*If any one cometh unto you, and bringeth not this teaching, receive him not into your house, and give him no greeting: for he that giveth him greeting partaketh in his evil works.*"—Saint John.

§ 158. In a church society with members, officers, worship, sacraments, limitations of action, it is manifest that the divine instructions respecting its nature, materials, management, and relations need to be gathered into a creed, covenant, and rules, which may be called its book of discipline. Such a standard promotes not only decorum, but also justice, purity, peace, and efficiency. If the discipline be not formulated in some recognized standard, confusion and decay follow. That standard may be written or traditional, long or short, rigid or free; but no church can long survive without such recognized rules of procedure. We call such standard the discipline of that church. It includes the general management as well as the dealing with offences, and may consequently be divided into two departments.

So uniformity of procedure among churches is desirable; not an enforced uniformity such as drove our ecclesiastical fathers out of England, but a voluntary uniformity, such as independent, yet affiliated, churches may agree upon. Otherwise unnecessary confusion arises. Thus, though fleeing from enforced uniformity, the General Court of the Colony of the Massachusetts Bay, in 1635, entreated "the elders and brethren of every church within this jurisdiction" "to consult and advise of one uniform order of discipline in the churches, agreeable to the Scriptures, and then to consider how far the magistrates are bound to interpose for the preservation of that uniformity and peace of the churches."[1]

§ 159. The general conduct of the affairs of a church comes under the comprehensive name discipline. We may notice briefly a few things here.

(1) The order of church services concerns the church more vitally than many imagine. As those services are for edification (§ 144: 2), and not for the convenience of the pastor, it is for the church to determine what shall go into the order of worship, and how that order shall be arranged. No material change should be made in that order without the vote of the church.

(2) So the times of regular and special meetings, whether for worship or for business, should be fixed by the church — regular meetings by rule, and special meetings by vote; so that the church will feel that such meetings are theirs, to be attended and sustained.

(3) The pastor is the presiding officer in all church meetings that do not concern himself. Meetings held about a call, discipline, dismissal, and salary of a pastor are matters in which the pastor is so intimately concerned that propriety forbids his presiding while they are under consideration. The pastor needs to be versed in parliamentary usages, that he may observe the rules that make for peace. If he trample on rules of order, he thereby trains the church to lawlessness. Instead, he should train all to do the business of the church in a legal way. Hence the church should adopt rules to guide him.

The church should adopt and give to every member and officer rules for their guidance, called standing rules, defining what, when, and how business should be done. And such rules ought to be scrupulously observed in times of peace, that they may be observed in times of trouble; for rules broken in peace can not be enforced in strife. A church well disciplined in this regard is like a ship manned by trained men, able to weather storms that wreck others.

[1] Records of the Colony, I, 143.

STANDING RULES. 231

(4) The importance of regularity in all business meetings of the church needs to be emphasized. These meetings ought not to depend upon the presence of a pastor, but be held whether he be present or not, whether the church has a pastor or not. Most unhappily the thought of some churches is so centered on their pastors that the church, as an organization, has little consideration. The church becomes a congregation, to do as the pastor wills without regard to its standing rules or organic interests. This is so common that for a church to assert its right to determine its rules, worship, and affairs is sometimes regarded by a pastor as cause for resigning. Yet the church, not the pastor, is clothed with the power of government. Where there is a dual organization, a church and its ecclesiastical society, there is great danger that the church will fail in organic development and regularity of procedure. The society, in fact, absorbs in some instances the functions of the church, so that church officers are elected by the secular society and all church business meetings cease to be held. If such cases are rare, they are numerous enough to warn against the fatal neglect. The efficiency and prosperity and peace of a church are largely dependent upon its thorough organization and prompt attention to business matters. Hence churches, like regiments of the great Captain's army, should be trained by their officers into such discipline that all things will be done decently and in order, whether they have pastors or not.

But church discipline is more specifically and generally confined to

DEALING WITH OFFENDERS.

§ 160. And here certain preliminary matters need to be considered.

(1) The mode of discipline will be determined by the theory of the church which is held. As there are four such theories (§§ 44, 79, 80), there will be four methods or processes of discipline in some essential particulars. A disci-

pline foreign to a theory can not be engrafted upon it; for either it will transform the theory into another or be thrown off as a foreign element. Discipline may be lax or rigid, but its form is determined by the theory of the church that is held.

(2) Defects in administration are of little weight. Human nature, even when renewed, is faulty, and no administration of discipline, under any theory, can escape defects. The primitive churches, under the eyes of the apostles, were not blameless here. Even the apostles were found fault with (Acts 6 : 1–6). It avails nothing, then, to cite slips in discipline against any church polity, unless it can be shown that those slips arise from the polity and not from man's common infirmities.

(3) Yet there is a drift in the discipline of any communion, determined by the theory of the church that is held, which makes for purity or for corruption, and so a polity may be judged by that drift. This drift requires long periods to be fully developed, but when developed, it is decisive; for it arises from the nature of the theory itself. If that drift makes for purity in faith and life, it proves the theory, so far forth, to be true; but if the drift be to compromise with error or corruption, it proves the theory, so far forth, to be false. Herein the history of churches becomes a test by which to judge of the theories held by them, after due allowance is made for the civil, social, and moral environment of the age and country. "The primitive communities were what they were mainly by the strictness of their discipline."[2] This strictness gave way to looseness when the primitive theory of the Church was perverted into the Episcopal and the Papal Theories of the Church.

(4) Special study of church discipline in its dealing with offenders is needed by the members and officers of free churches. It needs to be studied historically and practically, and that for two reasons: —

[2] Hatch's Org. Early Christ. Chhs. 68.

(*a*) Discipline is ever needed. There is no church so pure as not to require it. No polity, and no stage of piety yet attained, can escape either the duty or the test of discipline. And what is ever needed, both the members and the officers of a church should be ever ready to perform. They are culpable, especially the officers, if they neglect to study discipline.

(*b*) For mistakes in discipline rend churches as nothing else can rend them. Mistakes work injustice and divisions, which can not be remedied. Right action in the right spirit may stir up a church, but time quiets and heals; for there are no wrongs to be righted, no injustice to be remedied. Hence both officers and members owe it to Christ and to their future peace and prosperity to make no mistakes here. They must proceed with a sure step. It is better to study the case up in all its bearings before beginning, so as to make no mistake, than to spend nights in study and call a council to help the church out of the whirlpool into which a single mistake may plunge matters. Church and officers, but especially the pastor, should know the authority, the principles, the ends, the rules, the subjects, the limits of church discipline, that they may walk with a sure foot in every step of the procedure.

(5) The Congregational Theory of the Christian Church requires the same essential form of discipline, though the details of the process may be variant. This we shall set forth.

§ 161. The authority of church discipline lies, since the death of the apostles, in the particular, or local, congregation of believers. Since each believer can come boldly unto the throne of grace with no mediator but Christ, it might be claimed that he is, therefore, responsible to Christ alone for his belief and conduct. Were there a human priesthood to mediate for him, he might be called by it to account; but this priesthood being absorbed in Christ, the believer can be in subjection to no other authority. This is true when taken in the right sense, as we shall see; but when taken, as it sometimes is, it is disintegrating, destructive, forbidden. Christ did not thus resolve his manifested kingdom into unaffiliated, irresponsible, individual integers, but gathered those personal integers into responsible relations, one to another, in local churches, with the power and command of discipline (§ 99).

(1) The authority which a church has to discipline its members is not original, but derived from the Lord Christ. It is true that every organization has the inherent right and power of self-protection, of excluding unfit persons. Churches, like associations of churches (§§ 209, 210), have this common and essential right and power. But church discipline is much more than this. A local church can do what no other body, not even an association of churches, can do, namely: apply to a member the grace of discipline for his spiritual edification. Church discipline is a means of grace as really as the preaching of the Word, prayer, and the sacraments, committed by the Master to local churches. Associations of churches are not empowered to exercise it, though they can clear themselves of unworthy members (§§ 211, 212); but churches, though composed of only two or three, have had given them this power of the keys (Matt. 18: 15-20). Thus the power of exclusion is natural, belonging to all organizations; but the authority of discipline is conferred by Christ Jesus. Whatever body has this commission from Christ, the Head, acts therein as Christ's vicegerent on earth, whose action he expressly ratifies (Matt. 18: 18); (§ 99: 2, 3).

(2) That Christ has made the local church the repository of this authority of discipline, and not the Pope or the Episcopacy or the General Assembly, we have abundantly shown (§§ 106, 107, 108). The power of the keys given also to the apostles for the founding of churches (§§ 115: 5) ceased when they died, since they left no successors (§ 116: 3). The sole authority to administer discipline in the

name of Christ and by his commands is, therefore, permanently deposited with local churches (§ 99).

(3) The extent of this authority is limited. It may be carried, if the offender be incorrigible, to the extent of entire separation from the Church, but not to fines and imprisonment. These belong to the State, from which the churches have been separated (§ 225). For the force of "binding" and "loosing" see § 99 : 3.

§ 162. We need say little as to the subjects of church discipline. Each church has authority over its own members, whether officers or not, but not over the members of other churches or over those not members. Its jurisdiction is limited by its own full membership.

(1) Election to office does not release laymen from discipline. They can be dealt with as any other offenders, removed from office and excommunicated, for cause. Deacons, clerks, treasurers, committeemen, can be disciplined; and excommunication removes from office.

(2) Ministers, in virtue of their Christian character and ministerial function, require a twofold process. As church officers they can be removed from office by their respective churches, like other officers. Thus the church at Corinth removed its elders.[3] As church members they can be dealt with as other members. But as ministers, whose divine call to the work has been recognized in ordination by the churches, they can rightly claim that their ministerial standing thus secured shall not be jeopardized by the action of a single local church. Ministers, though subject to discipline, are not to be treated like private members (§§ 122, 131 : 5).

(3) Baptized children are not made thereby full members (§ 153), and so do not fall under the censures of a church. There should be the discipline of nurture but not of censure, until by confession of Christ in public they become full members (§153).

§ 163. The offences demanding notice in the way of

[3] Clement Romanus, Ep. Cor. xliv.

discipline need to be carefully considered. For not all offences call for church action. Love that suffereth long and is kind, that seeketh not her own but the good of others, must cover a multitude of sins. For some are too trivial to be noticed. Common sense ought to teach churches not to arraign members for trifles. "The putting on of gold and costly apparel" is against the "Discipline" of the Methodist Episcopal Church; yet that church long since wisely ceased trying to enforce plainness in dress. The General Court of Massachusetts Bay, in 1639, took notice of and forbade the wearing of lace, "immoderate great sleeves," bare arms, etc., but stayed direct proceedings, in the expectation that the churches would deal with such offences by way of discipline.[4] It is a greater evil to try to uproot such matters by church discipline than to let them alone. True, the standard of Christian living should be lifted high, but this can be done in the teaching of the pulpit better than in the discipline of every trivial offence. Much must be left to Christian liberty and consecration. Otherwise, while we gather up the tares we shall root up, also, the wheat with them (Matt. 13 : 29). Paul also says: "Him that is weak in the faith receive ye, but not to doubtful disputations." "Let every man be fully assured in his own mind" (Rom. 14: 1, 5). Discipline must not invade the realm of indifferent things.

If a serious offence can not be proved by witnesses or common fame, the church can take no action. When men do wrong they seldom take witnesses with them that will testify to the truth. To institute proceedings without probable proof is to bring discipline into contempt by failure. The old Jewish law required that there be two or three witnesses or their equivalent. Common fame is a very uncertain ground of action, since the best men have been persistently lied about; yet sometimes, with proper precautions, a member may be dealt with and excommunicated without other evidence of guilt than common belief. The offences demanding action are : —

[4] Colonial Records, 1, 274.

(1) The denial of the cardinal doctrines. The New Testament and the history of the Christian Church make it clear that some doctrines are of vital importance. They can not be denied without subverting the gospel and destroying the churches. If one denies the Lord that bought him, what has he to do in the Church? So the denial of any essential doctrine is ground for discipline, as an offence against the life and Head of the church-kingdom. The warrant for this is both natural and Scriptural. Such denial, if unnoticed, is subversive of the existence of the Church, which should protect itself from destruction. But the apostles enjoin action in such cases (Gal. 1: 6–10; Titus 3: 10; 2 John 9-11). These doctrines were at length formulated in the so-called Apostles' Creed; but they have been recently more elaborately set forth in the creed of the Evangelical Alliance.[5] In applying these doctrinal tests to individual members, great forbearance should be observed; for many a true Christian has been caught in some speculation which has carried him away for a time, to return again as soon as the speculation has revealed its emptiness. Greater rigor is required as regards ministers (§ 119) and teachers. But heresy is certainly one offence that should be dealt with by way of discipline, but with charitable discretion.

(2) Scandalous offences and gross crimes are causes of discipline (1 Cor. 5: 2; 10: 20; 2 Thess. 3: 6, 14); so also

[5] This Doctrinal Basis was adopted in 1846, and is as follows: —
1. The divine inspiration, authority, and sufficiency of the holy Scriptures.
2. The right and duty of private judgment in the interpretation of the holy Scriptures.
3. The Unity of the Godhead, and the Trinity of the persons therein.
4. The utter depravity of human nature in consequence of the Fall.
5. The incarnation of the Son of God, his work of atonement for the sins of mankind, and his mediatorial intercession and reign.
6. The justification of the sinner by faith alone.
7. The work of the Holy Spirit in the conversion and sanctification of the sinner.
8. The immortality of the soul, the resurrection of the body, the judgment of the world by our Lord Jesus Christ, with the eternal blessedness of the righteous, and the eternal punishment of the wicked.
9. The divine institution of the Christian ministry, and the obligation and perpetuity of the ordinances of baptism and the Lord's Supper. — Schaff's Creeds of Christendom, iii, 827, 828.

private wrongs (Matt. 18 : 15–18), and violations of the church covenant. On joining a church each member enters into a covenant, either written or understood, to attend, support, fellowship it; to commune with it, and to seek its peace and welfare. Now, if he neglect any part of this covenant, he has broken his solemn agreement, and may be disciplined as a covenant-breaker. Thus, for heresy, immorality, private injury, and violation of the covenant, a member may be brought to discipline.

§ 164. But it may not always be the duty of a church to discipline a member even when the offence may warrant it. A case of discipline, as we have said (§ 160 : 4), stirs up a church and may hinder much good. The members may sometimes be reclaimed by patient waiting. Hence a church needs not only to look at offences as tares, but also to consider all the near and remote issues, lest the wheat be rooted up also.

(1) The grant of authority to discipline does not remove the duty of discretion in the exercise of discipline. The keys were not given for ornament, it is true ; nor do they deny a wise discretion. The Church is to be kept pure by their use, and the process began with fearful rigor (Acts 5 : 1–11) and was often enjoined (Gal. 1 : 6–10 ; 2 John 9–11 ; Titus 3 : 10, etc.) ; and neglect of discipline has ever tended to corruption. As early as A.D. 251, Novatian divided the churches on this issue. He would have ruled out all discretion from the duty of discipline, holding that any church neglecting to keep itself pure ceased, in the act of neglect, to be a true church.[6] This ultra position is not imposed by the grant of the authority to enforce purity.

(2) Nor does the function of the churches as the salt of the earth and the light of the world prevent the exercise of proper discretion. If the salt lose its savor, and the light become darkness, the churches cease to fulfill their divine function. They then become blind leaders of the blind.

[6] Neander's Church Hist. 1, 246.

They can not, therefore, be or do what they ought without laying great stress on discipline. But even this does not relieve them from wise discretion in its exercise.

(3) This discretion makes the duty of discipline somewhat variable. Churches exist in varying conditions of environment, and the duty of discipline varies somewhat with those conditions. There are certain offences which can under no circumstances be overlooked, but must be proceeded against at once. There are other offences which are more culpable in one age and land than in another; so that the standard of practice and the duty of discipline should vary a little. God has acted on this principle in the three dispensations, and Christ expressly taught it in the doom of certain cities (Matt. 11: 20-24), in the parable of the tares and wheat (Matt. 13: 24-30), in the matter of divorce (Matt. 19: 8), and in the revelation of truth (John 16: 12). Any other rule than this which respects the light one has and the environment in which one lives would be manifestly unjust. The discipline should be wisely matched to the light and environment.

Take the matter of temperance as an example. The colonial records contain repeated enactments against intemperance; and yet every body used liquors — ministers, deacons, members, rulers, all. We can not carry the light and circumstances of our day back to the times of our Pilgrim and Puritan Fathers and judge a rum-selling deacon of the seventeenth century as we should judge him now in this century. This enactment, or order, of the Legislature of the Bay Colony, in 1647: " The court think it convenient that order be given to the auditor to send twelve gallons of sack and six gallons of white wine, as a small testimony of the court's respect, to the reverend assembly of elders at Cambridge,"[7] — the same that framed the Cambridge Platform, — would be deemed an insult, if passed to-day by any Legislature in reference to the National Council or a state

[7] Colonial Records, ii, 194, 195.

association. And even now churches should remember that not all men nor all churches look upon the sale and use of liquors as our churches do. Some are nearly where our fathers were, of whom we may use the words: "Of some have compassion, making a difference" (Jude 22). For love will win them to the principle of total abstinence, when harshness and discipline will only harden.

Hence the duty of discipline is under discretion, in some degree, and the highest wisdom and gentleness are needed in a church in dealing with offences, lest the best intended discipline fail of reaching its true ends through rigor or through laxness.

§ 165. This liberty of discretion keeps ever before a church the ends of church discipline. Were the duty without discretion, there would be no need of asking, What end should ever be had in view in dealing with offenders? But now all cases are to be conducted with reference to a double end.

(1) Discipline should aim first at reclaiming the offender. This is true of all proper discipline, private or public, parental or civil, ecclesiastical or providential. In this it differs radically from punishment. Discipline in the church is therefore a potent means of grace when properly conducted. It aims at recovering the wayward, never at expelling him. It should not, therefore, be entered upon in haste, in malice, in revenge, but after patient waiting, much prayer, and with the most earnest and tender desire and purpose to bring the wayward member in penitence back to an orderly life and sound belief.

(2) But the ultimate end of discipline is the purity of the church. This end is best secured by the reclamation of the offender; but, that failing, it requires his expulsion. In either result the Church protects its purity and vindicates its character as a holy body. The moment that a church, through fear or ambition or policy or indifference, covers sin, it is shorn of strength and vacates its mission in part.

It must thereafter tread like Samson in the mill of the Philistines. Its discretion in the duty of discipline (§ 164: 3) has respect to the best way of securing the ends of discipline, not how to avoid it. As purity is essential to the power of the ministry, so purity is essential to the power and permanent prosperity of any church.

§ 166. So important did Christ regard the ends of discipline that he detailed the steps by which those ends can best be attained. He gave a rule of discipline with steps of progress (Matt. 18: 15-18).

(1) The first step in the process of discipline for private offences is this: "If thy brother sin against thee, go, shew him his fault between thee and him alone: if he hear thee, thou hast gained thy brother" (v. 15). The margin says: "Some ancient authorities omit *against thee;*" this would make the rule universal, if these two words should be omitted. This first step is so plain that it would seem to need no explanation; but the history of discipline enforces the necessity of dwelling upon it with the greatest particularity of detail. (*a*) The injured party must begin the process. He takes the initiative because he has suffered wrong. If the wrong-doer shall first come and confess his fault, the process can not begin. The case is closed. (*b*) The wronged goes to the offender. There is special significance in that little word " go ; " a casual meeting will not do. An interview must be sought and obtained, if possible. The injured does not meet the requirement if he write a letter or send another person to the one who wronged him. (*c*) The interview must be secret or private, " between thee and him alone." No third person should be present. This rests on human nature. A man will relent and confess and make amends in such an interview, who would not if a third person were present. (*d*) The injured must show the wrong-doer his fault, without enlarging it or diminishing it, by giving a fair and full presentation of it. It is not merely to be told him: it must be shown him, that he may see it.

(e) And all in a tender spirit of love. To go in any other spirit might increase the injury. To go to him in order to reach the next step is itself a wrong. There must be a love that forgives, if need be, seventy times seven (Matt. 18: 21–35), and it will probably win the man. (f) "If he hear thee, thou hast gained thy brother." The end has been gained. To gain, and not to cut off, is the aim. (g) His penitent confession and reasonable reparation ends the case. Purity is secured in penitence. The grace of God has triumphed. No more should ever be said or done about it.

(2) But a second step is sometimes necessary. Hence it is given in these words: "But if he hear thee not, take with thee one or two more, that at the mouth of two witnesses or three every word may be established" (v. 16). (a) Here the spirit and end are the same as in the preceding step. Forgiving love trying to reclaim inspires the interview. (b) The one or two taken along are witnesses of the loving fidelity of the party wronged and the conduct of the wrong-doer. They should be discreet, full of wisdom and love, having the confidence of all, especially the wrong-doer. (c) In the presence of these witnesses the fault must be shown again, for the purpose of bringing the offender to see and confess it. (d) His confession before these witnesses ends the case, and all are to keep silent about it.

(3) If this interview fail, then comes the third step: "And if he refuse to hear them, tell it unto the church," or "*congregation*" (v. 17). (a) This shows what part the witnesses take in the preceding interview. They must use all Christian endeavor to reclaim the offender; for it is only when he refuses to "hear them" that (b) the offence must be told unto the church, or congregation. This must be done in an oral or written complaint. (c) This church, or congregation, is the local church to which the offender belongs (§ 99: 1). The whole membership must now hear the case.

(4) The fourth and final step is this: "But if he refuse to

hear the church also, let him be unto thee as the Gentile and the publican " (v. 17). (*a*) The offender reveals his incorrigible heart in refusing to hear first, the wronged; second, the witnesses; and third, the whole Church; all laboring to save him, not to cast him out of their fellowship. (*b*) Hence they have no alternative but to cast him out of the Church, to excommunicate him. He is thence to be as a Gentile and a publican; that is, cut off from all privileges of membership in the Church of God, and denied participation in the Lord's Supper (§§ 155: 2, 3; 156). (*c*) Further than this the Church may not go; nor should the State interpose to punish him.[8]

(5) These steps are complete, and make a final end of the case so far as authority to discipline goes. (*a*) The offender is dealt with step by step until reclaimed or cut off, with no appeal from the beginning to the end. And the issue is final and complete exclusion from church privileges. The four steps leave the process finished. (*b*) This issue is ratified by Christ, the Head and King: "Verily I say unto you, What things soever ye shall bind on earth shall be bound in heaven: and what things soever ye shall loose on earth shall be loosed in heaven" (v. 18). This estops all right of appeal (§ 99: 2, 3). (*c*) Yet if wrong is claimed to have been done in thus issuing the case, the church and the aggrieved may ask the advice of churches in a council (§ 194: 10), what redress, if any, is required, and may act on that advice. This advice is not of the nature of a command, for it has none of the authority of discipline, which was permanently committed to local churches alone (§§ 99: 1, 3; 106, 107, 108). (*d*) If the offending member be also a minister, another principle comes in (§ 162: 2) to modify his discipline by a church. He has been recognized in ordination as a minister called by

[8] The General Court of Massachusetts, in 1638, "ordered, that whoever shall stand excommunicate for the space of six months, without laboring what in him or her lieth to be restored, such a person shall be presented . . . and proceeded with by fine, imprisonment, banishment, or further, for the good behavior, as their contempt and obstinacy, upon full hearing shall deserve." But the law was repealed the next year. Records, 1, 242, 271.

the great Head of the Church unto the preaching of the Word. His excommunication by a local church impairs, if it does not destroy, his character and influence as an ambassador of Christ,. which, as his call to the ministry was not recognized by one church alone, ought not to be jeopardized by the action of one church alone (§§ 121, 122, 124). But both these apparent exceptions are treated elsewhere (§§ 200, 201, 202).

Such is the plain interpretation of Christ's rule for church discipline; but many queries arise, which we will consider under the head of

SOME QUESTIONS RESPECTING CHURCH DISCIPLINE.

§ 167. Should all cases of discipline be treated alike? There is a great difference between a private offence and a public scandal, and must they always be treated the same? We reply: (1) The ends of all church discipline are the same. The guilty are to be reformed, if possible, and the church kept pure either by reformation or by exclusion. In no case should this dual end be overlooked. (2) Yet public scandals should be treated more summarily than private offences. The private steps (§ 166: 1-4) may not always be required; hence Paul indicates public action at once (1 Cor. 5: 4, 5, 13), which our Platforms recognize.[9] The reason is that such offences are known to the community, and the church may hasten to clear itself of complicity with the crime. (3) Such scandalous offences are those which are "infamous among men," "condemned by the light of nature," which are "of a more heinous and criminal nature."

§ 168. When should the first private step in discipline be taken? It should not be taken in a hurry. Passion should have time to cool, and conscience time to assert its claims to control. This may require a full year or more. The most favorable time for gaining the wrong-doer must be chosen. Not until after a full year was Nathan the prophet sent to

[9] Camb. Plat. xiv, 3; Boston Plat. part ii, viii, 4.

David the king. In case of doctrinal errors, a longer time may be needed. When the heart begins to relent or hungers for the truth, then a word, gently spoken, may win and save. God is patient, and the child of his love should also wait in patient hope and constant prayer to win a brother. Yet he must not wait too long.

§ 169. Should a second private interview with the offender be sought? No intimation is given of such renewed attempt in case of failure; but as the prime object is to gain a brother, a second and a third interview may be had in the spirit of the rule. It is better to save by loving labors not expressly required, than by strict interpretation to lose. It is better to be good than to be simply just (Rom. 5: 7).

§ 170. Does the asking for a letter of dismission forestall discipline? The guilty party sometimes seeks to anticipate action of discipline by asking for a letter of dismissal before his offence is made public, or while the church or the wronged party is waiting to take the proper reclaiming steps. How does such a request affect the case? (1) The request for a letter is not a letter of dismissal. It is only a request, which the church may grant or not as each case may come before it. If any cause be known to exist why the letter should not issue, the party knowing it is bound to reveal the fact to the pastor or deacons or church, and thus to prevent the issuing of the letter until the matter is satisfactorily settled. A simple request of a member for delay for the taking of private steps stops the church from issuing the letter. (2) For a case of discipline takes precedence of a request for dismissal. It were a great wrong for a church to override a notification of complaint against a member by issuing a letter of dismissal. If notice of an offence be given it, the request for dismissal must lie on the table until the discipline be had. (3) And the said notice of complaint need not contain, and ordinarily should not contain, the nature of the offence committed; otherwise, there might be a premature exposure of the fault.

§ 171. Does the granting of a letter of dismissal preclude discipline? If the sin be hidden altogether until the letter is issued, the church can call the offender to account in one of two ways, namely: (1) If he has received his letter, but has not been admitted on it to some other church, he remains still a member of the church granting the letter, and is subject to its discipline. Hence the church, if the case shall warrant it, can recall the letter and begin process of discipline as though no letter had ever been issued. (2) But if he has been already admitted to another church before the detection of his guilt, the church so receiving him should bring him to discipline the same as if the crime had been committed while he was a member of it. If, however, by reason of distance, his trial be inconvenient or impossible in said church, that church can ask the church where the deed was done to act as a commission, or to appoint from its membership a commission, to hear the case, record the evidence, formulate its judgment, and report. On which report the man may be acquitted or censured by the church to which he then belongs. (3) To prevent, as far as possible, such cases, letters of dismissal ought not to issue immediately. A request for dismissal, like an application for membership, should lie over for a week or two; and for the same reason precisely, namely, that any one may have opportunity to stop action if he deem the party to be unworthy either of admission or of dismissal.

§ 172. How should the case of discipline be brought before the church? The rule is: "Tell it unto the church," or, as the margin has it, "the congregation." This would imply only an oral statement of the case; and no church can demand more than this before action. (1) If an oral complaint be brought, the church, by its clerk, should reduce it to writing, read it to the complainant for his endorsement, and preserve it on the records and on file. (2) As this takes time, it is better to prepare written charges beforehand, as definite as they can be made, and thus tell it unto the church.

(3) Such complaint should cover the wrong that is complained of, the time when committed, the names of witnesses, the steps taken to secure redress, and the request that the church deal with the offending member as he may deserve.

§ 173. How should the church conduct the case? It must hear the complaint as made, whether it vote to entertain it or not. The complaint may be so trivial that it would be wrong to dignify it with a church trial. For, as we have shown (§§ 163, 164), a church must carefully discriminate between what impeaches a man's Christian character and belief, and what belongs to Christian liberty or to immaterial infirmities. Hence, in the exercise of a wise discretion, the church must vote either to entertain or to dismiss the complaint. But in either case the complaint should go upon the record, with the action taken. If the church vote to dismiss the complaint, the case is ended. If it vote to entertain the complaint, then it should attend to these several things: (1) It should fix the time and place of the trial, allowing ample time for preparation. (2) It should order its clerk to give due notice of the time and place of trial to all the parties and witnesses, to send a copy of the charges, with the names of the witnesses, to the accused; and the church should appoint one or more to conduct the case on its behalf, and allow the accused to select one or more of the members to assist him at the trial. The church should also summon the accused and request the witnesses to appear at the trial. (3) The church tries the case at the time and place designated. If the accused refuse to appear, either in person or by representative, the church may, at its discretion, adjourn to some fixed day, and notify him of the adjournment; or it may proceed without him to the trial. The reason of this is that a church, unlike the State, can not compel the attendance of the accused or of witnesses, or the production of documentary evidence; so that if the absence of the accused could stop proceedings, he might prevent a trial altogether, and thus subvert church discipline. (4) In the trial, the pastor, unless a party in the case, directly or indirectly, is the presiding officer. If he be absent or disqualified, a deacon, or any one best versed in the principles and usages of our polity and in parliamentary law, unless he be disqualified by interest or partisanship, should be chosen to preside. (5) The church clerk should keep a full record of the doings of the trial for the journal of the church. He should also record and preserve on file the testimony of witnesses and other proof submitted, reading said testimony for correction to the witnesses, which must remain unaltered thereafter, unless corrected by the witness himself before the church. (6) Witnesses may be put under oath.[10] The oath gives sacredness and a needed sanction to testimony. Witnesses will sometimes testify under oath what they will not otherwise. (7) When the evidence is all in and summed up, if pleadings shall be deemed best, the church votes on the specifications of a charge first, and then on the charge itself, and so of every charge in the complaint; the question being put by the moderator: Is this specification (or charge, as the case may be) sustained? On the result of the voting the church founds its verdict of guilty or not guilty. If none of the specifications or charges are sustained, the case is ended by the acquittal of the member. If any or all the charges are sustained, the church proceeds, in due time and form, to its censure, which should be delayed a little. (8) The confession of the guilty party, if deemed genuine and ample, arrests proceedings at any stage of the trial; for the ends sought are thus secured. The church has no right or power to punish for guilt confessed. Its function is discipline, not punishment. (9) There must be throughout the proceedings not only impartiality, but the utmost care lest the

---

[10] The oath or affirmation should be administered to a witness by the moderator, in the following, or like, terms:—

"You solemnly promise, in the presence of the omniscient and heart-searching God that you will declare the truth, the whole truth, and nothing but the truth, according to the best of your knowledge, in the matter in which you are called as witness, as you shall answer it to the great Judge of quick and dead." This is the Presbyterian form. Discipline, chap. vi, 9; Moore's Presby. Digest, 1873, 530.

charge of partiality or unfairness be made with some degree of credibility. The church must heed in its discipline the words of Paul: "Take thought for things honourable in the sight of all men" (Rom. 12: 17).

§ 174. May not the church hear the case through the church board (§ 135), or by a special committee or jury? As this mode of discipline is Congregational in principle, has been adopted in England, and is sure to be adopted by our churches in difficult cases, if not in all cases, we will explain it somewhat fully. (1) A church board, special committee, or chosen jury, if appointed and authorized to act in any matter by vote of the church, has all the authority therein of the appointing power. The Church, like the State, may, for good reasons, commit the hearing of a complaint, the taking of evidence, the formulation of censures, and whatever else is necessary in the trial of a member, to its church board, or to a select committee or jury, which shall submit its action to the church for final ratification. It can do this in matters of discipline as it does it in other matters. And any church can do it, if it so elects. (2) Certain cases demand such a trial: (*a*) Sexual scandals are bad enough without gathering a whole church, and the public too, to listen to their sickening and demoralizing details. The trial of such cases, for decency's sake, should be had in a small room before a jury of a few men, good and true. (*b*) Long trials require that a few, and not a whole church, be gathered, night after night, in patient hearing and recording of testimony. A jury of six men is far better here than a whole church. (*c*) Some cases are so difficult, because of the points of business or of polity involved in them, that few in the church are qualified to pass upon them. Those few ought, therefore, to be chosen as a jury to act for the church, and report. (*d*) Justice demands that only those who are present to hear the evidence should vote upon the charges. Yet if a trial should last a few evenings, many who have not heard a word of the evidence may come in at the close of the trial and determine the result. (e) There may be also great prejudice against the accused, or he may be related to a large part of the church, or connected with a majority of the church in a business way; so that the church may be an unfit body so far forth to hear the case, when a jury chosen from among its members could act calmly and impartially. These cases, separately and collectively, present a strong reason why our churches should modify their discipline by the introduction of what may be called the jury system. (3) This jury should be chosen by the church itself. The accused can not nominate any part of it, nor can he challenge any member of it. He can not refuse to be tried by the church to which he belongs; and hence he can not refuse to be tried by any jury chosen by that church, since that jury is the arm of the church disciplining a member. The church acts in and through the jury. Such a jury is not a board of arbitration, nor a committee of reference, where each party has equal voice. The accused is not a party as against the church, but a member of the church on trial whether or not he shall be debarred church privileges. The church should consequently elect the whole jury that acts for the church in said trial. If the church should allow the accused the opportunity of challenge, it is of grace, not of right, and can be limited or denied again at pleasure. It were abhorrent that the accused should either dictate who should try him or else stop all proceedings. (4) The jury should report to the church its findings and recommendations for ratification or rejection. The church, by approval, makes the doings of the committee its own. The case can not again be opened, though all the records made and evidence taken by the jury may, on demand, be read before the vote is taken upon the report of the jury. There is no possible danger to the liberty of the churches in this jury trial, which avoids the evils above indicated. It ought to be universally adopted.

§ 175. What rules control the admission of evidence in church trials? A correct answer is of the greatest practical value. (1) It is manifest that legal rules can not be allowed, though some writers have asserted their application.[11] One fact is conclusive against their use, that they are framed to regulate evidence in courts which can compel the attendance of witnesses and the production of evidence, neither of which falls within the power of a church. This one fact so separates civil and criminal trials from ecclesiastical that the rules for the admission of evidence must vary to suit the different conditions. (2) In fact, the rules governing evidence in ecclesiastical trials have been very comprehensive. "The best kind of testimony need not be produced, or its absence accounted for, before secondary evidence can be offered. Parties in interest are not excluded, on account of bias, from giving their testimony; husbands and wives are not prevented from testifying for or against each other; hearsay evidence is not excluded. But every thing is admissible that the council choose to admit, that will help them come to an understanding of the case. The Supreme Court has never qualified this license of proof, or been called to qualify it."[12] (3) The civil courts are approaching somewhat this ecclesiastical liberty, by admitting testimony that once was excluded. It is not because hearsay evidence is unworthy of belief that legal rules so generally exclude it. Sir James F. Stephen, the author of A Digest on the Law of Evidence, says: "But it must not be supposed that the law admits as evidence all facts which are, in a strictly logical sense, relevant. The most considerable and important exception is that of hearsay evidence. In ordinary life we should regard a statement made to us at second-hand not only as relevant to the fact it asserts, but as sufficient and satisfactory proof, if both of our informants are persons of creditable character and intelligence. In point of fact, the immense bulk of our knowledge and belief on all sorts of subjects is founded on

---

[11] Dexter's Congregationalism, Revised Ed. 390; Harvey's The Church (Baptist), 60, 61; Canon 9, iv [4], of Prot. Epis. Ch. Digest, 83.
[12] Buck's Mass. Eccl. Law, chap. xvii, § 10, p. 227.

hearsay evidence many times more remote than in the case we have supposed. The general rule of law excludes all such evidence. . . . The reason is sufficiently obvious. A deponent in court tells his story under securities for its truthfulness. He may be cross-examined. He may be punished for telling lies. But for these securities it would hardly be safe, considering the consequences attaching to every issue in a court of justice, to act upon any testimony whatever."[13] These issues in fines, imprisonment, and death justify the exclusion of hearsay evidence from state courts, where the law brings both witnesses and documents into the court and compels testimony; but neither such issues nor the impotence of a church to compel testimony can be claimed as a reason for excluding hearsay evidence from church trials. They, on the contrary, justify its admission. (4) This liberty of proof covers all ecclesiastical trials, whether before a church, or before a council or association of churches. For the reason of it exists in all such cases. We have seen no instance where the civil courts have set aside ecclesiastical action because legal rules of proof were not observed. The principles which have governed the courts in Massachusetts, above referred to, have governed all courts, so far as we can learn.

§ 176. May legal counsel be admitted to plead in church trials? Paul's question: "Dare any of you, having a matter against his neighbour, go to law before the unrighteous, and not before the saints?" (1 Cor. 6 : 1) has not lost its force altogether by the nominal Christianization of a nation. He felt that in pagan countries the least in the church, "who are of no account," were better than pagan magistrates (v. 4). We may answer the question, then, in this way: (1) Men should not be permitted to plead in church trials as professional counsel. Lawyers are court officers, with certain special privileges which it would not be wise to grant them before churches. They should have no privi-

[13] 8 Ency. Brit. 740.

leges not accorded unto others in conducting a case or in pleading. But (2) as Christian counselors lawyers may conduct cases of discipline. Their experience and wisdom can thus be used in the interest of justice. If a member of the church, a lawyer may assist the accused or conduct the case of the church. He acts as a church member in either case, not as a lawyer, and is amenable, like any other member, to the church. In consequence of conducting the trial, he rightly loses both voice and vote in making up the result of the trial. (3) Lawyers who are not church members in any communion ought not to be admitted to conduct a church trial. This is the general, if not universal, rule in other communions. It is said for the Baptists that "it would not be proper for any member on trial before the church to bring a person who is not a member to appear as his advocate and plead his cause." [14] The Episcopal Methodists limit counsel to "any member in good and regular standing in the Methodist Episcopal Church." [15] The Presbyterians and Reformed Churches have this rule: "No professional counsel shall be permitted to appear and plead in cases of process in any of our ecclesiastical courts. But if any accused person feels unable to represent and plead his own cause to advantage, he may request any minister or elder belonging to the judicatory before which he appears to prepare and exhibit his cause as he may judge proper. But the minister or elder so engaged shall not be allowed, after pleading the cause of the accused, to sit in judgment as a member of the judicatory." [16] The Protestant Episcopal Church says that "the accusers may, if they choose, select a lay communicant of this church, of the profession of the law, to act as their adviser, advocate, and agent, in preparing the accusation, proofs, etc.;" and the board for trial "shall also appoint a church advocate, who must be a lay communicant of this church, and of the profession of the law," to repre-

[14] Hiscox's Baptist Directory, 1871, 100.
[15] Discipline, 1872, § 347. [16] Discipline, chap. iv, § 21.

sent the church in the trial of a bishop.[17] We should not, in our liberty, imperil the peace of our churches by admitting non-church members to plead or conduct process in them. (4) The same may be said of councils and associations of churches, although the reasons are stronger for the exclusion of professional counsel from trials before churches than from trials before councils and associations. The arts of a lawyer pleading as such are more likely to bewilder a church than to confuse a council and association; and hence the greater the danger. But brethren versed in law may, as unprofessional counsel, render inestimable assistance in church trials wherever held.

§ 177. What censures may be administered? The rule for private offences, heresy, and public scandals (§§ 163 : 1, 2) seems to be one, that of exclusion from the church. The apostolic power "to deliver such an one unto Satan for the destruction of the flesh" (1 Cor. 5 : 5 ; 1 Tim. 1 : 20) was never conferred upon the local church. If the accused be found guilty by the church, and the offence be light, the end of purity may be secured by the censure of admonition. The guilty party is admonished of his guilt, the injury done Christ and his cause, and enjoined to penitence and reformation. If the offence be more grievous, there may be added to this admonition suspension from communion for a fixed period. When this period is elapsed, the offender, without further action by the church, is restored to good and regular standing again. If the sin demand the extreme censure of excommunication, the church may wait a short time before pronouncing it, that the man may repent and confess; but, if he still remain incorrigible, he must be cut off entirely from church standing and become to the church "as a Gentile and a publican."

If after his excommunication he becomes penitent and asks for restoration, and the church be satisfied with his repentance and reparation, he can be restored to full mem-

[17] Digest of the Canons, Can. 9, §§ 2 [3], 4 [3].

bership again by a vote, reciting the fact of repentance and reparation, and lifting or removing the censure. This is not a reconsideration of the vote of excommunication, which vote still stands as a part of the record, but a lifting of the censure, by which action he is restored to full membership again without public profession or further action.

§ 178. Should the act of censure be publicly announced? This was our former custom, and two considerations seem to determine the answer. (1) If members are admitted publicly, as they are, they ought to be cast out publicly, if cast out at all. If admitted with joy and thanksgiving, they should be cut off with sorrow and lamentation. If they enter through the front door, they should not be sent out through the back door. For (2) equity requires that reparation should be as wide and public as the injury done. This law lies at the bottom of Christ's rule of discipline. So long as an offence is private, private reparation is all that is required. If it be extended to the one or two witnesses in a second interview, the confession must be before them. If it be carried to the church, the reparation or excommunication must be before the whole church. If members are admitted in church meeting, when the congregation, as distinct from the church, is absent, their excommunication need only be announced in a similar meeting; for neither equity nor policy requires the advertising of church troubles, whether in prayers, in sermons, or in other public announcements. The church and pastor may lament the existence of troubles, but let their lamentations be in private, not in the social meetings or in the pulpit, lest strangers ask, What is the trouble here? and the worship be marred and embittered by needless personal reflections. In all worship, let thoughts of God and love and peace and truth drive out the petty quarrels and needed censures of men. Yet an announcement of the excommunication of a member is not so unauthorized as to be a public libel or slander.

§ 179. Are persons taking part in church trials protected

by the law of the state? All who take part, whether as witnesses or as moderator, or in any other capacity, if they act in good faith, are protected from suits for slander or libel. This extends to the reading of an excommunication from the pulpit. The state recognizes the right of a church to administer its discipline,[18] so long as it keeps to its proper province. It will not even interfere to restore an irregularly expelled member.[19]

§ 180. When do irregularities in procedure invalidate church proceedings? As important as this question would appear to be, in view of the frequent appeals based on this ground, both in state courts and in the judicatories of other polities, we find that it has been omitted from all the writers on Congregationalism that we have consulted. We have considered it briefly in other manuals.[20] It demands a more elaborate treatment. (1) Irregularities often occur. They do in civil and criminal procedures, in the hands and under the eyes of trained lawyers. They occur also under polities with elaborate books of discipline which are the inflexible standards of procedure. They can not be less frequent under our free and independent polity with no authoritative standard but the Bible, although we have books of principles and usages. (2) The force of irregularities in civil and criminal procedure has been elaborately discussed and the precedents formulated into the rule, that a mistake or irregularity, to find relief in equity, must be of a material nature, and the determining ground of the transaction.[21] (3) Irregularities in Presbyterian procedure rest on the same principle. Thus the General Assembly has decided that " an irregularity in the call does not necessarily invalidate the election ; " that " irregularity in the mode of election

---

[18] Buck's Mass. Eccl. Law, 70, 71; 13 Wallace (U. S. Supreme Court), 722-734; 5 Cushing (Mass.), 412; 51 Vt. 501 (31 Am. Repts. 698-707).
[19] 37 Mich. Repts. 542.
[20] Ohio Manual, 23; Pocket Manual, § 110.
[21] Kerr on Fraud and Mistake, 399; Parsons on Contracts, 555; Story on Contracts, 330.

does not invalidate the ordination;" that "the superior judicatory shall judge how far the irregularity vitiates the proceedings and defeats the ends of justice;" that "a dismission may be irregular, yet valid;" and that a decision may be reversed in part, on grounds of irregularity, and sustained in the rest.[22] A mere irregularity does not here invalidate, unless it be of a material nature and the determining ground of the transaction. (4) The same principle will hold in our polity. And we may give as a rule in Congregationalism: That an irregularity, to invalidate proceedings, or to be a ground of relief, must be of a material nature and the determining ground of the transaction. If it can be shown that the censure or the transaction would not have occurred if the irregularity had not occurred, the irregularity is material and invalidates the action. But if the censure or transaction would have been the same if the irregularity had not occurred, the irregularity is not material and does not invalidate the transaction. This seems to be a rule of equity and common sense.

§ 181. Who may vote in cases of discipline and on other church matters? This question is of grave importance, involving as it does the purity, peace, and prosperity of our churches. Shall any limitation be put upon the right of suffrage in the churches? and if so, what limitation? (1) The best time to answer this question is when no other issue is pending. When the stress of trouble is upon a church and parties are excited, and a few votes may turn the trembling scales and determine the gravest questions, it is no time to settle who shall be entitled to vote and who shall not. Rules already made can be and should be enforced; usages may be called in to limit the right of suffrage; but all attempts in a quarrel, by either party, to pass a rule defining those limits will be bitterly resisted. (2) The rules of discipline should exclude minors from the right of suffrage in the church, as custom excludes them. The

[22] Moore's Presby. Digest (1873), 338, 339; 142; 540; 624; 572.

reasons for such a rule are conclusive: (*a*) Minors can not give a free vote. They are legally, morally, and Scripturally subject to the will of their parents. "The rule of the common law that *infants* can not vote in civil corporations is applicable to religious corporations," says Judge William Lawrence, of Ohio.[23] The parents can punish minor children for not voting as they command, as for any other disobedience. And the Bible requires obedience of children to parents (Eph. 6 : 1 ; Col. 3 : 20). These reasons apply as strongly to the uncorporate action as to the corporate action of churches. To submit to the vote of minors the question of creed, of pastorate, of discipline, or the question of salary, expenditures, church building, etc., is the absurdity of liberty. There is untold evil in it. Religious liberty does not involve it. Children are subject to their parents until of age. The courts so hold in religious matters. Hence a Baptist minister in Pennsylvania was held to have "interfered with the lawful authority of the father" by immersing a daughter, aged seventeen years, against the prohibition of her Presbyterian father.[24] (*b*) Children can not give a mature vote, even if allowed to vote as they please. The civil law in its treatment of them rests partly on this immaturity, and churches can not ignore it. Hence (*c*) the vote of minors, being immature and subject to the will of parents, will not long be endured. The questions at issue are too momentous, such as creed, discipline, pastorate, salary, expenditure, building and repairing churches, fellowship. Wise men will not give liberally to churches if all their gifts and labors are to be put in jeopardy by the votes of children. Hence the usage which excludes minors from voting should be put into the rules of discipline of every Congregational church. (3) Women were formerly denied by usage the right of suffrage in our churches, both

---

[23] The Law of Relig. Soc. and Church Corporations in Am. Law Register, New Series, xii, 201, 329, 537; xiii, 65, where a multitude of precedents are cited on all points involved. [24] Ibid. 538.

in England and in America.[25] The prohibitions of the New Testament (1 Cor. 14: 34, 35; 1 Tim. 2: 11–15) have been held to cover voting as well as speaking in the churches; but female suffrage in the churches has increased until now it is common. State laws sometimes allow it in religious societies or corporations. (4) In cases of discipline the accused and the man who brings the complaint and they who conduct the case on both sides should not vote. Great care must be had that an impartial verdict be rendered; and yet, as an offence may be against the whole church, all parties in interest can not be excluded.

§ 182. What is the validity of a vote when the majority present fail to vote? This condition of things is quite common in all bodies. Men are indifferent, or there is no division over a measure, and so only a few take the trouble to vote, the majority not voting. Important laws are thus passed. For such a vote is valid if a majority of those voting are in the affirmative. Judge Lawrence, in his articles above referred to, cites cases to show that "an election is valid if the majority neglect to vote."[26] The same would be true of any other action, provided there were no rule or constitutional provision to the contrary.

§ 183. Can members of a church be dropped from the roll without censure? We may answer here: (1) Members can not be dropped at their own option. A member can not cease to be a member by voluntary withdrawal. This is impossible from the nature of covenant church membership. (2) Nor should a member be dropped while charges against him are pending. If a man be under charges, the case should go to trial, that the man may be acquitted or condemned. To drop his name, even at his own request, under charges, would be the perversion of discipline. (3) If a man prefer charges against a church member or the pastor, the matter can not be evaded by dropping the complainant, either with or without censure, until such charges have been

[25] Buck's Mass. Eccl. Law, 68, 213. [26] 12 Am. Law Register (New Series), 549.

properly disposed of. It were abhorrent thus to punish a man for beginning process of discipline; and the dropping of his name under such circumstances would properly be held to be a confession of guilt or of fear of conviction on the part of those doing it or permitting it to be done. If charges are preferred against a man or officer through spite or persecution, the motive should be exposed in the trial and the false accuser of the brethren should he punished by proper church action. (4) But absent members may sometimes be dropped from the roll. Such members should be hunted up and labored with, and so induced to take letters; but if they will not join another church, they should be dealt with severally as they deserve; if they desire to retain the old connection, let it be retained under such conditions as the church may deem best to impose; if they are indifferent or repellent, let their names be dropped with or without censure as the church may deem best. (5) But unconverted members who have joined the church under a mistake, and perhaps under moral pressure, whose lives are free from scandal, may, if they desire it, be dropped without censure. To excommunicate such, with all the dishonor attaching thereto, were unjust and cruel. It damages the discipline of a church by putting no difference between a mistake and a sin, but meting out to each the same penalty, and publishing both in the minutes under the same head.[27] Such moral members, mistaken as to their conversion, should be urged to make their covenant vows real by repentance and faith; but, failing in this, the church should drop their names without censure. The utmost gentleness must be exercised towards them in the whole matter, that, if it be possible, they may be won, and not alienated. (6) The dropping of such members appears to be a just, and consequently a growing, custom among our churches. This appears from a

[27] Down to the year 1878 the Year Book recorded all who had been dropped under the head "Excommunicated;" but in the statistics for that year the more comprehensive term "Disciplined" appears, which includes every degree of censure and dropping names without censure.

partial consensus of church usages therein,[28] and from other sources.[29]

§ 184. What part should a pastor take in the discipline of members? (1) He should not take part either as the offended in the preliminary steps or as the prosecutor. Let the parties immediately concerned attend to all such matters. If he himself has suffered wrong, it is ordinarily better for him to bear it for Christ's sake than to bring the offender to discipline; but if the wrong demand public redress, he must begin and conduct the case as a private member, not as a pastor. He must not preside, or claim, or use any privileges as pastor in the trial. (2) Yet, as in other cases, he is to see to it that the proper steps have been taken, and all things necessary for the hearing of the case (§§ 166, 172) have been done before the trial begins. (3) In all things he is to show himself impartial and non-partisan. He in other cases is the presiding officer; as such he must give rulings on points that may arise. Hence he should not only be impartial, but he must appear to be impartial, which he can not be if he interest himself for any party. A civil judge can not sit on a case in which he has been or is an attorney. The pastor should be as scrupulous in church trials.

§ 185. When the pastor is the accused, can a local church complete the discipline? (1) According to the pastoral theory of the ministry (§ 111), the church can first remove him from office, when he becomes a layman again ;[30] and he can then be disciplined as a layman.[31] But this theory is false (§§ 111, 113),[32] hence (2) a church may deal with a minister as respects his Christian character and conduct (§§ 131: 5; 162: 2) and excommunicate him, in virtue of its authority to discipline all its members (§§ 99, 161). But since a minister is more than a member, since his ministerial function has been recognized by the churches

[28] Brooklyn Council, 1876.
[29] Roy's Manual, art. iii, § 4; Ross's Pocket Manual, § 117.
[30] Dexter's Congregationalism, 150, and Note.
[31] New Englander (1883), 461, 462.   [32] 43 Bib. Sacra, 403.

in ordination (§ 121), and since church censures would impair his ministerial recognition and standing (§§ 122, 123), justice and the law of fellowship require that even in church censures the voice of neighboring churches should be had before judgment is passed by the church. As, however, the methods of ascertaining the voice of said churches depend upon the fellowship of independent churches, we must postpone the further consideration of this subject to the next Lecture (§§ 200, 201, 202, 211, 212).

§ 186. If a church do wrong in its discipline, is there any redress? (1) When it obeys Christ in spirit and in the letter of discipline, it will not be likely to do wrong. It will do nothing that sanctified human nature, enlightened by the Spirit of God, can ever hope to better. But a church sometimes acts hastily, passionately, and so commits wrong in dealing with members which ought to find redress in some way. (2) Other polities allow appeals to be taken to higher judicatories, even to national tribunals, in some of which the wrong, it is hoped, may be righted. The want of similar right of appeal might be urged against our polity as a grave defect, if we had no method of redress equally good, and if the Master, in the rule itself, had not precluded such " higher courts." Since he has forbidden them (§ 99 : 2, 3), no satisfactory redress from wrongs inflicted by local church action can be expected ; for whatever gain may be claimed for such judicatories, the gain is more than counterbalanced by the loss of liberty. (3) Our polity preserves the primitive liberty, while allowing councils of advice in cases of grievance or claimed injury. If the church desire light before issuing the case, as when a minister is on trial before it, or when the offence of a layman has been peculiar; or if a member has been unjustly censured and desires redress or vindication, the proper council can be called to inquire into the matter fully and give advice. This way is open without involving the whole community or denomination in the affair. (4) This is in harmony with Christ's rule, which does not.

exclude light and advice, but external authority. It leaves the action of a local church, though advised, final. (5) If the church refuse the advice sought and obtained, the aggrieved can use the advice, if favorable, in vindication of his conduct and in admission to another church. (6) This method is the best in experience. The advice of the wisest men can be sought and secured. This has in practice worked so well that the decrees of General Assemblies have been confessed to be little more than advice. Our method conforms to Christ's rule, and is best in rightly balancing purity and liberty.

Before completing, therefore, the discipline of ministers by local churches, we must consider the bearing of fellowship upon it.

LECTURE X.

THE DOCTRINE OF THE CHRISTIAN CHURCH.—
FELLOWSHIP.

" A new commandment I give unto you, that ye love one another; even as I have loved you, that ye also love one another. By this shall all men know that ye are my disciples, if ye have love one to another." — Jesus Christ.

" Neither for these only do I pray, but for them also that believe on me through their word; that they may all be one; . . . that the world may believe that thou didst send me." — Jesus Christ.

§ 187. CHRIST'S church-kingdom appears chiefly in little democratic bodies called churches, independent one of another in matters of control and authority. Each can elect and install its own officers, control its own worship and discipline, and manage its own affairs; yet all in subjection to the will of Christ Jesus, the Head and King. These free and independent churches, having individually the same relation precisely to Christ and his church-kingdom (§§ 97, 98), stand fundamentally and essentially in the closest relations of fellowship one with another.

§ 188. The definition of church fellowship may be derived from that of Christian fellowship. One article of the Apostles' Creed defines the church to be "the communion of saints," the fellowship of believers. This is its chief visible manifestation, first, in local churches; then in association of churches. We may, therefore, define church fellowship to be the communion of churches. As saints in local churches have "mutual association on equal and friendly terms," so churches have mutual association one with another on equal and friendly terms, which constitutes church fellowship. As saints hold fellowship for their mutual edification in worship, coöperation in labors, and sanctification in spirit, so churches hold fellowship for the same purposes.

§ 189. Church fellowship is a necessity as truly as Christian fellowship. The church-kingdom is one, and not many. Hence all believers every-where are united by faith and love to Christ and to one another in one only spiritual household. This spiritual unity compels the formation of local churches, but it is not limited by the boundaries of these particular congregations of believers. It necessitates also the fellowship of churches. And as the spiritual unity becomes visible unity in local churches, it must also, for the same reason, become visible unity in associations of churches, and will not be satisfied until all churches are, in some tangible sense, visibly one. Isolation is as contrary to the nature of churches as it is contrary to the nature of saints, because churches have their existence and continuance in the life and love of the one church-kingdom. Hence the new commandment given by Christ to his disciples, that they love one another as Christ has loved them (John 13: 34). This love and life makes them all one. But Christ had more that spiritual unity — which can not be broken (§§ 32: 2; 97) — in mind when he gave the commandment and prayed his sacerdotal prayer. This unity must become visible unity, that all may know that members are true disciples of Christ (John 13: 35), and the world may believe that God sent him (John 17: 21). It is an unwarranted concession to the spirit and fact of schism, to limit the unity for which the great High Priest prayed before his offering up to spiritual unity, which is by nature indivisible. It expressly refers to a unity that can be seen, which convinces the world of the divinity of our Lord Jesus.

§ 190. Hence church fellowship is not peculiar to any polity, for all polities are built upon it. Each polity must, indeed, have a peculiar method of using this common element when it passes over from "the communion of saints" to the communion of churches; but the element of fellowship is in all systems the same. No polity has such a preemption of it that it can truly call the fellowship of churches a peculiar principle. What is peculiar is not fellowship itself, but the way of using it, of exhibiting it. One polity has one way; another has another way; all, some way. Fellowship is not, therefore, peculiar to Congregationalism [1] (§ 43).

§ 191. This element of fellowship, arising from spiritual oneness, and being therefore necessary, has been the chief vehicle on which centralized and false theories of the Christian Church have ridden into power. Each has claimed to express the unity of the church-kingdom in the normal way (§§ 52, 55, 59, 67, 81), and that way ends in unity by force. The churches retained, in large degree, their independence and liberty down to the union of the Church with the Empire under Constantine (§ 226). Since then unity of fellowship has been sought under force. But ecclesiastical force is divisive. It divided the Greek and Roman Churches, A. D. 381–1054. It cast out the Reformation in the sixteenth century. Later it ejected the Puritans and the Pilgrims. In the eighteenth century it drove out the followers of Wesley. Fellowship endures force and corruption, until the life of God in the heart can bear it no longer, then the life of love must break fellowship or perish. Such has been the origin of divisions under theories that use force. Tyranny has been endured long because of fellowship, and fellowship has been abused in the interest of hierarchies, until rebellions and separations have arisen. Thus there are five Presbyterian Churches in Scotland and nine in the United States; and there are nine Methodist Churches in the United States (§§ 70: 1; 247).

§ 192. Church fellowship may exhibit itself fully under the polity of liberty. It was "the plan of the apostles to establish many churches absolutely independent one of another," but yet in visible fellowship, according to the prayer of Christ (John 17: 21). It has been thought that unity in fellowship could not co-exist with liberty; but it is

[1] New Englander, 1878, 514–520.

coming to be seen that force, and not liberty, is the great foe of unity, and that the fulfillment of the prayer of Christ can be had only in the spontaneous, free, equal, and universal association of local churches. In such association each church can retain freedom, while all Christendom becomes one in visible manifestation. This is the divine model. The primitive churches, though perfectly independent under Christ (§§ 98, 99, 100, 109), were not isolated. They had the most fraternal interest in one another, as we have shown (§ 101). They recognized their unity, and began to manifest it in ways suited to their environment. We may do the same. All the churches of Christ may do the same, their methods varying within the Scriptural independence conceded by church historians (§ 109), that each local church has the right and authority to manage its own affairs without interference or control from without. Beyond this limitation no church fellowship may pass; for then it enters the realm of force. We shall see that this liberty under fellowship conduces to unity (§ 247), as force produces divisions.

There are two ways, or systems, of fellowship within the above limitation, which we will detail: one local and occasional and limited; the other stated, comprehensive, and ecumenical.

CHURCH FELLOWSHIP IN OCCASIONAL COUNCILS.

§ 193. The origin of this system of fellowship in occasional councils needs notice.

(1) It has its germ and warrant in the Scriptures. The prayer of Christ, that all might be one and might exhibit their unity (John 17: 20-23), and the consultation at Jerusalem (Acts 15: 1-29) are the germ and warrant of fellowship by occasional councils wherever needed. The conference of the churches of Antioch and Jerusalem and the Apostles, over the continuance of the rite of circumcision, suggested undoubtedly similar consultations of churches without inspired apostles.

(2) There arose in the second century, local and advisory assemblies, or synods, whose decrees did not bind the minority, but were merely the mature expression of opinion by the majority. There were also general councils in the early days, beginning with that at Nice, A.D. 325, and ending with one, A.D. 869, whose creeds and decrees were enforced by the temporal power. These may have aided by example in the origin of the system of occasional councils.

(3) The system, as such, has, however, a late and provincial origin. Robert Browne and his followers held to fellowship in councils for "counsel and advice." They confessed "that particular churches are 'by all means convenient to have the help of one another in all needful affairs of the church, as members of one body in the common faith, under Christ, their only Head.'"[2] But the system, as such, originated in New England. It has been supposed, but without careful inquiry, that the system of councils for the organization of churches, the installation and dismissal of pastors, had a purely normal and ecclesiastical origin and development. But there are some things that go to show that the system had largely a political origin, or, if not this, certainly a politico-ecclesiastical origin. (a) It is reasonable to believe that if the system be a normal outgrowth of church life and forces under our polity, it would have appeared in other lands. But churches of our faith and order in other countries have never developed a similar system. (b) If the system were the normal expression of church fellowship, its spread, when once originated, would have been rapid and complete, certainly in this country, if not in others; but instead, it has not prevailed largely out of New England, and has lost ground lately in New England. Installations cover less than one third of the pastors in the country, and but little more than one half in New England. The stated associations of churches began early in the present century; but they now embrace nearly every Congregational church in the

[2] Hanbury's Memorials, i, 542.

land, as in foreign lands. The stated meeting of churches has become universal, because it expresses and meets the normal fellowship of the churches in the most comprehensive way; but the occasional meeting of churches in councils has decreased, because it does not, and can not, meet and satisfy the demands of church fellowship, which are much wider than advice. How, then, did the system of councils come into being? (c) We think its general acceptance in New England is due to civil or political causes. When councils first came into prominence there, none could vote in two colonies, Massachusetts Bay and New Haven, except church members; while in Plymouth and Connecticut the suffrage was carefully restricted. In the former and controlling colonies the Legislatures were composed of laymen elected by the several churches, empowered by the Cambridge Platform to suppress heresy, immorality, and schism.[3] The General Court of Massachusetts "was but the whole body of the church legislating for its parts."[4] This General Court, in 1631, enacted that only church members should be allowed to vote;[5] in 1636, that no church should be gathered without first acquainting "the magistrates and the elders of the greater part of the churches in this jurisdiction with their intentions, and have their approbation therein;"[6] in 1658, "that henceforth no person shall publicly and constantly preach to any company of people, whether in church society or not, or be ordained to the office of teaching elder, where any two organic churches, council of state, or general court shall declare their dissatisfaction thereat; . . . and in case of ordination . . . timely notice thereof shall be given unto three or four of the neighboring organic churches, for their approbation."[7] Thus, no church could be organized without the approval of the magistrates and of the majority of the churches in the colony; and no man could preach regularly

[3] Camb. Plat. chap. xvii.
[4] Palfrey's Hist. N. E. ii, 40.
[5] Mass. Col. Records, I, 87.
[6] Ibid. 168.
[7] Ibid. iv, part i, 328.

or be ordained if two churches, or the council of state, or
the General Court objected. It is clear that some method of
obtaining the consent of the churches was needed at every
formation of a church or ordination (the same then as installation) of a minister. In this need was the birth of councils
for these purposes, and their development into an established
system. Under these and other laws, the State, in its protection of the churches, needed an eye of inquisition, that it
might use wisely its arm of strength. It was careful not to
trench on the liberties of the churches beyond the warrant
given it in the last chapter of the Cambridge Platform ; and
how could it guard these liberties and watch over all interests better than to make a council of churches its eye of inspection, even in church troubles. Hence the General Court
repeatedly called councils, naming churches and time, and
in some instances ordering them, as a commission by the
State, to report to itself.[8] That these laws had time to develop a system of councils appears from the reply which the
General Court made, in 1665, to the king's commissioners, in

[8] The following are some of the cases: In 1655 the General Court called a council of twelve churches, which it named, to adjust the troubles of Ipswich. Each church is ordered to send "two messengers." (Mass. Col. Records, iv, part 1, 225.) Again, in 1671, it ordered a council to be held at Newbury, to settle troubles, and named the churches and ordered the council to report to the General Court or to the council of the state. (Ibid. part ii, 487.) Again, in 1677, the General Court ordered the church and town of Rowley to arrange their controversy before the next term of court, or all parties were to appear before the Court. (Ibid. v, 149.) As the unruly town and church failed to come to terms, the Great and General Court said: "This Court do declare that they will not countenance any procedure or actings therein contrary to the laws of this Court, having therein made provision for the peace of the churches and a settled ministry in each town, and that all votes passed by any among them contrary thereunto are hereby declared null and void, and do order the actors therein . . . to be admonished, and to pay costs, six pounds seven shillings and eight pence." (Ibid. v, 172, 173.) As still the strife continued between the church and town of Rowley, the Court, in 1679, ordered that ten churches, which it named, "be written unto by the secretary, in the name of this Court, to assemble . . . to give their solemn advice and issue to the said differences, as God shall direct, and make return to the next General Court." (Ibid. v, 245.) The Court, in 1675, appointed a committee to adjust troubles in Salem between the church and town, which reported to the Court. (Ibid. 67.) Again, in 1677, the Court ordered a committee to settle troubles civil and ecclesiastical in Salisbury, whose advice all were required to submit to. (Ibid. 144.) In 1679 the Court ordered the inhabitants of a precinct to apply themselves to the church of Ipswich " for reconciliation," for " erecting a meeting-house," " which being done," the Court " do grant them liberty to procure a minister . . . provided he be pious, able,

which it is said, in reference to ecclesiastical institutions and regulations, "that all proceedings in this kind be done openly with the approbation of the civil government and of neighboring congregations, the Court directed to the observation thereof, the which practice having been now attended among us near forty years, we have had experience of the good effect thereof." [9]

(4) Such being the origin and provincial nature of councils, and the limitations of advice imposed upon them by the letters missive being so rigid and narrow, we may conclude that the functions of councils will in the future be greatly restricted, being confined largely to the settlement of controversies. Yet councils deserve a detailed treatment.

and orthodox, as the law directs, with the advice of the following committee" [which is named]. (Ibid. 225.) In 1681 the Court appointed three laymen and the elders of four churches to heal an Andover quarrel, and to report to the Court. (Ibid. v, 325.) Even the county court, in 1653, forbade the new church in Boston to call a man to the pastorate, because it judged him "unfit in abilities, learning, and qualifications;" but afterwards, in 1654, the General Court recommended a fit man to the said church. (Records, iv, 177, 210.)

[9] Mass. Col. Records, iv, part ii, 220, 221. We catch glimpses of the "observation" had, not only from what is said in the preceding note, but also from the following facts: In 1660 the General Court removed a minister, and enjoined a church to obtain another. (Ibid. iv, part i, 434.) The Court claimed "the power by the Word of God to assemble the churches," but from prudential reasons it refrained from the use of the power. (Ibid. ii, 156.) Yet it, in 1679, exercised the power of calling synods, and commended the result of said synod so called. (Ibid. v, 215, 244.) It recommended the renewing of the covenant, the enforcement of discipline, and the filling of all offices in the churches. (Ibid. 470.)

The Plymouth Colony was more tolerant, yet, in 1679, on petition for uniting two churches in Scituate, the Court denied the request, and ordered one to rebuild its meeting-house, and appointed four men to locate it and fix the rate of assessment for the same. (Records, Plym. Col. vi, 26, 27.)

The commissioners of the United Colonies wrote a letter, in 1656, to the church at Hartford, Conn., urging it to settle its great trouble. (Plym. Records, x, 175, 176.) They provide also, in case of "a council or synod," for settling "any question" "of common concernment," "that the members of such council or synod may consist of the churches indifferently, out of all the United Colonies by the orderly agreement of the several general courts." (Ibid. x, 328.) The United Colonies provided also, 1656, for the maintenance of "an able, orthodox ministry," as "a debt of justice and not of charity," by "the whole society jointly, whether in church order or not." (Ibid. 157.)

It seems strange to us that the general courts had so much to do in church matters; but the members of those courts in two colonies were at first the representatives of the churches, as much so as the members of our state associations. They were elected to rule ecclesiastically as well as civilly and politically. The churches did not entrust their interests to councils alone.

§ 194. The description of the system of church councils as developed in America.

(1) A church council is the assembly of such churches by pastor and delegate (and of such persons) as may be invited and named in the letter missive, to inquire and advise respecting a specified matter.[10]

(2) A council can be called by those who wish to organize a church, by a church or churches, by an aggrieved member or members of a church, when the church refuses to join in a mutual council, or by any party or parties whose case is of common concernment or is important enough to demand advice from sister churches.

(3) A council is assembled by issuing proper letters missive to the churches and individuals invited. These letters should always give: (*a*) the names of the churches invited; (*b*) the individuals invited, if any; (*c*) the object or objects of the council; and (*d*) the time and place of meeting.

(4) The parties calling a council fix and define the membership in the letters missive. No one not covered by the letters can sit on the council. Not even the church calling it is a member of it; for it asks for advice, and should not therefore have part or power in determining what that advice shall be. A council can not, therefore, from the way it is called, properly enlarge itself, not even by honorary membership in it. This rule is so essential to the nature of a council that it should never be broken.

(5) Any invited party has a right to sit in a council. If the composition of the council be such that he can not conscientiously sit in it, he should decline to attend it and notify the parties calling it to that effect, as also the council; but neither the church itself, by letter or delegate, nor any individual member of the council, can challenge the right of another church or of an individual to membership therein,

---

[10] The rules given respecting councils are those that have grown up by usage, and have come to be recognized as valid though they have never been formally adopted. Hence they are somewhat flexible.

if covered by the letters missive. The council itself can not exclude a member, except for misconduct in the sessions. This arises from the nature of a council, as chosen by the parties desiring it.

(6) A quorum of a council consists of a majority of all who have right to sit in it. A minority of two members, possibly of one, may organize provisionally and adjourn to a fixed time and place, but can not transact any other business.

(7) The objects of a council are: (*a*) to advise respecting the organization of a church;[11] (*b*) or the dissolution of a church; (*c*) the ordination, installation, dismissal, discipline, or deposition of a minister; (*d*) the redress of aggrieved members; (*e*) church troubles or necessities; (*f*) the apostasy or disorderly walk of a church in fellowship; and (*g*) any matter requiring the combined wisdom of the churches in council to settle. There needs to be added another object: (*h*) redress of grievances when a church or minister has been unjustly excluded or expelled from an association, the association and the church or minister being parties with equal rights and privileges in calling the council (§ 194: 10, *c*).

(8) The scope of councils is limited by the letter missive to the specific object for which the council is called. A council should not inquire into matters nor act upon questions

[11] When the Shepard Church, Cambridge, was organized, in 1636, the eleventh in Massachusetts Bay Colony, they acquainted the magistrates with their purpose to form a church, "who gave their approbation" and "they sent to all the neighboring churches for their elders to give their assistance," and asked "the churches, that if they did approve them to be a church, they would give them the right hand of fellowship," which was done (Manual (1872), 8, 9). So when the Woburn church, Mass., was formed, 1642, the magistrates were present, and the elders of the churches questioned the members to their satisfaction, and gave them the right hand of fellowship in the name of the churches. The church was constituted with a covenant, which was assented to or joined in before the messengers of the churches. There appears to have been no distinct creed. In the covenant occur the words: "And all this, both according to the present light that the Lord hath given us, as also according to all further light, which he shall be pleased at any time to reach out unto us out of the Word by the goodness of his grace," etc. (Johnson's Wonder Working Providence, book ii, chap. xxii.)

This care about new churches was in the interest of uniformity enforced by law, as well as, if not more than, an expression of fellowship among churches. The same is true of installation in the early days of New England.

not directly or indirectly covered by said letters. The letters are held to be the charter of a council, beyond which inquiry may not be made or action had. Whatever is necessary to a complete judgment and result as to the one specific object of the council can be and should be thoroughly examined; but being called for one purpose, it may not inquire into another matter not germane.

This limited scope of councils — which, however, seems necessary to liberty — utterly prevents them from ever becoming able to meet the wants of church fellowship. Communion is more comprehensive than advice, and true fellowship can not be limited to occasional expressions upon the few topics of forming churches, installing, dismissing and disciplining ministers, and adjusting church troubles. This limited scope of councils exhibits their essential inadequacy to satisfy church fellowship.

(9) The size of councils is determined by the party or parties calling them. They may range from a few up to a hundred churches or more. They should generally consist of all neighboring churches within easy access. Ten churches make a good-sized council.

(10) There are several kinds of councils. When viewed in respect to the object mentioned in the letters missive, they may be called councils of recognition, whether of a church or of a pastor; councils of dissolution of a church; councils of ordination, installation, dismissal, or discipline of a minister; councils of illumination or of admonition, etc.; the purpose of the council giving the name to it. When viewed in respect to the parties calling them, councils may be classified more exactly, as, councils called by one party, *uni parte* councils; councils called by two parties in agreement, *duo parte* councils; councils called by parties in controversy, mutual councils; and councils called by one party to a controversy, *ex parte* councils. We will treat fully each of these four kinds of councils, though we have explained them elsewhere.[12]

[12] Pocket Manual, §§ 48–51.

(a) Councils called by one party may be called, from lack of a better name, *uni parte*. There is in connection with them no opposition, nor other party in agreement. When persons agree to form a church and call a council to advise in the matter, or when a church desires light and advice in troubles, or in a case of discipline or of doctrine, or when any single party calls a council for any purpose whatever, councils so called by one party constitute a class by themselves, to be distinguished from all other councils.

(b) When there are two parties in agreement, standing in no opposition to each other, it produces confusion and evil to call a council convened by them a mutual council. Another name ought to be found for it, and one which will distinguish it from all other classes of councils. No better word than *duo parte* councils has been found or invented for them. This class includes councils of ordination, installation, or recognition, and often of dismission of a minister. A council called by a minister and a friendly church, in agreement, to inquire into any matter, as the minister's standing, or into the action of a third party with which the minister may have had a controversy or by which he may have been censured, is not a mutual, but a *duo parte*, council, because called by parties in perfect agreement. To call such a council mutual is misleading.

(c) A mutual council is one called by the mutual agreement and selection of two or more parties in controversy. Each party selects an equal portion of the council. The rule is: " In a difficulty or controversy between the church and its elder or elders, or between the church and some other person or party in the church, if a council is desired, and the church consents, the churches to constitute the council are selected by agreement between the parties . . . and this is called a mutual council." [13] " Cases of controversy in general between a church and its pastor ; cases of controversy between a church and a private member or members," call

[13] Boston Plat. part iii, chap. ii, 4.

for mutual councils. "Occasions calling for the formation of mutual councils are always understood to imply the existence of two parties which sustain to each other such a relation as to render it expedient to deviate from the common practice."[14] "Such as are assembled by the coöperation of two parties standing in any sort against each other are called mutual" councils.[15] A council, therefore, is a mutual council only when called by parties in controversy; if called by parties in agreement, it is not a mutual council.

(*d*) An *ex parte* council holds an important place in our polity. Punchard calls such councils "courts of errors, to which the humblest member of a Congregational church may appeal. This appeal, can not however, be made until a mutual reference has been refused."[16] Cotton Mather calls them "a remedy for oppression." When a member or members have been wronged by the action of a church, they should ask the church to join in calling a mutual council. If the church refuse by vote or neglect to join in such council, the aggrieved may then, but not till then, call an *ex parte* council, to review the case and give advice.

This same right, as we shall see (§ 199), belongs to a church or minister that has been improperly cut off from connection by action of the conference or association to which either belonged.

The conditions necessary to the calling of an *ex parte* council are: a valid complaint of wrong actually done which calls for redress. Irregularities in procedure may not constitute a ground of complaint (§ 180). Redress of this wrong through a mutual council must be courteously requested of the offending body. An insolent request demands refusal, but such refusal is not a ground for calling an *ex parte* council. But if the body refuse a courteous request for a mutual council, the aggrieved has right to redress through an *ex parte* council.

[14] Upham's Ratio Disciplinæ, §§ 158, 159.
[15] Dexter's Congregationalism as seen in its Literature, 527.
[16] View of Congregationalism, 124.

(11) Different councils are sometimes confounded to the peril of good order. Hence careful discrimination needs to be made and observed between the kinds above given, which include all. Yet we need to note more particularly: (*a*) Councils of advice on the discipline of laymen are easily confounded with *ex parte* councils, though having no characteristic elements in common. A church in the progress of trying a lay member needs advice, and calls a council to give it. Is that council *ex parte?* No; it is *uni parte.* One party not in controversy calls it, and not a party in controversy, as in *ex parte* councils. A layman undergoing trial by the church is not a party in controversy, but a party on trial; he has no grievance in the trial, and can have none, until his case is issued. And the church, having complete jurisdiction, can issue the case without calling any council, or, if it choose, it can call a council to advise it what to do in completing the trial. A layman on trial can not ask the church for a mutual council. Not until the case is issued, and wrong be done him, can he request such council. A council thus called to aid the church in dealing with a layman on trial has none of the characteristics of an *ex parte* council. (*b*) There may be three parties in a church: a pastor, whose ministerial standing (§ 122) is questioned or destroyed; the majority of the church, that stands by him; and a minority, that stands opposed to him. The pastor and the majority call a council to inquire into the pastor's standing. What is such a council? It is not a mutual council, because the parties calling it are in agreement. And to call it such is both misleading, as respects the whole fraternity of churches, and unjust, as respects the opposing minority in the church, which has been ignored. Such a council is *duo parte*, because called by two parties in friendly agreement and concurrent action. (*c*) When a church walks disorderly and two neighboring churches, after due labor, call a council to withdraw fellowship from it, is such a council *ex parte* or mutual? This process constitutes "the third way of the

communion of churches,"[17] which was approved by the action of our churches, in 1865.[18] It is *ex parte*, as the churches in laboring with the disorderly church should ask it to join with them in calling a mutual council, and only on the refusal of which request can the supposed council properly be called. This process, to make it successful, as experience shows, needs the authority of the magistrate behind it to enforce it, as in the early days, when it was first formulated.[19] It is not likely to be tried often, if ever again, as a more peaceful and efficient way has been opened to the churches (§§ 209, 211).

(12) The mode of procedure in councils is usually as follows: The oldest pastor reads the letter missive, calls the council to order, and presides while a temporary moderator and scribe are chosen. The roll is then made out. If a quorum (§ 194: 6) be not present, the council, after due delay for arrivals, adjourns to a fixed time and place. If a quorum be present the council should elect by ballot a permanent moderator and scribe, and proceed to the business before it. In conducting its business, the ordinary rules of deliberative bodies are used,[20] except where superseded or modified by special rules or Congregational usage. In all sessions of the council the best order should be observed and the utmost impartiality shown, as becomes the churches of the Lord Jesus Christ assembled to learn and do his will.

(13) The result of a council is the formulated action of the body, both as to what is called "the findings" and as to the advice given. This result is formulated and adopted in private session after the case has been fully heard. If the council be fairly chosen and acts impartially, its result is conclusive as to facts, usages, and jurisdiction. The civil courts will respect it and will protect the parties acting on said advice, as in church trials, and will enforce the action of the

---

[17] Camb. Plat. chap. xv, 2, 3.
[19] Camb. Plat. xvii.

[18] Boston Plat. part iii, chap. ii, 11.
[20] See Pocket Manual, §§ 151-161.

council in matters coming within the jurisdiction of said courts.[21]

But the advice given in the result may be accepted or rejected by either party or by both parties, since it is only advice. But if either party accept the advice, the other party is so far forth holden by it. If a council advise the dissolution of the pastoral relation, the acceptance of the advice by the pastor or by the church society dissolves the pastoral relation and stops salary. If the council advise the dissolution of the pastorate and the payment of a sum of money to the pastor by the church society, the acceptance of the advice by the pastor closes his pastorate, but does not compel the church society to pay the advised sum. It can not be collected in law,[22] unless the society also accepts the advice.

(14) Councils are temporary bodies called on special occasions for specified objects. If they do not meet when called, or on the day to which they are adjourned, they can not meet at all, except as new councils on new letters missive. If during the proceedings or at the close they adjourn without day, they are dissolved, and can not meet again except on new letters as new councils. They may for cause adjourn to a fixed time and place, or at the call of the moderator or scribe, and assemble again; but they are occasional bodies and can not become permanent.

SOME QUESTIONS RESPECTING COUNCILS.

§ 195. What is the force of usage in Congregationalism? The above rules have been established as convenient by

[21] Buck's Mass. Eccl. Law, 240; Watson vs. Jones, 13 Wallace (U. S. Supreme Court), 679. This decision is so important that it is quoted in full in Moore's Presb. Digest (1873), 251-262.

"The Court always look behind the adjudication; and before the result can be received as evidence, or allowed to have any validity, they will examine the proceedings to ascertain whether there was a suitable case for the convocation of an ecclesiastical council; whether the members were properly selected; whether they proceeded impartially in their investigation; whether their adjudication was so formally made that it might be seen that they acted with due regard to the rights of the parties, and that they founded their decision upon grounds that will sustain it." Thompson vs. Rehoboth, 5 Pick. 471; 7 Pick. 163. Quoted in 1 Cong. Quart. 176.

[22] Rev. A. H. Quint, D.D., gives a valuable discussion on these points in 1 Cong. Quart. 173, seq.

usage, as we have said; but what force has usage among independent churches?

Usage is the common practice; a few instances do not make a usage; but the common practice even for ages can not prevent changes without destroying liberty. To say at any time of any thing that it can not be done because usage is against it, is to attempt to bind the polity of free churches in the swaddling clothes of infancy or the small garments of childhood for all the future. Independent churches can do any thing, consistent with the New Testament, demanded by the expanding interests of the church-kingdom. For usage is only a guide to orderly development. Custom should not be set aside in a spirit of license, or without sufficient reason, and then only in lines of truth, unity, and liberty. The extension of church fellowship into stated associations, district, state, and national, has been accomplished against usage, and may require changes in our customs in some other respects. We need to guard on the one hand against an antiquarian rigor of usage, and on the other hand against innovating license, and make only such changes in usages as the Scriptures allow and growth and reason demand.

§ 196. Is the result of a council divisible? It is manifestly divisible into the findings and the advice; and the advice may be accepted without endorsing the findings. So also if two or more things are advised, that advice is divisible, and may be accepted in whole or in part by either party, since it is simply advice and not a mandatory decree.

§ 197. In calling a mutual council has either party a right to challenge the selections of the other party? Such a right of challenge might be used to prevent a mutual council or to pervert it, and hence justice and equality deny the right. Neither party can challenge the selections of the other. Each party should choose fair-minded men, while duly looking after its own interests.[23]

§ 198. Is there not danger of councils being chosen from

[23] Buck's Mass. Eccl. Law, 219.

churches and men of known bias? It is unfortunately too true, if not fatally true, that a council may be thus directly or indirectly packed to do a desired thing. This objection lies especially against the councils which we have designated *uni parte, duo parte,* and *ex parte,* but not against mutual councils, unless packed by limiting them to the churches of a specified district. If a church wish to ordain or install a man of questionable orthodoxy or character, and it itself be of easy virtue, it may select a council by careful picking that will ordain or install him. If one council refuse, a second or third may be called, until the thing desired be done. Or if there be no other way, the church may ordain or install him, and ask the invited churches, not to examine and advise, but to assist in the ordination or installing exercises. None of these things supposed goes beyond the actual facts in rare cases. Railroads have immensely enlarged the area from which councils can be conveniently drawn, and hence have increased the temptation. Yet if a territorial limit be put upon the calling of councils, it may, in certain cases, work as it did with the elder Edwards,[24] in giving a packed council. If a party appeal against such packed council, it is council against council, with no state authority, as in the early days of New England, where and when the system grew up, to interpose and settle the controversy.[25]

The danger to our polity from this liability is very great. It impairs the advice of councils, and if it should be held as sound Congregationalism that an ordaining council, called for the purpose, by laying hands on a man puts him into good and regular standing in the Congregational ministry, from which he can not be removed but by a council duly called for that very purpose, as has been maintained,[26] then not only purity but also fellowship is endangered by such packed councils.[27]

[24] Life of President Edwards, Works, i, 36.
[25] Hubbard's History N. E., 16 Mass. Hist. Col. 608, 609.
[26] Result of Stanton (Mich.) Council. The Congregationalist, May 24, 1882.
[27] New Englander, 1883, 485–487.

For these reasons, as for others (§ 185), a minister's standing (§ 122) should be held in an association of churches, secured by vote on proper credentials (§§ 122, 124, 213), to which he is amenable as a minister, but not as a church member (§§ 162: 2; 185); and he should not be held or treated as in full connection with the fraternity of Congregational churches until this standing has been secured. If any association unjustly refuse to admit him into such ministerial standing or wrongfully expel him from it, he has the right of asking it to join him in calling a mutual council, to consider the whole case from the beginning, in order to advise his admission or restoration or to depose him from the ministry. This method provides a complete remedy from packed councils of ordination and installation, and ample security and relief if a minister be unjustly deprived of ministerial standing, with full freedom from centralization.

§ 199. Can an association be a party in the calling of a council? We may answer: (1) That whatever concerns the churches may be the ground of a council. If a thing be of common well-being, the churches may sit in council upon it. And the parties most affected or involved are the ones that should invite the churches to give their advice in the matter. (2) Past usage can not prevent needed changes (§ 195). If it could, then a living infallible pope were better than an unchangeable custom. Usage is not superior to principle and growth, and hence it must change, since Congregationalism is a living organism. (3) The past has had similar councils. We have already shown how the General Court of Massachusetts Bay, which was also a general association of the churches, called councils (§ 193: 3, c, note). Besides, councils have been called by associations of ministers, by towns, and by missionary societies.[28] There is nothing to hinder the calling of such councils, if there be a general need of them. (4) That there is such need is easily made apparent. Ministerial standing of some

[28] Dexter's Congregationalism in Lit. 526, 527; Upham's Ratio Disciplinæ, § 93.

sort is now held largely in associations of churches or of ministers.[29] Ministers have been expelled from them, either after a fair inquiry or without a fair hearing, possibly no notice having been given them; and their expulsion is published in the papers to their great damage. If they are unjustly dealt with in such exclusion, how shall the wrong be ascertained and redressed? There is only one ecclesiastical way of redress in our polity equal and fair to both the parties involved (§ 124: 7). If redress be sought in the civil courts on a suit for libel or slander, or in a *mandamus* ordering their restoration to membership, the expense is great, the result probably adverse,[30] and our polity is put to shame. If a church call a council on the case, its action therein is indirect and inadequate. Each such case can be covered and full redress rendered only by a mutual council called by the two parties involved, the minister suspended or expelled or excluded and the association or conference doing the alleged wrong. Neither civil courts nor other councils meet the requirements of the case. Hence justice and polity alike demand that in such cases at least associations be parties in the calling of councils. Nothing else will satisfy. (5) This change adjusts our polity to its expanding conditions. Installation, if it were universal in the pastorate, could not be the security necessary, because such councils are liable to be packed. But installation reaches only a third of our pastors and less than one fourth of our ministers. There is a demand, founded in ordination itself as the recognition of the ministerial call and function, that ministers hold somewhere a constant accountable standing. Our principles place that accountable standing in associations of churches (§ 124: 6). In some places it is held in associations of ministers.[31] These associations can certify their members to the State Minutes and the National Year Books; and can receive, dis-

---

[29] 43 Bib. Sacra, 416–420.
[30] Shurtleff vs. Stevens, 51 Vt. 501; 31 Am. Reports, 704; 37 Mich. Reports, 542.
[31] 9 Cong. Quart. 194; 51 Vt. Repts. 501.

miss, try, and expel them for cause. And lest injustice be done a minister by refusal to receive or by expulsion, the right of appeal should be had, not to the State Association and then to the National Council, but directly to the churches, in and through a council mutually chosen, which may review the whole case and advise restoration or deposition from the ministry. Such a council is in harmony with our principles, meets a defect in our polity, satisfies the necessities arising from the wide extension and rapid increase of our churches, and gives both purity and liberty without centralization. It has received national recognition (§ 124: 8).

§ 200. What part have councils of churches in the discipline of ministers?

(1) In respect to Christian character and belief ministers are amenable to the churches of which they are members (§§ 131: 5; 162: 2), which may deal with them in that regard as with other members, with (§ 194: 10, *a*, 11, *a*) or without calling in the advice of a council. But while churches have this right, they need to remember that those called into the ministry of the Word have far higher qualifications (§ 119: 1–6) than believers need, to become church members, which qualifications are recognized in their ordination (§ 121: 1–6). Their ordination thus places them in peculiar relations with all churches, since it is not the recognition of a pastoral relation (§ 121: 4), but of a divine call and ministerial function (§ 113). Thereafter they are recognized as ministers by all churches in connection, whose peace and welfare are largely dependent on the belief and conduct of said ministers. On this relation is properly built up in all polities accountable ministerial standing (§§ 122, 123), which takes their discipline, as ministers, out of the hands of the local churches of which they are members, and puts it into the hands of some association or council of churches.

(2) This principle was definitely affirmed with only one dissentient vote, by our churches in National Council at St. Louis, in 1880, in the passage of the following resolutions: —

"*Resolved* (1), That a *pro re nata* council is the origin of ministerial standing in our fellowship, and the ultimate resort in all cases of question.

"*Resolved* (2), That the continued certification of ministerial standing may well be left to the ministerial associations or the organizations of churches.

"*Resolved* (3), That the body of churches in any locality have the inalienable right of extending ministerial fellowship to, or withholding fellowship from, any person within their bounds, no matter what his relations may be in church membership or ecclesiastical affiliations, the proceedings to be commenced by any church, and to be conducted with due regard to equity."[32]

This is a clear and emphatic enunciation of ministerial accountability, as ministers, to the body of churches in any locality where they may labor, whatever their relations as church members may be. It is so certain and real a thing that it is "the inalienable right" of the churches in any locality to bring them to account for heresy or misconduct. This right resides in the body of the churches in the locality where the offence is committed.

(3) The method of putting this inalienable right into operation for clearing the churches of unworthy ministers is manifestly separable from the right itself. The right may be exercised in one way at one time and place, and in another way at another time and place. The right must not be confounded with the method of exercising it. The method indicated in the resolutions is through a council called for the purpose, the proceedings to be commenced by any church. This method is so defective as to render the right which is inalienable practically inoperative. (*a*) A church may possibly, in rare instances, deal with its own pastor in discipline, but it is safe to say that it will never begin proceedings against the pastor of a neighboring church. If asked to do this, it will demur. (*b*) No better

[32] Minutes National Council for 1880, 17.

device for stirring up strife between two churches was ever imagined than the one given in these resolutions of the National Council, making it the duty of one church to begin proceedings against the pastor of a sister church. (*c*) A similar process for dealing with a wayward church,[33] instead of its pastor, has been tried a few times, stirring up the bitterest animosity and utterly failing of good results. A recent attempt closes this method.[34] The more difficult task of one church attempting to discipline by a council of churches another church's pastor has, we believe, never been undertaken; and it is safe to predict that it will never be undertaken. For: —

(4) This inalienable right of the churches in any locality to give or withhold fellowship may be exercised in a far easier and better way. It is by requiring that ministerial standing be held in the association of churches of any locality, in order to full connection in the Congregational ministry. If a minister be not in such associational connection, though ordained by a council of churches and a pastor of a Congregational church, he should be reported in Minutes and Year Books as not in connection, and for whom, consequently, our associated churches are not to be held accountable. If he be expelled from such connection, he may, if aggrieved, find redress in a mutual or *ex parte* council.

(5) Councils have, therefore, an important part to act in the discipline of ministers. If a minister still be in ministerial standing and a church begin process against him as a church member, it should not complete it without asking him to join in calling a mutual council, since he is more

---

[33] Camb. Plat. xv, 2 [3].

[34] The Church of the Pilgrims and the Clinton Avenue Congregational Church, Brooklyn, N. Y., united in beginning process against the Plymouth Church, Brooklyn, in 1873, which resulted in a large council called by them in 1874. This council accomplished nothing. Other attempts were made or suggested, when the Plymouth Church called a council, in 1876, which closed the case. This conspicuous failure of "the third way" will prevent any church from beginning proceedings against the pastor of another church through a council of churches.

than a church member, and his wider relations as a minister require this wider treatment of his case. If any church should begin process against him as a minister, it should ask him to join in a mutual council to try the case. If an association expel him or refuse to admit him, he should ask the association to join in calling a mutual council, to review the case. If in any case a mutual council be refused, an *ex parte* council may be called. Thus in every form of process the ultimate resort is to a *pro re nata* council of churches.

So if a church be unjustly excluded or expelled from an association, it may, on the same principle and inalienable right, ask the association for a mutual council, and that being unjustly denied, may call an *ex parte* council (§ 194 : 10).

§ 201. May a council of churches depose from the ministry? In order to answer this question, we must refer back to the ministerial function and ordination.

(1) The ministerial function is far more than the pastoral relation, as we have shown (§ 113). It is not something conferred by man, and it can not, therefore, be taken away by man.

(2) Ordination is the ecclesiastical recognition of the ministerial function and call (§ 121 : 4). If we make the ministerial function identical with the pastoral relation, then ordination becomes only inauguration, and removal from office is deposition from the ministry. Any church may then depose its pastor. This was the case in the pastoral theory of the ministry, held for a time by our churches, but soon abandoned as untenable. While this theory was held, deposition was strictly removal from office, by which the pastor was made a layman again; but this theory of the ministry was so narrow that writers found great difficulty in keeping within it so as to be consistent in their statements.

(3) If ordination were a conferring of the Holy Ghost, the imprinting of a character, the imparting by the laying on of hands of a special grace, then deposition, whether by a church or by a council of churches, would be the withdrawal

of the Holy Ghost, the erasure of the character, and the removal of the grace. But our churches have never believed in such ordination and deposition.

(4) Hence, as ordination is the recognition by prayer and the imposition of hands of the qualifications, the call, and the function of a minister, as conferred by Christ, so the deposition of a man from the ministry is the withdrawal of such ecclesiastical recognition (§ 121: 3, 4) when once given. And this should be done by a council of churches, if the recognition in ordination was so given, which has of late years been the case. But

§ 202. May not councils give place to associations of churches in ordaining and deposing ministers?

(1) There is nothing in the nature of the case to prevent this change. The churches in any locality may, in the exercise of their inalienable right, extend fellowship to a man in ordination or withhold it from him in deposition through an association that meets statedly, as well as through a council that meets occasionally. The same churches do it in either case, and a council has no greater warrant than an association, if as good.

(2) There are reasons why an association can ordain and depose better than a council of churches. These reasons are: (*a*) The association embraces the churches in any locality, while the council may include only a part of them, or go entirely beyond their number. Thus the inalienable right of the churches in any locality to extend or withhold fellowship finds a far safer expression in associations than in councils. Indeed, councils sometimes not only ignore this right, but contemn and defy it. (*b*) If an association make a mistake in ordination or deposition, it can correct it, and both will be recorded in the same journal for preservation and inspection — the same body correcting its own mistake. But if a council, doing the same things, commit a blunder, it can not after adjournment correct it. Another council must be called to do that. So it is one council against

another council. Besides, the results of both councils, being nowhere recorded, unless by the churches calling them, are soon lost altogether, or no one knows where to find them. True, in some states efforts are made to preserve them, but probably in no state are the collections complete, while in many states no effort is made to preserve them. (*c*) The independence of the churches is not interfered with by either method. Each church can have whom it pleases as pastor. If the association will not ordain whom the church wants, the church is in the same condition precisely as if the same churches in council had refused to ordain him. If the church, to ordain a man under such circumstances, go beyond the boundary of the association for a council, or pick a council from within the association, it defies the inalienable right of those churches in the locality, which can not be held to be a gain for councils. Instead, it is better for the church to fall back upon its own inalienable right to elect and inaugurate its own officers by ordination, remembering that it may itself be cut off in consequence from the association and all church fellowship for violation of its covenant with the churches in connection. (*d*) In case of ordination by the association of churches, expulsion after trial by a similar body would be deposition from the ministry. It would be the withdrawal of recognition by the churches of the man's call and function as a minister, from which action, as we have seen (§ 200: 5), appeal may be taken to a mutual council. (*e*) The expense in time and money of councils of ordination and deposition, when the churches have stated meetings in associations, becomes a reason why the association should do the work, if consistent with principle. This reason is apparent in the western states and territories.

(3) The objections to ordination and deposition by associations do not, in our judgment, outweigh the reasons in favor of such action. If it be said that it be centralizing and Presbyterianizing, the denial is ample, and will be given hereafter (§§ 210, 249).

§ 203. May not councils of installation give place to councils of recognition? Installation is re-ordination, and came into vogue partly in consequence of the pastoral theory of the ministry, which made a pastor a layman when out of office, and required re-ordination when taking another church, and partly as a guard to purity. It has two elements, a legal and an ecclesiastical element. Installation in some states legally binds a church society in a contract with its pastor which can be dissolved only in one of the following four ways: (1) by death; (2) by mutual consent; (3) by a mutual council; and (4) by an *ex parte* council, a mutual council having been refused.[35] This legal element is easily separable from the ecclesiastical element as foreign, unnecessary, and disturbing; it can be dropped and leave the ecclesiastical in full force. But if a council be necessary to dismiss an installed pastor in an ecclesiastical sense, then installation should give place to recognition; for when a pastor's resignation has been accepted, there is nothing for a council of dismissal to do but to advise what has been already done and to give papers that may serve as credentials. If councils of installation are to be continued, they should drop their legal element and require no dismissing council, except in cases of trouble or charges of heresy or immorality; that is, they should become councils of recognition.

§ 204. Are councils adequate safeguards of purity? It was said in the report of a committee made to the National Council, in 1883, that "the churches of the East have depended entirely upon the action of councils for ordination and installation as the safeguards of the purity of the ministry." [36]

(1) Councils of installation reach but a fraction of the ministry in active pastoral work. In 1886 the installed pastors in New England were only fifty-one per cent. of those in pastoral work, and only thirty-seven per

[35] Buck's Mass. Eccl. Law, 212, 213.   [36] Minutes, 162.

cent. of all Congregational ministers; while out of New England in the United States, installation reaches only twenty per cent. of our pastors, and fourteen per cent. of all the ministers.[37] That is, in New England a bare majority of our churches, and in the rest of the country only one fifth of them, are protected by the safeguard of installation. In 1857, when the statistics of our churches were first published, seventy-three per cent. of our pastors in New England were installed, and fifty-four per cent. of all our ministers there. Such being the facts, the churches there can not much longer depend entirely on councils of ordination and installation for safeguards of purity. Indeed, wisdom demands that those states begin finding some better safeguard, or soon their churches will be defenceless.

(2) This decadence in installations has come about in the face of the most persistent efforts to encourage the churches to call such councils. As a means to this end reports in our Year Books have divided pastors into two classes, "pastors" and "acting pastors," and the Boston Council, in 1865, declared installation necessary to the recognition of a preacher as a pastor.[38] It can hardly be hoped that since the churches have stated fellowship in their associations, they will ever return to councils in addition as safeguards of purity; since a comprehensive, inexpensive, normal, and adequate safeguard is found in ministerial standing in associations of churches.

(3) No safeguard which reaches only a small proportion of ministers and churches, and is failing in spite of every

[37] During the last thirty years strenuous efforts have been made in papers, associations, and councils to induce the churches to install their pastors. The result is indicated in the following table, in the making of which the "unspecified" for the years 1857 and 1867 are divided one third to "pastors," and two thirds to "acting pastors."

Per cent. of the installed:

Year.	Pastors.	Acting Pastors.	Ministers.	Of Pastors.	Of Ministers.
1857	1,025	706	2,350	59.2	40.5
1867	887	1,111	2,879	44.4	30.8
1877	889	1,474	3,406	39.0	26.1
1885	954	1,910	4,043	33.3	23.6

This shows a steady and great relative decline in installations.

[38] Boston Plat. part iii, chap. ii, 7 [2].

device to sustain it, can be adequate, and no such safeguard should be relied on any longer than is needful for adjustment to a better way. The ease with which councils can be packed, their unfitness for careful inquiry on the eve of installations, their tendency to stir up strife by hasty action, the fact that if one council fail to do the will of a church another can be called to do it, their narrow scope, their expense in countries with few churches, their politico-ecclesiastical origin, — these and some other things render it evident that councils, except for adjustment of troubles and the discipline of ministers or churches, will ultimately cease.

CHURCH FELLOWSHIP IN MINISTERIAL ASSOCIATIONS.

§ 205. Ministerial associations only indirectly express the fellowship of the churches; but as they stand between occasional councils and stated associations of the churches, for which they prepared the way in this country, we call attention to them.

(1) When the ministers within a small or large district organize into an association with or without a written constitution or rules or covenant, the body so formed is a ministerial association.

(2) Such associations sprang out of the unity of the church-kingdom conjoined with the circumstances in which our polity developed in this country. They originated in the conflict of the law of fellowship with the fears of centralization, natural in those separating from persecuting state establishments. The exact date of their formation is unknown. There is notice of one as early as 1633.[39] These

[39] "We find the following in the journal of Governor Winthrop, under the early date of 1633: 'The ministers in the Bay and Saugus did meet once a fortnight at one of their houses by course, where some question of moment was debated.'" — Hist. Essex North Ass'n of Mass., by Rev. S. J. Spaulding, 9. "In 1641-1642 Letchford, in his Plain Dealing, says: 'Of late, divers of the ministers have had set meetings to order church matters; whereby it is conceived they bend toward Presbyterian rule.' In 1643 there was an assembly called at Cambridge of all the pastors in the country, some fifty in all. 'The principle occasion' of which, says Winthrop, 'was because some of the elders were about to set up some things according to the presbytery, as of Newbury, etc.' The assembly concluded against some parts of the presbyterial way." — Ibid. 10.

meetings of ministers were, however, soon discontinued, through the fear, on the part of the churches, of ministerial power. The first whose existence can be traced in a regularly organized form probably embraced the ministers in and around Boston, and whose earliest recorded date is 1655. The synod of Cambridge met in 1647, and issued in 1648 a platform of church discipline which allayed the fears of the churches lest a presbytery should be set up over them. Thereafter ministerial associations flourished.[40]

(3) The object of ministerial associations was at first and chiefly professional, and not ecclesiastical. Rev. Thomas Shepard, 1672, described their object in these words: "Nothing that was difficult or questionable or weighty or new, or that had an influence upon the whole, but they were wont to consult with one another."[41] The object is thus stated in the oldest constitution extant, we believe: "For promoting the gospel and our mutual assistance and furtherance in that great work"; "yet the members were bound 'to submit to the counsel, reproofs, and censures of the brethren so associated and assembled in all things in the Lord.'"[42] This rule implies that said association was more than a professional club.

(4) Ministerial standing came to be held in some of these associations. The General Association of Connecticut, in 1812, appointed a committee to consider the question of the ecclesiastical standing of ministers dismissed from churches, who were members of associations, and report. That committee reported, in 1813, declaring that a dismissed minister is amenable to the association to which he belonged, after dismissal from a church the same as before. This report was adopted.[43] This confirms the implication above expressed,

[40] 2 Cong. Quart. 203, seq. Yet John Wise said, in 1710: "About thirty years ago, more or less, there was no appearance of the associations of pastors in these colonies and in some parts and places there is none yet." Hist. Essex North Ass'n, Mass. 10.
[41] 2 Cong. Quart. 204.
[42] Ibid. 205. They were bound also not to "relinquish the association, nor forsake the appointed meetings, without giving sufficient reason for the same."
[43] Contrib. Eccl. Hist. Ct. 323; 9 Cong. Quart. 194.

and is an important action, as it is the first instance we have seen of asserted responsible ministerial membership in associations. It is in line with the subsequent decision of the Supreme Court of Vermont, which held that membership in some ministerial association, where they exist, is "considered among the churches as evidence of good ministerial standing."[44] Such associations receive members on credentials (§ 213), give credentials on dismissal, try and expel them for cause.

Rev. John Mitchell said, in 1838: "But though an association is not competent to depose a minister in form, it may do that which is virtually equivalent. It may declare him to have forfeited his standing with his brethren, and publish him as unworthy of the public confidence."[45] But no association can do this justly without a careful examination into the case.

It is contrary to the principles of Congregationalism for ministerial standing (§ 124: 5) to be held in ministerial bodies, thus separating it from the churches.[46] Hence the practice above referred to is dangerous, and ministerial standing should be held only in associations of churches (§ 124: 6).

(5) Ministerial associations are temporary in our polity. They were the stepping-stones in this country between the independency that relied on the state [47] and associations of independent churches. They secure the fellowship of the clergy, not of the churches, except through their pastors. So far as pastors acting in concerted coöperation could exercise authority over churches of our order, ministerial associations gave opportunity for ministerial rule, instead of prelatical. And this opportunity they did not fail, occasionally, to improve, and try to exercise authority.[48] The churches, however, are now coming more and more to the front, until

[44] Shurtleff vs. Stevens, 51 Vt. 501; 31 Am. Repts. 704.
[45] Guide to Princip. and Prac. Cong. Chhs. N. E. 234.
[46] Pocket Manual, §§ 80, 83; New Englander (1883), 477–483.
[47] Camb. Plat. xvii. [48] 7 Cong. Quarterly, 35, seq.

all our churches, in this and other lands, are gathered into fellowship through church associations,[49] supplanting ministerial associations.

But it was not until the latter bodies had long existed in this country without exhibiting any natural and fatal tendency to centralization, or in any way endangering the liberties of the churches, that the churches ventured to enter upon a fuller, more normal and comprehensive form of fellowship in associations of their own by pastors and delegates, which is destined to supplant ministerial associations and abide as the permanent form.

CHURCH FELLOWSHIP IN ASSOCIATIONS OF CHURCHES.

§ 206. An association of churches is the stated meeting of churches by pastors and delegates, and of such other ministers as may be members of it, under a constitution or covenant, expressed or understood, limiting its membership, objects, and functions. They are named differently in different places. An examination of the local associations reveals the general name conference in this country, while elsewhere they are called with rare, if any, exceptions unions or associations. The state bodies are generally called associations. The national bodies are called National Council in the United States, and Unions elsewhere. An ecumenical gathering has not yet been held, and so has not been named.

§ 207. The importance of church associations can not be over-estimated. They are the normal expression of church fellowship without the narrow limitations of councils. Hence they must increase while councils and ministerial associations must decrease. They bind all our churches together in free and equal fellowship and labor, without damage to their liberties. Each church, without dictation, inspection, or review, may still manage its own affairs, conducting all business pertaining to itself, and at the same time hold stated

[49] 43 Bib. Sacra, 417-420.

fellowship with all other churches and coöperate with them in all common concerns, as educational, benevolent, and missionary work. In these church associations the greatest liberty and the widest unity are combined, with a possible comprehension equal to the church-kingdom on earth of our Lord Jesus Christ — a solution which all churches for eighteen centuries have been seeking.

§ 208. The origin of church associations is not found in the council held at Jerusalem in the times of the apostles (Acts 15: 1–29), for those churches probably never met in council again. Yet that one act of conference for the common good is in part the warrant for stated meetings of the churches. The full warrant is found in the unity of the church-kingdom, the law of fellowship, and the sacerdotal prayer of Christ (John 17: 20–23). The churches in the early centuries had their informal synods, beginning in the second century. "Some prominent and influential bishop invited a few neighboring communities to confer with his own." "Not even the resolutions of the conference were binding on the dissentient minority of its members."[50] "But no sooner had Christianity been recognized by the state than such conferences tended to multiply, to become not occasional, but ordinary, and to pass resolutions which were regarded as binding upon the churches within the district from which representatives had come, and the acceptance of which was regarded as a condition of intercommunion with the churches of other provinces."[51] It was the state, not fellowship, that gave such associations authority.

(1) In Massachusetts Bay Colony, for many years, the General Court was a stated ecclesiastical body as well as a legislative assembly. "It was but the whole body of the church legislating for its parts; and this, with the important peculiarity that all the legislators by whom the church exercised its supreme power were of the laity. The system had no element of resemblance to prelacy or presbytery. It

[50] Hatch's Org. Early Chhs. 166, 167.   [51] Ibid. 168.

was pure democracy installed in the ecclesiastical government."[52] This court was clothed with authority civil and ecclesiastical,[53] which it freely exercised.[54] Our polity took its form under this ecclesiastical coercion, and when a separation occurred between the Church and the State, it was left crippled and defenceless in some important particulars.[55] In 1641 Massachusetts Colony adopted a code of laws, giving permission both for ministerial associations and for church associations. "It shall be lawful for the ministers and elders of the churches near adjoining together, with any other of the brethren, with the consent of the churches, to assemble by course in each several church," "once in every month of the year," and after a sermon "the rest of the day may be spent in public Christian conference about the discussing and resolving of any such doubts and cases of conscience, concerning matters of doctrine or worship or government of the church, as shall be propounded," etc.[56] The same General Court, in 1662, in ordering a synod to be held, ordered it to settle, among other questions, this: "Whether, according to the Word of God, there ought to be a consociation of churches, and what should be the manner of it?" "This . . . question was, unfortunately, returned to the secretary [of state] by the elders."[57] The elders stifled this attempt of the laymen for church association. Had they answered, as did the Saybrook synod of Connecticut, in 1708, they might have combined, as they desired, "our churches in such a bundle of arrows as might not be easily broken;"[58] and that too without the Presbyterian element of the Saybrook Platform, or any foreign element whatever.

(2) The earliest associations of churches in America, of our order, are, we believe, the following: The Susquehannah Association, 1803;[59] and the Black River Association,

[52] Palfrey's Hist. New Eng. ii, 40.
[54] New Englander, 1883, 468–473.
[56] Felt's Eccl. Hist. New Eng. i, 440.
[58] Felt's Eccl. Hist. New Eng. ii, 296.
[59] 16 Cong. Quart. 285, 286.
[53] Camb. Plat. xvii.
[55] Ibid. 473–476.
[57] Col. Records of Mass. iv. part ii, 38.

1808;[60] both of New York. The Brookfield Ministerial Association, Mass., in 1820, invited the churches severally to send a lay delegate annually to its June meetings. The churches have done so since 1821.[61] The York County Conference, Maine, was organized with lay delegates in 1822.[62] Others soon followed.

Of the state bodies, the Convention of Vermont, in 1817, appointed a committee to investigate the question of admitting lay delegates, which reported the next year no decisive recommendation. But in 1822 the constitution of the body was so altered as to admit laymen. The Conference of Rhode Island bears on its roll for 1823 lay delegates. The General Conference of Maine was organized in 1826, and admitted laymen, followed by others.

There seems to have been a general and spontaneous movement for the stated fellowship of churches in the first quarter of this century. And those first formed had in themselves the potency and promise of state, national, and ecumenical associations of churches.

(3) We have never fully inquired into the origin of this system in England and her colonies. At a conference held in Jacob's Church, in 1616, it was declared: "We acknowledge . . . that on occasion there ought to be, on earth, a consociation of congregations or churches . . . but not a subordination," etc.[63] But the oldest existing district association of churches in England was formed in 1781; that in Ireland, in 1829; that in Scotland, in 1872.

§ 209. The membership and functions of church associations are defined in the articles of agreement or covenant on which they are formed. Each church is entitled to the same number of representatives, because it is the church as such, and not its membership, that constitutes the ground and law of fellowship. A rule regulating the number of delegates by the size of the church in whole or in part, we have else-

---

[60] 20 Cong. Quart. 577, 578.
[62] 6 Cong. Quart. 187, seq.
[61] 20 Cong. Quart. 535.
[63] Hanbury's Memorials, 1, 295.

where denominated a dangerous principle in Congregational fellowship.[64] These associations manifest forth the individuality of the churches by giving the same membership in them to a small church as to a large, and at the same time show forth their unity in essential life, belief, and labor. They may do this in enlarging circles, until they attain ecumenical comprehension. They are not confined to one specified object, as councils are, but can embrace whatever business concerns the churches in common, while guarding jealously the rights and liberties of each as an independent body under Christ Jesus.

It is held as "an inalienable right of the churches in any locality" to extend fellowship to, or withhold it from, any minister or church (§ 200 : 2). This can be done as safely, more economically and certainly through stated associations than through occasional councils (§ 202: 2). If this be the right of the whole body of churches in any locality, it is an infringement of this right for a church to select a council either from abroad or from a part of the neighboring churches. Yet in calling many councils there is this infringement. Members may be gathered from Boston to Kansas into a council which shall in fact defy the churches in the vicinity. Hence, as we have shown (§ 202 : 1-3), ordination, ministerial discipline, and deposition (§ 201: 1-4) may be wisely committed to churches in association; rather, may be wisely assumed by them. Then the churches in the locality would be, and would be held to be, responsible for the standing of ministers and churches therein. If any wrong be done, a mutual council may be called.

This is not a new doctrine; for "some of the Baptist churches have an association with only *advisory* jurisdiction to which an appeal is made, leaving each congregation independent and supreme;"[65] and their polity is like ours. An

---

[64] New Englander, 1878, 514.
[65] Hon. Wm. Lawrence in 12 Am. Law Reg. N. S. 332, note; Baptist Ch. vs. Witherell, 3 Paige, 296.

association logically should extend or withhold fellowship, as being in the locality and most concerned in the matter. This was seen by our ecclesiastical fathers, who would not ordain a minister or form a church without the consent or approval of neighboring churches.

The same principle or inalienable right that applies to the extending or withholding of fellowship as respects ministers [66] applies also to churches that desire to join our church associations.

§ 210. There is no authority over churches involved in such action by church associations. These associations recognize the right of each church to administer its own affairs, free from external control or inspection, even to the calling and ordaining and installing of its pastor; and they by constitutional limitations refuse, in any case, to assume or exercise legislative power or juridical authority over churches or ministers, or to become a court of appeal. All this should be stoutly maintained.

But in ordaining a man the association does not put him into any church or pulpit, as ordination once meant in early New England,[67] but simply recognizes his call by Christ, and his ministerial qualifications and function. No church need call him in consequence. His ordination does not in the least infringe upon the rights and liberties of the churches. If any church prefer a layman, it can call him to its pastorate and ask the association to ordain him, as it now asks a council to do the same; and in either case it is the call and its acceptance that constitutes him a pastor, and not his ordination or even his installation. If the association refuse to ordain him, as a council might, the church may itself, in the exercise of its inherent right, ordain him and make him pastor. It has this right in all its plenitude; for it is complete in itself under Christ to do all churchly acts. No one will interfere with this right. But when its pastor thus ordained applies to the association for membership, the associa-

[66] Minutes National Council, 1880, 17.   [67] Camb. Plat. ix, 2.

tion that refused to ordain will refuse to admit him to ministerial standing therein, unless the impediment be removed. It will not interfere with his relation to the church that thus ordains him, but it will see to it that that church does not infringe upon the inalienable right of the other churches to extend or withhold fellowship as they may deem best. That church can not demand his recognition by the association; but the association may, if the case warrant it, after patient waiting, proceed to expel the church itself for breaking covenant in ordaining and keeping a pastor whom the association can not fellowship. There is no exercise of authority here, but the application of a common right which all bodies possess.

So if a member of an association, whether a church or a minister, violate the constitution of the body or its creed or covenant, that member may be tried, convicted, and expelled for the offence, in the exercise of the common right that a body has to enforce the terms of membership upon its members. This is true if such expulsion be held to depose a minister (§ 201). In none of these cases is there the exercise of authority over a church.

§ 211. In case of expulsion the process should be the same for a church as for a minister. It may become necessary for an association to expel a member, either a church or a ministerial member, to clear itself from complicity in heresy or immorality, and it should act as becomes a body of Christian churches, with due regard to forbearance and justice and mercy.

(1) In either case the mode of expulsion depends upon the mode of admission. If the churches of any locality could, in virtue of their calling themselves churches, associate together without condition, each one forcing itself upon the rest with all its isms, and they having no right to exclude it, then of course the association so formed would be helpless. It could not exclude the most heretical and disorderly gathering calling itself a church. But such a

claim as this is unscriptural (§ 94 : 1–8) and irrational and impossible. There must, then, be a covenant of union, either embodied in a constitution or understood, on which the association of churches is effected, to which every member assents. If any member becomes a covenant-breaker, that member, whether church or minister, may be expelled as such from the body.

As a matter of fact churches and ministers join the association on credentials (§ 213) and by the special vote of the body. Usually the application, with the credentials, is referred to a special committee to report upon. If that committee have reason to question the fitness of the applicant, it can and should take ample time to ascertain the facts, if it takes six months or a year, and report. On their report the application is accepted or rejected, and the church or minister admitted or excluded. The inquiry covers creed, belief, ministerial character and standing, whatever is needful to be known.

(2) If a member, whether church or minister, violates the conditions of membership, the association is in duty bound to notice the offence and deal with the offender. But as such associations are not strictly voluntary societies, but are required to express the law of fellowship and the unity of the church-kingdom, the association is required to labor with the offender according to Christ's rule (Matt. 18: 15–18), if possible to win the church or minister back to truth and purity. It were both unbrotherly and unjust to expel, except for public scandals (§ 167), without trying to reclaim and save. If these labors fail to reclaim, the case should be reported to the association, tried, and the proper censure passed. It were unchristian to read letters criminating the party and then to act on them without giving the accused a full opportunity to be heard. The trial should be conducted as a church trial (§ 173).

(3) We need here to distinguish between pastoral representation and ministerial membership or standing in an

association of churches. A church in connection is usually entitled to be represented in the meetings of the association by its pastor and one or more delegates. The church is the member of the body, and the pastor and delegates are its representatives; and its pastor, as such, has no more right and membership in the body than the delegates possess. Such membership gives him no standing in the body and entitles him to no credentials. His church has standing and can be dismissed with credentials or expelled; and such dismissal or expulsion takes its pastor and delegates out of the body, unless the pastor has also ministerial membership or standing therein. This ministerial standing and membership (§ 122) is effected by vote of the association on credentials (§ 213), and it entitles a minister to credentials on leaving the body, or to a trial and expulsion. This membership is distinct from any relation he may sustain to a church, and should not, therefore, be confounded with it. A minister may indeed be expelled from an association as a ministerial member, and yet appear as the pastoral representative of his church in the same association, in virtue of his pastorate, until the association shall deal with the church for having as pastor an expelled minister. This anomaly will, however, rarely occur.

(4) If a church or minister, after trial, be expelled from an association, they are cut off from connection and standing with Congregational churches. They remain a church and, possibly, a minister still, but we withdraw our recognition from them (§ 121: 3, 4), and can not be held accountable for them. A church so expelled should be dropped from our minutes and Year Books as no longer a Congregational church; and a minister so expelled should be dropped from the minutes and Year Books as no longer a Congregational minister. If a church in connection employ or call such a minister as pastor, his name should go into the statistical tables against the name of that church, but marked with a star (*), with a foot-note giving the fact of his expulsion;

as, " Expelled from —— Association ; " but it should not go into the list of Congregational ministers for whom our churches are responsible. Such a note accords with the fact, and brings a constant pressure upon the church and its minister to recover, if possible, his ministerial standing again. If a minister has not joined an association, he should be designated by a foot-note as unconnected or as a member of some other body. Thus our churches in any locality are made responsible only for those in connection, who should be reported in the minutes in an alphabetical list, as also the churches.

§ 212. If in either exclusion or expulsion injustice be alleged to have been done, relief may be had, as we have before stated in case of ministers (§ 200: 4), in a mutual council called by the association and the minister or church aggrieved, or claiming to be aggrieved, from churches beyond the bounds of the association, whose findings and result shall be final.

If the action of the association be approved by the council, the church or minister remains disfellowshiped; if the action of the association be condemned, the association should restore or admit the party to membership, but if it refuse, the action or result of the mutual council becomes good credentials, on which any other association is warranted in receiving the aggrieved.

§ 213. And by credentials we mean such papers and documents as the creed and standing rules of a church; ordination, installation, and dismissal papers, if issued by a council; certificates of transfer from one association or coördinate body to another, and the favorable result of a mutual or *ex parte* council duly called for relief, as given under the preceding head. All papers that define a minister's standing or a church's standing in some association or coördinate body as good and regular are credentials.

A minister's credentials, if given by a presbytery or similar body, contain both his church membership and his ministerial standing and membership; and hence they are not discharged of their true and full contents until the bearer of them is admitted on them both into membership in a local church and into membership in an association of churches. A minister bringing them should not, therefore, unite with a church on profession of faith, but on his credentials.

Our churches have been slowly feeling their way to this associational method of fellowship and security. We have noted the late origin of church associations in this country (§ 208 : 1, 2), and their rapid spread. In 1850 the General Association of the Congregational Churches and Ministers of Michigan changed its constitution, so that since then no minister has had membership therein unless a member of a local association or conference within the state, and in 1855 it began publishing a list of such responsible members, which it has continued to the present time. Care in making up lists of ministers responsible through associational connection will render this safeguard of purity of the utmost value. A star (*) should mean more than it does.

§ 214. The National Council at its organization, in 1871, declared that "all ministers in our denomination ought to be in orderly connection with some ministerial or ecclesiastical organization which shall be able to certify to their regular standing in the ministry," and warned the churches against employing any others.[68] It repeated the warning in 1877.[69] These warnings still stand. The lists of ministers in our Year Books have recognized this standing in associations of ministers or of churches. The same is true in England. There the list is expressly limited to "only such names as are officially furnished from year to year by the secretaries of county associations or unions." The method has been found needful in the natural working of the fellowship of untrammeled, independent churches. It has had only a recent statement. But the principle will develop into com-

[68] Minutes, 60.   [69] Minutes, 24.

pleteness; for there is not in it a single element borrowed from another and foreign polity. It leaves the churches free and independent, while exhibiting in fellowship their unity and coöperation. There has been no case that we have heard of where an association of churches has attempted to exercise authority. When associations of churches ordain and discipline and depose under the limitations above given, our fellowship will be simplified. One step more remains to be added to the system,[70] then our churches will meet in occasional or stated ecumenical councils. The isolation of our missionary churches demands this bond of fellowship. And the sooner it is established, the better for freedom and life.

NOTE ON THE ORIGIN OF THE NATIONAL COUNCIL.

We have already referred to the character of the general courts of the New England colonies as both civil and ecclesiastical (§§ 123, 208), and to the action of the General Court of Massachusetts in 1641 in favor of church conferences for the resolving of doubts and cases of conscience (§ 208). Had this action grown up into associations of churches, as both Cotton and Hooker desired, the history of the Pilgrim polity would have had a more honorable place; but it failed.

In 1642 the four New England colonies formed a confederation under the name "The United Colonies of New England." This union was both civil and ecclesiastical, "a firm and perpetual league of friendship and amity for offence and defence, mutual advice and succor, upon all just occasions, both for preserving and propagating the truth and liberties of the gospel, and for their own mutual safety and welfare."[71] As this union was the forerunner of the United States in its civil relations, it was also the forerunner of the National Council in its ecclesiastical relations.

General councils of our churches have been held occasion-

[70] 16 Cong. Quart. 291-303.   [71] Palfrey's Hist. New Eng. 1, 630.

ally: One at Newtown, now Cambridge, Mass., in 1637; another at Cambridge, Mass., 1646-1648; a third at Albany, N. Y., 1852; a fourth at Boston, Mass., 1865. There have been also some important local councils, or synods: the Boston synod, 1662; the "Reforming synod," 1679, 1680; the Saybrook synod, 1708; the Michigan City convention, 1846, called by the General Association of Michigan. It is claimed that this convention led directly to the calling of the Albany convention, six years later, and more remotely to the triennial National Council.[72]

In 1818 the General Association of Connecticut attempted to unite all the general associations of New England, not in an association, but in a "Committee of Union," to meet annually. Massachusetts approved; New Hampshire and Vermont declined the proposal. The committee met in 1819, but in 1821 it recommended its own dissolution. Dr. Dexter calls the plan a fifth wheel;[73] but Dr. Quint says: "Had it succeeded it would have essentially united all our Congregational associations in one compact body, and changed our whole polity."[74] It was purely ministerial, and rightly died.

The Congregational Union of England and Wales, organized in 1833, was naturally suggestive of a similar national body in the United States and other countries.

Next to the influences of the Holy Spirit, who makes all believers one and draws them into suitable manifestations of that unity, the Congregational churches of the United States owe an incalculable debt of gratitude to the founders and editors of The Congregational Quarterly. Their labors made the National Council possible, and fostered all the elements which brought it into being and which have given permanency to it. Their names are worthy to be mentioned here: Reverends Joseph S. Clark, D.D., Henry M. Dexter, D.D., Alonzo H. Quint, D.D., Isaac P. Langworthy, D.D., and

[72] Introduction to Reprint of Minutes, by Rev. L. Smith Hobart, 5.
[73] Congregationalism, 226, note. [74] 1 Cong. Quart. 48, 49.

Christopher Cushing, D.D. Without their labors the National Council could not have been organized when it was. This Quarterly was begun in 1859 and died an untimely death in 1878. Its twenty volumes are a thesaurus of ecclesiastical information.

But so far as is known to the writer, the honor of having first suggested the idea of a stated national gathering of the Congregational churches in this country belongs to Rev. Richard B. Thurston, whose youth and early ministry was spent among the founders of the Maine Conference. He then removed to Massachusetts and aided in the formation (1860) of the General Conference of that state, which was united with the General Association in 1868. Removing thence to Connecticut, he took an active part in the organization of the General Conference therein (1867). Through these labors there arose in his mind the idea of a national stated meeting of our churches, which he broached to others in conversation. At length a call for the Pilgrim Memorial Convention was issued. Mr. Thurston, in reading it to his church, made known his hope respecting a permanent national conference; his church, the First Church of Stamford, Conn., sent him as delegate to the said convention, which was held in Chicago April 27, 1870. He attended, and offered through the business committee of the body, the following: —

"*Resolved*, That this Pilgrim Memorial Convention recommend to the Congregational state conferences and associations, and to other local bodies, to unite in measures for instituting, on the principles of fellowship, excluding ecclesiastical authority, a permanent national conference."[75]

The resolution was adopted, we believe, unanimously and without discussion. In the June following the General Associations of Iowa and Indiana adopted similar general resolutions of approval. But "the General Conference of Ohio was the first to propose definite action. That conference appointed

[75] Introd. Minutes National Council, 1871, 8; 12 Cong. Quart. 392; 13 Cong. Quart. 235.

a committee (Rev. A. Hastings Ross being made chairman) to correspond with other state organizations and propose a convention to mature the plan."[75] The plan here referred to was prepared and presented by the writer, and was unanimously adopted by the conference and the committee appointed. It is as follows: —

" *Whereas*, The cause of the Master demands united counsels and efforts; and, *whereas*, our churches and polity have neither obtained [attained] the efficiency of which they are capable, nor exhibited the unity for which Christ prayed; therefore,

" *Resolved*, That we hail with delight the movement to establish a national council of Congregational churches in the United States, to meet at stated times, but to have and exercise no ecclesiastical authority whatever.

" *Resolved*, That we appoint a committee of seven to make overtures to the Congregational conferences and associations of the several states, and the officers of our denominational societies, respecting the formation of such national Congregational council on such basis of representation as shall be deemed best, and in accordance with the principles of our polity.

" *Resolved*, That said committee be authorized to represent this Conference in any convention or conference which may be called before our next meeting, to mature this plan; said committee to report to this Conference."[76]

These resolutions were adopted on June 16, 1870, only fifty days after the action at Chicago. They were communicated to all the state bodies by the chairman of the committee appointed for the purpose, with the request for action thereon. All the state bodies, therefore, acted expressly with reference to the establishment of a national council meeting "at stated times." " The several state organizations approved of the proposed national organization, and appointed

[75] Introd. Minutes National Council, 1871, 8; 12 Cong. Quart. 392; 13 Cong. Quart. 235.
[76] Minutes, Conf. Ohio, 1870, 12, 13.

committees."[77] The writer suggested to the General Association of New York the propriety of calling the several committees to meet on December 21, 1870, "and its committee (Rev. L. Smith Hobart, chairman) issued circulars to that effect." This proposal and date were in the original Ohio resolutions, but were stricken out before presentation, on the suggestion of Rev. Samuel Wolcott, D.D., as premature. On the invitation of the committee of the General Association of Massachusetts, a convention of committees was held in Boston, Mass., December 21, 1870. This convention, after hearing "the substance of the action taken by the several state conferences on the subject of a national council," adopted the following: —

"*Resolved*, That it is expedient, and appears clearly to be the voice of the churches, that a national council of the Congregational churches of the United States be organized."[78]

This convention prepared a draft of action necessary to the organization of such a body, which included name, ratio of representation, doctrinal and ecclesiastical basis, objects, permanency, etc. It also

"*Resolved*, That the churches throughout the country be notified of the action of this convention, and be requested to authorize their representatives in conferences to choose delegates as above."[79]

Every step in these preliminaries looked to the formation of a national body meeting statedly. As such, the churches approved it by electing delegates in response to the call. These delegates met as a council of the Congregational churches of the United States, in Oberlin, Ohio, November 15, 1871. They organized provisionally, adopted a constitution, providing for triennial sessions, under which they organized as a permanent national council.

The Ohio resolutions suggested the membership of our national societies in the council, which membership was also

[77] Introd. Minute Nat. Council, 1871, 8. [78] Ibid. 10. [79] Ibid. 12.

advocated in The Congregational Review for September, 1870 (437, 438).

But the growth of fellowship among free churches can not stop at national boundaries. That fellowship must extend to ecumenical unity, according to the prayer of Christ, that all may be one. Hence the writer has advocated an ecumenical, or general, council of Congregational churches, in his lectures, since 1872, in the Oberlin Theological Seminary, in The Congregational Quarterly for 1874 (291–303), and in the Pocket Manual (1883). The time is near when such general council will be held, that the scattered free churches, and especially the mission free churches, may be strengthened by the bonds of a common fellowship.

LECTURE XI.

THE DOCTRINE OF THE CHRISTIAN CHURCH. — ACTIVITIES AND RELATIONS.

"*Go ye therefore, and make disciples of all the nations:* . . . *And lo, I am with you alway, even unto the end of the world.*" — Jesus Christ.

"*Render therefore unto Cæsar the things that are Cæsar's; and unto God the things that are God's.*" — Jesus Christ.

"*Ye are the salt of the earth.*" "*Ye are the light of the world.*" — Jesus Christ.

§ 215. A CHURCH does not live for itself alone, nor even for sister churches. All churches unite in one church-kingdom, whose great commission is to "make disciples of all the nations" (Matt. 28: 19), to "preach the gospel to the whole creation" (Mark 16: 15). This comprehensive duty rests in its degree upon every believer and every church. It is enforced by the pertinent question of Paul: "How shall they hear without a preacher?" (Rom. 10: 14). At first ambassadors went every-where preaching, until all lands had heard of the gospel (Col. 1: 6, 23).

Christ has made the local churches the nerve-centers of Christian life and activity, the integers of organization and of evangelization (§ 42), and he will require the accomplishment of the work at their hands.

§ 216. Some parts of this evangelization are laid upon each individual church to do separately. Each church controls its own worship (§ 159). It trains its own children in doctrine and in duty. Hence its Sunday-school, being a part of the church work, is under the control of the church in matters of lessons and of management. The church school is not an independent body, but is subject to church control.

(1) The churches early gave great attention to the Christian training of the young and ignorant. "To guard against the hasty admission of unworthy men, the churches, soon

after the age of the apostles, gradually instituted a severe and protracted inquiry into the character and views of those who sought the privileges of their communion. They were put upon a course of instruction and discipline, more or less extended, before being received into the communion of the church."[1] The earliest manual of instruction extant is probably the "Teaching of the Twelve Apostles," going back nearly to the beginning of the second century. The later manuals must have been more elaborate and profound. The catechumens constituted a church school, whether held on Sunday or on week-days.

In the Pilgrim Church at Plymouth, as early as 1694, "the pastor attended the catechising of children on Sabbath noons, and continued it during his ministry." This was nearly a century before Robert Raikes began his ragged schools on Sunday, out of which the Sunday-school system is generally supposed to have grown. "In 1783 the church requested the deacons to catechise the children between meetings, which they did, and also the next year."[2] The importance of this system is indicated by its rapid spread in all communions, and by the vast apparatus employed by it. Yet the school must not take the place of the church, or draw the children from the church services; for in either case it weakens the church, if it does not destroy it. The undue working of the Sunday-school system in this regard has produced a reaction; for it has been feared that the school has been emptying the churches. The church must control the school and train its children to attend the church services regularly.

(2) Each church must attend also to the evangelization of those within its immediate care or parish. No other church should crowd into this its special field, so long as it does the work well and is sound in the faith. A church should care for its own congregation and the waste places in its vicinity, but not rob other churches.

[1] Coleman's Prim. Christ. Exemplified, 118.   [2] New Eng. Memorial, 433, 434.

§ 217. Yet no church can do all that is required of it without coöperation with others. Many things belong to the churches in common, in the doing of which they need to join hands.

(1) The churches must see to it that the ministerial function of the church-kingdom be properly trained. They must prepare men for the ministry. The chosen apostles while in training lived from a common treasury (John 12: 6; 13: 29), which was replenished by the gifts of the pious (Luke 8: 3). It remains a duty to aid those called of God into the ministry of the Word. "What soldier ever serveth at his own charges?" (1 Cor. 9: 7), or trains for war at his own expense? Whatever preparation be needed for the pastorate and missionary work, the churches should provide in whole or in part, as necessity may require, for the candidates.

(2) It is the duty of each and every church to aid in evangelizing the country in which it is planted. Home evangelization is laid upon them, until every city, town, and hamlet is brought under the benign influences of the gospel. Owing to the rapid settlement of our own country, this home labor becomes the paramount duty of our churches, enforced by patriotism as well as religion.

(3) But the great commission is wider than any country. To make disciples of all the nations is included expressly in it. National and racial lines are not to stop the grace of God or the love of his people. The gospel is ecumenical, and the churches must preach it to every tribe, nation, and race. This is their business.

To train the ministry, to evangelize the country, to preach the gospel to all the creation, are parts of one and the same work and duty of the churches.

§ 218. This common work demands coöperation. Nothing would seem to be more self-evident. Both economy and efficiency, both harmony and permanency, demand unity of action in plan and execution. Their money, their agencies, their administration, must flow together, that there may be concentration, permanence, and no waste. What no one church can do alone many churches can do together, and do with ease and with the best results. And there must be some normal method for the coöperation of independent churches, since Christ ordained such and the apostles planted only such (§§ 98, 109). Their essential nature is for each to manage its own affairs; and having been commanded to make disciples of all the nations, there is a normal way for them to coöperate in doing it. What is that way?

(1) The primitive churches were not in circumstances, while under persecution, to exhibit the law of coöperation in systematic, organic missionary work. Driven from Jerusalem, the disciples went about preaching the Word (Acts 8: 1, 4). Later the Holy Ghost, through the church at Antioch, separated Barnabas and Saul expressly to preach the gospel to the Gentiles (Acts 13 : 2). While in this and subsequent missions Paul sometimes earned his support in whole or in part by his trade (Acts 20 : 34), and sometimes received assistance from the churches he had planted (2 Cor. 11 : 8, 9; Phil. 4 : 15), there appears to have been no systematic and organized attempt made to sustain missionaries. The zeal of the churches was abundant, and the gospel was soon preached every-where (Col. 1 : 6, 23), but each church and missionary acted alone largely, and not with concerted action. Persecution constrained such a course.

(2) In the systematic efforts put forth near the beginning of the present century, in this country, individual believers became associated in societies, as many or more than there were objects of endeavor. The foundation of such voluntary societies is not the churches but individuals, who generally purchased the membership of control in them by one small pecuniary contribution. These generally were union societies embracing members of different denominations. Some of our Congregational societies are of this sort, which, consequently, recognize the churches in no organic way in their management.

(3) Another method of organized labor was in and through a permanent board, small, select, perpetuating itself, a close corporation. Most of our colleges and seminaries, and one of our missionary societies, are of this kind. The close corporation manages the school or society in all respects by its own wisdom. The churches give the money and the board of trust expends it or holds it in trust as required by the bequest. The churches have no control over either school or society, except that which comes from the cruel withdrawal of funds. If either should become endowed so that its income would sustain it, it could defy the churches that planted and fostered it, in doctrine, polity, and labor. While such a method may conduce to efficiency, it risks the loss of the college, seminary, or society to the faith and polity that planted and endowed it. Our churches have already more than once suffered this loss by defection, and are liable to the risk in every case; for it lies in the method. Besides, the method puts a gulf between the school or society and the living heart of the churches. The management of the corporation is separated from the great working doctrines of the churches, on which alone the gospel has ever obtained success. Alienation and loss are the fruits of this method, when matured.

(4) There are mixed plans which also exist certainly in one society, and in some schools. In the schools it consists in allowing the alumni to nominate or elect a part of the board of trustees, or the school is connected with a clerical union or convention in some responsible relation. In the case of the society, the final power of control vests in life members, made such by a small gift of money, and in delegates from churches and general associations, annually chosen. This brings the society into closer relations to the churches than the preceding methods are able to do. But this plan, like that of individual membership, owing to the many thousands of voting members, must confine the management almost wholly to the officers. A change in the place of

meeting renders the membership present at the annual gatherings too unacquainted with the affairs of the society to be efficient; while the permanency of that meeting in one place gathers about the officers their personal friends. Hence this method practically reduces the management to the officers and the smallest fraction of the voting membership.[3]

(5) Another method of coöperation is through the association of the churches, which becomes itself a board or society for educational, benevolent, and missionary operations. Some of our state associations and foreign unions thus coöperate, the churches doing their Master's work without any intermediary agency.

We have among our churches all these methods, a delightful variety, if confusion can ever be delightful. There is management, *first*, by association of individual believers; *second*, by close corporate boards; *third*, by mixture of life members and delegates from the churches; and, *fourth*, by association of churches. No wonder that there are symptoms of unrest, under this confusion and the losses it has occasioned, lest even worse things come upon us. This unrest has already modified charters and altered constitutions, and must find expression until some normal and safe way shall be reached by which independent churches can fulfill Christ's commission to make disciples of all the nations.

§ 219. The normal method of conducting the common interests of independent churches needs both statement and adoption. The liberty of these churches can not be infringed upon. Each must choose its own channel of operation, and freely give, as it has freely received, the gospel of eternal redemption. But several or many churches receiving a commission that renders coöperation not only desirable but necessary, would naturally do, as the church at Antioch did in a doctrinal controversy, choose messengers to meet

---

[3] The society may hold its annual meetings in rooms where not one in a hundred of its many thousand life and voting members can find admittance. The evil is but little removed if the society meet in the largest churches.

together and to act for them in devising and executing plans for the accomplishment of the work. They would not commit their trust to boards or societies not accountable to themselves. If the assembly of delegates be too large to act most efficiently in any respect, it would do, as the so-called council at Jerusalem did, "choose men out of their company" (Acts 15: 22), to do the work for the churches and in their name. This way would seem to be natural and normal as well as Scriptural. There is in it no surrender of the corner-stone of our polity, the independence under Christ of each church; no separation between the churches and their commanded work; no transference of responsibility to a third party; and therefore no feeling that the men doing the work are not the chosen representatives of the churches. This method brings the schools and the missions into direct contact with the life and working doctrines of the churches. It does not establish and endow cloistered centers of independent life, sure to grow away from the churches, unless held by annual contributions, as are the majority of our societies and theological seminaries. In this associational management of all common interests, our churches only fulfill their divinely given trust, and that without damage to their Scriptural autonomy. They manage all their affairs.

We are glad to find that this normal method of conducting the common affairs of independent churches is employed elsewhere. The affairs of "The Congregational Church-Aid and Home Missionary Society" of England are "managed by a Council," and this Council, numbering not more than two hundred members, is elected annually by "the several Confederated Associations." These Confederated Associations are "such County Unions as may agree to confederate for the objects" specified in the constitution of the society, and "such other Associations of Churches as may from time to time be received by the Council." Thus the churches have exclusive control of the management of this Society through their representatives chosen annually in their Confederated Associations. The foreign missionary society of the English Congregationalists, called the London Missionary Society, formed in 1795 by long and repeated conferences of pastors and laymen of the churches, is "thoroughly democratic." Its income is much larger than that of our foreign missionary society. The mission work of Victoria in Australia is managed by the Congregational Union or association of churches. Contributing churches have representation in the corporation of the Congregational College of British North America, and in the Canada Congregational Missionary Society. Voluntary societies appear to be peculiar to this country. Why should not our societies come into closer relations to our churches?

§ 220. There are certain obstacles to a return to this normal method which must be regarded, if they can not be removed. These obstacles are: —

(1) Reverence for the ways of our fathers, who organized our societies and schools on different principles. But they did so largely to make them union societies, in which individuals, not churches or denominations, naturally became the basis of organization. Other denominations have withdrawn and constituted their own boards or societies, leaving the old societies in our hands, and so the chief reason for the original method no longer exists. And reverence for the founders ought not, therefore, to prevent a return to the normal and true, so far as it can now be effected without legal risks.

(2) Regard must be had for present charters and trust funds, so that no alterations may be made which shall annul or forfeit them. Yet alterations may be made bettering the methods of carrying out the ends of schools and societies. And charters may be amended for the greater efficiency of their working. Membership may be limited or changed in these ways. True, vested rights may not be taken away from members, but life members need no longer be made, and delegate membership may be secured, so that in a gen-

eration or so there will be no voting members but the delegates of the churches. And even from the introduction of the change the control of the society or board would be in the hands, practically, of the churches. Then when once all life members have ceased, the charter and constitution may be changed so that the churches shall have the sole right of control.

(3) There is no unwarranted centralization in this normal method. The churches are controlling their own common affairs, while each is free and equal and independent under Christ. There is always more danger from the introduction of a foreign element than from the right use of a normal power. Our societies and schools, with rare exceptions, are foreign to our polity, since our churches are deprived in them of managing their own affairs; and there has been introduced by them a concentration of power that is dangerous. This power is in the hands of a few men who may again, in the case of schools, as they have done in the past, pervert trust funds and institutions and paralyze the energies of the churches that fostered them. Men separated by natural taste and special training into a cloister, each desirous of making prominent his own specialty, need frequent contact with the vital energies of the churches to keep them from going off into profitless speculations. Cut off from this responsible connection, as in state establishments, it is no wonder that their schools, planted in prayers and manifold self-denials, desert the faith and pull down what they were founded to build up. A wrong principle can not be worked long with good results.

§ 221. These obstacles are not insuperable. They can be removed or remedied. We suggested, in 1882, a method of adjustment,[4] which we will re-produce. It preserves all vested rights, secures the perpetual legal continuity of the societies to which it applies, and brings the societies into close and responsible relations to the churches. (1) Let no more

[4] The Advance, June 15, 1882; see also 44 Bib. Sacra, 417–420.

members be made on a pecuniary basis, as wrong in principle, and as giving temptation, in certain emergencies, to increase membership thereby for partisan ends, or the suspicion that majorities are sometimes so made. (2) Let members and officers, however they may have been made, remain undisturbed until their terms shall expire by limitation in time or by death. (3) Let the board of control, by whatever name called, be limited to a fixed convenient number, and divided into three or five classes; the first class to serve one year, the second, two years, and so on, from the time of the first election, but each class thereafter to serve three or five years, according to the number of classes. (4) Let the members of this board of control be distributed among our several state associations proportionately, according to the number of churches; the said members to be nominated (in cases where their election would endanger trust funds) by their respective state associations to the board of control or society which shall elect them members, thus preserving the legal continuity of the corporation beyond a technical peradventure. (5) Let the said board constitute the legal society which shall elect the proper officers and transact the business of the body, electing its own corporate members on nomination as above. (6) Let no members or officers of auxiliaries have membership in the body. (7) Let honorary membership, if continued, be based on pecuniary gifts.

This plan is conservative, if revolutionary, preserving the charters and franchises and legal status of the societies, while bringing them into virtual control of the churches, to which appeals may legitimately be made for support, since the societies will then be theirs.

§ 222. The advantages of this normal relation of the churches to their educational and missionary work may be stated. Any thing, even a good thing, out of its true relations produces friction and strife. It is so with our societies and schools until they become the direct agencies of the churches. Then delegates will be responsible to the churches, can be questioned as to their management, instructed, censured, without violating the courtesy which should exist between an officer of an independent institution speaking by grace, and churches having no voice in the management of said institution. Then, too, appeals for money or for students or missionaries could be made to the proper constituents. If a school or society be wholly controlled by trustees, or by corporate or life members, it becomes the affair of those trustees or members, like a business firm; and in pinching emergencies, as at all times, the proper appeal is not to the churches, but to its own managing constituency. If the school or society be the agent of the churches for doing a common work, why should not that fact appear in its management? Is it the whole duty of the churches to give money and men and prayers? It becomes them as independent churches, able and required to manage their own affairs, to manage their common business as their individual affairs, and so to make the work wholly their own.

§ 223. It may be objected that the giving is individual, and that, therefore, the educational, benevolent, and missionary institutions should rest on individual membership. But if this be true of one part of the Christian service, why does it not also cover all parts, as praying, singing, worship, and so abolish church organizations? Besides, if the duty and work be purely individual, why should churches and associations be called upon to take action thereon? Why are resolutions desired from such bodies? The fact is that missions began in churches. The church in Jerusalem was scattered abroad that it might the better preach the Christ. When the Holy Spirit would send out Paul and Barnabas, he did not directly call them, but laid the duty upon the Antiochian church to separate them and ordain them for the missionary work. It was the church that "laid their hands on them" and with prayer and fasting "sent them away" (Acts 13: 1–3). On their return Paul and Barnabas reported to the assembled church "all things that God had done with them"

(Acts 14: 27). Missions then were sustained by church collections. "I robbed other churches, taking wages of them that I might minister unto you" (2 Cor. 11: 8). In matters, too, of benevolence "the churches of Macedonia" contributed liberally for the impoverished saints of Judæa (2 Cor. 8: 1–4). The churches appointed an agent to aid Paul in administering their gifts (2 Cor. ˜8: 19). The churches were active also in other benevolences (Acts 6: 1–6; 1 Tim. 5: 16). Churches worship, act, and labor only through individual members. Yet churches are ordained by Christ to carry on evangelization in all its departments as certainly as to conduct worship, administer sacraments, or do any thing else.

Paul had this view of the matter when he wrote: "Now concerning the collection for the saints, as I gave order to the churches of Galatia, so also do ye. Upon the first day of the week let each one of you lay by him in store, as he may prosper, that no collections be made when I come" (1 Cor. 16: 1, 2). This was addressed to a church, as Paul had ordered the Galatian churches. The individual is to work in and through the church, as the local churches are the life centers and the organic integers of Christian labors and growth. Individualism is not the law of Christ, even in missions. Disintegration and death follow all attempts to reduce Christianity to individual endeavor and life. Christianity is union, communion, fellowship, in labors as in creed and life.

LEGAL RELATIONS OF CHURCHES.

§ 224. It is manifest that churches, though independent, must hold some tangible relations to the civil power. They acquire and convey real estate, raise and disburse moneys, erect and own buildings, and must therefore appear in court as subject to the law in certain respects. Under the patriarchal dispensation the Church and State were combined in the family, and there was no need of exact relations between them as respects property. Under the ceremonial dispensation the civil and ecclesiastical codes mingled, and so the relation of the one to the other was most intimate and mixed. We have to do with the church-kingdom as manifested in local churches. As it is both spiritual and ecumenical, it can not be divided up into national segments, nor can it have a civil and political rule among the nations it brings into discipleship.

§ 225. The churches are independent of the State as to their spiritual function, but dependent upon the State as to their property matters. The Christ and his apostles and disciples were rejected both by the ecclesiastical (Mark 14: 61–64; John 9: 22) and by the civil authority (Matt. 27: 1, 2, 26; Acts 4: 27). And the infant Church was confronted by both these powers (Acts 4: 1; 12: 1, 2); but in defiance of both, the apostles asserted the supreme right and duty of preaching the gospel, if need be, against the civil and ecclesiastical power (Acts 4: 19, 20; 5: 29). Nevertheless, they taught obedience to the civil powers as to an ordinance of God (Rom. 13: 1–7; Titus 3: 1; 1 Peter 2: 13–17). The explanation is to be sought and found in Christ's own teaching: "Render unto Cæsar the things that are Cæsar's, and unto God the things that are God's" (Mark 12: 17). Hence, while asserting their right and duty to preach the gospel in all its fullness, the apostles rendered unto Cæsar the things that belonged to Cæsar, though the Cæsar was a Nero. Consequently they put forth no civil laws, as Moses did; and they never attempted to govern the churches planted by them in a civil or political way. They founded churches, in their functions independent of the State as they were independent one of another, but subject to the civil power as the ordinance of God in matters within its jurisdiction. "He that resisteth the power, withstandeth the ordinance of God" (Rom. 13: 2). And believers are "subject to every ordinance of man for the Lord's sake:

whether it be to the king, as supreme ; or unto governors, as sent by him," etc. (1 Peter 2: 13, 14). Thus the apostles separated between the ecclesiastical function and the civil function, regarding each as an ordinance of God, and forbidding each to trench on the province of the other.

§ 226. The apostolic teachings controlled the churches down to the conversion of Constantine and the union of Church and State under this Cæsar. This was a relapse into Mosaism. Constantine published an edict of toleration in A.D. 313. He also restored the property taken from Christians in the persecutions. He interdicted heathen worship in private, but tolerated it in public. He forbade officers to sacrifice, and finally forbade the erection of images and the performance of religious sacrifices. He invested the church with the power to receive and hold landed property, which led to the slow but sure accumulation of wealth and power. He decreed, A.D. 321, the observance of Sunday. He enforced uniformity in obeying the decrees of the Council of Nice, A.D. 325. He thus introduced the sword of the State to enforce the decrees of the Church. The change from advice to authority in the decrees of synods, or conferences, came not from polity, but from State intervention.[5] "Whatever weakness there was in the bond of a common faith was compensated for by the strength of civil coercion."[6] It prevented schism, and therefore reform. The Donatists arose, A.D. 313, and continued long after the death of Constantine. "Their soundness in the faith was unquestionable. They resolved to meet together as a separate confederation, the basis of which should be a greater purity of life; and but for the interference of the State they might have lasted as a separate confederation to the present day."[7] "'Let all heresies,' says a law of Gratian and Valentinian, 'forever hold their peace: if any one entertains an opinion which the Church has condemned, let him keep it to himself and not communicate it to another.'"[8] This was, A.D. 381. We see

[5] Hatch's Org. Early Christ. Chhs. 166, 168.   [6] Ibid. 177.   [7] Ibid. 175.   [8] Ibid. 176.

here the sad return to Mosaism which led to the Papal tyranny. That Church still holds as an infallible utterance, that the Church ought not to be separated from the State, and the State from the Church.[9]

§ 227. The Great Reformation was but a partial return to the primitive separation of Christian churches from the civil power. The reformers announced and defended the right of private judgment in religious matters, the cornerstone of Protestantism, but past habits of thought and of life, conjoined with the doleful excesses of religious fanatics, prevented the full realization in practice of their fundamental principle. They could not adjust matters so as to "render unto Cæsar the things that are Cæsar's, and unto God the things that are God's." Probably an entire separation then between Church and State would have prevented the success of the Reformation. It was better to gain a foothold for a complete return than to have attempted completeness at first and have failed. Yet Luther[10] apprehended the true idea of the church-kingdom as separated from the State, as did Zwingle[11] and other reformers;[12] but neither he nor they could effect an entire separation.[13] Calvin used the temporal power to suppress heresies.[14] Had it not been for the aid which the State gave the reformers, the Reformation would probably have perished altogether under the terrible persecutions and wars which the Roman Church instituted and instigated, as it perished in Italy, Spain, France, and Bohemia. A foothold was gained for future conquests; and soon a nearer approach was made in the Puritan reformation in England and America. The Puritans included two wings, the Presbyterian and the Congregational, or Independent. The Presbyterians clung tenaciously to the union of Church and State, uniting the two in Scotland, and attempting it in

---

[9] Syllabus of Errors, No. 55.   [10] Fisher's Hist. Reformation, 488, 489.   [11] Ibid. 495.
[12] Augsburg Conf. art. xvi.   [13] Palfrey's Hist. New Eng. ii, 71.
[14] Fisher's Hist. Ref. 496, seq.; D'Aubigne's Hist. Ref. of Calvin, iii, 197.

England.[15] They failed in England only through the more rapid growth of the Congregationalists under Cromwell, who gave a larger liberty to that country. After the Restoration the persecutions confirmed them in their love of free churches separated from the State. From the first, both wings of the Puritans were persecuted, and one reason may be found in the favorite expression of Queen Elizabeth, who, when she had any business to bring about among the people, used, as she said, "to tune the pulpits."[16] For she found it harder to tune free pulpits than those of the Established Church, which, like their organs, were easily tuned by one who held in her hands appointments, promotions, and salaries. Thus dependent, ambitious prelates sung the tune ordered by ambitious politicians or by the crafty queen.

§ 228. The return in America to the Scriptural relation between the Church and the State requires notice. At first the Puritan settlers of the Massachusetts Colony attempted a church-state, in which none but church members could vote and hold office, the Church thus ruling the State. The same was true of the New Haven Colony. The Plymouth and Connecticut Colonies were a little more liberal, though there the suffrage was put under special limitations. The general courts were the annual assemblies of the churches in the respective colonies, enacting ecclesiastical and civil laws. The churches ruled through the civil power. "After all that may be said," wrote Hutchinson, "of the constitution [of the churches in Massachusetts], the strength of it lay in the union . . . with the civil authority. The usual way of deciding differences and controversies in churches, it is true, was by a council consisting of the elders and other messengers of neighboring churches; and where there was a general agreement in such councils, the contending parties generally acquiesced; but if the council happened to differ in apprehensions among themselves, or if either of the contending parties were contumacious, it was a common thing

[15] Palfrey's Hist. New Eng. II, 79, 101.   [16] Hanbury's Memorials, 1, 478.

for the civil magistrate to interpose and put an end to the dispute."[17] The churches gave them their warrant to interpose;[18] and the frequency and nature of their interposition have been noted (§ 193 : 3, note).[19]

But while "there was a real union between Church and State," there was "a radical difference in the form of the connection between the State and the churches here, and between the Church and State in the mother country. Here there were many churches, nearly independent of each other; there the Church was one body. Here the churches elected their own pastors; there ministers were imposed by the civil government or by patrons. Here the civil government never assumed or exercised the power of deciding on matters of doctrine and discipline, but always called together representatives of the churches freely chosen to determine such matters; there they were determined and established ultimately by the civil power. Here, if the proceedings of the magistrates were supposed to bear hard on the liberties of the churches, they could be, and sometimes were, displaced at the next annual election; there, there was, in such cases, no redress."[20]

These elements of liberty finally worked a complete separation between Church and State in New England, as in the rest of the United States. But the union entailed upon the Congregational churches that established it evils from which they have not yet cleared themselves. The chief of these evils we must dwell upon.

§ 229. The town church was changed into the parish system of church and society. A town meeting in any town in Massachusetts and New Haven was also at first a church meeting. In it the members of the church assembled -to transact both ecclesiastical and civil business, to build a meeting-house and to build a bridge, to elect a deacon and to choose a member of the General Court, to call a pastor

[17] Hist. Mass. 1, 383.   [18] Camb. Plat. chap. xvii.   [19] New Englander, 1873, 468–473.
[20] Wisner's Hist. Old South Church, Boston, 2, 70.

and to tax the inhabitants. But under the liberty they had introduced, the few church members in a town found it difficult to govern and tax for church purposes the many who were not members; so in 1664 the law passed in 1631, limiting the suffrage to church members, was repealed. Thereafter persons who were Englishmen could become freemen by presenting a certificate from their minister that they were orthodox; a certificate from the selectmen that they were freeholders, ratable "to the full value of ten shillings, or that they are in full communion with some church amongst us;" by presenting "themselves and their desires" to the court for admittance to the freedom of the Commonwealth; by being voted in by the General Court; and by being twenty-four years old.[21]

It was then that the parish became wider than the church; for it included all the voters in the town, whether church members or not. From 1631 to 1664 the church and the town in the Bay Colony were one in membership, though dual in function. After 1664 they were dual in form and function, though closely united. The church admitted its own members and elected its own deacons, but not its pastor, except in concurrent action with the town. For the town still claimed and exercised the same right it had before of calling a minister, since it taxed the whole township to pay him, as also to build and repair the meeting-house. There arose at once questions about the limitations of the church in choosing and ordaining its pastor, which the General Court, in 1668, imperfectly answered;[22] for from 1664 to the present time the relation of church and parish has caused untold trouble and loss.[23]

[21] Col. Records, iv, part ii, 118.
[22] Ibid. 396.
[23] The troubles referred to in § 193: 3, and note 8, were partly of this nature. But more: "The committee of New Haven for settling the town of Wallingford, which was settled in 1669, for the safety of the church obliged the undertakers and all the successive planters to subscribe the following engagement, namely: ' He or they shall not by any means disturb the church, when settled there, in their choice of minister or ministers or other church officers, or in any other church rights, liberties, or administrations; nor shall withdraw due maintenance from such ministry.' This shows how

The town parish gradually passed over into our present ecclesiastical society, owning all the church property and collecting and paying all moneys for church buildings, salary, and running expenses; while the church admits, disciplines, and dismisses members, fixes the order of services, adopts a creed, elects deacons, and has a concurrent vote — which amounts only to a nomination — with the parish or society. The parish society controls the church edifice and holds the purse-strings. Thus the church-town became a dual system of church and society, as abnormal as the Siamese twins.

In nearly every state in the Union the laws provide for the incorporation of churches as such without an ecclesiastical society. In a few states the qualifications of voters in religious corporations are determined by statute laws; but in the other states the religious corporations define their own voters in by-laws. In all cases conditions are required for member-

strongly the churches in this part of the colony were at that time opposed to town and parishes having any thing to do in the choice of a minister, or in any church affairs." — Felt's Eccl. Hist. New Eng. ii, 561. The same trouble arose in the Bay Colony. In 1719 it was said: "Many people would not allow the *church* any privilege to go before them in the choice of a *pastor*. The clamor is: *We must maintain him.*" The churches had then become so helpless in the hands of the parish, that it is said, "they do sometimes, by their *vote*, make a *nomination of three or four* candidates; for every one of whom the majority of the brethren have so voted that whomsoever of these the *choice* falls upon, it may still be said: *The church has chosen him.* And then they bring this *nomination* unto the other inhabitants to join with them in a *vote* that shall determine which of them shall be the man." — Mather's Ratio Dis. art. ii, §§ 2, 3.

The same abnormal condition of independent churches has been lately (1885) expressed in a compact between a church and its society, in these words: "In calling a pastor, the society and church shall act as concurrent bodies, a majority of each being necessary to constitute a call; the vote of the church shall be considered as a nomination which shall be confirmed or rejected by the vote of the society."

But this bondage is not even the worst phase of the evil inherited from the union of Church and State. It is easy for a parish to exclude evangelical preaching from the pulpit, and so bring in heresy and apostasy. The parish system played a fatal part in the Unitarian defection in Massachusetts in the early part of the present century, by which "one hundred and twenty-six places of worship, with their appurtenances of parish and church funds, were lost to the cause of evangelical religion and gained to its opposite." — Clark's Cong. Chhs. in Mass. 270.

Our churches did not see the bearing of the law they passed enlarging the suffrage and so bringing in the parish system. The law reduced them from complete control in town and state to bondage to the town parish; and they did not take to their degradation kindly. For in 1697 "a letter of admonition was voted by the second church [Boston, Mass.] to the church in Charlestown, for betraying the liberties of the churches in their late putting into the hands of the whole inhabitants the choice of a minister." — Robbin's Hist. Second Church, 1852, 42.

ship, as, stated attendance on divine worship, regular contributions to the support of said worship, adult age, and enrollment. The conditions are other than church membership. This ecclesiastical society is the legal corporation, having officers, records, and meetings distinct from those of the church in connection with it (§ 138: 3).

§ 230. The parish, or society, in Massachusetts contained the legal existence of the church in connection with it. This was not seen until the Unitarian defection brought the relation between the church and its parish into court, when, in the celebrated Dedham case,[24] 1820, the court held that in Massachusetts a church could not exist without a parish. Their words were: "A church can not subsist without some religious community to which it is attached." "Churches can not exercise any control over property which they may have held in trust for the society with which they have been formerly connected." " As to all civil purposes, the secession of a whole church from a parish would be an extinction of the church; and it is competent to the members of the parish to institute a new church, or to engraft one upon the old stock if any of it should remain; and this new church would succeed to all the rights of the old in relation to the parish."[25] This decision was re-affirmed in 1830.[26] These decisions of the Supreme Court still stand as the proper interpretation of the relation of a church to its parish, as inherited from the original union of Church and State. The churches protested against the decision, but no relief has come, unless through statutory laws.

Whatever should be the decisions in other states, the fact would still remain that wherever this relic of the union of Church and State exists, the parish or society has power to dead-lock the church in the call of a pastor, and so to embarrass the church, if not to turn it out of the church edifice. No other churches anywhere, under any polity, were

[24] Baker vs. Fales, 16 Mass. Repts. 488.   [25] 16 Mass. 503, seq.
[26] 10 Pick. 171.

ever more completely in subjection to a power largely outside and independent of themselves. The parish could legally bar the door of the pulpit against the pastor the church had chosen, and strip the church of every item of property, funds, communion service, and life itself, if it would not yield. The result of union with the State was that the Church was bereft of liberty and independent life.

American Congregationalism has had an abnormal development: — (1) in the dual organization of church and society, and (2) in the voluntary societies for missionary labors. The first is the direct outgrowth of the union of Church and State, and the second is the indirect outgrowth of the same. Our fathers relied on the civil arm, then on the parish system, until they held the churches incompetent to transact their own affairs in evangelizing the world. Our English brethren were fortunately kept from all these aberrations.

§ 231. It is time to return to the Christian relation of churches to the State. We have shown (§ 129) that the Church is an ordinance of God, and that the State (§ 225) is also an ordinance of God; and each is to be kept to its proper function. The State may not say what the churches shall believe and preach, or when, or where, or how, or by whom; only so that the creed and teachings be not immoral, like polygamy. And the churches may not say what the State shall do or not do, in constitutions, laws, policies, and courts; only so that it do not trench on morality and church rights. Each ordinance must fulfill its function, judging of its own proper jurisdiction. Between the two realms there is a border-land of doubt which only experience can settle.

The State is not irreligious, because its own sphere is not to preach the gospel; and the Church is not lawless, because its own sphere is not to legislate and divide inheritances (Luke 12: 14). The State, as an ordinance of God, is bound to rule in righteousness and to foster religion; and the Church is bound to obey the laws and to teach loyalty; and both co-operate in securing the well-being of men in time and in eternity. To combine them into one, or to make either subordinate to the other, works disaster, as fifteen and a half centuries prove. Yet these ordinances of God must touch each other in these several points: —

(1) The State must regulate the holding of church property. Property falls within the legitimate function of the State to regulate and protect. The churches must acquire, hold, and convey real and personal property so far as these things are necessary for its proper function. To carry on business or to accumulate vast wealth does not fall within the sphere of church life, and they are prejudicial to the public welfare; and so the State may limit church activity and acquisition. Whatever property is needful for necessary uses the State may bring under its laws of acquisition, tenure, and transfer.

(2) The State may regulate the taxation of church property. It may exempt it altogether from taxation, as has been the almost universal custom in Christian lands, because the Church serves the State in morals, good order, and prosperity, and because the Church, like the State, is a divine ordinance; or it may tax church property when it exceeds a certain amount, in order to prevent the massing of great wealth in churches; or it may tax all church property the same as other property. Whatever exemption is allowed must be defended not on the ground of evangelization, nor on the ground that the property is taken from business channels and devoted to moral and religious culture, but on the ground of public benefit, the churches being the best nurseries of morals, good order, loyalty, and peace.

(3) The State may regulate the teaching of religion and morals in its schools. It does not fall within the sphere of state schools of any and all grades to teach religion or morals, for spiritual ends; yet as morality, more than education, is essential to good citizenship, good order, and permanent prosperity, the State is more bound to teach it in its schools than to teach literature or science or even the common

branches. But as morality, to be effective, must have the sanction of religion in its grand doctrines of God, sin, and retribution, the State is bound to teach this needed sanction. Hence the Bible, or selections from it, should be a text-book in every state school, as teaching the highest morals and giving the best sanction of morality. This is needed to keep our schools from godless secularity and refined corruption. Certainly, whatever moral and religious instruction is necessary to give purity and permanency to the State, the State has the divine right to teach, leaving to the churches the rest.

(4) The State may regulate the worship of the churches in some respects. Hence church assemblies are protected by the State from disturbers, in some states the church officers being empowered to arrest at sight and deliver for trial those who disturb the worship. But, on the other hand, the churches or religious assemblies must not themselves become disturbers of the peace in their doctrines, their worship, their discipline, and their practices. The State protects the day of rest and of worship. The original Sabbath was a religious day solely (Gen. 2: 2, 3). The Mosaic Sabbath was both a religious day (Ex. 20: 8–11; 31: 13–17) and a civil institution (Ex. 16: 23–30; 35: 3). The Christian Sunday is a religious institution (Matt. 24: 20; Acts 2: 1–4; Rev. 1: 10) which the State might not regulate or interfere with but for the fact that a day of rest every week has also a physical and moral foundation. The cessation of labor on Sunday, or on some other week-day, is necessary to the welfare of a people, and hence the State may not only foster the religious observance of the day, but also enforce the cessation of labor upon it.

(5) The State may regulate the discipline of the Church in some particulars. It may keep the discipline within ecclesiastical limits, and prevent the infliction of fines, corporal punishment, imprisonment, and the like. It will protect parties acting in good faith within the proper limits of

church discipline (§ 179). Majorities may not violate "particular and general laws of the denomination to which they belong," nor transcend the scope of their jurisdiction.[27]

(6) The State may regulate the alienation of church property. And here we will quote from the Hon. William Lawrence, of Ohio, who fortifies his statements by an abundance of legal authorities and references: —

"The religious congregations which adopt the independent form of church government generally recognize some standard of faith or creed, but not one which is unchangeable. Some congregations may be so constituted as to have definite articles of religion, with property held for those who adhere to them, unchangeable entirely or in part by the action of any church authority. But generally property is held by or for each congregation, subject to its right to control it and change the doctrines for the propagation of which it is designed to be used according to its policy and usage."[28]

"In independent congregations generally, a majority control the use of property, and a change of religious tenets does not affect the right of the majority unless otherwise clearly provided by special trust." "'Courts will interpose to prevent the diversion of funds appropriated to promote the teaching of particular religious doctrines,' even if sanctioned by a majority of a church." "An independent society may have property devoted for specified doctrines, which a majority can not pervert." "The Legislature and the courts have in some instances gone far in sanctioning a change or perversion of trusts."[29]

A change in the creed of a church does not vacate title to property where the title vests in the said church by purchase in fee simple; nor does change in ecclesiastical connection; but if the title vests in the church as holding a particular faith or polity, the majority can not change the faith or polity

[27] See cases 12 Am. Law. Reg. N. S. 344, 345.   [28] Ibid. 332–335.
[29] Ibid. 356, seq., notes 53, 54.

and hold the property.[30] A denominational name, with contemporaneous acts, may define the trust in respect to doctrines deemed fundamental.[31] The church may before change and division agree upon an equitable partition of property, but not for private purposes.[32]

The law protects a church from seceders, as seceders forfeit all rights in property by withdrawal, and that, too, whether they are a minority or a majority of the body.[33] The title to the church property of a divided church is in that part, though a minority, which adheres to the ecclesiastical laws, usages, and principles of the denomination under which the church was constituted.[34]

The same principles apply, we may suppose, to union voluntary societies (§ 218: 2) and their funds. The withdrawal of any denomination from such societies cancels all the rights legal and moral of that denomination in the property and funds of said societies, and leaves the denomination that remains in these societies the sole and complete owner of all the property, with the full right to use all trust funds as it may deem wise, subject only to special conditions imposed in the bequests conveying the trust funds.

If a church unite with the Methodist Episcopal Church, for example, the act of uniting places both the property of the said church under the control of the Methodist Conference, and also its pulpit. Its building and land "no longer remain under the direction and control of the members of said church, but under the direction and control of the Methodist Episcopal Conference." The refusal of the trustees of a Methodist Episcopal Church to receive a preacher appointed by the bishop is an act of insubordination to the ecclesiastical tribunals of that Church, and the violation of one of the injunctions of its discipline; and so the

---

[30] 6 Ohio, 363; 16 Ohio, 583; Hale vs. Everett, 53 N. H. 9.
[31] 53 N. H. 9; 16 Am. Repts. 124, 125.   [32] 14 Ohio, 44.
[33] 14 Ohio S. 31, 44; 5 Ohio, 289.
[34] 67 Penn. St. 138; 5 Am. Repts. 415; 69 Penn. St. 462; 13 Am. Repts. 275, 283; 12 Am. Law Reg. N. S. 359, note 55, where many cases are cited.

courts will issue a peremptory *mandamus*, commanding them to admit the preacher thus appointed as pastor of the church.[35]

COMITY AMONG CHURCHES.

§ 232. Since the different theories of the church-kingdom develop inevitably into separate communions or denominations, and since, through the imperfection of the saints, denominations are formed on other issues, the local churches of any one communion, as well as the associations of those churches, must come into some sort of relation with churches of other communions and with their ecclesiastical assemblies. Hence we can not complete our view without considering the relations of comity.

(1) Comity assumes the right of private judgment as the foundation of disagreements among churches, and the unity of the church-kingdom and its manifestation as the basis of fraternal relations. All believers in Christ are "a royal" and "holy priesthood, to offer up spiritual sacrifices, acceptable to God through Jesus Christ" (1 Peter 2: 5, 9), and they must judge what sacrifices are thus acceptable; and being assured in their own minds (Rom. 14: 5), others can not interfere with their beliefs and cultus, since they stand or fall to their own Lord (Rom. 14: 4). Yet this Christian principle has had a hard and long combat to regain its divinely appointed place. The primitive churches enjoyed this right of private judgment, but when the Church and State were united under Constantine, uniformity began to be enforced. From the fourth to the nineteenth century this inalienable right has been denied, as it is now expressly denied, by the Roman Catholic Church, which calls it "the insanity."[36] As an instance of its denial by Congregationalists in this country, take the law passed in 1742 in Connecticut, forbidding a man either to preach or to exhort within

[35] Guild vs. Richards, 16 Mass. Gray, 309; People vs. State, 2 Barbour, N. Y. 397.
[36] Ency. Letter, Pius IV, Dec. 8, 1864; Syllabus of Errors, No. 15.

the bounds of a parish, unless the consent of the minister of the same and a majority of the parish was first obtained.[37] Under this law "eminent and excellent men, like Rev. Dr. Finley, afterwards president of Princeton College, were arrested and punished."[38] When liberty was finally secured in this country, as it has been, the pent-up isms multiplied denominations into wasteful divisions with slight and non-essential differences. A wholesome reaction towards union has already begun, and will go on until the unity of the church-kingdom will be organically manifested.

(2) Comity must divide communions according to their essential beliefs. It must place on one side all that hold the essential doctrines of Christianity, and put on the other side all that deny those doctrines. The line of separation is a creed, and those on the one side are called evangelical, while those on the other side are called unevangelical, denominations. The criterion by which doctrines and practices are to be determined as fundamental or not may be found in Acts 11: 17; 15: 8–10. It is, in brief, God's recognition of churches by the gift of the Holy Spirit. Those which God so recognizes, his churches must also recognize; and those that God does not so recognize as his churches, his churches must not recognize in their fellowship. This is the criterion given; its application depends upon the written Word and experience. The evangelical doctrines are held by the Orthodox Greek Church, the Roman Catholic Church, and the Armenian Church, though overlaid by many perverting doctrines and practices, and by almost all the Protestant churches. The unevangelical doctrines are held by Unitarians and Universalists, and such like communities.

(3) Comity requires the limited fellowship of the evangelical denominations. Differing only in matters which are not essential, these churches may exchange members, ministers, and pulpits; may unite in communion services; may invite the communicants of one another to the Lord's table; may

[37] Contrib. Eccl. Hist. of Conn. 119.   [38] Ibid. 438.

and should respect one another's ordinations, parishes, people, and mission fields; may form evangelical alliances; and may join in meetings and labors. In union meetings and labors, however, it should be remembered: —

(*a*) That the Lord established local churches as the centers of life and nurture and the organic factors in evangelistic labors. Union meetings generally run across this line of labor and violate the plan of the Master. Great union tabernacle services leave the converts without any particular church home, and surround them for a brief period with a spectacular environment which can not be repeated in any church; and hence their results are disappointing. No one can hope to improve upon Christ's plan of worship and labor, namely: to work and worship in local church homes, where converts can be known and cared for; and to go out from these spiritual households in labors of evangelization.

(*b*) It must be remembered also that all union efforts end in denomination results, so far as they are successful. It is so logically; it has been so historically; it can be otherwise only sentimentally. For every believer that joins a church must join some church that has a particular creed and polity, a denominational church. Every dollar given for union purposes turns up at last with a denominational stamp, within denominational folds. It can not be otherwise; for every church that is formed must organize into itself some theory of the church-kingdom (§§ 44, 45), which theory gives it at once a denominational trend, though called a union church, or simply a church of Christ, and which in time brings it into denominational connection. If mission churches in Japan or elsewhere vote to discard denominations and plant only churches of Christ, this law will hold them like gravitation, and have its way, until those churches are carried to Rome, or to Episcopacy, or to Presbyterianism, or to Congregationalism. And the constitutive principle (§ 48) most dominant in their organization and their environment will determine which road they shall take. By no device can it be otherwise, for a principle of polity is stronger than love. It has destroyed nearly all distinctive union societies that have been established.

(c) We should remember also that independent churches under Christ are what Christ planted and what all other polities seek to destroy. Such churches are the germs of civil democracies. It was "the plan of the apostles" to plant them, to leaven the world. Comity does not require a true polity to aid and abet the theories that seek to destroy it. Through mistakes here, thousands of churches, in their origin and principles free, have been carried over into a centralized polity. Charity does not require that churches should thus commit suicide to please polities that subvert the conceded independence of the primitive churches. We should care for the form of polity that Christ chose, which is giving liberty to the world.

Remembering these things our churches should exhibit in love the comity that should ever exist between churches of Christ which can not yet walk together because they are not agreed.

(4) Comity can not go into fellowship with unevangelical denominations. Over the line of separation there can be no exchange of members, of ministers, or of pulpits, and no invitation to the eucharist or exchange of fraternal greetings. Loyalty to Christ demands this. He said: "He that is not with me is against me" (Matt. 12: 30). The "destructive heresies," "denying even the Master that bought them," bring "swift destruction" (2 Peter 2: 1), and can not be recognized in fellowship. "Whosoever goeth onward and abideth not in the teaching of Christ, hath not God," and must not receive even the "greeting" of Christ's followers (2 John 9, 10). The word of Christ thus limits recognition. Reason puts the same limitation upon fellowship. There can be no true fellowship where there is no community of belief, life, and sympathy. Two can not walk together in fellowship except they be agreed. When a minister had

renounced even the name Christian, another minister of the denomination left was reported to have written and published these words : " I had rather go to hell with Emerson and Abbot than to heaven with any who would shut them out; *because theirs is the better spirit."* Yet the Christ whom Abbot denied said: " No one cometh unto the Father, but by me " (John 14: 6). What fellowship is possible between those who worship Christ and those who refuse his name? or the denomination that tolerates such utterances? None is possible; and, if any were possible, loyalty would forbid it.

Yet love, not coercion, must be shown them. The "swift destruction" to come upon them must not be inflicted by the churches or by the State. They have the right of private judgment as well as others. The Master cares for his own. And the " all things " that work for the good of his own (Rom. 8: 28) work also for the overthrow of his enemies (1 Cor. 15: 25). Our attitude must be loyal but Christian. Love, Christian love, that admits the right of all men to form their own opinions under their personal accountability to God; that seeks to give them truth for error, Christ for self; that labors to win them unto the Saviour of the world, — this love that wins while it disfellowships, — is the privilege and duty of all the churches of Christ. That love, to be loyal, must disfellowship all who deny the Lord Jesus.

THE RELATION OF CHURCHES TO THE WORLD.

§ 233. The church-kingdom has been set up in the world, which fact brings its churches into relations with the world. And we mean by "the world" unrenewed humanity, the world that lies in wickedness, or " the evil one " (1 John 5: 19), for whose redemption God sent his only Son (John 3: 16). The churches of Christ touch this world. They stand in relation to it as a divine institution established for the very purpose of converting it, of turning it unto God, of lifting it out of sin and misery into holiness and joy. For this end the Church has been endued with the gift of the Holy Ghost, with a ministerial function, and then commanded to make disciples of all the nations. It is likened to leaven, the mustard seed, and is called the salt of the earth, the light of the world. The churches are to do more than teach the world of God and Christ and salvation — a creed; they are to bring into the world righteousness, purity, brotherly love — a life, begotten of God, which shall remove sin and misery. They are commissioned with a new religion, revealed from God, which they are to live and proclaim. "Religion, in the eye of a Pagan," said De Quincy, "had no more relation to morals than it had to shipbuilding and trigonometry."[39] It is the sublime mission of the churches to unite religion and morality in a reign of "righteousness and peace and joy in the Holy Ghost" (Rom. 14: 17). To do this they must condemn whatever is sinful in itself and in its tendencies, and put it away. They must go before all others in good deeds. They must not conform to any evil customs. They must proclaim the truth in love, and preach Jesus Christ and him crucified.

The churches must keep clear of all alliances with the world. They must not take the world into membership, nor into partnership. They must keep themselves pure, whose members must be saints by regeneration, not merely by baptism; and they must carry their holy standard into all business, socials, fairs, pleasures, amusements, and recreations. They must not present to the world a commercial aspect,[40] but the aspect and acts of the Good Samaritan and of ambassadors of the Lord Jesus Christ. No monkish garb should be theirs, but modest apparel with pure hearts and loving

---

[39] Theol. Works, i, 8.

[40] We mean by the commercial aspect of the churches the various methods of indirection or devices for raising money — fairs, socials, singing, and preaching, whatever presents the churches as money-getting instead of soul-saving institutions. This attitude has called out the remark: "The church cares more for getting my money than for saving my soul." The power of any church is crippled to the degree in which this may be truly said of it. Its mission is salvation, a free gospel to all men; and it should appeal directly to men to support it in this divine work.

deeds. The churches must not in any way be in alliance with the world; but they must refine and purify whatever can be made fit for the Master's service, and destroy the rest. The leaven must leaven the lump.

We have now compassed all the relations save one which the churches sustain to the kingdom out of which they spring; to one another, and each to the whole; to their officers and the ministry of the Word; to their members; to fellowship with those in connection; to those of other faiths and polities; and to the world. Thus through the Church the manifold wisdom of God is made known to a world lying in the evil one. We have not considered yet the relation of churches to doctrinal standards, except in the matter of comity (§ 232: 2). We reserve this relation and certain objections to our final Lecture.

LECTURE TWELFTH.

THE DOCTRINE OF THE CHRISTIAN CHURCH. — CREED. — OBJECTIONS.

" Hold the pattern of sound words which thou hast heard from me, in faith and love which is in Christ Jesus." — Saint Paul.

" Upon this rock I will build my church; and the gates of Hades shall not prevail against it." — Jesus Christ.

§ 234. THE matter of church creeds is of the utmost importance, and has indirect relation to polity. Indeed, it has been affirmed that the polity we have presented tends to unsoundness in the faith. If this charge be true, it is a strong, if not insuperable, objection to Congregationalism, either in its principles or in its workings. For no organization has ever done, or can ever do, much good either for itself or for the world without a creed of principles. It was said of the Liberal Republicans, in 1872: "Harmony is a very good thing, as far as it goes, but it is by no means the principal thing; indeed, it is only a means to an end. *The first thing for a new party or a reform party to provide itself with is a body of doctrines; a party without this is a simple absurdity.*"[1] Parties in their state and national conventions issue platforms as their creed; and this they do repeatedly. And if a party must have "a body of doctrines" in order to escape an "absurdity," how much more a communion of churches, and even a single congregation of believers. "A system of religion, to be worthy of a sane man's faith, must . . . *be* a system. It must have concinnity. It must have a beginning and a middle and an end. A jumble of incoherences commands as little honor from faith as from reason."[2] If any polity tends to ignore or reject creeds, or substitutes

[1] New York Nation, No. 356.
[2] Prof. Austin Phelps, D.D., Am. Home Missionary, xlv, 3.

for doctrinal formularies a jumble of any sort, or carries the churches away from the faith once for all delivered to them, that polity stamps itself as inadequate for the evangelization of the world. Its career must be short.

§ 235. The general confessions of the Congregational churches set forth sound doctrine. This will appear from a reference to them. Some of the leading men in the Westminster Assembly (1643–1649), which issued that masterpiece of doctrinal statement, the Westminster Confession of Faith, were Congregationalists. They did their full share in framing this confession, and they heartily assented to all its doctrinal teachings. So the Cambridge Synod that framed and issued the Cambridge Platform, in 1648, gave the Westminster Confession its "professed and hearty assent and attestation to the whole confession of faith (for substance of doctrine)."[3] The English Congregationalists, in 1658, met in synod and issued the Savoy Declaration, as it is called, the doctrinal part of which is identical in substance and almost in word with the Westminster Confession.

[3] There were at that time fifty-one Congregational churches in America, distributed as follows: two in New Hampshire; nine in Plymouth Colony; thirty in Massachusetts Colony; five in Connecticut Colony; and five in New Haven Colony. The term, "for substance of doctrine," whose meaning has sometimes been disputed, was very restricted at that time. The Synod excepted polity, of course, in their endorsement, and then added: "We may not conceal that the doctrine of vocation, expressed in chap. 10, § 1, passed not without some debate. Yet considering that the term vocation and others by which it is described are capable of a large and more strict sense and use, and that it is not intended to bind apprehensions precisely in point of order or method, there hath been a general condescendency thereto" (Felt's Eccl. Hist. ii, 5). The subsequent action shows that no essential doctrine was then in dispute. After the said approval, in 1648, the General Court of the Massachusetts Colony, in 1649, commended the Cambridge Platform to the several churches for "their judicious and pious consideration," desiring the churches to return the Court answers "how far it is suitable to their judgments and approbation" (Records iii, 177, 178). Objections being returned to the Court, they were referred to Rev. John Cotton to answer (Ibid. 235, 236). Then in October, 1651, the General Court, composed wholly of lay church members, and elected only by church members, "gave their testimony to the said Book of Discipline, that for the substance thereof it is that we have practised and do believe" (Ibid. 240). Increase Mather, in his preface to his son's Ratio Disciplinæ, published in 1726, says: "It is true that for certain modalities there has been a variety of practice in these churches: as there was in the primitive; but in essentials, both of doctrine and of discipline, they agree" (iii).

By no stretch of the term can "substance of doctrine" be made to cover any doctrinal unsoundness. It excepted only matters of minor importance.

This Savoy Declaration was in 1680 approved by a synod at Cambridge, Mass. Thus our churches in England and America endorsed as their belief a confession whose doctrinal statements are given in thirty-four chapters, each chapter containing from one to ten articles. There are in it one hundred and sixty-one sections.

But in 1691 the Congregational and Presbyterian churches of England formed a basis of agreement, which was that "the Articles of the Church of England, or the Confession or Catechisms, shorter or longer, compiled by the Assembly at Westminster, or the Confession agreed on at the Savoy,"[4] should be tests of fellowship. The Congregational Union of England and Wales adopted in 1833 a doctrinal basis covering the fundamental doctrines.[5]

The American Congregational churches, in 1865, in council adopted the Burial Hill Declaration, after re-affirming their "adhesion to the faith," "substantially embodied in the Confessions" of 1648 and 1680. In this declaration our churches present "the great fundamental truths in which all Christians should agree" as the basis "of Christian fellowship." And when the National Council was organized at Oberlin, in 1871, it, by constitutional provision, rested the doctrinal basis of fellowship on the Scriptures as interpreted by the evangelical faith and set forth by former General Councils. In 1880 the National Council appointed a large commission to form a creed or catechism, or both, and to report the same to the churches. This commission reported in 1883 a statement of doctrine and a confession of faith.

These confessions and declarations, and heads of agreement, and statements of doctrine and creeds, give no uncertain sound. Some are elaborate; some are brief; all are thoroughly evangelical (§ 232: 2).

§ 236. The doctrinal bases of our state associations are also evangelical. They range from the word "evangelical" up to the Burial Hill Declaration of 1865, and even to the

[4] Heads of Agreement, art. viii.   [5] New Eng. Memorial, 452.

Shorter Catechism. Nearly all have a creed as the basis of membership in them. Not one repudiates the consensus of Christian doctrines held by Christendom. Instead, they are all associated in the National Council, whose doctrinal basis is "belief that the holy Scriptures are the sufficient and only infallible rule of religious faith and practice," our interpretation of which "being in substantial accordance with the great doctrines of the Christian faith, commonly called evangelical."

§ 237. If we turn to church creeds we find a great variety; for each church chooses or frames and adopts its own. It has authority to do so as independent under Christ. Of the thousands thus adopted, none in connection is heretical. When a church joins a conference or association, its creed is a matter of inquiry before admission. Its doctrinal soundness is therefore a test of admission, as well as the doctrinal basis of the conference or association to which it gives its assent.

§ 238. Every member on joining the church publicly assents to a creed; and every pastor in accepting the call to any church makes its creed a part of his covenant and contract with the said church, which he can not honorably break by preaching another doctrine. Every church and minister on joining an association either expressly or impliedly assents to a creed and covenant, both of the district body and of the state and national bodies. In this way any doctrinal unsoundness in church or minister is likely to be detected. There is no slighting of creeds. Our general confessions, it is true, are mere declarations, to which no formal assent is required; for assent to church creeds, associational bases, and inquiry by committee or council are sufficient to secure soundness in the faith. The Congregational churches of England are less rigid than those in America in this regard of doctrinal tests.

The credal tests of admission to church membership should not, however, go beyond the Scriptural requirement of "repentance toward God, and faith toward our Lord Jesus Christ" (Acts 20: 21). Whom the Lord receives in regeneration his churches are to receive (Rom. 14: 1-5). The creed and covenant for admission should be constructed on this principle; and hence no elaborate articles of faith or rigid examination should stand as tests of admission. There should be, therefore, a form of admission to membership separate from the creed of the church, and much more simple, that children and the weakest believer may enter the nurturing home of the saints and be trained in the church up to the doctrinal perfection of its creed. The church creed should be read at communion seasons, but members should be admitted on their assent to a simpler form. This position was taken in the Ohio Manual in 1874, and in the creed and confession of faith prepared by the commission of the National Council, and issued in 1883. Our churches, in placing an elaborate creed as the condition of church membership, depart from their principles and early practice.

§ 239. Our system of church councils has been a safeguard to purity, and is yet to some extent, though the stated meeting of the churches in associations renders councils of less vital importance. Councils have been called to recognize a church, to ordain, install, and dismiss ministers, etc. (§ 194: 7), which inquired into the faith of both churches and ministers. They may be called also to discipline both churches and ministers in case of heresy or immorality (§ 200).[6] Councils do these things now wherever called, and so form an additional security to those above given.

§ 240. The history of our churches shows that they have kept the faith with unusual firmness. Time tests all things, and history is but the record of its testings. Polities do not escape. How do they stand the ordeal? Towards the close of the eighteenth century a wave from that deluge of infidelity which had submerged Europe broke upon the

[6] Minutes National Council, 1880, 17.

shores of New England, unmooring many churches, which during the first quarter of the present century drifted upon the bleak shores of heresy. The wave came from Europe; its damage was chiefly done in Europe, — in the comparison the defection in New England was slight, — and yet the country and polity that suffered least from it have been charged with its origin. Nothing could be farther from the fact. "No great heresy was ever generated by our polity." Let us examine the facts more closely, a thing we would not do but for the charge so persistently made against Congregationalism. In the Revolution a French army came over to assist us, which brought with it the infidelity of Voltaire. In consequence of its influence, of the influence of the Halfway Covenant, and of the parish system, inherited from the union of Church and State, ninety-six churches in Massachusetts out of three hundred and sixty-one became Unitarian. Only twenty-six per cent. of them apostatized.[7] But in England, out of two hundred and fifty-eight Presbyterian churches, all but twenty-three lapsed into Unitarianism; which was ninety-one per cent. of the whole.[8] In Connecticut no Congregational church was lost to the faith;[9] but in Ireland two Presbyterian synods became Unitarian.[10] In England, only six, or at most ten, churches of our order became unsound in the faith;[11] while in Scotland the whole body of Presbyterian churches fell away into Moderatism, a term which included all shades of unbelief from bald deism up to the evangelical faith.[12] There were not many Congregational churches in Ireland, but no one of these apostatized;[13] while the Presbyterian and Reformed Churches of Switzerland, Holland, and Germany lapsed almost wholly into rationalism and heresy, leaving even the cradle of

[7] Clark's Cong. Chhs. in Mass. 270.
[8] Tracts for the Times, 1, 403, quoted from A Churchman's Reasons, 181, 182.
[9] Bacon's Hist. Address, in Contrib. to Eccl. Hist. Ct. 70.
[10] Hall's Hist. Presby. Ch. III, 454, 472.
[11] Spirit of the Pilgrims, III, 537; iv, 46.
[12] Hetherington's Hist. Ch. of Scotland, ii, 362, 363; chap. x, 367, 377.
[13] Spirit of the Pilgrims, iv, 97.

Presbyterianism without a church in the faith of John Calvin.[14] The Lutherans,[15] the Episcopalians, and the Roman Catholics suffered equally or even worse from this deluge of unbelief. About two hundred and fifty clergymen of the Anglican Church, including a bishop and an archdeacon, petitioned Parliament to be released from subscribing to the Thirty-Nine Articles, because they had become Unitarian.[16] The Roman Catholic churches in France and Italy were even less sound in the faith.

We believe that impartial history will show more heresy under centralized forms of church government than under the liberty of independent churches. We believe it to be true and proved by history, that ecclesiastical courts rising in appellate jurisdiction have not proved to be the best guards of purity in faith. Liberty and sound orthodoxy go naturally together.

§ 241. For the people are the best custodians of the faith as of liberty. The oracles of God were committed unto his people. The gospel was entrusted to free, independent churches, governed by the popular vote of their members, with the command to evangelize all nations. It is a conceded fact that the membership of the primitive churches resisted, and sometimes by riots, the encroachments upon their liberties that ended in the Papacy. Those churches were robbed of their rights against their will by the clergy fortified by the civil power. So bitter was the contest for their liberties, that a semblance of their inalienable rights was left the people for centuries after the substance had been insidiously taken away from them.

We have said that in Ireland two synods of Presbyterians lapsed into Unitarianism; but the rest were preserved by the people in this way as told by their Presbyterian historian: "For a quarter of a century before the commence-

---

[14] Dorner's Hist. Prot. Theol. ii, 475; Pond's Church of God, 1040; Spirit of the Pilgrims, v, 532, seq.
[15] Pond's Church of God, 1037.
[16] Spirit of the Pilgrims, iv, 44.

ment of the Arian controversy, congregations had been scanning with increased vigilance the doctrines propounded from the pulpit; and on the occurrence of a vacancy the very suspicion of 'New Light' was almost sure to destroy the prospects of the candidate. In 1827, when the synod began fairly to grapple with the question, the people themselves had already performed so effectually the process of purgation, that only a comparatively small fraction of the body was tainted with Unitarianism." " The synod always recognized the right of the people to elect their minister, and the enlightened exercise of this privilege tended greatly to impede the progress of anti-evangelical principles." [17] The Moderatism of Scotland, which carried all the Presbyterian churches away for a long period, had its origin partly in the union of Church and State. " Early in its progress it showed itself favorable to soundness of doctrine and laxity of discipline, and strongly opposed to the rights and privileges of the Christian people." [18] In Germany there is a union of Church and State. Hence it is said that " the great Coryphæi of rationalism have sprung from the very bosom of the Church . . . and, at the same time that they were endeavoring to demolish the superstructure of divine interpretation, they were in the eyes of the people, its strongest pillars, the accredited spiritual guides of the land, teaching in the most famous universities of the continent, and preaching in churches which had been hallowed by the struggles and triumphs of the Reformation." [19] The pious members of all churches, whatever their polity, care little for doctrinal speculations, but they do care for the grand doctrines of the gospel by which men are brought to Christ and saved. These great working doctrines, which have carried the churches through persecutions and controversies, the storms of the centuries; which have brought in reformations and

[17] Hall's Hist. Presby. Ch. of Ireland, iii, 487.
[18] Hetherington's Hist. Ch. Scotland (7th ed.), ii, 362.
[19] Hurst's Hist. Rationalism (6th ed.), 27.

revivals; which have given spiritual victories at home and in foreign mission fields; which satisfy the deepest wants of the soul, and convict men of sin and the need of salvation, and which consequently hold within themselves the redemption of the world until the end,—these doctrines the true believers cling to even unto death, and they are the best custodians of them, and ever will be.

§ 242. The people stand also as the best guardians of the independence of local churches. It is hardly too much to say that the ministry would have given our polity away altogether out of New England, but for the laity. "The most injurious practical mistake made in the working of our church order in this country was an affair of the ministers. The Plan of Union (1801) is a notable instance of the ill effects which may follow when ministerial meetings take upon themselves to manage affairs without deferring them to the judgment of the churches."[20] Probably a greater mistake was the failure to find and use true remedies for the defects in discipline when the reliance of the churches on "the coercive power of the magistrate" ceased. This we have shown in another place.[21] This failure to supply a needed remedy in time led men to distrust our polity as unfit for the West, or, indeed, any place but New England. Ministers and churches were advised to join the presbytery, and home missionary committees almost forbade the organization of Congregational churches. The missionaries were instructed that it was expected that they should join the presbytery; "that it would not be either desirable or wise to organize any Congregational churches;" and "that, while Congregationalism did well enough for New England, it was not adapted to the recent settlements of the West."[22] That was in 1831. In the subsequent revival of Congregationalism it has been said that "the ministers have not led in this matter, but followed. Congregationalism in Illinois is

[20] Prof. Ladd's Principles Ch. Polity, 319.   [21] New Englander, 1883, 468–476.
[22] 2 Cong. Quart. 192.

very largely the result of a spontaneous movement of the people themselves."[23] In Ohio, Congregational churches "originated with the laymen, and not with the ministers." The pastors carried the city churches over to the presbytery.[24] The same was true in New York,[25] in Michigan,[26] and in other states.[27]

In the Unitarian apostasy, our churches in England, by insisting on the examination of candidates for the ministry and by requiring credible evidence of experimental religion from them, preserved themselves, with the rarest exceptions, from the heresy which swept nearly all the Presbyterian churches away.[28] It was the pious people that withdrew from apostate parishes in New England in order that they might preserve the faith in its Scriptural integrity.[29] "It is probably the Unitarian controversy which served to fix the custom, as it now exists, of examining every candidate for ordination as pastor of a Congregational church."[30] This examination had previously been neglected. A foot-note of a sermon preached by Dr. Samuel Hopkins, in 1768, expresses the fear that ordaining councils were beginning "to neglect the examination of candidates for the ministry with respect to their religious sentiments."[31] Where the churches have insisted on a converted and orthodox ministry, they have preserved their soundness in the faith, but the inspiration of such tests has been in the pious laymen rather than in the ministry.

§ 243. The way the Congregational churches deal with heretics conduces to purity of the faith. There are two ways of dealing with them. One method retains them in

---

[23] 17 Cong. Quart. 403.
[24] Defence of Ohio Congregationalism, by Dr. Henry Cowles, 1, 2. The planting of Congregational churches had to be defended.
[25] 1 Cong. Quart. 151, seq.; 2 Cong. Quart. 33, seq.
[26] 2 Cong. Quart. 190, seq.
[27] 10 Cong. Quart. 201, seq.
[28] Wilson's Hist. Dissenting Chhs., quoted in Spirit of the Pilgrims, III, 537.
[29] Clark's Cong. Chhs. in Mass. 299, seq.
[30] Prof. Ladd's Principles Ch. Polity, 237, 238.
[31] Ibid. 237.

fellowship, that they may be reclaimed; but after long forbearance casts them out, if not brought back to the faith. The other way is to make the unity of the body paramount to its purity. This latter method, as history abundantly proves, corrupts often the whole body past recovery; for it seems to put no difference between truth and error, the essential doctrines and "destructive heresies." The Scriptural way (§§ 94, 164) is the former method, which our churches have followed. As soon as Unitarian heresies became public in Massachusetts, the churches began the work of purgation, and it was soon completed. Whether there was undue haste in casting out or not, we are unable now to say. But the method of free churches was far more prompt and decisive than that pursued by centralized churches, whose unity would be destroyed by withdrawal of fellowship. No Moderates were cast out of the Presbyterian Church of Scotland; no Unitarians from the Established Church in England; no Rationalists from the continental churches. Had the Unitarians in Ireland chosen to remain in the Presbyterian Church, they would not probably have been cut off from fellowship.[32] The Puritans and Methodists were driven out from the Anglican Church, as the earlier Reformers were from the Roman Catholic Church, not for heresy, but because they laid the axe at the root of those hierarchical systems in church polity.

§ 244. The system of guards among independent churches is complete. Let us repeat them. Members, whether baptized in infancy or not, are received into our churches on profession of their faith in Christ and repentance of sin; and are expelled for denying the faith called evangelical as for immorality. Churches are recognized by council or received into associations of churches on condition of assenting to an evangelical creed, and they can be dealt with by council or expelled from the association to which they belong for heresy or any violation of the cove-

[32] Hall's Hist. Presby. Ch. in Ireland, iii, 487.

nant of their fellowship. Ministers are examined at ordination, recognition, or installation, as to their soundness in the faith; and on joining an association of churches or of ministers they bring credentials and assent to the creed and covenant of that association, from which they may be expelled if they violate either creed or covenant, and be brought before a council of churches for vindication or deposition in case they feel aggrieved. And this covenant may be either written or understood. Our general associations have generally doctrinal bases, and our National Council re-affirms the great confessions. No system is more complete. Authority without the civil power to enforce it adds nothing to it. It is as a Presbyterian is reported to have said: "Congregationalism politely invites a man to leave, and — he leaves; Presbyterianism tells him to go, and — he goes. The result in either case is the same." That is, the withdrawal of fellowship is as potent a method of discipline as the most terrible censures of ecclesiastical power. We think it impossible for one who distinguishes between essentials and incidentals, between rigor within the evangelical circle of doctrines and liberty of belief beyond that circle, to charge the conceded polity of the primitive churches with a tendency to unsoundness in the faith.

SOME OBJECTIONS TO CONGREGATIONALISM CONSIDERED.

§ 245. In answering objections to any thing, we need to know the force of objections; for many men seem to think that any objection is destructive.

(1) But some objections have no force whatever. Such are many objections drawn from church troubles against any and every form of church government. For they lie rather against imperfect, though regenerate, church members. There is a great deal of human nature in Christians. Were members perfect in head and heart, church troubles could not arise; but being imperfect in both head and heart, "it is im-

possible but that occasions of stumbling should come" (Luke 17: 1); and therefore no church polity can escape troubles. One polity may deal with church troubles better than another, but the fact of such troubles is no objection against a polity. To give the objection the least force whatever, it must be shown that the trouble can not be met as well under that polity as under some other polity.

(2) Some objections have force only against a faulty administration of church government. In no form is there perfect administration, since regenerate human nature is imperfect. Hence in studying a polity we must separate it, as far as possible, from faults in administration. A faulty church government well administered may for a time appear to better advantage than a faultless polity badly administered. If an objection lies against a faulty administration, it is illogical to urge it against a polity. A mistake in administering discipline is no objection against that discipline, unless the polity tends to multiply mistakes or neglects.

(3) Some objections have real, but not conclusive, force. Were this not so, what could stand? It is a real objection against civil government that injustice is sometimes done and justice sometimes fails to be done. Yet this objection is not conclusive against the ordinance of God, the State. The worst administration in the state is better than anarchy. It is a real objection against the climate of this earth, that it shortens man's life so much by its extremes and changes; but the objection does not prove either the imperfection or the malignity of God's government of nature. The existence of sin is a real objection urged against God's moral government, but no one can claim that it is conclusive. Objections may lie against every form of church government, yet some form must be had. The church-kingdom can not exist in this world without some method of combining church with church in fellowship and coöperation.

(4) Objections can be used, therefore, only as tests by which to ascertain what form of church polity is the best.

And here no one will be so hardy as to deny that the plan of the inspired apostles, as respects polity, whatever that plan was, is on the whole freest from real objections, and must be the best. What the primitive polity in principle was is now generally conceded (§ 109). And that polity, when drawn out in detail, is not to be set aside either by objections against its faulty administration or real objections against its most perfect administration. The force of objections needs ever to be kept in mind, lest we mistake in judging polities.

§ 246. It has been objected that public discipline before the whole church is not the best way either for purity or peace. Discipline is like a storm, and we know of no storm that does not cause greater or less commotion. But we seek to follow Christ's rule exactly, and he is supposed to know what is best for his churches. The responsibility of keeping the church pure is not laid upon a few in the church, but upon the whole membership, which sobers and trains each member. But in certain, or even in all, cases the trial may be had before the church board or a jury of the church (§ 174), which limits, if it does not destroy, the objection. Then again our polity does not provide a series of judicatories, by which the strife or discipline of one congregation may become the strife and discipline of the whole church or community of churches. Congregationalism, following the Master's rule, confines the trouble to the narrowest limits. And in case of alleged grievance councils may be called to redress the grievances, if any exist (§ 186).

§ 247. It has been said that Congregationalism lacks unity. And it is true that the visible signs of our unity have not been conspicuous. From the landing of the Pilgrims down to the organization of the National Council, in 1871, there was no stated expression of the union of our churches in this country. They had met in occasional synods or councils, as in 1637, 1648, 1852, and 1865; but these meetings were neither frequent nor imposing enough to express the oneness of our churches. And district and state associations are of late origin (§ 208). "Strict independency clearly fails to give just prominence to the Scriptural doctrine of the fellowship of the churches, and the sacred unity of all in the one great Church of God on earth."[33] What is here affirmed of strict independency is true, but the same can not be affirmed of Congregationalism; for our polity is unifying. It fosters the life of Christ in the heart, which is unifying; it rests not on sacramental, but on spiritual, regeneration and sanctification, which is unifying; it rejects divisive force, which is unifying; it seeks fellowship with all the saints, which is unifying. We are not surprised, then, to learn that within the evangelical lines, the Congregational churches of no one country have ever been divided into different communions. But this can not be said of other communions. The Western, or Latin Church, separated from the Eastern, or Greek Church. The Lutheran and the Reformed Churches were broken off from the Roman Catholic Church. The Puritans, Congregational and Presbyterial, and the Wesleyans were driven out from the Anglican Church. The cleavage of force still went on. Scotland was divided into five independent national Presbyterian bodies; the United States into nine such bodies. Methodism breaks up into eleven distinct bodies in the United States; five in Canada, recently united; and nine in England and Ireland. This cleavage under authority, but oneness under liberty, is a final answer to the objection. The force of this unifying love of Christ in free churches was early foreseen. Captain Edward Johnson wrote from Massachusetts Bay, A.D. 1654: "Could your eyes but behold the efficacy of loving council in the communion of Congregational churches, and the reverend respect, honor, and love given to all teaching elders, charity commands me to think you would never stand for classical injunctions any more; neither Diocesan, nor Provincial authority can possibly reach so far as this royal law of love in communion of churches: verily it

[33] Prof. Morris's Ecclesiology, 137.

is more universal than the Papal power, and assuredly the days are at hand wherein both Jew and Gentile churches shall exercise this old model of church government, and send their church salutations and admonitions from one end of the world unto another, when the kingdoms of the earth are become our Lord Christ's; then shall the exhortation of one church to another prevail more to reformation than all the thundering bulls, excommunicating lordly censures, and shameful penalties of all the lording churches of the world; and such shall be and is the efficacy of this entire love one to another, that the withdrawing of any one church of Christ, according to the rule of the Word, from those that walk inordinately, will be more terrible to the church or churches so forsaken than an army with banners."[34]

§ 248. It has been said that Congregationalism lacks efficiency, and our past history in this country has given occasion for the objection. In the number of churches the Congregationalists were first in 1776, but seventh in 1876. This showed great inefficiency in home growth and evangelization, but that the causes were other than those of polity is clear from the fact that the Baptists, who are as free and independent in polity as our churches are, retained the second place in the number of churches during the entire century.[35] We must therefore look for the causes of the inefficiency of our churches, as measured by growth, in other things than church government.

(1) Our churches cherished more than any others the spirit of union. Hence they gave their energies for a long time, and that too at the beginning of missionary and benevolent operations, to the formation and support of union societies. Had their labors here been wise, they would have been noble; but they had not studied the problem profoundly, or they would have seen that two polities can not long walk together unless they be agreed; that is, become one, and that

[34] Wonder Working Providence, book i, chap. xliv; Mass. Hist. Col. vols. 12, 14, 17, 18. [35] Centennial No. North Am. Rev. 1876, 36.

consequently all union efforts end in denominational results (§ 232: 3, *b*). By reason of this union sentiment our churches neglected their golden opportunity, and built up other denominations.

(2) The early union of Church and State, and the desperate tenacity with which our churches clung to every shred that bound them to the State, were causes of early and late inefficiency. The Congregational churches were the established churches, for whose support all were taxed, though supporting other churches. This induced an aristocratic temper and a separation between these churches and all other churches and the non-church going population. When the liberty they had established produced a cleavage between the civil and the ecclesiastical powers, our churches clung desperately to the early but vanishing connection, even down to the present century. Their reliance on the State damaged both spiritual aggressiveness and popular favor, and so hindered growth.

(3) And when the separation was finally effected, the parish system was retained, whose dual arrangement permits an adverse parish to dead-lock the church and drive it out stripped of all its property. This occurred ninety-six times in the Unitarian defection in Massachusetts. The parish system became a clog to growth.

(4) The Plan of Union, a child of the Saybrook Platform of Consociationism, surrendered our polity to another. The Hartford Association of Ministers issued in 1799 a declaration affirming that the standards and usages of the Connecticut churches were not Congregational but Presbyterian in their fundamental principle.[36] It was natural, therefore, that the general association of ministers should propose to the general assembly of the Presbyterian Church coöperation in conducting missions throughout the West. Out of this proposal grew, in 1801, the plan of union which continued in operation fifty-one years, and which carried over more than

---

[36] Gillett's Hist. Presby. Ch. 1, 438, 439, note.

two thousand churches, in origin and habits Congregational, to the Presbyterians. These churches being planted in places where great cities grew up, became generally strong and of commanding influence. It is no wonder that the denomination receiving these churches should charge us with inefficiency, since it has so many proofs of it on its rolls.

(5) Neglecting to care for their own, to remedy the defects in their discipline, and to work their own principles, our leading men soon distrusted their own polity. They discouraged the organization of Congregational churches out of New England, and advocated the desertion of its principles. "There is no more self-convicting and mortal, nay, cowardly and suicidal, heresy regarding this polity than to claim its fitness only for provincial uses, selected classes, opportune seasons, and favoring circumstances."[37] Had it not been for a few ministers true to the faith and polity of their fathers,[38] and for the faithful laity (§§ 241, 242), our union labors and the ministerial distrust of our polity would have prevented the planting of Congregational churches west of the Hudson. When the golden opportunity arrived for efficient work in the West, our churches were devoting, largely, their energies to the building up of other polities. They left their own vineyard to cultivate those of neighbors. It is a wonder that Congregationalism was not swallowed up and lost in this current of its own making. Those who reaped the fields of our planting and put the golden grain into their own granary admired our suicidal benevolence, but held the polity that could do such things in contempt.

(6) Efficiency arises partly from using the wisdom of the wise. There are still diversities of gifts, but the same Spirit. Hence some men have greater wisdom and executive ability than others. They can lay plans for the centuries, and work out results the greater the longer the centuries continue. Some polities make such men bishops, cardinals, popes. We

[37] Prof. Ladd's Prin. Ch. Polity, 325.   [38] 2 Cong. Quart. 192, seq.

can not surrender liberty that a hierarchy may govern. The polity of the New Testament trains the rank and file as well as the officers in the army of the Lord; but this does not prevent the wisdom of the wisest from directing affairs by counsel though not by command. With a trained membership meeting in associations where the wisest may make their plans the concern of all, our polity may become the most efficient of all.

(7) Efficiency arises partly from using the resources given us. We, as churches, have been very benevolent and active, but we have been wanton in the use of these elements of power. Some have so feared denominational tendencies that they have preferred union societies to our own, never dreaming that every cent they gave turned up somewhere with a denominational stamp on it (§ 232: 3, b). This scattering through catholic channels into denominational folds has done good; but it would have done more good, if liberty counts for any thing in the churches or nations, had free churches been planted by it. Disguise it how men may, independent churches can not foster centralized polities without loss. We have societies as ably and wisely administered as any, and when we learn, as we are learning, to put all our resources into these channels, our efficiency will no longer be questioned. The Baptists, with the same free polity, have had no union with the State; have been free from the parish system where the law allowed; have worked through no plan of union, but have used their wisdom and resources in the extension of their faith and polity; and the result vindicates their wisdom and efficiency. A Baptist writer says: "Our principle of obedience to Christ makes us, first, Baptists ourselves, and then immediately sets us to making Baptists of others. If we cease to make proselytes, it is because we, so far, cease to be Baptists. We become Baptists and we become propagandists of Baptist views by one and the same almighty creative act of God."[39] Had our churches been

[39] Dr. Wilkinson's The Baptist Principle, 8.

possessed of a similar spirit, or even a spirit of caring for their own, our history would have been our vindication for efficiency. Possessing at the outset well-nigh the Republic, we should have well-nigh possessed it to-day. Of late years our churches have been gaining in efficiency without narrowness, and this objection begins to lose its force.

(8) Complete efficiency is secured by the union of wisdom and resources. We do not require for efficiency the sword of Peter in the garden, but the sword of the Spirit; not coercion, but love; not ecclesiastical courts, but Christian graces; not bigotry, but husbandry. To elevate the few and debase the many; to compel assent against the right of private judgment; to lord it over the charge allotted; to be master and lord in the Church of Christ, — these and such as these are not the ends of church government; and for these "Congregationalism is a rope of sand," neither strong nor efficient. But for all the divine ends of church government — to foster the growth of Christian graces in the membership; to hold fast and forth the true faith; to stimulate the missionary spirit by laying the whole responsibility upon the local churches; to balance liberty and security in even scale; to join believers in one unbroken front of unity against all enemies — Congregationalism is, we believe, the best, the strongest, the most efficient. It preserves purity, liberty, unity. It secures universal fellowship, coöperation, and efficiency. "It was the plan of the apostles," therefore, "to plant many absolutely independent churches." This is Congregationalism, " a rope of sand" as respects authority; but the Lord's appointed cord of love, to bind in truth and liberty all churches into one in Christ Jesus. We believe it to be the weakest for evil and the strongest for good of any form of church government.[40] May it soon fill the world with truth, liberty, and unity.

§ 249. It is said that the form of Congregationalism given in these Lectures is centralizing, and is therefore subversive of church independence. Let us repeat our denial of it.

[40] 12 Cong. Quart. 560, 561.

(1) The centralization of unity is not dangerous; for the Author of Christian liberty prayed that all his followers might be one, that the world might believe on him — a unity that is visible and that exhibits the oneness of the indivisible church-kingdom. The evils of the past centuries have not arisen from the associations of churches in district, state, national, and ecumenical bodies, the centralization of love in free fellowship; but liberty was lost in the union of Church and State; the centralization of love was coerced by the civil power. Wherever there has been a separation between Church and State, the movement in centralized systems has been among the people to greater liberty. Even the State can no longer enforce uniformity. We must not forget that force in the churches came from the State, and falls with the separation of Church and State. It was not born of fellowship. For

(2) Fellowship is devoid of authority. It is the association of equal and free churches. Authority is excluded by constitutional provision, and no case of attempted coercion by associations of churches has ever come to our notice.

(3) Votes of associations are void of authority. We express opinions by votes and resolutions. Editors express their opinions in their papers, speakers in their speeches. If church liberty forbids the expression of an opinion by vote or resolution, it must also prevent editors and speakers and preachers and others from uttering an opinion. Voting is only a quick way of ascertaining opinions. If the force of a vote depends on the reason for it, as does the force of a speech or editorial, the vote of an association of churches through chosen messengers is more likely to be wise and more likely to command the assent of free churches than an editorial or speech which represents only one man. But a free uniformity among independent churches, secured by means of public discussion and vote, is not a dangerous element. It is not the uniformity of force and proscription, and hence can never create a schism; it is the uniformity of truth and

love. Under our present system of associations there is greater liberty and closer fellowship than ever before in our history.

(4) Our churches, in their closer fellowship, have escaped the bondage of personal leadership. In the past, individuals by commanding influence have obtained great personal following, and have founded schools of thought, making larger or smaller eddies in the great stream of religious life and belief, which eddies absorbed the thought and energies of the churches until they passed away. Against the consensus of all our churches expressed in state and national bodies, the voice of leaders will now be faint. The rise of the religious paper would give increased force to this dangerous element of personal leadership but for the associations of churches. The churches will call such leaders as once dominated New England thought from their speculations and peculiar isms back to the great working doctrines of the gospel of Christ. The churches care little for criticism or speculation, but they do care for the grand doctrines of the historic faith of Christendom, which have flowed through the centuries like a crystal river from the throne of God, burying, except for the historian, system after system of philosophical theology. Eddies are beautiful, but they are in shallow water or near the shore, never in the deep river. The church members care little for the side attractions, but they will lay down their lives for the grand doctrines of redeeming grace. And they can now make their voice heard as never before. Hence our method of associations of churches is favorable neither to personal rule nor private interpretation, whether by pastor, professor, or editor.

(5) There is no danger to liberty in our escaping from ministerial guidance. Ministerial associations (§ 205) have exerted considerable influence over their members and over churches. The state association of Connecticut was formed in 1709; that of Vermont, in 1796; that of Massachusetts, in 1803; and those of New Hampshire and Rhode

Island, in 1809. These bodies were for a time composed wholly of ministers, and acted for the churches in many things, as in the plan of union (§ 248: 4). They constituted a form of clerical government. Surely associations of churches are as much less dangerous as they are more normal modes of fellowship than these clerical bodies.

(6) There is no danger to liberty in escaping from the perils of consociationism. In 1708 twelve ministers and four laymen met by order of the Assembly or Legislature of Connecticut at Saybrook, to devise a remedy for the evils of lax discipline consequent upon the growing separation of Church and State. They framed and issued the Saybrook Platform, which the said legislature, without any further approval of the churches, made the established ecclesiastical order of Connecticut.[41] This Platform consociated the churches of a county, or of a definite part of a county, into an ecclesiastical body called a consociation. Cases of discipline could be carried to a council composed of the churches consociated together, which should give "a final issue, and all parties therein concerned shall sit down and be determined thereby"; or, if the case were too large or difficult for one consociation to handle, another might join with it in determining the final issue.[42] This Platform has had a double interpretation, one of which regards it as purely Congregational in principle and results; but the other regards it as subversive of the independence of the local churches and as introducing into consociations the fundamental principle of Presbyterianism.[43] The latter was the view of the Hartford North Association of Ministers.[44] This Platform, by going too far in remedying "the defects of discipline in the churches" occasioned by the partial but growing separation of Church and State, hindered the introduction of a better method, until the system of consociated churches had been largely neglected in Con-

[41] Bacon's Hist. Address, in Contrib. to Eccl. Hist. Ct. 38, 39.
[42] Saybrook Plat. art. v, 7.
[43] Contrib. Eccl. Hist. 40, seq.
[44] Gillett's Hist. Presby. Ch. 1, 438, 439, note.

necticut, and prevented its spread into other colonies and states. Yet the Saybrook Platform saved every church in Connecticut from the Unitarian apostasy, which carried over so many of the unassociated churches of Massachusetts. This plan of consociation now embraces only four bodies, and these are in Connecticut.

(7) Our present method of church associations avoids all centralization but that of united fellowship. Our churches are relieved from personal leadership, from civil and clerical control, from consociationism; and our system of church associations, with redress in mutual councils, gives unity without loss of liberty. These associations include all our churches. If a church violate its covenant which it entered into on joining the association, it may be expelled for the same, or fellowship may be withdrawn from it. But there is here, as in the case of ministerial standing in associations, no exercise of authority over the church; for all the association does is to clear itself in self-protection of an unworthy member. The church may manage all its own affairs, even to having whom it will as pastor; but it may not presume to manage the affairs of other churches and force itself upon their fellowship in association; for that would be the exercise of authority by one church over other churches. To deny an association of churches this common right of self-protection, under the cry of centralization, is the absurdity of license; is to make one wayward church supreme in power; it is to give the said church the right and power to compel others to fellowship it. Fellowship is reciprocal, between equals, and it is no centralization to exclude the unworthy from fellowship.

(8) Our present method of church associations rightly balances liberty and unity. It leaves each church to manage its own affairs in all respects, while it gives to all a free, equal, visible fellowship together in counsels and labors. Each church can worship God as it judges best; may have its own creed and discipline; may choose and install its

pastor; may do whatever it likes within its own organization. But when the inherent law of fellowship causes it to look beyond itself in communion with other churches, it must show an evangelical creed and a Christian walk as the condition of that wider fellowship. If ever it lapse from the faith or violate in other ways its covenant, it has given cause for disfellowship and should be cut off as unworthy. If it feel aggrieved by the action, it can ask for a mutual council to review the whole case and give advice as to restoration or exclusion, which advice shall be final. This gives liberty under unity, and unity in liberty.

Thus the centralization presented in this ecumenical system is only the centralization of the life of God in the hearts of redeemed and renewed sinners, which manifests the unity of the church-kingdom in harmony with the constitutive principle of its manifestation. In it the prayer of Christ Jesus may be fully answered, that all may be one, while liberty is assured unto the feeblest church.

§ 250. It has been said that Congregationalism was an anomaly in the days of the apostles. "The presumption that a pure democracy was at once established in every instance where a church was organized, whether on Gentile or on Jewish soil — that one uniform mode was inflexibly followed, in whatever form of civil society, and without regard to the antecedent experience or culture of those uniting in the organization; and especially that a type of government which had literally no representative, or even suggestion, among the civil governments then existing, and which neither the Jewish believer trained in the synagogue system, nor the Gentile believer disciplined under the imperial sway of Rome, could possibly have comprehended at the outset, was invariably instituted wherever Christianity was carried — is certainly one which it is difficult for any mind that appreciates these conditions even to entertain."[45]

(1) If Christianity were an evolution, it could hardly have

[45] Prof. Morris's Ecclesiology, 1885, 135, 136.

appeared in the world under this reasoning; but it was a revelation, not a mere evolution, and as such it would naturally take in its beginning, whatever its environment, the essential form in doctrine and polity of its final completeness. The leaven hid in the meal is the leaven that leavens the whole lump.

(2) The gospel was an anomaly in the world, and it were not strange if its polity were also an anomaly. True, the preceding dispensations had prepared the way for it, and so had they prepared the way also for the polity of independent churches. Professor Morris admits that the Scriptural conception of the church is an anomaly: — " Not as an empire or an oligarchy, but rather as a spiritual democracy — a holy brotherhood of saints, in which the principle of equality is the fundamental law, and in which those who rule, in whatever station, are still the servants of all, in the name of Christ." [46] This anomalous equality made the churches independent because equal.

(3) The Jews were well acquainted, and had been for centuries, with synagogues, each independent of each and all the rest. Each elected its own officers and conducted its own discipline. In this conceded equality and independence are found the elements of Congregationalism (§§ 41: 3; 102).

(4) But no presumption can set aside a fact. It is conceded that the primitive churches were independent democracies (§ 109); that it was "the plan of the apostles to plant many churches each absolutely independent of the rest." And this they did. Within there may have been, and the oldest liturgies prove that there were, minor diversities of worship and order, but without all were independent one of another, as were the Jewish synagogues. They were democracies; no point connected with them is more fully demonstrated or more generally conceded, which no presumption drawn from an unfavorable environment can be allowed to set aside.

[46] Prof. Morris's Ecclesiology, 1885, 135.

§ 251. Removing what is common to other polities from Congregationalism, the remainder is said "to be too casual and too slight to sustain the extensive fabric of inferences based upon it."[47] But its conceded constitutive principle will bear the load of inferences even unto ecumenical unity. Nothing more is needed; for fellowship is able to construct, after many past experiments, on this one principle, a complete and permanent method of exhibiting the unity of the church-kingdom. The temple is rising upon this one foundation.

§ 252. And this anomalous democratic polity gives ample scope for the exercise of all the authority deposited in the churches. Professor Morris says: "There is conveyed in this theory an inadequate conception of the true province and worth of government as a central feature of all church organizations."[48] He cites in support of the worth of government as the central feature of all church organizations these passages: 1 Cor. 12: 28; 2 Peter 2: 10; Rom. 12: 8; Heb. 13: 7, 17; 1 Tim. 5: 17; Acts 20: 17, 28; and the Corinthian Epistles. Congregationalism heartily uses all the authority and government here referred to. It exhausts the panel.

These are all the objections given by Professor Morris in his recent work referred to, save the one given in § 247 on fellowship. They lie forcibly against independency, but not against Congregationalism, and so are easily answered as not relevant.

§ 253. As a final resort it is said that church government is left by Christ and his apostles to the discretion of believers in every age. The objection leaves the Papacy, Episcopacy, Presbyterianism, and Congregationalism as equally authorized. If the objection were true, our polity would have a better claim than any other, for it is the conceded polity of the apostles, who had the spirit of Christ. They planted independent churches, and so gave this polity the preference in act, if not in word. But the objection is not true.

[47] Prof. Morris's Ecclesiology, 1885, 136. [48] Ibid.

(1) Polity is of the essence of the Church. The Church is the communion of saints, who are citizens of one and the same church-kingdom. That communion rests on some normal principle and must take a form consistent therewith. Form here, as in nature, is determined by the life, and the same stage in life does not produce many forms. The holy life of faith, the reign of Christ in the hearts of men, must manifest itself in some form built after the essential nature of that life and reign. It can not fundamentally be one thing here and now and another thing at another time and place. In the divine mind the church-kingdom has but one normal development into visible churches, and hence but one normal relation of church to church (§§ 47, 98). Church polity can not be incidental and discretionary, therefore, but of the essence of the Church. Polity is the mould or form which the church-kingdom takes in manifestation; and as there can be, in God's thought, but one mode of manifestation in exact accord with the nature of the church-kingdom, there can be but one true polity. Hence church polity is not discretionary.

(2) This is the conviction of men. Not one of the four great polities but claims or has claimed a divine warrant for it. All instinctively feel that human expediency or discretion touching the organic form of a divine revelation is unwarranted. Hence they search the Scriptures as with a lighted candle for some word or phrase or text which may support their theory. And it must be confessed with shame that often the holy Scriptures have been perverted into support of a particular polity. The Revised Version of the New Testament removed several such perversions from the Authorized Version. These perversions and the persistency with which men return to the Bible for proofs reveal the deep-seated conviction that polity is not discretionary. It is not until they are driven from the revealed Word in confusion that they resort to the claim of expediency and discretion for refuge.

(3) The New Testament gives the constitutive principle of one of the great polities with sufficient clearness to indicate conclusively what polity the church-kingdom requires. That principle deposits the permanent power of discipline in the local churches (§ 161: 2); it forbids prelatical rule; it shows that the apostles planted independent churches. This is so clearly proved that it is conceded by those who hold other polities. Archbishop Whately calls it "the plan of the apostles." Now if this one constitutive principle be conceded, all else follows; but the proof compels the concession. With this concession all questions of expediency and discretion are swallowed up in the divine plan.

(4) It is the duty of all Christians to obey the will of Christ in polity as in doctrine. If appeal be taken to tradition, decrees of councils, papal bulls, inner light, reason, discretion, expediency, or any thing else, it can be done as well for doctrine as for polity, and the churches are cut loose from Christ their Head and King at once. Once out on such a sea, shipwreck is certain. The will of Christ, when made known, is our only law and safety. The churches, through an unfavorable environment and union with the State, broke away from the plan of the apostles, and since then have tried every form of polity; but the corruptions in doctrine and morals, and the oppressions and persecutions under authority, have proved that in church polity the way of the transgressor is hard. And so they are slowly returning from their wanderings unto the primitive polity again.

(5) The future belongs to the primitive church polity of unity in liberty. If our reasoning in these Lectures be correct, the ecumenical unity of the Mediator's prayer will be reached not through the polity of an infallible primacy, or of apostolic succession, or of authoritative representation, but through the polity of church independency or liberty. And since the right of private judgment has been vindicated, the drift has been setting strongly towards that liberty both in Church and in State. "And the most significant fact of

modern Christian history is that, within the last hundred years, many millions of our own race and our own [Anglican] Church, without departing from the ancient faith, have slipped from beneath the inelastic frame-work of the ancient organization, and formed a group of new societies on the basis of a closer Christian brotherhood and an almost absolute democracy."[49] Democratic institutions are in the air as never before. A ground-swell has begun which will not cease until liberty in Church and State is assured unto all the people in all lands. Our fathers brought liberty to this continent at great cost; they put liberty at first under restraint; and they complained of those who kept "buzzing our people in the ear with a thing they call liberty, which when they have tasted a smack of, they can no more endure to hear of a synod or gathering together of able and orthodox Christians, nor yet the communion of churches, but would be independent to purpose, and as for civil government, they deem religion to be a thing beyond their sphere."[50] This "thing they call liberty" has been buzzed in the ear of the people to some purpose in this and in other lands. "Sixty years ago [1820] Europe was an aggregate of despotic powers, disposing at their own pleasure of the lives and property of their subjects, maintaining by systematic neglect [of common schools] the convenient ignorance which renders misgovernment easy and safe. To-day [1880] the men of western Europe govern themselves. Popular suffrage, more or less closely approaching universal, chooses the governing power, and by methods more or less effective dictates its policy. One hundred and eighty million Europeans have risen from a degraded and ever-dissatisfied vassalage to the rank of free and self-governing men." " Never since the stream of human development received into its sluggish currents the mighty impulse communicated by the Christian religion has the condition of man experienced ameliorations

[49] Hatch's Org. Early Christ. Chhs. 215.
[50] Johnson's Wonder Working Providence, book 1, chap. xliv.

so vast. . . . The nineteenth century has witnessed the fall of despotism and the establishment of liberty in the most influential nations of the world. It has vindicated for all succeeding ages the right of man to his own unimpeded development. . . . The growth of man's well-being, rescued from the mischievous tampering of self-willed princes, is left now to the beneficent regulation of great providential laws." [51] "The people are every-where and in every thing coming to the front, and in the front henceforth they are destined forever to remain." [52]

The labor ferments reveal a determined movement on the part of the people to share in some just and equitable way in the management and profit of business. The laborer is no longer content with his wages while his employer pockets the profits, but he too claims a share in the profits, and he will not rest until he obtains it and stands on a level with his employer. There is, in fact, to be in the future no governing class in business, in the State, and in the Church, whose function it is to rule the people. There is to be a brotherhood including all on terms of equality. This movement touching business, the State, and the Church may be hindered, but it can not be stayed. It is born of the Fatherhood of God and the brotherhood of man. And those forms of government, wherever found, which raise a class of rulers into an aristocracy or a hierarchy over the ruled are destined to perish from the earth. The Papacy, the Episcopacy, and Presbyterianism thus separate the rulers from the ruled, but each in its degree. No bridge can unite the ruled and the rulers under those systems and make them one. The rulers must come down to the people and become one with them in a democracy. There is no other way. The king of England cried out: "No bishop, no king," and harried the Puritans out of his kingdom. Events are justifying the wisdom of his mad cry. For a free Church ends in a free State;

[51] Mackenzie's Hist. Nineteenth Century, 459, 460.
[52] Prof. Ladd's Principles Ch. Polity, 331.

religious liberty is the mother of civil freedom. Christianity builds democracies; for it teaches the brotherhood of man and the equality of all churches and Christians. This world-movement towards liberty was begun at Calvary and will end only in the ecumenical millennial glory. "Christianity's unaccomplished mission is to re-construct society on the basis of brotherhood. What it has to do it does, and will do, in and through organization. . . . But the framing of its organization is left to human hands. To you and me and men like ourselves is committed, in these anxious days, that which is at once an awful responsibility and a splendid destiny — to transform this modern world into a Christian society; to change the socialism which is based on the assumption of clashing interests into the socialism which is based on the sense of spiritual union; and to gather together the scattered forces of a divided Christendom into a confederation in which organization will be of less account than fellowship with one spirit and faith in one Lord — into a communion wide as human life and deep as human need — into a Church which shall outshine even the golden glory of its dawn by the splendor of its eternal noon." [53]

[53] Hatch's Org. Early Christ. Chhs. 216.

INDEX.

Aaronic priesthood, 13, 132.
Abrahamic Call and Covenant, 7, 8, 10, 11, 12, 31, 208, 211.
Accountability of ministers, 154–165, 175–178.
Activities, church, 312–323; coöperation in, 314; determined by polity, 93, 94.
Acts 9: 31, meaning of "church" in, 166–168.
Advertising church troubles, 255.
Advice changed into decrees by the state, 296, 325.
Alford, Dean, on apostolical succession, 141, 142.
Alliance between church and the world, 331, 332, 342, 343.
Alliance, Evangelical, Creed, 237.
Alliance, Presbyterian, 74; abandons constitutive principle, 74, 75; number of churches in, 76.
American churches and the State, 327–337.
Anabaptists and the ministry, 134.
Andrews, Prof. E. B., 31, 40.
"Angels," the, of "the seven churches," 146, 147.
Anglican Church and the Bible, 66; and fellowship, 66; its standard of faith, 66, 99; origin, 66; Prayer Book of, 66; visible church, 4.
Apostates from the kingdom, 110.
Apostle, election of an, 114, 115.
Apostles, the, 138–142; administration of sacraments by, 226; authority of, 140; authority of, over churches, 124; completed church order, 142; equal in rank, 140; founded churches everywhere, 37; inspired, 139, 140; meaning of their name, 124; miraculous gifts of, 140; number of, 138; qualifications of, 138–142; selected by Christ, 138; successors of, 141, 142; taught by Christ, 139.
Apostolate, the, temporary, 140–142; vacancies in, 124, 141, 142.
Apostolic, churches, composed of saints, 107, 108; Fathers, on independence of churches, 118, 119; succession, 62, 63, 85, 86, 141, 142.
Apostolical constitutions, 60, 135, 173, 200, 201, 212, 221.
Appeals, associations and, 160–163; churches and, 112, 113; Presbyterian, 71–74
Association, church, a law of the kingdom, 38–40; ecumenical, needed, 38, 82, 311.
Associations of churches. 295–306; authority of, 300, 301; avoid centralization, 284, 295, 296, 363–368; conditions of membership in, 302, 347; councils and, 282; covenant of, 296, 298, 302; deposition by, 288, 289; discipline by, 301–304; district, 81, 82; early, in America, 297, 298; English, 298; expulsion from, 163, 164, 282, 283, 301–304; fellowship in, 295; importance of, 295, 296; Massachusetts Colony on, 295, 296; membership in, 298, 299, 305; mistakes and, 160, 288; national, 82; normal, 269; origin, 296–298; participate in councils, 282–284; pastoral delegates in, 302, 303; representation in, 298, 299; state, 82; warrant of, 296; Year Book and, 283, 284, 286, 305.
Associations of ministers, 292–295.
Attempted return to Patriarchal Church, 17, 18.
Augustine and the Donatists, 49; on bishops and elders, 145.
Authoritative representation, constitutive principle of Presbyterianism, 72.
Authority of synods under Constantine, 325, 337.

Bacon, Dr. Leonard, 21.
Bancroft, George, on the Puritans, 89.
Baptism, 207–216; administered by whom, 225–228; adult, 211; Christian, required, 32, 33, 207; confession of Christ and, 215, 216; confirmation and, 214; essential elements in, 207; in distress, 226, 227; infant, 211–213; infant, and church membership, 213–216; infant, more than consecration, 216; initiatory rite, 208, 219; intent essential, 209; John's, not Christian, 33, 208, 209; mode of, 210, 211; nature of, 207, 208; only once to be administered, 210; prerequisite to the Eucharist, 219; purity of the churches and, 107–109, 211–216; Roman Catholic, 209, 210; salvation and, 29, 54, 212, 227; subjects of, 211–213; superseded circumcision, 108, 207–209, 212; symbol of a changed life, 105, 106, 207, 208; Unitarian, 209.
Baptismal regeneration, 50, 213.
Baptist view of the covenant and children, 211, 216.
Baptists, efficiency of, 359, 362; standard of faith, 99.
Baptized children, discipline of, 235; relation to the church, 213–216.
Barnabas, called an apostle, 138, 141.
Basis, doctrinal and ecclesiastical, of the National Council, 346, 347.
Bases, doctrinal, of state bodies, 346, 347.
Believers and visible churches, 171.
Bible, the, inspired, 33, 34; other standards than, 98, 99; sole standard, 99.
Bigotry, polities not due to, 41, 94.
"Binding" and "loosing," 113, 114.
Bishops, primitive, same as elders, 60, 61, 124, 145; presiding, 61, 62.

378 INDEX.

Brotherhood, primitive churches a, 96; Christian, and polity, 127, 130; Christian society to be built on, 374, 375.
Browne, Robert, and polity, 91, 268.
Buck, Edward, Esq., Mass. Eccl. Law, admissibility of evidence, 251; legal elements in installation, 290.
Bunsen, independence of primitive churches, 126.
Burial Hill Declaration, 346.
Business, church, demands order and regularity, 229, 231.

Calvin, John, author of Presbyterianism, 71; his Institutes, 18; used temporal power, 326.
Cambridge Confession, 346.
Cambridge Platform and the General Court, 345 n.
Candlish, Dr. J. S., 28, 43, 90.
Catechumens, 221, 312, 313; early manual for, 313.
Censures, church, 254; public announcement of, 255; vote to lift, 254, 255.
Centralization, dangers avoided, 367.
Ceremonial Church, 11-17; covenant of, 11, 12; inadequacy of, 16; developed into the Christian Church, 32, 33, 128; unity of, 12, 13.
Ceremonial Dispensation, a Theocracy, 14; covered all codes, 12; development from the Patriarchal, 11, 12; bound to the Patriarchal, 31; national form of the Church of God, 11-17; temporary, 16, 17; unity of, 12, 13, 15, 16.
Ceremonial Law abolished, 120; inadequate, 16; minute and fixed, 13.
Challenge, no right of, in trials, 250, 280.
"Chiefs," in New Testament, 146.
Children, church duties towards, 213-216, 235; may not vote, 257, 258.
China, government of, older than the Papacy, 47.
Christ Jesus a High Priest, 132, 133; assumed regal power, 24; superseded other priesthoods, 133; taught for churches, 111-113.
Christian Church, 98; early confusion of thought respecting, 47-51; priesthood in, 133, 134.
Christian Dispensation, 21; bound to the Ceremonial, 31; not a succession but a continuance, 30, 31.
Christianity, adjustments of, 94-96; not an evolution, 131, 342, 368, 369.
Church, meaning of, 166; Matt. 18: 17, 111-113.
Church, a, 110, 111, 170, 171; in Episcopacy, 64, 65; not a congregation, 107; not a voluntary society, 171; parity in, 171, 172; tests of admission to, 105.
Church board, 185; duties of, 186; importance of, 186; trial by, 219, 357.
Church of God, conditioned in apostasy, 6; forms of, 3, 4, 21; origin of, 6, 7; what it is, 5, 98; without cleavage, 32, 33.
Church of Christ, the, 4, 5, 98; a development in part, 32, 33, 109; doctrine of, one, not many, 44, 45; manifests the kingdom of heaven, 42, 43, 98, 104; theories of, 40, 45, 46, 84, 85; true theory, 41, 97, 98, 118, 119, 126-130; visible and invisible, 4, 49, 50; importance of this distinction, 50; manward side of the kingdom, 103.
Church government, force of faulty administration of, 356.
Church-kingdom, the, 103, 104, 121.
Church meetings, importance of regular, 231.
Church polities, narrow lines separate, -41; origin of, 39, 40.
Church relations, all Israel entered, 12; no salvation out of papal, 29, 48.
Church taxation, 333.
Churches, activities of, 312-323; authority of democratic, 355, 364; baptism admitted to primitive, 105, 106; boards of control in, 185; city, of New Testament, 168-170; coöperation of, 314; discipline of, 111-113; discipline of primitive, 106, 107; doctrinal soundness of Congregational, 347, 349, 350; divine factors in fellowship, 39, 364; holy assemblies, 104-108; independence of primitive, 110-130; independent of the State, 324, 325, 332; life-centers of evangelization, 312, 339; manifest the kingdom of heaven, 36, 37, 104; materials of, 100, 104-108; members of, equal, 171, 172; mission of, never abandoned, 95; multiplied not through bigotry, 41; number of in New England, in 1648, 345 n; organs of the Holy Spirit, 126, 152. 153, 323; planted everywhere, 37; primitive intercourse of, 116, 117; property of, 324, 335-337; relation of, to kingdom of heaven, 43-45; relation of, to State, 323-337; in Connecticut, 337, 338; in New England, 328; in papal countries, 57, 58; relation of, to the world, 341-343; subject to no Episcopacy, 123-125; nor to a General Assembly, 125, 126; nor to an infallible Primate, 121-123; terms of admission to, 105; training for the Scriptural polity, 94-96; troubles of, should not be advertised, 255; true factors of evangelization, 312, 339; union of, with the State, introduced force, 325; unity of, essential, 110, 119; worship essential to, 194, 195.
Circumcision admitted to the *kahal* of Israel, 101; of the heart, 12; rite of, 8, 13.
Civil Courts, look into constitution and proceedings of councils before enforcing result, 279 n.
Civil law, churches are subject to, 324, 325, 332-337.
Cleavage produced by force, not liberty, 76, 77, 266, 358.
Clement Romanus, 70, 107, 112, 113, 118, 126, 153, 235.
Clerk, church, 186; duties of, 187, 191; qualifications, 187.
Clubs, heathen, prepare for the church, 36, 38.
Coercion and reform, 266, 358, 359.
Coleman, on independence of primitive churches, 126, 127.
Comity, church, 337-341; and creeds, 338, 340; criterion in, 338, 340; respects polity, 340; rests on private judgment, 337, 338; unevangelical bodies excluded from, 338, 340.
Commercial aspects of churches, 342, 343.
Committees, appointed by a church, 189, 190.

INDEX. 379

Communicants in the Eucharist, 218-224; must be baptized believers, 219; and church members, 219; these terms confirmed, 220.
Communion, the, of churches, 38, 39, 264-266; of saints, 3, 5, 12, 36, 38, 39, 42, 80, 264.
Complaint, the, in cases of discipline, 242, 246, 247.
Conditions of church membership, 105,106.
Conferences of churches (see Associations), 295-306; district, state, and national, 81, 82; express stated fellowship, 81; may be parties to councils, 273, 282-284.
Confirmation, Episcopal, by a bishop, 64, 65; sacrament, so-called, of, 205.
Confession, effect of, on trial, 248; on joining a church, 215, 216, 222, 347, 348.
Confessions, general, of Congregationalists, 345, 346.
Confusion of thought, Papacy arose from, 47-50.
Congregation, not the church, 107; of Israel, 12, 100, 101 (see also *kahal*).
Congregational churches, 83; in New England in 1648, 345 *n*; their guards to purity, 345-355; unity of, 357-359.
Congregational Puritans, 90, 326.
Congregational Quarterly, influence of, 307, 308.
Congregational theory of the Christian Church, 79-84; the oldest, 79; secures unity, 82, 311, 357-359, 375.
Congregational Union of England and Wales, 307; creed of, 346.
Congregationalism, abnormal development of, in America, 332; an "anomaly," 368, 369; constitutive principle of, 80, 372; development of, 81, 82; future prospects, 130, 372-375; historical, studied, 22; not infallible, 84; not a narrow theme, 1; proof of, 83, 110-128; republican, 93; revolutionary, 84; saved in the West by laymen, 352, 353, 361; shuns independency and authority, 79; unifying principle in, 39, 40; unity of, 357-359; wanting in no element, 83, 84.
Congregationalists, distrusted their polity, 361; national churches rejected by, 90; standard of faith, 99, 345-347; who are, 83.
Connecticut, ministerial standing in, 155, 293; restraint of liberty in, 337, 338; Unitarianism in, 367.
Consociationism, 86, 297, 360, 366, 367.
Constantine and the church, 325, 337.
Constitutive principle, defined, 40, 45, 46; of Congregationalism, 80; of Episcopacy, 62; of the Papacy, 52; of Presbyterianism, 72.
Coöperation among churches, 314-323; matters included in, 314; methods of, 315-317; through church associations, 317, 318; through close corporations, 316; through voluntary contributors, 315; through combining these, 316, 317; normal method, 317-319; advantages of the normal method, 321, 322; obstacles to a return, 319-321; required, 314-317; primitive method, 315, 317, 318; English method, 318, 319.
Corinthian Church, discipline in the, 112, 113.

Corporation, church, 330, 331.
Council, authority of the, of Jerusalem, 124.
Council of churches, a, 272; an association a party to, 273, 282-284; called by whom, 272; letters missive, 272; membership in, 272; quorum of, 273; rights of members in, 272, 273.
Councils of churches, 267-292, 327; abnormal system, 268, 269; accounted for in New England, 269-271; associations parties to, 273, 282-284; associations may supplant, 288, 289; called sometimes by the State, 270, 271; confounded one with another, 277, 278; courts and, 278, 279; earliest, 124; *duo parte*, 275; *ex parte*, 276; fellowship in, limited, 81, 274; final resort, 287; functions of, limited, 81, 273, 274; general, 124, 268; inadequate as safeguards, 160, 161, 178, 281, 290-292; installing and ordaining, 273, 290; kinds of, 274; limited use of, 160, 161, 291; ministerial discipline by, 284-287; mistakes by, not easily corrected, 160; mutual, 275, 276; no right of challenge, 280; objects, 273; origin of, politico-ecclesiastical, 268-271; packing, 281, 282; procedure in, 278; quorum in, 273; recognition, 290; result of, 278, 279, 280; scope of, 273, 274; size of, 274; temporary, 279; *uni parte*, 275; warrant for, 267.
Covenant, Abrahamic, 7, 11, 12; church, 170, 171.
Coxe, Bishop, abolition of episcopate in Roman Church, 58, 59, 86; priority of the Greek Church, 47.
Creed, assent to, 347, 348; importance of a, 106, 344; of Ceremonial Church, 14; of Evangelical Alliance, 237; of Patriarchal Church, 9; property affected by change of, 335, 336; required, 106.
Creeds, of associations of churches, 346, 347; of churches, 347, 348; of ethnic religions, 9 *n*; preserved best by laity, 350-352; primitive norm of, 106; tests of membership, 347, 348, 354, 355.
Credentials, 302; contents of, 304, 305; defined, 304.
Cromwell, Oliver, on State, Church, and liberty, 90.
Cross-examination, 252.
Cyprian, church and the kingdom, 48; election of church officers, 172, 173; primacy of Peter, 122.

Deacons, 178-181; authority of, what, 180; duties of, 178, 179; election of, 115, 178; laymen, 179, 226; ordination of, 180; origin of the office of, 178; qualifications of, 180; removal of, 180; rotation in office of, 180, 181.
Deaconesses, 179, 180.
Dead-lock between church and society, 330-332, 360.
Decrees, church, a standard of faith, 99.
Dedham decision, 331, 332.
Delegates of primitive churches, 115, 116; of Congregational churches, 303.
Deposition from the ministry, 176, 287, 288; by associations, 283, 284, 288; by councils, 284, 287, 288; papal and prelatical, 287, 288; under the pastoral theory, 287; revokes ordination, 288.

De Quincy, 342.
Development, Biblical *versus* Vedic, 9 *n*; Congregational and ecclesiastical, 130; dispensations and, 30, 31; normal, of the kingdom, 43–45; religion not a mere, 131; righteousness and, 109.
Dexter, Dr. Henry M., 21, 157, 175, 251, 261, 276, 282, 307.
Diaconate, origin of the, 178.
Disciples, baptism and Christ's, 32, 33.
Discipline, 229–263; associational, 163, 164; authority of, limited, 235; whence derived, 234; where deposited, 233, 234; baptized children under what, 235; church officers subject to, 235, 261; complaint in, 246, 247; defects in, when of little weight, 232; discretion needed in, 238–240; drift in, 232; ends of church, 240, 241, 244; evidence in, 250–252; evils of, restricted in Congregationalism, 357; excommunication in, 243, 254; final when, 113; first step in, when to be taken, 244, 245; general and special, 230, 231; irregularities in, 256, 257; letters of dismissal and, 245, 246; jury in, 249, 250; means of grace, 240; meetings of a church and, 231; ministerial, 51, associations endorsed, 161, 162; ministerial, twofold, 177, 235; mistakes in, rend churches, 233; offences demanding, 235–238; parties protected in, 255, 256; pastor's province in, 248, 261; polity determines mode of, 231, 232; polity judged by, 233; principle governing ministerial, 154, 175, 176, 235, 243, 261, 262; proxy used in, when, 246; purity through, 238–241; ratified in heaven, 113; redress of grievance in, 262, 263; regulated how by the State, 334, 335; rigor of early, 106; rule of, 111–113: rules needed, 230; steps in, 241, 247; study of, demanded, 232, 233; subjects of, 235; supreme when, 113, 114; temperance and, 239, 240; testimony in, to be preserved, 248; uniformity in, desirable, 229; varies with circumstances, 239, 240; voters in, 257–259; witnesses in, 247.
Discretion in discipline, 238–240; in doctrine and polity, 370–372.
Dispensations, Ceremonial and Christian, confounded, 18, 49; bound together, 16, 31; preparatory, sifted for the final, 19, 20, 31, 32, 111, 114 (see *kahal*).
Divisions caused by force, 76, 358, 359.
Doctrinal, basis of the National Council, 346, 347; of state associations, 346, 347; reforms and polity, 2, 3, 18, 358, 359.
Doctrine, meaning of the term, 43, 98; of the Christian Church, 3, 43, 98; one and not many, 43–45.
Doctrines, the great working, 316, 351, 352, 365.
Donatists, 49, 325.
Dropping church members, when, 259, 260.
Duo parte councils what, 275.

Ecclesia, 36, 37, 112, 120, 121, 127, 128, 166; winnowed from the *kahal* of Israel, 32, 111, 114, 136, 208; used for *kahal*, 107.
Ecclesiastical infallibility, 26; rationalism, 128, 129.
Ecclesiastical society, 328–332; usurpation of, 231, 330, 331.

Ecumenical Association, 82; rightly balances liberty and unity, 88, 367, 368; needed, 38, 82, 311.
Elders (Presbyters), 70, 71, 145; accountability of, dual, 176, 177; appointed or chosen, 116, 172, 173; church officers when, 172; duties of, 173, 174; membership of, dual, 174, 175; plurality of, in primitive churches, 70, 71, 169, 170, 173; presiding officers, 175; removed by Corinthian church, 176; synagogues-elected elders, 117, 118.
Efficiency, church, of Baptists, 359, 362; of Congregationalists. 359–363; objects of true, 363; unites wisdom and resources, 363.
Election of an apostle, 114, 115; of deacons, 115; of delegates, 115, 116; elders, 116; primitive churches and the, of officers, 114–116, 172, 173; removed from office, 176.
Emmons, dictum of Dr. Nathaniel, 86.
Encyclopædia Britannica, democracy and autonomy of the primitive churches, 127, 142; hearsay evidence, 251, 252; identity of elders, pastors, and bishops, 146; infallibility of Greek Church, 52; invisible and visible church, 4; priority of Greek Church, 47; rise of Episcopacy, 61, 63, 65; tradition in Anglican Church, 66.
English Congregational societies, 318, 319.
Environment, 51, 239, 267, 368, 369.
Episcopal, convocations, 64; jurisdiction, 64; orders in the ministry, 64.
Episcopacy, 59–69, 123–125; aggressive and exclusive, 68; constitutive principle of, 62, 63; development of, 64, 65; forms of, 65–67; older than the Papacy, 59; origin of, 59–62; proof of, 63, 64; reformable. 68; undeveloped, 59, 68, 69; unifying principle of, 40.
Episcopate, churches not subject to an, 123–125.
Eucharist, the, early communicants in, 107, 108, 220, 221; not a sacrifice, 54, 133, 134.
Europe, progress of liberty in, 89, 90, 373.
Evangelical churches and comity, 338–340.
Evangelical Alliance, creed of, 237.
"Evangelists," 144, 145.
Evangelization, coöperation of churches in, 314–317.
Evidence, admissibility of, 250–252; hearsay, 251, 252.
Evolution, ecclesiastical, 11, 31–33, 94–96.
Examination, of ministers, 353; value of cross-, 252.
Excommunicate, how to restore an, 254, 255.
Excommunication, 243, 254; final, 243; of ministers, 286, 287; redress in, 262, 263; synagogue, 102.
Ex parte councils, 276.
Expulsion from associations and standing, 163, 164, 283, 301–304.
Extreme unction, so-called sacrament of, 206.

Faith, standards of, in Christendom, 98, 99.
Family form of the Church, 6–11; at-

tempted return to, 17; lacked fellowship, 11.
Family, the, honored in all dispensations, 6, 15, 33.
Fan, Christ's winnowing, 32, 109, 111, 114, 136, 208.
Feet-washing, rite of, among the Mennonites, 205, 206.
Fellowship of churches, 38, 39, 264–267; basis of, 108, 264; channel of blessings, 36, 87, 266, 267; councils inadequate to express, 81, 274; definition of, 264; devoid of authority, 266, 267, 364; essential, 37, 38, 265; exhibited on four principles, 40, 265; expressed in Congregationalism, 81–83, 358, 359; impossible where, 340, 341; liberty in, 266, 267; limitation of, 338–341; methods of, 267; peculiar to no polity, 80, 81, 265, 266; prime factors in, 39; unites all believers, 38; unity sought in, 40; vehicle of oppression, 266; visible, required, 265; withholding, from ministers, 155.
Felt, J. B., Eccl. Hist., quoted, 153, 156, 157, 297.
Fiction, papal, of imprisonment, 58.
Fisher, Prof. Geo. P., D.D., on good done by the Papacy, 95; on Lord's Supper, 218.
Force, ecclesiastical, divisive, 76, 266, 267, 358, 359, 364.
Foreign missions, coöperation in, 314, 323; when begun, 322.
Form essential to organic life, 2, 30, 371.
Francis I., Calvin wrote his Institutes for, 18.
Froude, J. A., on the Puritans, 89.
Future, the, belongs to the primitive polity, 130, 372–375.

General Assembly, 74; powers of, 74; churches not subjected to a, 125, 126.
General Councils, State gave authority to, 64, 325, 337; Congregational, 307.
General Court of Massachusetts, an ecclesiastical body, 296, 297.
General Courts of New England, ecclesiastical, 156; relation to councils, 269–271.
Gladstone, Hon. Wm. E., the Papacy, 58.
Gospel of the kingdom, 23; an anomaly, 369.
Greek Church, 65, 66; older than the papal, 47, 59; standard of faith, 99.
Guards of purity complete in Congregationalism, 344–355.

Hanbury's Memorials, 21, 181, 268, 298, 327.
Harris, Prof. George, D.D., unit of society, 6.
Harris, Prof. Samuel, D.D., definition of the Church, 5.
Harvey, Prof. H., D.D., ordination by ministers, 152; relation of polity to heresy, 2, 3.
Hatch, Vice-Prin. Edwin, equality within churches, 172; identity of elders and bishops, 61; independence of local churches, 127; ordination, 151, 152; polity of the future. 96, 273, 372, 375.
Heads of Agreement, 346.
Hearsay evidence, 251, 252.
Heresies, early, began in changes of polity, 2, 3.

Heresy, disciplinable, 237; liberty hinders, 350, 351; ways of dealing with, 353, 354.
High Priest, Christ the Christian's, 132, 133.
Hitchcock, Prof. R. D., D.D., 183, 184, 185.
Homburg, synod of, 91.
Home Missions, coöperation in, 314.
Hooker, Richard, 185.
Hume, the Puritans, 89.
Hutchinson, early use of councils in Massachusetts, 327, 328.
Hutchinson's Hist. Mass. on duties of ruling elders, 181, 182; ordination, 153; polity derived from Pilgrim Church, 227, 228; strength of churches in civil power. 327, 328.

Ignatius, 48, 69, 71, 126, 180.
Imprisonment, papal fiction of, 58.
Inalienable right of churches in any locality, 158, 160, 163, 164, 283, 286, 299; expressed in associations, 285, 286; imperfectly guarded in councils, 299, 300; should be respected, 303, 304; when infringed upon, 299, 300.
Inauguration of pastors, 177, 178.
Incorporation of churches, 330, 331.
Indelible character and ordination, 136, 151, 152.
Independence of local churches, 80, 110–119; arises from unity, 110, 111; conceded, 126–128; hated, 340; proof of, 110; by the rule of discipline, 111-114; by the election of officers, 114–116; by their relation one to another, 116, 117; by their relation to the synagogues, 117, 118; by statements of the Apostolic Fathers, 118, 119.
Independent churches, guards of purity in, 345–355; modeled after clubs and synagogues, 34–36, 38, 198, 199; power of, 300; property of, 335, 336; subject to no centralized authority, 119–126, whether Pope, 121–123, or Episcopate, 123–125, or General Assembly, 125, 126; this point conceded, 126–130.
Independents, Congregationalists in England called, 83.
Individuals not factors in common labors, 126, 322, 323.
Indulgences, 54.
Inequality in representation, dangerous, 298, 299.
Infallibility, papal, 26; dogma of, 51, 52; when decreed, 52, 53; of the Greek Church, 52; of the kingdom of heaven, 26; of the Popes, 51, 52; ecclesiastical, 26.
Infallible Primacy, active and passive, 53; constitutive principle of the Roman Church, 52; churches not subject to, 121–123.
Infant baptism, 108, 211–216; Congregationalists and, 215; reformed churches and, 214; when corrupts a church, 214.
Infant damnation, 227.
Injustice in censures, remedied, 260, 262, 276.
Inner Light, standard of faith, 99.
Installation, 290; decadence of, 160, 291; elements in, 290; inadequate guards, 160, 290–292; unessential to the pastorate, 177, 178; urgency of its advocates, 291.

Intemperance and church discipline, 239, 240.
Invisible Church or visible, Christendom divided over, 4.
Invitation to the Eucharist, 224, 225.
Ireland, Presbyterian churches in, expurgated heresy, 350, 351.
Irenæus confounded church and kingdom, 48.
Irregularities in procedure, 256, 257, 276.
Isolation of churches, abnormal, 38–40, 264, 265.

Jeroboam, how caused Israel to sin, 13, 14.
Jerusalem, council at, 124, 139.
Jewish Christians and independent synagogues, 118.
Johnson's "Wonder Working Providence," 358, 359, 373.
Jurisdiction, ecclesiastical courts determine their own, 278; lawful, in Episcopacy, 64.
Jury trial of offences, demanded in churches, 249, 250, 357.
Justin, Martyr, 107, 108, 221.

Kahal, or "congregation of Israel," 12, 32, 100, 111, 114, 115, 119, 120, 121, 128, 136, 167; became the Christian ecclesia or Church, 111, 112, 114, 115, 120, 121, 128, 167, 208; oneness of the, 119, 120; relinquished authority in becoming Christian, 128.
Keys of the kingdom, where deposited, 113, 114.
Kingdom of heaven, the, 22–30; appears chiefly in churches, 36; characteristics of, 24–28; Christward side of the Church, 103; conditions of admission to, 28; confounded with the church, 28, 29; Congregationalists and, 21 n; constantly coming, 30; contrasted with Ceremonial law, 33; also with previous dispensations, 23, 24; defined, 24, 27, 28; distinguished from the Church, 28, 29, 103, 166, emerges in local churches, 42, 43; equality in, 27; established already, 22–24; everlasting, 27; evolved from preceding dispensations, 30, 31; foundation of the Christian Church, 21; gives place to "church," and "churches," 42, 43; gospel of, 23; holiness of, 25; indivisible, 25; infallible, 26; invisible, 25, 26; loyalty to Christ in, 24, 25; manifested in organic forms, 30, 36, 38; materials of, 31, 32, 102; misunderstood by the Jews, 31; reign of Christ in, 24; notes of, 24–28; partly on earth and partly in heaven, 29; peculiar, 27, 28; preached, 23; predicted, 22, 23; separated from the State, 120, 121, 324, 325, 332; subjects equal, 27; synagogue worship appropriated by, 35, 36; term, how used by the apostles, 42, 43; unity of, 25, 38; universal, 27; writers on Congregationalism neglect, 21 n.

Ladd, Prof. G. T., D.D., doctrine and polity, 3; democracy to the front, 374; examination for ordination, 353; mistaken policy, 352; provincialism suicidal, 361.
Laity, custodians of faith and polity, 350–353; distinguished from the ministry, 134–136; saved Congregationalism in the West, 352, 353, 361.
Laud, Archbishop, the Puritans, 90.
Lawrence, Judge Wm., alienation of church property, 335, 336.
Lawyers in ecclesiastical trials, 252–254; rules respecting, 253.
Lay Eldership, Presbyterian, 181–185; duties of, 181, 182; unscriptural, 182, 183; being rejected by Presbyterians, 183, 184; Presbyterianism then reduced to a clerical despotism, 184.
Leadership, personal, escaped, 365.
Legal, counsel in trials, 252–254; elements in installation, 290; obstacles to church coöperation, 319, 320; relations of churches, 323–337; rules of evidence and ecclesiastical trials, 251, 252.
Legislation, all ecclesiastical, vests in Christ, 24, 25.
Letters, of dismission and discipline, 245, 246; missive, 272.
Liberty, associations and, 82, 266, 267; called "the insanity," 54, 88; Consociationism and, 366, 367; endangered by personal leaders, 365; polity and, 18, 19, 82, 88–93; progress of, 88–93, 373; Puritans and, 88–90; relation of, to unity, 266, 267, 367; union of Church and State destroys, 296, 330–332; unity and, balanced, 295, 296, 367, 368.
Licentiates, 226.
Life manifests itself in organisms, 2, 30, 371.
Lines, narrow, separate polities, 41; also visible from invisible Church, 4.
Liturgies, early, 201; independent of polity, 204; New Testament and, 197–203; sermon versus, 202; value of, 202–204.
Local churches, powers of, 80, 81, 111–119, 312, 322, 323.
Lord's Supper, the, 216–228; administered by whom, 225–228; both kinds in, 218; communicants, 218–224; conditions of partaking, 218, 219; must be Scriptural, 222–224; enforced by local churches, 224, 225; Boston Platform and, 222; discipline and, 221, 222; elements used in, 217, 218; invitation to, 224; not controlled by the pastor, 225; Judas Iscariot and, 220; meaning of, 217; mode of, 218; names of, 217; primitive churches and, 220, 221; repeated often, 217; supersedes the passover, 14, 217, 220; unrestricted admission to, fatal, 222, 224.
Lord's Table, like the Church, 224.
Lutherans, Congregational in polity, 83; standard of faith, 99.
Luther's, Martin, idea of the Church, 326.

Macaulay, Lord, the Papacy, 46; the Puritans, 89.
Mackenzie, progress of liberty in Europe, 89, 90, 373, 374.
Majority, discipline by, in primitive churches, 112, 113; what such a vote is, 259.
Marriage, so-called sacrament of, 205.
Mass, held to be a literal sacrifice, 54, 133, 134, 227.
Massachusetts Colony, called councils,

270, 271; ordination and preaching and, 156; regulated the churches, 156, 327, 328.
Materials, of a church, what, 100; of the Ceremonial Church, 100, 101; of the Christian Church, 103, 104; of churches, 104-108; of the kingdom of heaven, 102, 103; of the Patriarchal Church, 100; of synagogues, 161, 102; unity of, in all dispensations, 109.
Matthew 16: 18, 19, interpretations of, 122, 123.
Matthias, how chosen an apostle, 114, 115, 139, 141.
Mediators, priests are, 132.
Members of churches, on dropping, 259, 260; equality of, 171, 172; tested by what, 104-108, 222, 347, 348.
Messengers of the primitive churches, 115, 116.
Methodist Episcopal Church, the, polity of, changing, 76, 77; Presbyterian, essentially, 76; property and pulpit of, 336; rejected by Episcopacy, 65.
Methodists, standard of faith, 99.
Metropolitan bishops, 61.
Michigan, general association of, defines ministerial standing, 156; constitution of, and ministerial standing, 305.
Milman, Dean, on primitive churches, 126.
Ministerial accountability, 154, 155, 284-287.
Ministerial associations, 292-295, 365; liberty and, 295, 365, 366; objects of, 293; origin of, 292, 293; standing in, 293, 294; temporary in nature, 294, 295.
Ministerial membership and pastoral representation, 302, 303; where held, 174, 175.
Ministerial discipline, 177, 235, 284-288.
Ministerial standing, 154-165; associations of churches and, 158, 160, 161, 282, 286; defined, 155, 156; in England, 305; ministerial associations and, 159, 294; National Council on, 161, 162; New England and, 157; redress when, is impaired, 163, 164, 282, 283; required to be held somewhere, 155, 163-165; single and unassociated churches can not hold, 157, 158, 159.
Ministerial training, 314.
Ministers, guides, 191, 192; membership of, dual, 174, 175; responsibility of, dual, 175-177; removal of, 190.
Ministry of the Word, the, 131-149; called of God, 131, 132, 135; as custodians of doctrine and polity, 350-353; distinguished from the laity, 136; function of, 132, 133, 134-136, 190; independent of the churches, 136, 137; not exclusive, 135; not an official relation, 131, 137; not a priesthood, 132-134; ordination of, 149-154; parity of, 137; pastoral theory of, 131; permanent, 138, 143-147; perpetual, 149, 150; precedes churches, 131, 136; prelatical, unscriptural, 137; preparation for, 148; qualifications of, 147-149; restrictions of, in New England colonies, 156; temporary, 138-143.
Minors not voters, 257, 258.
Mistakes, discipline and, 233; when vital, 257.
Mitchell, Rev. John, membership of ministers, 174; standing in ministerial associations, 294.
Moderatism in Scotland, 349, 351, 354.
Moffat, Prof. J. C., D.D., primitive religions, 9, 10.
Moravian Church, 67.
Morris Prof. E. D., D.D. Apostolic succession, 142; proof of Presbyterianism, 75; lay eldership, 183; primitive type, 368, 369, 370.
Mosheim, primitive churches, 126; worship after conversion of Constantine, 201.
Müller, Prof. Max, relation of religion to history, 2.
Mutual councils, 275, 276, 283, 304.

Nation, The (New York), political creeds, 344.
National Church, intolerable, 15, 16; return to, perversive, 18.
National Council, doctrinal basis, 346, 347; origin of, 306-311; recognizes ministerial standing, 161, 162, 305; stated body, 309, 310.
Neander, parity of church members, 172; visible and invisible Church, 49; Novatian, 238.
New England, Church and State united in, 327, 328; effect on Congregationalism, 332; peculiar, 328.
Noah renews a godly seed, 7.
"No bishop, no king," 88, 89, 374.
Notice in cases of discipline, 247.

Oath for witnesses, 248 n.
Objections, force of, 355-357; tests, 356, 357.
Offences, disciplinable, 235-238; scandalous, 237, 238, 244, 249.
Officers, church, authority of, 190-193; no veto power, 190, 191; removal of, 190.
Offices, distribution of, among members, 192, 193.
Ohio General Association and National Council, 309.
Orders, the so-called sacrament of, 205.
Ordination, 149-154; Ceremonial, 132; Christian, 137, 150; authority conferred by, 153, 154; deposition and, 176, 289; ecclesiastical recognition in, 152, 153; Episcopal, 64; modes of, 151; performed by associations of churches, 288, 289, 306; by churches, 152; by councils, 273; relations caused by, 154, 155; Scriptural, 150, 151.
Original, the, polity, the final polity, 96, 372-375.
"Out of the church there is no salvation," 48, 49, 171.

Palfrey, churches as towns, 91.
Pan Anglican Conferences abnormal, 68.
Papacy, the, 46-59; an absolute monarchy, 54; absorbed the Episcopate, 59; Augustine might have strangled, 49; clerical government wholly, 54, 55; constitutive principle of, 52; good fruits of, 95; irreformable, 56; liberty denied by, 53, 54, 57; temporal power must be recovered, 57, 58; visible and invisible Church confused in, 49, 50.
Papal infallibility, 51, 52; when located, 53.

Papal theory of the Church, 51; alternative of victory or death, 56, 57; cleavage fatal to, 56; comprehension of, 59; development of, 53, 54; environment of, 51; grandeur of, 46; irreformable, 56; matured when, 52; origin of, 47-50; power of, 56; primacy in, 50, 52; unassailable by argument, 56; vitality of, 56.
Parliamentary rules, binding, 191; councils and, 278; pastors and, 230.
Parish system, 328-332; churches in bondage to, 330-332; church property and, 330; efficiency hindered by, 360; influence on faith, 349; legal existence of churches in, 331, 332; origin of, 328-330; strifes and remedies under, 329, 330; unscriptural, 332; voters in, 329-331.
Parity in the laity, 171, 172; in the ministry, 137.
Passover, Jewish, 14; communicants at, 220.
Pastoral representation, 303.
Pastoral theory of the ministry, 131.
Pastorate, the, essential elements of, 177, 178; National Council and, 161, 162.
Pastors, 145, 146; churches may ordain their own, 153, 177; councils unnecessary to constitute, 177, 178; discipline of, 159, 261-263; impartiality required in, 261; more than church officers, 177; presiding officers, 175, 230, 248, 261; should not attend certain church meetings, 175, 230; when representatives of churches, 303.
Patriarchal Dispensation, 6-11; creed of, 8, 9; degeneracy of piety under, 7, 9, 10; divisive, 9; initiatory rite introduced into, 8; purity of, 10; worship of, 8.
Patriarchal theory of society, 6.
Penance, so-called sacrament of, 205.
Pentecost, Christian Church inaugurated on, 111; converts at, 169.
People, best guardians of faith and polity, 350-353.
Permanent ministry, 143-149; lists of, 144; names of, 144.
Peter, St., called to account, 114, 176; primacy of, 121-123.
Phelps, Prof. Austin, D.D., necessity of creeds, 344.
"Pilgrim convention" of 1870, and the National Council, 308.
"Plan of the Apostles, the," 128, 130, 340, 363, 369, 372.
Plan of Union, 352, 360, 361.
Plurality of elders in churches, 70, 71, 169, 170, 173.
Political elements in the Ceremonial Law, 128.
Polities, œcumenical, 87, 88; exclusive, 85-87; origin honorable, 39-41; simple, four, 40, 84, 85; union labors and, 93, 94, 339, 362; utility of, 94-96.
Polity, church activities determined by, 93, 94; covers the revelation of redemption,1; development in, 94, 95; not discretionary, 370-372; essential, 371; involved in every church act, 94; liberty and, 18, 19, 88-93; not detailed in New Testament, 44, 45; obedience to, required, 372; principles of the true, revealed, 43-45, 129, 372; relation of, to civil government, 18, 19, 88-93; study of, needed, 1, 2, 3, 18-20; theology molded by, 2, 3, 50.
Polycarp, 71, 118, 126, 180.
Prayer, Book of Common, conflicting elements in, 66.
Preaching, open to laymen, 135; right of, found in Christ's call, 137.
Prelate, 137.
Presbyterian Alliance abnormal, 74, 75.
Presbyterian Churches, number of, 76.
Presbyterian Puritans, 90, 326.
Presbyterian, theory of the Church, 70-79.
Presbyterianism, 70-79; adjusted easily to new light, 129, 130; constitutive principle of, 72; abandoned where, 74, 75; development of, into sessions, 72; presbyteries, 73; synods, 73; general assemblies, 74; and the Presbyterian Alliance, 74; infallibility not claimed by, 78; lay eldership not essential to, 77, 78; not republican, 91-93; originated in a wrong interpretation, 71, 183, 184; principle of unity in, 40, 72; proof alleged for, 75, 76; reformable, 78; representatives may be laymen, 72; yielding to the light, 74, 78, 129, 130.
Presbyterians favored a national church, 90; standard of faith, 74, 99.
Presbyteries, 73; powers of, 74.
Presbytery in particular churches, 60, 70, 71, 76, 125, 173, 185.
Proselytes, 102.
Priesthood, the Aaronic, 13, 132; Christ's, 132, 133; Christian ministry not a, 132-134; Patriarchal, 8; Roman Catholic, 134, 135; Greek Church, 134.
Priests, what, 132; ministers not, 132-134.
Primacy, infallible, 52.
Primacy of St. Peter, 50, 51, 122, 123.
Primitive churches, discipline of, 232; worship of, 199-201.
Primitive religions, 10.
Principle, domination of, in polity, 40, 45, 46, 128.
Private judgment, corner-stone of liberty, 18, 337, 338.
Proof, liberty of, in ecclesiastical trials, 251.
Property, church, regulated by civil law, 333; alienation of, 335-337.
Prophets, New Testament, 142, 143; Old Testament, 13, 14, 142; priests of Israel not, 13; school of the, 14.
Protestant Episcopal Church, 67.
Proxy, discipline by, when, 246.
Public discipline not necessary, 249, 250, 357.
Purgatory, nature of, 54.
Puritan Reformation, a theory of the Church, 326, 327.
Puritans, Congregational and Presbyterian, 90, 326; influence in civil governments, 18, 19, 88-91.
Purity, inability to attain, no objection, 108; ministerial, tested by examinations, 353; Patriarchal Dispensation did not favor, 10.

Quakers, ministry rejected by, 134; sacraments and, 206, 207; standard of faith, 99.

INDEX. 385

Queen Elizabeth, tuning pulpits, 327.
Quorum in councils, 273.

Rationalism, ecclesiastical, 128, 129, 185.
Reason, a standard of faith with whom, 99.
Reciprocal relation of polity and life, 2, 30.
Recognition, councils of, 290.
Records, church, 186. 187; of trials, 248.
Redress of grievances, 262, 263.
Reformation, the great, effect on worship, 201, 202; partial return to primitive polity, 326, 327; sprung from a theory of the Church, 3, 18, 19.
Reformed Episcopal Church, 67.
Reformers depended on the State, 326, 327.
Reforms, religions, saved by ecclesiastical, 18, 19, 354.
Relation of Church and State, 323-328; true, 332-336.
Religion, history molded by, 2; morality and heathen, 342; revealed, requires a called ministry, 131; State may teach, when, 333, 334; studied in organic manifestations, 2, 38-40.
Religions, primitive, one in origin, 9, 10.
Religious liberty denied by the Papacy, 57; called "the insanity," 88.
Representation of churches equal, why, 298, 299; pastoral, 302, 303.
Republican, the polity most, 91-93.
Resolutions of National Council on ministerial standing, 158, 161, 162, 285.
Result of councils, 278, 279; advisory, 279; divisible, 280; validity in civil courts, 278, 279.
Ritual, Jewish, 13, 14, 198, 199; none in New Testament, 197; value of, 202-204.
Robinson, John, on sealing ordinances, 227.
"Rock," meaning of, in Matt. 16: 18, 122, 123.
Roman Catholic Church, 46-59; laity have no voice in, 54; reformable when, 58, 59; standard of faith, 99; visible Church, 4; no salvation out of the, 29, 48.
Rule of discipline, 111, 229-263; meaning of "church" in, 111-114; steps in, 241-243.
Rulers, in churches, 146; in Israel, how chosen, 13.
Ruling elders, 181-184; duties of, 181, 182; government by, 72, 73, 184, 185; laymen or ministers, 181-183, 220.
Ruling eldership, discredits the diaconate, 185; lay, being rejected, 183, 184; theories of, 181; unessential, 72.

Sabbath, 8, 15, 17, 33, 334.
Sacraments, the, 205-207; administered by whom, 225-228; laymen may administer when, 226-228; nature of, 206, 207; number of, 205; Quaker view of, 206, 207; validity of, 226, 227.
Sacrifices, eucharistic and expiatory, 7, 8.
Safeguards of purity, 290-292, 305, 306, 344-348; complete, 354, 355.
Saints, line of, 7; separation of, under the three dispensations, 10, 11, 12, 15, 104, 107, 109.
Salvation, no, out of the Church, 29, 48.

Savoy Declaration, 345, 346.
Saybrook Platform, 297, 360, 366; synod, 366.
Scandalous offences, 237, 238, 244, 249.
Schaff, Philip, D.D., LL.D., elders and bishops the same, 145, 174; liturgy, 197, 200; mode of baptism, 210; proselytes, 102; ruling elders, 183; separation of believers from synagogues, 168; synagogues modes of churches, 34, 35, 118, 135, 198, 199.
Schism, under the Papacy the greatest sin, 54.
Schools, state, the State may teach religion in, when, 333, 334.
Scott, Prof. H. M., primitive churches, 127, 128.
Scriptures supplemented, 33, 99.
Seceders forfeit all rights, 336.
Separation of Church and State required, 324, 325.
Sermon, place of the, in worship, 202.
Session, Presbyterian, 72; powers of, 72, 73.
Societies, ecclesiastical or parishes (see Parish), 328-332.
Socinians, standard of faith, 98, 99.
Spence, Canon, Apostolic succession, 142.
Standards of faith, various, 98, 99.
Standing, expulsion from, 163, 164, 286, 289.
Stanley, Dean, liturgy, 203; modes of ordination, 151; prophets, 14; relation of the Papal to the Greek Church, 47.
State, independent of the Church, 332; not irreligious, 332; regulates worship, 334; and property, 333-336.
Stone, Rev. Samuel, 192, 193.
Subjection, no, of one church to another, 117; or to others, 119-126.
"Substance of doctrine," meaning of, 345 n.
Sunday-school, 190, 312, 313; superintendent of, 190; Pilgrim Church and, 313.
Sword, the papal Church, claim use of, 57.
Syllabus, papal, of errors, 51, 57.
Synagogue discipline and Matt. 18: 15-18, 112.
Synagogue worship, 35, 198, 199; conducted by laymen, 35, 76; Congregational, 35; model of the Christian worship, 34-36, 198, 199; origin of, 16, 34; ritual in, 198, 199, 203; sanctioned by Christ, 35; supplemented the Mosaic, 16; universal in form, 34-36.
Synagogues, developed from a want, 16; elected officers, 35; independent, 35, 117, 118, 120, 369; Christians separated from, 37, 167; members of, 101, 102; origin of, 16, 34; rulers of, 35; spread of, 34, 35.
Synods, early, 124; authority of, 125, 268, 325; Presbyterian, 73.

Taxation, church property and, 333.
"Teachers," 144; layman may be, 135.
"Teaching of the Twelve Apostles," the, 107, 124, 141, 142, 143, 173, 176, 178, 209, 217, 220, 221, 313.
Temporal power of the Pope, 57; must be recovered, 58.
Tertullian, 122, 183, 212, 226.
Theories of the Christian Church, 40, 41;

Congregational, 79; Episcopal, 62; Papal, 51; Presbyterian, 71, 72; each ecumenical, 87, 88; efforts after the true, 43–45; influence on doctrine, 2, 3, 50; and practice, 50; mutually exclusive, 85–87; number of simple, 40, 45, 84, 85; subtility of, calls for charity, 94, 95; working out the truth, 94–96.
Third way, the, of communion, 159.
Thurston, Rev. R. B., and the National Council, 308.
1 Tim. 5: 17 explained, 183, 184.
Town church in New Egland, 91, 328–330.
Tradition, a standard of faith, 99.
Training, coöperation in ministerial, 314.
Treasurer, church, 187–189; permanent officer, 188; qualifications of, 188.
Treasurer, society or parish, 189.
Trials, ecclesiastical, 247–250; impartiality in, 248, 249; limitation of associational members in, 163; result how determined, 248, 250.
Tridentine council, 121, 145; abolished the order of bishops, 58, 59, 86.
Trinity Church catechism, 62, 63, 213 n.
Troubles, church, advertising, 255; force of, 355, 356; restriction of, 357.

Unevangelical bodies and comity, 338, 340, 341.
Union churches, 87, 339; trend in, 339, 340.
Union, committee of, in New England, 307.
Union efforts end in denominational results, 339, 362; hinder efficiency, 359, 360.
Union of Church and State, Constantine and, 325, 326, 337; hinders efficiency, 360; introduced force, 325; peculiarity of, in New England, 328.
Union societies and seceders, 336.
Uni parte councils, 275.
Unitarian, apostasy in Europe and New England, 348–350, 353, 354; Arlington, church, 222; stayed in Ireland, 350, 351.
United Colonies of new England, 306.
Unity of churches, attempted, 40, 87, 88; Congregationalism and, 266, 267, 357–359; force can not produce, 266, 267, 358, 350, 364; independency rests on, 110, 111; plurality can not express the, 43–45; rightly balanced by liberty, 367, 368; sought by all, 40, 110, 119.
Unity of the Ceremonial Dispensation, 15.
Universe, plan of the, one, not many, 43, 44.
Upham, Prof., on membership of ministers, 174; on presiding pastors, 175.

Usage, force of, 279, 280.

Vatican council, 52, 53, 57, 58, 121.
Veda, religion of the, 9 n.
Vermont, supreme court of, on duties of associations, 161; on ministerial standing, 155, 294.
Veto, no power of, 190, 191.
Voluntary societies, 315–317; churches are not, 171; property of, 336.
Vote, when pastors may break a tie, 175; validity of a, when majority refrain from voting, 259.
Votes, devoid of authority, 364, 365; in early synods, 125.
Voters, church, 257–259; disqualified when, 259; minors not, 257, 258; rule defining, needed, 257.
Voters in New England colonies, 269.

Waddington, on primitive churches, 126.
Westminster confession, 345, 346.
Whately, Archbishop, apostolic succession, 63; primitive churches, 126; "the plan of the Apostles," 128.
Wine, gift of, to Cambridge synod, 239.
Winer on the ministerial function, 134, 135; on Sacraments, 205, 207, 218, 225, 226.
Wisdom, denominational, how shown, 361, 362.
Wiseman, Cardinal, on constitutive principle, 46, 52.
Witnesses, church can not compel, 251, 252; protected by civil law, 255, 256; should be sworn, 248.
Women, when voters, 258, 259.
World, relation of churches to the, 341–343.
Worship, Christian, 194–204; conception of, 202; description of early, 199–201; early liturgies in, 201; elements of, 195; ends of, 196; essential to a church, 194; form of, unfixed, 197, 198; laymen may conduct, 199; liberty in, 198; model of, 198; nature of, 196, 197; perversion of, under Constantine, 201; perverted by exaltation of preachers, 202; protected, 334; reformation changed, 201, 202; social, largely, 194, 195; State may control, 334; variety in, 202–204.
Worship, eucharistic and expiatory, when begun, 7.
Worship, synagogue, model of the Christian, 198, 199.

Year books, and expelled ministers, 303, 304; ministerial standing and, 305.

Zwingle, on nature of the Church, 326.

www.ingramcontent.com/pod-product-compliance
Lightning Source LLC
Chambersburg PA
CBHW022116290426
44112CB00008B/689